BAGO REGION

YANGON AND THE AYEYARWADY DELTA

THE DELTA REGION

YANGON

MON AND KAYIN STATES

SOUTHERN MYANMAR

MYEIK REGION

GULF OF THAILAND

ANDAMAN SEA

INDIAN OCEAN

CAMBODIA

THAILAND

Bangkok

Viangchan (Vientiane)

Andaman Islands (India)

Myanmar

N

0   100 km
0   100 miles

MYANMAR

◉ Walking Eye App

YOUR FREE DESTINATION CONTENT AND EBOOK AVAILABLE THROUGH THE WALKING EYE APP

Your guide now includes a free eBook and destination content for your chosen destination, all for the same great price as before. Simply download the Walking Eye App from the App Store or Google Play to access your free eBook and destination content.

HOW THE WALKING EYE APP WORKS

Through the Walking Eye App, you can purchase a range of eBooks and destination content. However, when you buy this book, you can download the corresponding eBook and destination content for free. Just see below in the grey panels where to find your free content and then scan the QR code at the bottom of this page.

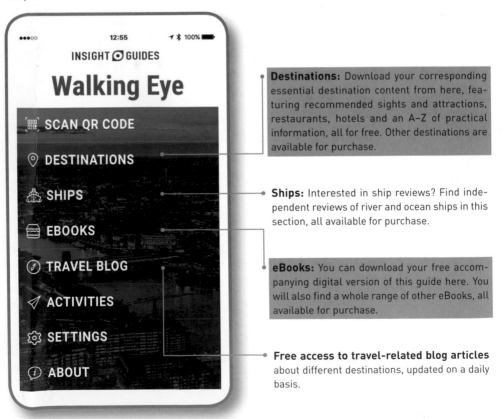

Destinations: Download your corresponding essential destination content from here, featuring recommended sights and attractions, restaurants, hotels and an A–Z of practical information, all for free. Other destinations are available for purchase.

Ships: Interested in ship reviews? Find independent reviews of river and ocean ships in this section, all available for purchase.

eBooks: You can download your free accompanying digital version of this guide here. You will also find a whole range of other eBooks, all available for purchase.

Free access to travel-related blog articles about different destinations, updated on a daily basis.

HOW THE DESTINATION CONTENT WORKS

Each destination includes a short introduction, an A–Z of practical information and recommended points of interest, split into 4 different categories:

- Highlights
- Accommodation
- Eating out
- What to do

You can view the location of every point of interest and save it by adding it to your Favourites. In the 'Around Me' section you can view all the points of interest within 5km.

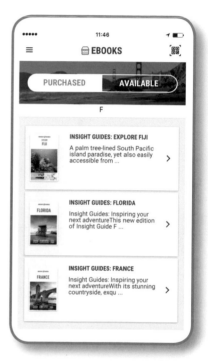

HOW THE EBOOKS WORK

The eBooks are provided in EPUB file format. Please note that you will need an eBook reader installed on your device to open the file. Many devices come with this as standard, but you may still need to install one manually from Google Play.

The eBook content is identical to the content in the printed guide.

HOW TO DOWNLOAD THE WALKING EYE APP

1. Download the Walking Eye App from the App Store or Google Play.
2. Open the app and select the scanning function from the main menu.
3. Scan the QR code on this page – you will then be asked a security question to verify ownership of the book.
4. Once this has been verified, you will see your eBook and destination content in the purchased ebook and destination sections, where you will be able to download them.

Other destination apps and eBooks are available for purchase separately or are free with the purchase of the Insight Guide book.

CONTENTS

Travel tips

Maps

LEGEND
🔎 Insight on
📷 Photo story

THE BEST OF MYANMAR: TOP ATTRACTIONS

△ **Amarapura, Mandalay**. Spread around a beautiful lake on the edge of Mandalay, this former Burmese royal capital is home to dozens of flamboyant temples and a spectacular, kilometre-long wooden bridge. See page 182.

△ **Shwedagon Pagoda, Yangon**. The supreme symbol of Burmese Buddhism and national pride, the gigantic golden stupa rising from the midst of Yangon (Rangoon) is a sublime spectacle, especially when floodlit at dusk and after dark. See page 126.

▽ **Bagan, Mandalay Region**. Over two thousand ancient religious buildings dating from the 11th century dot the arid plains of Bagan – one of Southeast Asia's greatest archaeological sites and Myanmar's principal visitor attraction. See it from the air on a magical balloon flight. See page 207.

△ **Inle Lake, Shan State**. "One-legged" Intha rowers, floating gardens and markets, pretty stilt villages, ancient Shan stupa complexes and beautiful scenery are just some of the attractions of serene Inle Lake in the Shan Hills. See page 246.

△ **Golden Rock Pagoda, Kyaiktiyo, Mon State.** Teetering on the rim of a clifftop high in the coastal hills of Mon State, this extraordinary gilded boulder ranks among the country's most magical pilgrimage sites. Getting to it involves a stiff hour-long hike up a sacred stairway. See page 295.

△ **Cruising the Ayeyarwady.** Whether you travel by luxury cruiser or creaky government ferry, a journey along Myanmar's mightiest river takes you deep into the country's rural heart – a watery world of shifting sand banks, remote jetties and bamboo-built villages. See pages 179 and 309.

△ **Ngapali Beach, Rakhine State.** Kick back at Myanmar's premier beach resort, whose brilliant turquoise waters, golden sand and superb seafood offer a welcome respite from the heat and dust of inland travel. See page 285.

△ **Mount Popa.** Climb the steps leading to the top of this spectacular rock outcrop, its summit and sides covered in shrines dedicated to the country's revered nat spirits, and commanding sweeping views over the Bagan plains. See page 233.

▽ **Hill-tribe treks, Shan State.** The hill-tribe trekking scene in Myanmar is nowhere near as commercialised as in neighbouring Thailand. Kalaw, a former British retreat near Inle Lake, and Hsipaw, further northeast, are the two main hubs. See page 251.

△ **Mrauk-U, Rakhine State.** Hidden away in the remote west of the country, Mrauk-U is an amazing lost city of ruined temples, palaces and shrines, set amid scrub-covered hills. Boats leave the coastal town of Sittwe daily to reach the site – an enjoyable three- to six-hour river trip. See page 278.

THE BEST OF MYANMAR: EDITOR'S CHOICE

The reclining buddha at Bodhi Tataung.

BEST BUDDHIST MONUMENTS

Shwedagon Pagoda, Yangon. Thousands of pilgrims stream daily around the precincts of Myanmar's most splendid religious monument – a structure of other-worldly beauty. See page 126.

Kyauk Htat Gyi Pagoda, Yangon. Gargantuan reclining Buddha not far from the Shwedagon Pagoda, combining superhuman size with lavish decoration. See page 136.

Shwemawdaw Pagoda, Bago. Bago's most magnificent stupa, smothered in gold and precious stones, outstrips even the Shwedagon for size. See page 153.

Shwethalyaung Buddha, Bago. This colossal, greatly loved reclining Buddha is regarded as the one that best expresses the Master's attainment of Nirvana. See page 155.

Mahamuni, Mandalay. Myanmar's most revered Buddha, this serene-faced giant was brought to Mandalay from Mrauk U in Rakhine as war booty in the 18th century. See page 177.

Shwesandaw Pagoda, Pyay (Bago Region). Though a provincial backwater now, Pyay was once a wealthy river port – as the scale and splendour of the great gilded Shwesandaw Pagoda testifies. See page 158.

Bodhi Tataung, Monywa (Mandalay Region). Among the most surreal sights in Southeast Asia are the two vast Buddhas – one standing, one reclining – on this hilltop to the east of Monywa. See page 194.

Pho Win Taung Caves, Monywa (Mandalay Region). An ancient complex of hand-hewn caves containing rows of ancient sculptures and murals, buried deep in the countryside west of the Chindwin River. See page 194.

Shwezigon Pagoda, Bagan. The most revered of Bagan's two-thousand-odd surviving shrines. Pilgrims pour through it year-round, but in particularly large numbers during the annual festival. See page 223.

Win Sein Taw Ya, nr Mawlamyine (Mon State). The country's largest reclining Buddha rests on a ridgetop near the former colonial capital of Mawlamyine – a diorama inside recounts moral tales and stories from the Master's life. See page 298.

Golden Rock Pagoda, Kyaiktiyo (Mon State). Balanced in an impossibly precarious position on the very edge of a clifftop, the remarkable Golden Rock is one of Myanmar's strangest but most compelling sights. See page 295.

Verdant landscape near Kalaw.

BEST WALKS AND TREKS

Kalaw–Inle Lake (Shan State). The country's most popular trekking route winds from the hill station of Kalaw to the shores of Inle Lake via a string of pretty ethnic minority villages and stretches of forest. See page 251.

Inle Lake–Pindaya (Shan State). Hike over the hilly western fringes of the Shan Plateau – home to several ethnic minority communities – to the Buddha-filled caves at Pindaya. See page 252.

Hsipaw (Shan State). Numerous day walks out of Hsipaw take you to Palaung minority villages such as Pankam, renowned for its tea cultivation, teak houses and animist traditions. See page 254.

Kengtung (Shan State). The market town of Kengtung, near the

Chinese border, serves as a springboard for a choice of routes to Eng, Akha, Palaung and Wa settlements. See page 253.

Nat Ma Taung (Chin State). A distinctive "sky-island" summit with its own peculiar jungle flora and fauna, Nat Ma Taung – aka "Mount Victoria" (3,053 metres/10,016ft) – is the target for a superb six-day trek. See page 286.

Hkakabo Razi base camp (Kachin). Close encounters with spectacular forest, abundant wildlife and some awesome snowy-mountain scenery characterise the trek to the foot of Burma's highest peak, Hkakabo Razi (5,889 metres/19,321ft). See page 267.

Jade for sale.

BEST JOURNEYS

Mandalay–Bagan. Take the slow, overnight government ferry or one of the faster and more comfortable modern cruise boats which ply the Ayeyarwady between Mandalay and Bagan. See page 179.

Mawlamyine–Hpa-an. The karst limestone mountains and outcrops of Kayin State make the ferry trip up the Thanlwin (Salween) River one of the loveliest in Asia. See page 301.

Pyin U-Lwin to Lashio, via the Gokteik Viaduct. It takes hours longer than by road, but the stop-start train ride through northwest

Shan State is worth making for the crossing of the spectacular Gokteik Viaduct alone. See page 201.

Myitkyina–Mandalay. A series of natural defiles gouged out by the river is the stand-out feature of the week-long journey by government ferry or private cruiser along the northern Ayeyarwady. See page 264.

Mandalay–Mingun. A short and sweet river trip, lasting just an hour and taking you from Mandalay through some idyllic countryside to the mighty ruined stupa at Mingun. See page 190.

BEST MARKETS

Bogyoke Aung San Market, Yangon. Known for its colonial architecture and stone-paved alleys, Bogyoke is the country's best source of antiques, handicrafts, jewellery and – famously – jade and rubies. See page 126.

Sittwe. An amazing array of Indian Ocean seafood can be seen at Sittwe's quayside fish market each morning, although you'll have to get up before dawn to catch it at its best. See page 276.

Five-Day Floating Markets, Inle Lake. Every five days, the

towns encircling Inle take it in turns to host the local market, where you can pick up lotus silk textiles, Shan bags and other handicrafts. See page 248.

Hsipaw. This weekly bazaar in the Shan Hills is a great place to see local tribal villagers dressed in the traditional finery. See page 254.

Bhamo. Head to the south end of Bhamo's lively riverfront market area for the town's main ceramic centre, where pots of all sizes and shapes are laid out for sale beside the water. See page 260.

BEST SCENERY & VIEWS

Aung's Puppet show, Nyaungshwe, Inle Lake region.

Mandalay Hill (Mandalay). Expansive views over the Konbaung Dynasty's former palace and across the city to the Ayeyarwady River extend from the hill where the Buddha is said to have preached. See page 171.

Sun U Ponya Shin, Sagaing (Mandalay). This whitewashed pagoda, crowning the top of sacred Sagaing Hill, affords an iconic vista over gilded stupa spires and monasteries to the river below. See page 188.

Shwesandaw Pagoda, Bagan. The upper terraces of this soaring stupa offer famous sunset views over the Bagan Archaeological Zone – though you'll have to jostle for space to photograph them. See page 218.

Mount Phonkan Razi (Kachin). Climb this 3,630-metre (11,900ft) snow-dusted summit in the far north for a superb view over the eastern arm of the Himalayas, including the country's highest peak, Hkakabo Razi. See page 267.

Mount Zwegabin, Hpa-an (Kayin State). Spend a night in the monastery at the summit of Mount Zwegabin, the largest of the limestone mountains near Hpa-an, to watch the sun rising over the coastal plain. See page 300.

Kyaikthanlan Pagoda, Mawlamyine (Mon State). This was the stupa memorialized by Kipling in his poem "Mandalay", and the panorama from its terrace across the port city and Andaman Sea is stupendous. See page 297.

BEST SOUVENIRS

Laquerware. Imported from Siam in the 16th century, yun laquerwork has since been refined into a distinctively Burmese art form. Myinkaba village, in Bagan is its major centre. See page 85.

***Htamein** and **longyis**.* The backlanes of Amarapura, near Mandalay, are filled with handlooms on which the elegant *htamein* and *longyis* (sarongs) worn by both Burmese men and women are made. See page 236.

Marionettes. Delightful string puppets, representing characters from much-loved myth and folk tales, are a common sight at souvenir stores in Yangon, Mandalay and Bagan. See page 88.

Parasols. Capital of the Ayeyarwady Delta region, Pathein holds a dozen or more workshops where traditional paper parasols are made in dazzling day-glo colours. See pages 86 and 149.

Kalaga tapestries. Beads, silver thread and sequins are used to make padded kalaga tapestries, featuring scenes from Buddhist Jataka tales. Mandalay is the main focus for this popular craft form. See page 89.

BEST BEACHES

Ngapali (Rakhine State). Ngapali is far and away Myanmar's most appealing resort, with a string of high-end hotels behind a bay of soft white sand and blue water. See page 285.

Chaungtha (Delta). On the western edge of the Delta, cheap-and-cheerful Chaungtha is where middle-class Yangonites come on weekends to party and eat seafood – although it's contrastingly quiet during the week. See page 147.

Ngwe Saung. Just down the coast from Chaung Tha, the more upmarket and peaceful Ngwe Saung attracts a mixed crowd of locals and foreigners thanks to its fine sands and excellent accommodation. See page 147.

Myeik Archipelago. Superb beaches and fabulous diving in Myanmar's deep south. See page 304.

Mountains in the Phonkan Razi National Park.

Ngwe Saung.

BEST HOTELS

Sandoway Resort, Ngapali Beach. Right on the sea, this sleek, village-style resort set between lush sands and gorgeous gardens is the perfect place to enjoy Myanmar's dreamiest beach. www.sandowayresort.com.

Governor's Residence, Yangon. Sip a gin sling on the verandah of this immaculately restored 1920s mansion, Yangon's most stylish place to stay. www.belmond.com/myanmar.

Hotel by the Red Canal, Mandalay. Blending sumptuous Burmese style with international boutique chic, this small hotel in the suburbs of Mandalay is a haven befitting the city's former royal connections. www.hotelredcanal.com.

Hotel @ Tharabar Gate, Bagan. Luxuriously furnished brick and thatch chalets set amid flower-filled gardens, only a short walk from some of Bagan's most striking landmarks. www.tharabargate.com.

Inle Princess, Inle Lake. Relax in regal fashion on the sunny northeastern shore of Inle Lake, with unbroken views over the water from its elegant pagoda-roofed buildings. www.inle-princess.com.

Strand, Yangon. Dating from 1903, the Strand is the granddaddy of Myanmar's luxury hotels, where the likes of Somerset Maugham and Rudyard Kipling stayed at the twilight of the British Empire. www.hotelthestrand.com.

ONLY IN MYANMAR

White elephants. Burmese royalty traditionally considered white elephants as auspicious – a superstition maintained by their military successors today, who collect albino pachyderms for good luck in elections. See page 200.

Thanaka. To protect themselves from the burning effects of the sun, Burmese women and children smear their faces in fragrant thanaka paste made from aromatic trees. See page 237.

Chinlone. Myanmar's own version of "keepy-uppy" is the national sport. You'll see it played informally on the streets and in competitions at temple festivals across the country. The Chinlone Festival at Mahamuni Pagoda in Mandalay is one of the best. See page 316.

Nat Pwe, Taungbyon (Mandalay). Drink-fuelled oracle rituals, music, dance and general mayhem accompany Myanmar's largest nat nature spirit festival. See page 192.

Thingyan festival. Welcoming in the Burmese New Year in mid-April, this three-day water festival is basically an excuse for teenagers to soak each other to the skin at specially erected stalls, or pandals. See page 77.

Mohinga. A spicy noodle broth flavoured with tasty fish stock is the quintessential Burmese breakfast, served at pavement cafés in all the major cities. See page 81.

Lahpet. The national delicacy, made of fermented or pickled tea leaves, most commonly served up in spicy lahpet thouq (tea-leaf salad), one of Myanmar's signature dishes. See page 82.

Governor's Residence.

Playing chinlone in Nyuang U.

A local sits outside his house in Twante, Delta Region.

Local Pa-O guide walking amongst the ancient pagodas of Kakku.

THE GOLDEN LAND

One of the least-known countries in Southeast Asia, Myanmar has been taking rapid steps towards long-overdue change in the past few years.

A monk crosses Taungthaman lake by boat.

Myanmar – as Burma was renamed in 1989 – is the most enigmatic country in Southeast Asia. Enfolded by jungle-clad hills, its central river valleys were for centuries the heartland of a classical civilisation little known by the out-side world – a tantalisingly exotic culture of gilded stupas, red-robed monks and elaborately carved teak palaces. Constant wars, civil unrest and chronic economic misman-agement by a repressive military junta compounded the country's isolation, although the much anticipated reforms kick started by Aung San Suu Kyi's release from house arrest in 2010 and the country's first democratic elections for half a century in 2015 are now steadily transforming the face of this captivating nation.

Even so, after fifty years in the economic doldrums Myanmar remains locked in a kind of time warp. The former capital, Yan-gon (Rangoon), may be sprouting skyscrapers, but elsewhere people live in dilapidated low-rise towns and villages made of mud brick and bamboo. Bullocks plough the paddy fields; horse-carts outnumber cars.

From a foreign traveller's point of view, this quirky, hand-made, old-world atmosphere makes Myanmar a charismatic place to travel. Traditions of the past remain very much to the fore. Walking the streets of Mandalay in the early morning, you'll see hundreds of shaven-headed monks queuing for alms, young women with fragrant *thanaka* paste smeared over their faces,

Stupa detail, Mahabodhi temple, Bagan.

elderly vegetable sellers puffing on oversized cheroots, and all manner of exotic headgear, from conical straw hats to burgundy turbans. Beautifully patterned batik *htameins* and *longyis* (sarongs) are worn by nearly all women – and most men. The everyday smells in the street can be just as strikingly unfamiliar, along with the wonderful flavours of Burmese cooking, with its pungent mix of spices, seafood sauces, limes and fresh green leaves.

Despite its manifold problems, Myanmar is ripe for exploration, with more world-class monuments than you could possibly see on a 28-day tourist visa, a wealth of vibrant arts and crafts traditions and, not least, inhabitants whose resilience, gentleness and hospitable attitude to foreigners impress every visitor to the country.

Note: we have used the name Myanmar instead of Burma, except for his-torical references. The adjective "Burmese" has been retained throughout.

Taking goods home from Taung Tho market by ox and cart, Inle Lake region.

LAND OF RICE AND RIVERS

Myanmar is roughly kite-shaped: a diamond with the long Tanintharyi peninsula as its tail and the Ayeyarwady as the controlling string.

The majestic Ayeyarwady (Irrawaddy) River is the lifeblood of the land, bisecting and watering the fertile rice-growing plains on which Myanmar's economy has always been based. Rising in the Himalayas, the river crosses the country from north to south for 2,170km (1,348 miles), emptying into the Andaman Sea through the Delta, where it splits into nine major tributaries (and myriad smaller waterways), like the frayed end of a gigantic length of rope. Called "the Road to Mandalay" by British colonialists, the broad river has also traditionally served as the country's major transport artery (at its peak in the 1920s the Irradwaddy Flotilla Company's 600 vessels carried around nine millions passengers annually up and down the river), though in recent times river boats have been largely supplanted in favour of transport by road, rail and, increasingly, air.

Travellers following the Ayeyarwady's entire course will experience the full range of Myanmar's climatic zones. Beginning at the far north, the river runs through the rugged Kachin Hills, outliers of the Himalayas. At Bhamo, the furthest point to which the Ayeyarwady is navigable by steamer (1,500km/930 miles from the delta), it enters the forested valleys and hills of the Shan Plateau. Further downstream, the waters emerge onto the broad dry plain of central Myanmar, the heart of classical Burmese civilisation. The Ayeyarwady then flows past sandbars to the ruins of Bagan and Sri Ksetra (Thayekhittaya), and enters its more fertile southern stretches.

In terms of surface area, Myanmar is the largest country in mainland Southeast Asia. Its population is estimated at around 55 million, of whom about 65 percent live in rural villages. After Yangon, with its population of around 6 million, the major population centres

Canoeing around Nampam village, Inle Lake region.

are Mandalay (1.3 million), Naypyidaw (1 million) and Mawlamyine (500,000).

THREE SEASON CYCLE

Myanmar is at its best during the dry and relatively cool period from late November to late February. This is the peak tourist season. From March onwards, humidity levels start to build ahead of the annual monsoons, with thermometers soaring well above 40°C (104°F) in the Ayeyarwady Valley around Mandalay by late April. The rains proper erupt in mid-May and last through to October – low season in tourism terms. Travel anywhere in the country at this time is problematic: roads are routinely washed away, rail lines flooded and cyclones can wreak havoc on the coastal plains and Delta.

INLAND NAVIGATION

Two rivers besides the Ayeyarwady are important to Myanmar's inland navigation and irrigation. One, the Chindwin, is a tributary of the Ayeyarwady, flowing through the northwest and joining the larger river about 110km (70 miles) downstream from Mandalay. Readily navigable for 180km (110 miles) upstream from its confluence, it opens up remote stretches of the Sagaing region, now served by occasional government ferries and luxury cruises.

Hills, reaching heights of 3,000 metres (10,000ft) on the southeastern edge of the Himalayas. On the Tibetan border is Hkakabo Razi, the highest peak in Southeast Asia at 5,881 metres (19,289ft). Deep valleys, many of them with subtropical vegetation and terraced rice fields, separate the mountain ridges. The chief inhabitants are the Kachin; Lisu are also common in the Chinese border region. The administrative centre of Myitkyina is the terminus of the railway from Yangon and Mandalay.

The Kachin Hills link with the Shan Plateau in the south, a vast area averaging 1,000 metres

Fertiliser made from lake-bed weeds is used to feed these floating gardens on Inle Lake.

In the east of the country, the Thanlwin (Salween) River slices through Shan State via a series of deep gorges. It has few tributaries between its source in the Himalayas and its exit to the Andaman Sea at Mawlamyine. It is navigable only for about 160km (100 miles) upstream due to its fast current and 20-metre (65ft) fluctuations in water level. It used to play an important role in the economy – as the route by which teak was rafted from the Shan Plateau to Mawlamyine, its export harbour – although teak is now exported via Yangon.

THE LIE OF THE LAND

Geographically, Myanmar can be divided up into several zones. In the far north are the Kachin

(3,200ft) in elevation. Deep valleys intersect the undulating surface of the plateau, and the Thanlwin (Salween) flows through it like an arrow. Once popular as a site for hill stations, the region still offers the flavour of a bygone era in its administrative centres of Pyin U-Lwin and Kalaw, while Inle Lake, in the southwestern part of the plateau, has developed into a major modern tourist centre. Fruit, citrus crops and vegetables thrive in the almost European climate, as does timber. Myanmar is the world's leading exporter of teak, most of which is harvested in the Shan State. Other crops include rice, peanuts, potatoes, tea, tobacco, coffee and cotton. The country is also the world's second largest producer (after Afghanistan) of opium, most of it grown in the Burmese section of the notorious "Golden Triangle", which encompasses much of the eastern Shan plateau, extending into neighbouring Thailand and Laos (see page 57).

East of the Gulf of Mottama, Myanmar narrows into the long, thin strip of land divided between Myanmar and Thailand and known as Tanintharyi on the Burmese side, with the forested Tanintharyi hills forming a natural border with Thailand. The coastland which follows this range down to the Isthmus of Kra is not easily accessible, for various reasons, but the coastal areas of Mawlamyine and Dawei are home to pockets of densely populated agricultural land.

Scattered off the coast of Tanintharyi are the islets of the Myeik Archipelago, one of Southeast Asia's least developed island groups. Long off limits for security reasons, the archipelago is now opening up for tourism, with day-trips from Myeik, plus a variety of live-aboard boat and dive cruises and a trio of luxury hotels on the islets themselves.

West of the Ayeyarwady Delta, on the seaward side of the Rakhine hills, Rakhine State comprises a flat, fertile coastal strip characterised by small rivers flowing out of mountains to the north, the highest of which is Nat Ma Taung (Mount Victoria) at 3,053 metres (10,016ft). Long sandy beaches, still largely undeveloped, run along the coastline.

The area surrounding the Ayeyarwady (and its tributaries the Chindwin and Sittaung) is the most fertile and densely populated part of Myanmar, and the traditional homeland of the dominant Bamar people, far and away Myanmar's largest ethnic group. The region is divided into two parts: Upper Myanmar, the area north of Pyay and Taungoo up to the Mandalay region; and Lower Myanmar, stretching south of Pyay and Taungoo down to Yangon.

FRUITS OF THE LAND

Myanmar remains a predominantly agrarian nation, with agriculture employing over two-thirds of the country's population (although contributing only 25 percent to the national GDP). From the later 19th century right through until 1962, Myanmar was the world's largest rice exporter, and rice remains the country's most important crop. More than 8 million hectares (20 million acres) of land are devoted to irrigated rice farming, although crop failures still occur, and before rice was available from

Lower Myanmar, famine was common in more arid parts of the country.

Most of Myanmar's rice is now grown in the fertile Delta region, home to around 3.6 million hectares (9 million acres) of irrigated rice farms, with a yield great enough to feed the entire population of the country.

When the British arrived in the mid-19th century, the Delta was an uncultivated expanse of jungle. Colonists were given land in the Delta which they then cleared of jungle to make way for wet-rice fields. It was during

Ploughing the fields around Bagan's Dhammayangyi temple.

this period that Burma became the world's largest rice exporter, and although production levels dropped during military rule, they have recently revived, and look set to improve even further with the introduction of high-yield strains, land reclamation, improved irrigation and more mechanised farming methods.

Rice cultivation in the drier regions of Upper Myanmar has always been more difficult. The ancient Bamar of Bagan developed a complex irrigation system of rivers and canals to irrigate their lands, while nowadays rice cultivation is combined with the farming of cotton, tobacco, peanuts, grain sorghum, sesame, beans and corn.

MINERALS AND FORESTS

Myanmar has huge, largely untapped mineral reserves. Oil, found mostly in the Ayeyarwady basin, has historically been the most important. Early British explorers visiting the town of Yenangyaung in 1795 found oil already being extracted from hundreds of hand-dug wells, while the country exported its first barrels of crude oil as early as 1853. The Burmah Oil Company (the forerunner of today's BP), founded in 1871, subsequently provided sufficient oil to meet most of the demands of Britain's Indian empire, producing over 6 million barrels a year. In recent years Myanmar has also become one of the world's top-twenty exporters of natural gas, largely through deals with Thailand and China.

Iron, tungsten, lead, silver, tin, mercury, nickel, plutonium, zinc, copper, cobalt, antimony and gold are found in significant quantities around the country. Myanmar's famed rubies and sapphires are mined in Mogok in western Shan State, while fine jade is extracted near the towns of Mogaung and Hpakant in Kachin State.

Over thirty percent of the country is still covered by forest – the largest area of tropical forest in Southeast Asia, home to some eighty endemic species. Deforestation is rife, however, and the country has lost over thirty percent of its entire tree cover since independence, both from the drive to create new agricultural land and to extract valuable teak and other hardwoods. Pockets of tropical rainforests can be found in wetter districts, and bamboo, used to construct many buildings, is common. Higher up, oaks, silver firs, chestnuts and rhododendrons thrive. In the central Dry Zone, cacti and acacia trees are common.

Taunggya (slash-and-burn) cultivation used through much of upland Myanmar has resulted in the depletion of the original forest cover, now replaced by a second growth of scrub forest. In *taunggya* agriculture, large trees are felled and the jungle burned to prepare for planting – often with 40 or more different crops.

When crops and torrential rains have depleted soil fertility (within a year or two), the clearing is abandoned and the land left to fallow for 12 to 15 years. In the past, villages often changed sites when the accessible land was exhausted, although nowadays the use of fertilizers means that land can be worked for much longer.

Red panda.

⊘ OPENING UP

In terms of ease of access and freedom of movement, there has rarely been a better time to visit Myanmar. Visas – which were unobtainable for much of the 1960s, limited to 24 hours in the early 1970s and to one week throughout the 1980s –are now readily available online and relatively easy to extend. Geographical restrictions on travel are also being steadily eased as large areas which were formerly off limits are opened to foreign tourists, although significant parts of the country (notably in the east and north) remain out of bounds as a result of political unrest and long-running clashes between the military and armed ethnic groups.

BURMESE WILDLIFE

The great variety of Myanmar's landscapes, climates and habitats – and a relative lack of exploitation – should be reflected in a rich and abundant biodiversity, although no one is entirely sure how many species survive, and in what numbers. Wars in remote border areas, in particular, have prevented naturalists from undertaking wide-ranging surveys. The one certainty is that over the past century, increased population, poaching and destruction of natural habitats by loggers and big businesses have, inevitably, had a negative impact on the local wildlife. Illegal hunting has also been encouraged by the booming market for exotic animal parts in the east of the country, particularly in the casino town of Mong La in Shan State, where Chinese tourists like to fortify themselves with libido-enhancing tiger's penis or bear's bile soup ahead of sex sessions with local prostitutes.

The willingness of the Burmese government to demarcate national parks and reserves in the 1990s and 2000s was a cause for optimism among conservationists, even if it is generally acknowledged that the junta's motivation stemmed less from a desire to save endangered species than to wrest control of peripheral zones – and their natural resources – from the enemy insurgent groups who formerly occupied them. One of the great hopes for wildlife conservation in Myanmar therefore rests with tourism. Generate sufficient income for local people (and the government) in parks – or so the argument runs – and the poaching, illegal mining and timber extraction will cease – though wildlife tourism as yet barely exists.

The gradual easing of travel restrictions in the remote corners of the country is particularly welcomed by wildlife experts because Myanmar's unspoilt forests keep turning up hitherto unknown species. These include the leaf muntjac (discovered in 1997), the world's smallest deer, weighing in at just 11kg (25lbs), and the snub-nosed monkey, discovered in 2010 when local hunters produced carcasses of the rare primate, which they claimed loathed the rain and spent wet days with its head between its knees to stop water dripping in its trademark upturned nose. A 2015 report by the World Wildlife Fund named a staggering 139 new species identified across the Greater Mekong region (including many in Myanmar), while a 2017 study sponsored by Fauna & Flora International identified no less than 15 new species of gecko in just two weeks.

The species most likely to attract wildlife tourists, however, is rather better known. An estimated 50 tigers inhabit an area of pristine forest in the Hukawng Valley, in the far north. Now protected by the government, this is the world's largest tiger reserve, though it remains under threat from logging, oil and gas exploration, uranium and gold mining – as well as poachers. At the opposite end of the country, in the Kachin Hills, the red panda is another great rarity that's been spotted in recent years. Myanmar is also home to a significant number of elephants – far and away the largest population in Southeast Asia – with around four to five thousand in the wild, and a similar number in captivity (see page 287).

With most tourism confined to the river valleys of central Myanmar and western fringe of Shah State, it's unlikely you'll spot any of the region's Big Five mammals – elephant, tiger, leopard, bear or gaur (Indian bison) – in the wild. You may, however, be lucky enough to encounter the critically endangered Irrawaddy dolphin. Resembling

Collecting palm sugar to make jaggery.

a small beluga with a distinctive round nose, this small cetacean has suffered terribly in recent decades from gill-net fishing and water pollution from gold mining in its stronghold area – a 45km (28-mile) stretch of the Ayeyarwady around Kyaukmyaung (see page 265), where a special protected area has been created. Only around 30 pairs survive today, though your chances of sighting one are good while cruising the river by ferry.

ENVIRONMENTAL ISSUES

Myanmar is one of the least environmentally protected countries in the world, and since 1988, when its military government opened the door to foreign investment in exchange for quick cash, threats to the country's forests, water, soil and biodiversity have spiralled out of control. Moreover, because most Burmese people are ignorant of the problems (the junta has long suppressed any reports of environmental issues), opposition is negligible, although this is now starting to change.

Laws to protect the environment do exist, but they're rarely enforced if there's a profit to be made, and logging companies have decimated the country's forests as a result. Between 1990 and 2015, nearly 15 million hectares (37 million acres) of forest and wooded land disappeared, giving the country the world's third highest rate of deforesta-

scheduled to be built with Chinese help over the coming decade. Opponents claim the schemes are merely a ruse to earn foreign exchange for the government and its cronies (most of the electricity generated will be exported to China), and will result in the forcible relocation of hundreds of villages, as well as the destruction of important fisheries and fragile ecosystems.

Opposition to the dam-building projects, however, began to gain the upper hand as the democratic reform process has gathered pace: work on the largest and most controversial scheme,

Boats arriving at Nampam market, Inle Lake.

tion, with an annual loss of forest cover approaching two percent annually. A 2014 government ban on the export of raw timber had little effect, while a further temporary ban on all logging introduced by the new NLD government in 2016 was similarly ineffectual. Much of the timber disappears over the Chinese border, while vast quantities of wood are also burned for fuel.

Further north along the banks of the Ayeyarwady, gold and gem-stone mining are having a disastrous impact on water quality, as tonnes of cyanide, mercury and other chemicals are spilled into the rivers. Dam projects pose another threat to the river system. Promoted by the government to produce hydroelectricity, dozens of barrages, including a handful of gigantic "mega-dams", are

at Myitsone in the Upper Ayeyarwady region, was suspended in 2011 in the face of pressure both from Burmese activist groups and foreign governments, although opponents claim that work on it is continuing in secret, and the NLD has yet to make a final decision on the dam's future.

In the rice-growing regions, soil depletion has also become a major issue. For the past three decades the military government has forced farmers to double or treble outputs, claiming the lion's share of the harvest at reduced prices for itself, and then selling the rice on the world market for huge profits. As a result, traditional crop rotation has fallen by the wayside, and yields are these days only maintained by costly, and environmentally damaging, inputs of fertilisers.

GEM STONES

Myanmar's rich natural bounty includes some of the world's largest deposits of precious stones, notably rubies and jade.

Ludovico di Varthema, an Italian who visited Burma in 1505, was the first European to report the existence in the country of a seemingly prodigious quantity of gem stones, among them sparkling star rubies which were at the time unknown to the rest of the world. Di Varthema was also the first Westerner to prosper from dealing in them. He presented the King of Bago with a gift of corals, and was rewarded with 200 rubies – worth about 100,000 ducats (about US$150,000) in Europe at that time. Today, it is not so easy to get rich in the gem business, but each spring hundreds of dealers from all over the world gather in Naypyidaw to try their luck at the famous Gems and Pearl Emporium, where lots are sold by bidding.

A BOOMING TRADE

Myanmar has historically been the world's main source of rubies, and still provides around ninety percent of all stones sold globally. The country's most famous mines are in Mogok, 110km (70 miles) northeast of Mandalay, celebrated since antiquity for their prodigious quantities of rubies and other precious gems. In earlier times, the kings of Burma appropriated many of the rubies found in their territories, leaving miners with only the smaller stones, while following the British annexation of Upper Burma in 1886, the London firm of Messrs Streeter & Co. became fabulously rich after having secured exclusive rights to the Mogok's gems. Today, nationalised mines at Mogok, Mong Hsu in central Myanmar, Namya in Kachin State and elsewhere provide a steady flow of foreign currency for Myanmar's government. Stones with the deep-red lustre (popularly described as "pigeon's blood") fetch the highest prices. Fakes also abound, however, and synthetic stones (often deceptively labelled) are also popular at tourist markets.

Myanmar is also known for its huge reserves of jade, most of which is mined in the remote hinterlands to the west of Myitkyina in Kachin State, near the towns of Mogaung and Hpakant. The riches of this region were well known to the Chinese as long ago as 2000 BC.

Most of Myanmar's precious stones are found in areas dominated by minority ethnic groups. The way in which revenues from the gem trade have been distributed remains a major source of conflict between central government and minority peoples. Opposition groups assert that while the trade has generated phenomenal wealth for the former military junta and its cronies, few, if any, of the benefits have trickled down to ordinary Burmese people in the regions affected by the mining. In addition, as well as filling

Polishing jade in Mandalay city's jade market.

government coffers, illegal trade in gem stones and jade has also provided the main source of income for various ethnic rebel groups fighting the government for greater autonomy.

The northern jade-mining districts attract prospectors from all over the country, who come in search of instant wealth. Some succeed, but most end up as day labourers in the larger pits, often controlled by ethnic Chinese. Stories of lawlessness and exploitation are rife, although difficult to verify given that the area remains off limits to Western visitors.

Rubies and jade are the most evident examples of Myanmar's precious mineral wealth, but sapphires, oriental aquamarine and emeralds, topaz, amethysts and lapis lazuli also lure buyers to the country.

Depiction of Bagan in the 19th century.

DECISIVE DATES

EARLY EMPIRES

5000–3000 BC
The lower-Palaeolithic Anyathian culture flourishes in northern Burma.

3rd century BC
The Mon, immigrants from Thailand, settle the Sittaung Valley and establish Buddhism.

1st century AD
The Pyu arrive in the northern Ayeyarwady Valley, gradually spreading south as far as present-day Pyay.

9th century AD
The Bamar people migrate into Myanmar from the China-Tibet border, settling in the rice-growing area around Bagan, from where they control trade between China and India.

THE BURMESE DYNASTIES

1044–1078
Myanmar's first empire, the Kingdom of Bagan, is

A British lithograph (1825) of Shwedagon Pagoda shows the British occupation during the First Anglo-Burmese War.

established under the rule of the legendary King Anawrahta.

1287
Fall of the Bagan empire following a series of invasions by Mongol armies from China.

1430
Mrauk-U, the last capital of independent Arakan (Rakhine), is established in northwest Burma.

1519
The Portuguese gain the first foothold of any European power in the region, founding a trading post at Mottama (Martaban) in southeast Burma.

1550–81
Bayinnaung, third king of the Taungoo Dynasty, subdues all of the country's rival dynasties, creating the largest empire in the history of Southeast Asia.

1784
Konbaung forces from Mandalay annexe Arakan, looting religious relics including the famous Mahamuni statue, and destroying much of the city.

COLONIAL PERIOD TO WORLD WAR II

1824–26
The First Anglo-Burmese War.

1852
Second Anglo-Burmese war. The British annex all of southern Burma, establishing their capital at Yangon (Rangoon).

1885
The British take the Burmese capital, Mandalay. King Thibaw and his family are sent into exile in India. All of Burma falls under British control.

1886–95
Insurgency breaks out across the country, but the guerrilla uprising is quashed with brutal force by the British.

1941
The Japanese occupy Burma, forcing the Allies northwest into India.

1945
The Burma National Army starts an anti-Japanese uprising as the Allies re-take Burma.

1947
Aung San signs an independence agreement with the UK, but is assassinated, along with six other members of the interim government.

INDEPENDENCE

1948
Burma formally regains independence, unleashing civil war and regional rebellions. U Nu becomes prime minister.

1962
Ne Win sweeps to power in a near-bloodless coup. He appoints a Revolutionary Council to rule by decree, and implements the economically disastrous "Burmese Road to Socialism". All political parties are banned and media strictly censored.

Aung San Suu Kyi speaks at a National League for Democracy demonstration near Sule Pagoda, Yangon.

1988

Following a period of civil unrest fuelled by economic hardship, major demonstrations erupt. On 8 August 1988 hundreds of thousands mount further protests calling for democracy – the so-called "8888 Revolution".

SLORC TAKES POWER

18 September 1988

A military coup places the State Law and Order Restoration Council (SLORC) in power and a massive crackdown is launched by the military, with thousands killed. Aung San Suu Kyi and colleagues form the National League for Democracy (NLD).

1989

Burma's name is changed by its military government to Myanmar. Some Western powers refuse to recognise the change.

1990

Aung San Suu Kyi placed under house arrest while general elections are held.

1991

SLORC refuses to accept the election results. Aung San Suu Kyi is awarded the Nobel Peace Prize.

1993

The Kachin Independence Organisation (KIO) signs a ceasefire agreement with the government, ending a 30-year war in the north.

2006

The military junta inaugurates a brand-new planned capital called Naypyidaw ("city of kings"), 320km (200 miles) north of Yangon.

THE "SAFFRON REVOLUTION" AND BEYOND

2007

A hike in the price of fuel leads to widespread anti-government protests, which are violently suppressed. Thousands of monks spearhead a growing campaign of civil resistance, dubbed the "Saffron Revolution".

2008

Cyclone Nargis wreaks devastation across the Ayeyarwady Delta in May, killing an estimated 200,000 people.

2010

As part of a raft of constitutional reforms, national elections are held, but the NLD condemn the result as fraudulent. Further reforms see a wind down of press censorship and the release of hundreds of political prisoners – among them NLD leader, Aung San Suu Kyi.

2012

Aung San Suu Kyi is one of 44 NLD representatives who enter the Burmese parliament following by-elections across the country. Tourist numbers increase rapidly as the tourism boycott is lifted.

2012–2013

Mobs attacks Burmese Muslims in Rakhine State and Meiktila, leaving at least a hundred dead, with thousands more driven into refugee camps.

2015

The NLD secures a landslide victory in Myanmar's first democratic elections in half a century, although Aung San Suu Kyi herself is barred from officially leading the new government and the military retain a large degree of autonomy.

2016

The Union Peace Conference between the government and most of the country's armed ethnic groups is held with the aim of bringing lasting peace to Myanmar – although shortly afterwards violence flares in Rakhine State.

2017

Ongoing violence in Rakhine State leads to widespread allegations of human-rights abuses against the Rohingya people, thousands of whom are massacred, and calls for Aung San Suu Kyi to be stripped of her Nobel Peace Prize.

2018

Renewed fighting between the government and Kachin Independence Organisation causes thousands to flee their homes, while the number of Rohingya refugees driven abroad approaches one million.

A 17th-century marble and gilded-lacquer Buddha statue.

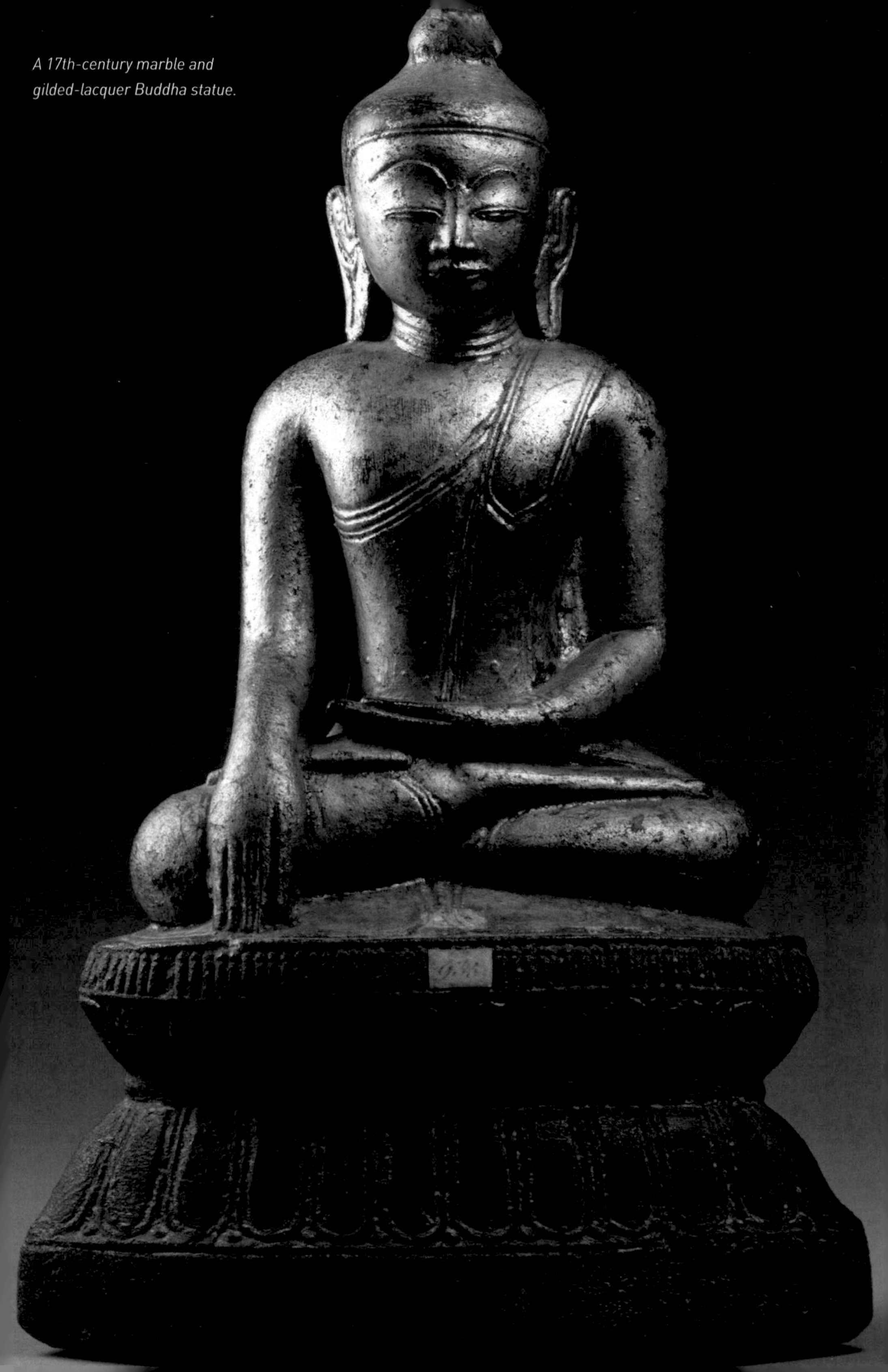

FROM EARLIEST TIMES

Settlement by the Bamar, Mon, Pyu, Tai, Shan and other peoples led to the development of a series of competing kingdoms, including the three great Burmese empires of pre-colonial times.

Early Burmese history is a murky affair. Solid historical and archaeological evidence is scant and open to widely different interpretations, and even some quite basic facts about the country's past remain fiercely contested.

THE "LAND OF GOLD"

The Mon (who can still be found in parts of Thailand and Cambodia today) were amongst the first ethnic groups to occupy the southern part of what is now Myanmar, over 2,000 years ago. Speaking a language belonging to the Mon–Khmer family, the Mon entered southern Myanmar from the east, settling along the estuaries of the Thanlwin (Salween) and Sittoung (Sittang) rivers, establishing a kingdom which Indian chronicles called *Suvannabhumi* ("Land of Gold") and which is also mentioned in ancient Chinese and Arab writings.

Legend says it was the Mon who laid the foundation stone of the Shwedagon Pagoda as far back as 2,500 years ago, while they also claim to have been the first people to have established the Buddhist tradition in Myanmar, enjoying close ties with the realm of Emperor Ashoka in India through the port of Thaton on the southeast coast by the 3rd century BC.

At the opposite end of the country, and at around the same time, the Pyu people migrated out of southern China and settled in Upper Myanmar, establishing a string of walled cities across the north. The largest was at Halin, although this was later superseded by Sri Ksetra (Thayekhittaya) (see page 159), close to present-day Pyay. The brick ruins here still clearly show extensive evidence of their brand of religious architecture – mainly Buddhist in style, but with a noticeably strong Indian influence.

A lithograph of the Golden Temple at Bago.

Pyu civilization had already been established in Upper Myanmar for a millennium when the Bamar people began migrating southward from their ancestral home in Yunnan, in southwest China. Bamar forces attacked Upper Myanmar on several occasions, capturing Halin in 832 and settling in the surrounding lands.

THE FIRST BURMESE EMPIRE

Having established themselves in Myanmar, the Bamar people began gradually to extend their lands and influence south down the Ayeyarwady, founding the city of Bagan in (legend has it) 849. It wasn't until two centuries later, however, under King Anawrahta (r. 1044–1077) that Bagan became the leading power in the land.

Anawrahta reformed the kingdom's agriculture and launched a series of attacks, conquering the remaining pockets of independent Pyu territory, before heading south. In 1057 he conquered the Mon capital of Thaton, returning to Bagan with 30,000 prisoners, including the Mon royal family and many master builders and craftsmen.

Ironically, despite the Mon's defeat, their culture became a leading factor in the development of the classic culture of Bagan. The Mon language replaced Pali and Sanskrit in royal inscriptions, and Theravada Buddhism became the state religion (the Bamar having previously practised a debased form of the religion known as Ari Buddhism). Through the close relations maintained by the Mon with Sri Lanka, at that time the centre of Theravada culture, "the way of the elders" spread throughout most of mainland Southeast Asia. Under this new influence, Anawrahta became a devout Theravada Buddhist, commissioning the building of the Shwezigon Pagoda in Nyaung U (near Bagan; see page 223), as well as other shrines on the plain.

Four of the 28 Buddhas in the Dhammacakka mudra, Payathonzu Temple, Bagan.

⊘ GLASS PALACE CHRONICLE

In 1829, King Bagyidaw of Burma appointed a committee of scholars to write a history of the Burmese monarchy, the *Hmannan Yazawin*, or "Glass Palace Chronicle", as it's known in English. The committee consisted of "learned monks, learned brahmans and learned ministers" who compiled a record "which they sifted and prepared in accordance with all credible records". The chronicle (named after Bagyidaw's Glass Palace in the royal residence at Mandalay where the history was written) recounts the story of Buddhism and of the Buddhist kings of ancient India, as well as the history of the early Burmese kingdoms up to the fall of Bagan.

BAGAN'S GOLDEN AGE

Having defeated the Mon, the Bamar were now in control of much of lowland Myanmar, and a golden age of pagoda building began. Many temples were constructed during the reign of Kyanzittha (1084–1113), who came to power after defeating a Mon rebellion during which Anawrahta's son and successor, Saw Lu, was killed.

Like Anawrahta, Kyanzittha was a deeply religious man. He ordered the construction of the Ananda Temple and – an indication of his vast wealth – sent a ship filled with treasures to India to assist in the restoration of the Mahabodhi Temple in Bodhgaya, the place of the Buddha's enlightenment. Kyanzittha gave his daughter away in marriage to a Mon prince, and chose their son, Alaungsithu, as successor to preserve the unity of the Bagan Empire.

The apogee of Bagan's culture and power came during the 12th century, when it acquired the name "city of the four million pagodas". In common with the other great civilisation in the region at the time – Angkor – the kingdom was supported by rice cultivation, made possible by a highly developed system of irrigation canals.

THE END OF THE EMPIRE

Unbridled temple-building slowly took its toll on the empire's economy, however, whose end was further hastened when the Mongol armies of Kublai Khan appeared on the scene in the later thirteenth century. Fresh from overrunning the Nanzhao Empire in Yunnan, Kublai Khan now demanded payment of tribute by the Bagan emperors. King Narathihapate, overestimating the strength of his own forces, refused.

When the Mongol forces invaded Myanmar in a series of battles in the late 13th century, advancing as far as present-day Bhamo, it is said that, in desperation, Narathihapate pulled down 6,000 temples to fortify Bagan's city walls. He died soon after, poisoned by his own son, the ruler of Pyay. The end result was the conquest of Bagan by the Mongols in 1287.

After the fall of Bagan, Myanmar was divided into several small states for almost 300 years. In Lower Myanmar, the Mon founded a new kingdom centred on Bago. Although they lost their grip on the southern Tanintharyi region during a mid-14th-century invasion by the Thai from Ayutthaya, they managed to hold the rest of their realm together. In Upper Myanmar, meanwhile, the Shan established sovereignty over an extensive network of kingdoms with their main capital at Inwa (Ava). In the west, along the Bay of Bengal, the Rakhine spread north, controlling large parts of what is now Bangladesh.

THE PORTUGUESE PERIOD

It was in the 15th century that Europeans first appeared in Myanmar. In 1435, a Venetian merchant named Nicolo di Conti visited Bago and remained for four months. Six decades later, in 1498, the Portuguese seafarer Vasco da Gama discovered the sea route from Europe to India. His countrymen were very quick to take advantage of his great success: Alfonso de Albuquerque

conquered Goa in 1510, and within a year Malacca, the spice centre of the Orient, was in his grasp.

It was from these two ports that the Portuguese sought to establish a monopoly over the commerce of the Indian Ocean. Antony Correa arrived in Mottama (in southern Myanmar near present-day Mawlamyine) in 1519 and signed a trade and settlement treaty with the town's viceroy which gave the Portuguese a base from which to trade with Thailand.

The most remarkable character from the Portuguese era in Myanmar was Felipe de Brito e

A Shan archer.

> *Despite his attempts to defend his empire, Narathihapate was branded Tarok-pyemin, meaning "the king who ran away from the Chinese".*

Nicote, who came to Asia as a cabin boy and later accepted a post in the court of King Razagyi of Rakhine, who had conquered Bago. De Brito was entrusted with the job of running the customs administration in Syriam (modern-day Thanlyin, near Yangon), but soon afterwards repudiated Razagyi's authority and placed the town under Portuguese sovereignty. After a trip to Goa, during which he married the viceroy's daughter, he returned to Thanlyin with supplies and reinforcements to withstand Burmese sieges and proclaimed himself king of Lower Myanmar.

De Brito's superior naval power forced all sea-going trade through the port at Thanlyin. He also displayed an utter contempt for Buddhist beliefs, plundering monuments and forcibly converting (it's said) some 100,000 Burmese to Christianity during his 13-year reign.

In 1613, Anaukpetlun of Taungoo stormed Thanlyin with 12,000 men. Around 400 Portuguese defended the town for 34 days but de

Filipe de Brito, Portuguese mercenary and governor of Syriam (Thanlyin), c. 1600.

King Bodawpaya suffered serious delusions of religious grandeur, claiming to be the future Maitreya, the next Buddha-to-be – a claim politely but firmly rejected by the country's monks.

Brito was captured and impaled: it took him three days to die.

In northern Myanmar, meanwhile, hill tribes razed the Shan capital of Inwa in 1527. Many Bamar fled to the small town of Taungoo, which suddenly rose to power under King Tabinshwehti (r. 1530–50), who attacked and defeated the

Mon kingdom, subsequently moving his capital to the former Mon centre of Bago. His successor King Bayinnaung (r. 1550–1581) extended the lands of the Taungoo dynasty down the coast to Dawei, and north to Pyay, before overwhelming the Shan and conquering the Thai kingdoms of Lan Na (around modern-day Chiang Mai) and (briefly) Ayutthaya far to the east, creating the second of Myanmar's three great pre-colonial empires.

During the 17th century, the Dutch, British and French set up trading companies in Myanmar's coastal ports. The long-running Taungoo Empire finally crumbled in 1752, when its capital (now moved to Inwa) fell to Mon forces.

Myanmar's third great empire emerged immediately out of the ashes of the second with the creation of the Konbaung dynasty by King Alaungpaya, a Bamar from Shwebo. Self-proclaimed leader of the Bamar, Alaungpaya assembled considerable forces and swiftly defeated the Mon, deported the French to Bayingyi, and got rid of British trading posts. Mon resistance ceased entirely, and the Mon people either fled to Siam or submitted to Bamar rule.

BRITISH CONTROL

Alaungpaya's second successor, Hsinbyushin, attacked Ayutthaya in Siam in 1767 and returned to Inwa with artists and craftsmen who gave a fresh cultural impetus to the Konbaung kingdom. King Bodawpaya (r. 1782–1819) moved the capital to Amarapura, not far from Inwa, on the advice of his soothsayers. He also conquered Rakhine, bringing the borders of his kingdom right up against the British sphere of influence in Bengal and leading to an increasing number of border clashes between Burmese and British forces.

Serious conflict was sparked after King Bagyidaw came to the throne in 1819. The Raja of Manipur, who had previously paid tribute to the Burmese, failed to attend Bagyidaw's coronation. The subsequent punitive expedition took the Burmese into the Indian state of Cachar in Assam, an intrusion which was used by the British as a pretext for what is now called the First Anglo–Burmese War.

The Burmese underestimated the strength of the British, and were soundly defeated. In the Treaty of Yandabo (1826) the Burmese were forced to cede Rakhine and Tanintharyi, plus the Assam and Manipur border areas they had controlled since 1819, to the European victors. The British thereby succeeded in making secure their exposed flank on the Bay of Bengal.

The Burmese were without a capable ruler through the first half of the 19th century, and this weakened the kingdom just at the wrong time. When British and French interests collided in Southeast Asia, Myanmar's independence was rapidly nearing an end. In 1852, two British sea captains registered a complaint

circumstances, to preserve Burmese independence while maintaining peaceful relations with Britain. A pious Buddhist, he welcomed Christian missionaries to his country and sent missions to the courts of Britain, France and Italy. In 1861, he introduced coinage and reorganised the tax system, greatly improving Burmese state finances. In the same year, commemorating the 2,400th anniversary of the Buddha's first sermon, Mindon transferred his court to the new city of Mandalay. He died at the age of 64, without choosing a successor.

The original Mandalay Palace compound was constructed between 1857 and 1859.

about unfair treatment in a Burmese court. The British Empire responded by sending an expeditionary force to Burma, leading to the Second Anglo–Burmese War and the rapid conquest of the whole of Lower Burma.

MINDON'S MANDALAY

It was about this time that King Mindon (r. 1853–1878) came to power in Amarapura, deposing his brother Pagan Min in 1852 and occupying Amarapura in 1853. His was a relatively enlightened rule, and he was the first Burmese sovereign to attempt to bring the country more in line with Western ideas.

Sources characterise Mindon as a man of high moral standards who did his best, in difficult

⊙ KING MINDON'S TRIPITAKA

Mandalay was sacred to the Buddhist faith, and in 1872 Mindon hosted the Fifth Great Synod of Buddhism, during which the revered Buddhist scriptures, known as the *Tripitaka*, were committed to stone. Mindon wanted the sacred scriptures to be preserved so that they would be available until the coming of the Maitreya Buddha, many thousands of years into the future. Some 2,400 scribes worked on the text, which was then chiselled onto 729 tablets of stone; a pagoda was built over each of the tablets at the base of Mandalay Hill. But even this appeal for a return to the values of Buddhism, which would sustain the Burmese state and people, could not alter the course of history.

British troops entering Mandalay during the Third Anglo-Burmese War, 1885.

BRITISH RULE AND WORLD WAR II

In the late 19th century, Myanmar was annexed as a province of British India, a move that still has repercussions today.

King Mindon was succeeded by Thibaw in 1878, and the new sovereign wasted little time in alienating the British. Most provocatively, he began negotiating an agreement with the French – who were seeking a direct trade route to China – for shipping rights on the Ayeyarwady. This was clearly contrary to the interests of the British. The final straw came when a British timber company became embroiled in a dispute with Thibaw's government; the king was given an ultimatum which he chose to ignore. Immediately afterwards, British troops invaded Upper Burma, encountering almost no resistance and overwhelming the capital with ease.

BRITISH BURMA

On 1 January 1886, Myanmar ceased to exist as an independent country. Thibaw and his queen, Supayalat, were sent into exile, and Burma, as the country would henceforth be known, was annexed as a province of British India.

To facilitate their exercise of power over all of Burma, the British permitted the autonomy of the country's many racial minorities. As early as 1875, they had enforced the autonomy of the Kayin (Karen) states by refusing to supply King Mindon with the arms he needed to put down a Kayin revolt. The repercussions of this and other similar political moves by the British still influence the country today.

Throughout Upper and Lower Burma, the British assumed all government positions down to district officer level. In the bordering states where Chin, Kachin, Shan and various other minorities predominated, they relied on indirect rule, permitting the respective chieftains to govern in their place. Military forces were largely recruited from India and the northern hill tribes.

King Thibaw of Burma in full court dress, c. 1900.

During most of the colonial period, Bamar were barred from admission to the armed forces.

British interest in Burma was principally of an economic nature, and there was, not surprisingly, a significant economic upswing after their occupation of the entire country. This economic transformation was particularly striking in the formerly marshy swamps of the Ayeyarwady Delta, which had been drained and opened up for cultivation following the British occupation of Lower Burma in 1852. A generation later, this move began to pay significant dividends, producing vast quantities of rice for export. This benefitted both the British, who controlled the exports, and the Indian moneylenders and merchants who financed and managed the trade, and who were far more familiar than the Burmese with the sophisticated workings of a modern cash economy. In particular, the *chettiars*, a caste of moneylenders from south India, profited greatly from Burma's agricultural expansion.

In the five years following the annexation of Upper Burma, a quasi-guerrilla war tied up some 10,000 Indian troops in the country. The guerrillas were led by *myothugyis*, local leaders of the old social structure. This resistance declined after 1890, however, and from this time on the Burmese attempted to adjust to the far-reaching social and economic changes that were taking place.

Following World War I, India was granted a degree of self-government by its British rulers, but Burma remained under the direct control of its colonial governor. This led to extensive opposition within the country, highlighted by a lengthy boycott of schools beginning in December 1920. Eventually, in 1923, the same concessions granted to India – known as the "dyarchy reform" – were extended to Burma.

The Quartermaster's Staff of the 1st Royal Munster Fusiliers, Rangoon, 1913.

⊘ SCOTT OF THE SHAN HILLS

Sir James George Scott (also known by his Burmese pseudonym Shway Yoe), was a prominent British administrator, soldier, explorer and writer who lived in Burma during the latter half of the 19th century. Scott was chiefly remarkable for his ability to assimilate Burmese customs and language, as well as for his love of the country and its people. The founder of Taunggyi (a place of respite for the British from the tropical heat) and one of the most respected colonial officers in the history of British Burma, Scott was a personal friend of King Thibaw, but later became a colonial administrator following the annexation of the Shan States in 1890. He is credited with introducing football to Burma, as well as for such major academic endeavours as producing the multi-volume Gazetteer of Shan State. His most famous work, *The Burman: His Life and Notions* (1882), published under the pseudonym "Shway Yoe – Subject of the Great Queen", presented so authentic an image of Burma that some contemporary reviewers mistakenly believed it to be the work of a prominent Bamar scholar. Scott went on to serve as British Commissioner of India in 1897. The book has been republished many times, and remains invaluable for understanding Bamar life cycles, society, religion and culture. Scott also provided the inspiration for two of the best modern books on Myanmar: Andrew Marshall's *The Trouser People*, and Rory Maclean's *Under the Dragon*.

THE RISE OF NATIONALISM

A major revolt took place in the Tharrawaddy region north of Yangon between 1930 and 1932. Saya San, a former monk, organised a group of followers called *galon* (after the mythical bird Garuda), and convinced them that British bullets could not harm them. Three thousand of his supporters were subsequently killed in fighting, and another 9,000 were taken prisoner, of whom 78, including Saya San, were executed.

Throughout the early 1930s, opinion was split in Burma as to whether the country should be

U Nu – boldly led another strike of university and high-school classes in opposition to the "alien" educational system.

The success of their movement in bringing about major reforms helped to give these men the confidence in the following decade to come to the forefront of the nationalist movement.

Meanwhile, however, war was brewing. The "Burma Road" made that inevitable. Built as an all-weather route in the 1930s to carry supplies and reinforcements to Chinese troops attempting to repulse the Japanese invasion, it was of

Japanese occupying forces, 1942.

separated from British India or not. The question was resolved in 1935 when the "Government of Burma Act" was signed in London. Two years later, Burma became a separate colony with its own legislative council. This council dealt only with "Burma Proper", however, and not with the indirectly administered border states.

However, as Burma was granted greater autonomy, the underground nationalist movement gathered momentum. In 1930, at the University of Yangon, the All Burma Student Movement emerged to defy colonial rule. The young men who spearheaded this group studied Marxism and called each other *Thakin* ("master"), a term generally used to address Europeans. In 1936, the group's leaders – Aung San and

> In Burmese the term *shikoe* means the act of touching one's head to the floor before the presence of an honoured person, a Buddha image or a Buddhist monk.

extreme strategic importance. As Allied forces moved to defend the road, Japan planned an all-out attack on the Burmese heartland.

The colonial government unexpectedly played into Japanese hands when it attempted to arrest leaders of the Thakin group in 1940. Aung San escaped by disguising himself as a Chinese crewman on a Norwegian boat. He arrived in

Amoy seeking contact with Chinese communists to help in Burma's drive for independence. But the Japanese arrested him, and although his movement was opposed to Japan's war on China, his release was negotiated on the grounds that he and other members of the Thakin organisation would collaborate with the Japanese.

In March 1941, Aung San returned to Yangon aboard a Japanese freighter. He secretly picked out 30 members of the Thakin group (the "Thirty Comrades") to be trained by the Japanese on Hainan Island in guerrilla warfare.

Chindits in the jungle.

A BRUTAL BATTLEFIELD

In December 1941, the Japanese landed in Lower Burma. Together with the "Burmese Liberation Army" led by Aung San, they overwhelmed the British, drove them from Yangon four months later, then convincingly won battle after battle. British, Indian, Chinese and American troops suffered heavy casualties and were forced to retreat to India. While World War II raged in Europe and the Pacific, the fighting was nowhere more bitter than in the jungles of Southeast Asia. Hand-to-hand combat was a frequent necessity, and tens of thousands of Allied soldiers were killed, along with hundreds of thousands of Burmese. The 27,000 Allied graves in the Taukkyan cemetery near Yangon are just one testimony to the horrors

that took place. Survivors of this conflict emerged from the jungle with stories of suffering, sacrifice and heroic deeds. They made household names out of such warriors as "Vinegar Joe" Stilwell, "Old Weatherface" Chennault, Wingate's Chindits and Merrill's Marauders.

STILWELL'S RETREAT

In February 1942, Joseph Warren Stilwell was sent by the US government as the senior military representative to the China-Burma-India theatre of war. Within two months of his arrival, Stilwell was struggling through Upper Burma, a mere 36 hours ahead of Japanese troops, trying desperately to reach the safety of the British lines in India.

There were 114 soldiers, mainly Chinese, in Stilwell's party. "Vinegar Joe" promised each one of them they would reach India. His retreat – which he called (citing a Chinese proverb) "eating bitterness" – involved 1,500km (930 miles) of trekking through formidable jungles with no hope of outside assistance. At about the same time, 42,000 members of the British-Indian army began to withdraw. The Japanese were right on the tail of the Allied retreat, burning every major town along the escape route. There were hundreds of thousands of civilian casualties, and only 12,000 British-Indian troops reached Assam safely. Some 30,000 perished.

All 114 of Stilwell's charges reached the haven of India, just as the general had pledged. But "Vinegar Joe" was riled. "I claim we got run out of Burma," he told a press conference in Delhi some days later. "It is humiliating as hell. I think we ought to find out what caused it, go back and retake it." Stilwell's words helped guide the Allied war effort in Burma from that point on. He and British General William Slim retraced their steps along the same difficult route – out of Assam, across the Chindwin River to Myitkyina, and down the Ayeyarwady River to Mandalay. Yangon was finally recaptured on 3 May 1945.

WINGATE'S CHINDITS

While Stilwell is perhaps best remembered for his retreat, others gained their greatest fame on the offensive. One of these men was General Orde Charles Wingate, a Briton whose deep-penetration teams used guerrilla tactics to slip behind the Japanese lines and block supplies.

Known as Chindits – after the mythological *chinthe*, the lions that guard temples throughout Burma – the troops were an amalgam of British, Indian, Chin, Kachin and Gurkha units.

The return to Burma of a large land force to combat the Japanese depended very much on a usable road. US Army engineers undertook the task with a unit consisting mostly of Americans. Called the Ledo Road, the new route was to reach from Assam to Mong Yo, where it would join the Burma Road and then continue into Chinese Yunnan.

FLYING "THE HUMP"

Until the Ledo Road was completed, supplies had to be flown to the Allied forces in western China. The air link over "The Hump", as it came to be known, was one of the most hazardous passages of the war. Between Dinjan air base in Assam and the town of Kunming in Yunnan lay 800km (500 miles) of rugged wilderness. Planes had to fly over the Himalayan outliers with its 6,000-metre (20,000ft) peaks, as well as the 3,000-metre (9,843ft) -high Naga Hills, the 4,500-metre (14,700ft) -high Santsung range, and the jungle-

A US Army cargo plane flies over the Himalayas, January 1945.

For more than two years, several thousand engineers and 35,000 native workers laboured in one of the world's most inaccessible areas. The war was almost over by the time the 800km (500-mile) road was completed. Japanese snipers killed 130 engineers, hundreds more lost their lives through illness and accidents, and the Ledo Road became known as "the man-a-mile road". Built down deep gorges and across raging rapids, it traversed a jungle where no road had passed before.

Despite the immense effort that went into the building of this vital link between India and Southeast Asia, today it is overgrown and virtually impassable to motor traffic. For more on the Ledo Road, see page 45.

covered gorges of the Ayeyarwady, Thanlwin (Salween) and Mekong rivers.

About 1,650 men and 600 planes were lost during the operation; so many planes went down on one of the many unnamed peaks of "The Hump" that it was nicknamed the "Aluminum Plated Mountain". The C-46, the workhorse of the operation, was often overloaded, and its pilots, flying up to 160 hours a month, were overworked. During 1944, three men died for every 1,000 tonnes of cargo flown into Yunnan.

CHENNAULT'S "FLYING TIGERS"

Another air unit to achieve fame in the Burma war were the "Flying Tigers" of "Old Weatherface" Chennault. Volunteer pilots from the

US Army, Navy and Marine Corps fought for only seven months under Chennault. But they became so feared by the Japanese that a Tokyo radio broadcaster called them "American guerrilla pilots" for their unorthodox tactics.

Chennault's tactics, however, put him in direct conflict with General Stilwell. While Stilwell pressed for an infantry-led reconquest of Burma, Chennault intended to win the war through air superiority. Ironically, both men had to leave the Asian theatre before the war had ended, but not before Chennault made his mark.

During their brief offensive, the "Flying Tigers" destroyed 1,900 Japanese aircraft, losing 573 planes themselves. Before they were incorporated into the 14th US Air Force, this band of heroic volunteers – who made their planes look like airborne sharks and painted Japanese flags on their planes' bodies for every enemy aircraft shot down – built a legend which remains today.

MERRILL'S MARAUDERS

While the US provided an estimated 50 percent of the air strength to the Allied counteroffensive in

Tombstones and the memorial at the Taukkyan British war cemetery.

⊘ ROYAL PALACE OF MANDALAY

The palace is located at the centre of a royal enclosure within Mandalay City, built by King Mindon in 1857. The former royal city is a mile square, surrounded by a moat 70 metres (225ft) wide and 3 metres (11ft) deep. The surrounding walls are 8.5 metres (27ft) high and 3 metres (10ft) thick. After annexation by the British, it was renamed Fort Dufferin, and parts of the wall were demolished to permit railway tracks to pass through the enclosure. In March 1945, the palace buildings were badly damaged by fire during fighting between Allied and Japanese forces. Now restored, the former royal palace is set amid lands used by the Burmese Army.

Burma, there was only one US ground unit involved in the theatre. It had an unmemorable name: the 5307th Composite Unit. But behind this title was one of the toughest volunteer fighting teams the US Army has ever assembled.

The troops called themselves "Galahad Force" but they were better known as "Merrill's Marauders", after their commander General Frank Merrill. Originally intended to join Wingate's Chindits, General Stilwell designated them for his own deep-penetration operations.

From the border of Assam to Myitkyina, these soldiers went head-to-head with Japanese forces. It was a formidable task. By the time the unit was disbanded in the summer of 1944, there were 2,394 casualties out of an original 2,830 men.

THE LEDO ROAD

The upper reaches of the Hukawng Valley may be a wilderness zone today, but in World War II the region was crossed by one of Asia's busiest transport arteries: the infamous Ledo Road.

One of the most impressive mountain routes in Asia, the Ledo Road (or the Stilwell Road, as it's also often called) snakes across the jungle-covered hills lining Myanmar's border with India. Beginning at the Indian railhead town of Ledo in Assam, the unsurfaced track snakes 61km (38 miles) uphill to crest the jungle-covered Patkai Range at the Pangsau Pass (1,136m/3,727ft), on the frontier, and from there runs via an impressive series of switchbacks to Tanai in Myanmar before continuing on to Myitkina and Bhamo, eventually connecting to the Burma Road, along which supplies were delivered to Kunming in China. In total the road runs for a little under 500 miles before joining up with the Burma Road north of Lashio, with a total overload distance from Ledo to Kunming of 1,079 miles (1,726km). You can just about trace its muddy course on Google Earth, but access nowadays is extremely difficult in this politically unstable region.

A VITAL ROUTE

A key component in US General Joseph "Vinegar Joe" Stilwell's military plans was the construction of a year-round, all-weather land link between northeast India and southwest China – the so-called Ledo Road (subsequently rechristened the Stilwell Road in honour of its creator). The aim was to help supply Chinese armies fighting the Japanese, who would otherwise have been cut off behind a wall of mountains for nine months of the year. Through the early phases of the war, the Chinese Nationalist Army (Kuomintang) had to be re-provisioned via a massive, and perilous, airlift over the treacherous eastern arm of the Himalayas, nicknamed "the Hump". Around 600 planes and their crews were lost flying this notoriously difficult route, and Stilwell was desperate to replace it. Churchill, however, disagreed, claiming the plan would prove "an

immense, laborious task, unlikely to be finished until the need for it has passed."

In the event, the British prime minister's prediction proved spot-on. Of the 15,000 US troops and 35,000 local Burmese coolies drafted in as a labour force, 1,100 American servicemen and a considerably greater number of Burmese lost their lives to landslides, dis-

U.S. Army trucks wind along the Ledo Road.

ease and Japanese snipers before the track was declared open for business in January 1945 – by which time the Japanese were in full retreat. More galling still for Vinegar Joe must have been the fact that the airlift proved capable of carrying ten times more supplies per day to the Chinese armies than could be carried by truck on the Ledo Road.

In spite of the suffering and death toll required to build it, the route gradually fell into disuse after the war. A plan to reconstruct the Burmese section of the road, announced in 2011, has so far come to nothing, although renewed calls in 2016 by China to reopen the entire highway suggest that the Ledo Road may eventually emerge back out of the jungle – although Indian security fears are likely to prove a major obstacle.

Burmese independence leader Aung San.

INDEPENDENCE AND MILITARY RULE

Post-war independence led to dictatorial leadership, economic hardships and conflict between the government and minority groups. Hard-won political changes, however, are finally bringing a measure of freedom to the long-suffering population.

By 1943, it was evident that the Japanese wanted to see Burma's government, which they had helped establish, become subordinate to the Imperial Japanese Army. Burma was declared "independent" in August of that year, with Dr Ba Maw, former education minister, as head of the puppet state. Aung San was named minister of defence, and U Nu was chosen as foreign secretary.

The Burmese nationalists, however, were not pleased with the arrangement. In December 1944, Aung San established contact with the Allies, and in March 1945 he switched sides, with his 10,000-man army now ready to fight the Japanese. Now called the "Patriotic Burmese Forces", they helped the Allies recapture Yangon. The Japanese surrender was signed in Burma's capital on 28 August.

RESULTS OF WAR

The war had completely devastated Burma. That which had not been destroyed during the Japanese attack was laid to waste during the Allied onslaught. There were, however, two positive results for the Burmese: their experience of nominal self-government, and the weakening of British power and prestige. It was clear Burma could no longer remain under the former colonial constitution. Yet the British, climbing back into the driver's seat after the wartime hiatus, had other ideas, having planned a three-year period of direct rule for Burma.

Meanwhile, Aung San was quietly building up two important nationalist organisations. One of these was the Anti-Fascist People's Freedom League, a Marxist-oriented group better known by its acronym (AFPFL). As the military wing of this political league, Aung San founded the

U Nu pictured in 1962 during his time under house arrest.

People's Volunteer Organisation (PVO), which, as early as 1946, claimed 100,000 (mostly unarmed) members.

Despite the growth of nationalist sentiment behind the AFPFL, the British remained firmly in control of Burma until September 1946. Then, a general strike, first by the police, then by all government employees plus railway and oil workers' unions, brought the country to a standstill. The colonial government turned to the AFPFL and other nationalist groups for help. A moderate national council was formed, and the strike ended in early October.

The AFPFL took advantage of the weakened position of the British to seize the political initiative. Aung San presented a list of demands to the British Labour government, which included the granting of total independence to Burma by January 1948.

A conference was promptly called in London in January 1947. Burma was awarded its independence as demanded, but there were several difficult questions to resolve in negotiations, especially concerning ethnic minorities. The AFPFL representative insisted upon complete independence for all of Burma, including the minority regions; the British were concerned about the consequences of

AFPFL won an overwhelming majority of seats. But on 19 July, as the new constitution was still being drafted, tragedy struck. A group of armed men burst in on a meeting of the interim government and assassinated nine people, including Aung San and six of his ministers. U Saw, right-wing prime minister of the last pre-war colonial government, was convicted of instigating the murders and executed.

U Nu, one of the early leaders of the All Burma Student Movement, and later of the AFPFL, was asked by the British colonial government to step

Watched by Indian soldiers, Japanese officers surrender their swords (1945).

continual friction between the Bamar and other groups.

In February, however, Aung San met with minority representatives at Panglong in Shan State. The result was a unanimous resolution that all the ethnic groups would work together with the Burmese interim government to achieve independence for the minority regions in a shorter space of time. After a period of 10 years, each of the major groups that formed a state would be permitted to secede from the Union if they so desired.

NATIONAL INDEPENDENCE

National elections for a Constituent Assembly were held in April 1947 and Aung San and his

into Aung San's shoes. U Nu became prime minister on 4 January 1948, at the astrologically auspicious hour of 4.20am, when the "Union of Burma" became an independent nation – as well as becoming the first former British colony to sever ties with the Commonwealth.

Newly independent Burma rapidly came face-to-face with the bitter realities of nationhood. The first three years of independence were marked by violent domestic confrontations and a militarisation of daily life. No less than five separate groups, including the Kayin, opposed to membership in the "Union of Burma" took up arms against the newly founded state.

One of the former Thirty Comrades, Lieutenant General Ne Win was appointed commander-in-chief of the armed forces, and soon thereafter minister of defence. The Bamar, who had not been allowed in the armed forces since the British took over in 1886, assumed all the high-ranking military posts, and all mutinous Kayin were discharged from active service.

ECONOMIC DISASTER

In economic terms, the first few years of independence were disastrous for Burma. Income from rice exports plummeted and tax revenue diminished, yet the expenditure that was needed to maintain the oversized military machine continued to grow.

U Nu and the AFPFL kept a firm grip on power during the 1951 national elections. But a schism within the party soon disrupted the government's programme of economic development. The Eight-Year Plan of 1953, produced by a team of US experts and called Pyidawtha (Happy Land), had to be abandoned in 1955 due to increasing intra-party disputes.

In 1958, the squabbling had become so serious that the government was virtually paralysed. U Nu was forced to appoint a caretaker government, with General Ne Win at its helm. The 18-month administration was stern, but made progress in cleaning up the cities, modernising the archaic bureaucracy and establishing free and fair elections.

The elections were held in February 1960, and the U Nu faction of the AFPFL, renamed the Pyidaungsu (Union) Party, regained power. U Nu's campaign promises inspired scepticism, however. He sought to have Buddhism recognised as the state religion and also promised the Mon and Rakhine people semi-autonomy. These promises spurred the Shan and Kayah to demand the right of secession granted them in the 1948 constitution, and again the U Nu government was thrown into turmoil. There was little resistance when Ne Win swept into power in a nearly bloodless coup on 2 March 1962.

THE BURMESE WAY TO SOCIALISM

Ne Win's first move was to appoint a Revolutionary Council made up entirely of military personnel. On 30 April, the council published its manifesto, entitled *The Burmese Way to Socialism*.

For 12 years, Ne Win ruled by decree, with all power vested in the Revolutionary Council.

Foreign businesses were nationalised, and the state took control of all businesses, including banks. The army was put in charge of commerce and industry. A foreign policy of self-imposed isolation and neutrality was pursued.

In May 1970, former prime minister U Nu announced the formation of a National United Liberation Front (NULF), an alliance between his followers, the Mon and Kayin, as well as a smattering of Shan and Kachin. He claimed to have an army of 50,000, although that figure may well have been exaggerated. In 1971,

General Ne Win, the first military commander to be appointed prime minister of Burma.

The term "U" is added to the names of senior figures in Myanmar to convey honour and respect.

the rebels launched successful raids from the Thai border, and, for a while, held territory inside Burma.

In Burma, meanwhile, Ne Win was reforming the government structure and introducing a constitutional authoritarianism. First, in an effort to "civilianise" the system, he dropped his military title. On 2 March 1974, the Revolutionary Council was officially disbanded and the

"Socialist Republic of the Union of Burma" was born. Ne Win became president of the nation and chairman of the Burma Socialist Program Party; various leaders of the armed forces filled 16 of the 17 ministerial posts.

Ne Win stepped down from the presidency in November 1981. U San Yu, a loyal disciple, was elected to succeed him. Ne Win, then already 71, continued as Burma Socialist Program Party (BSPP) chairman, and retained behind-the-scenes power. In December 1987, the United Nations general assembly approved LDC (Least

demonstrations in early 1988. These soon escalated, and heavy-handed government retaliation prompted the flight of thousands across the Thai border. In June 1988, a curfew was imposed in Yangon. In July, while proposing a referendum on a multi-party system, Ne Win announced his retirement as BSPP chairman.

On 8 August, a huge popular demonstration was crushed by the military, with thousands of demonstrators shot dead on the streets of Yangon. Following these huge country-wide

Students protesting in Yangon, 1996, demanding democracy.

China is the Burmese regime's principal ally, and its backing has been a major factor in allowing the generals to hold on to power for so long. How this relationship plays out following the end of military rule remains to be seen.

Developed Country) status for Burma, a source of much anger and embarrassment amongst the Burmese themselves.

A YEAR OF TURMOIL

Frustrated by a lack of freedom and the deteriorating economy, students started to stage

demonstrations, the new civilian president and BSPP chairman Dr Maung Maung lifted martial law and promised a referendum and general elections under a multi-party system.

Meanwhile, Aung San Suu Kyi, daughter of national hero Aung San, had returned unexpectedly from her home in the UK and entered the political scene, calling for a peaceful transition to democracy and the formation of an interim government.

SLORC IN POWER

On 18 September, the Chief of Staff, General Saw Maung, announced over the radio that the military had assumed power and set up the State Law and Order Restoration Council

(SLORC), with himself as prime minister. The next day the national parliament and other organs of power were dissolved. The general strike collapsed and thousands of students crossed the borders into neighbouring countries, later forming the Democratic Alliance of Burma (DAB) in which 10 ethnic resistance armies and 12 underground student groups united under the leadership of the Kayin leader Bo Mya. Opposition leaders formed the National League for Democracy (NLD), with Aung San Suu Kyi at its head.

In 1989, the English name of Burma was officially changed to that of Myanmar and the SLORC promulgated a new election law for the national parliament. Aung San Suu Kyi was barred from participating in the elections and was placed under house arrest (she received the Nobel Peace Prize in September 1991 while still in captivity).

When the general elections finally took place on 27 May 1990, the NLD captured 82 percent of the vote. However, the military demanded that a new constitution should first be drafted

The military has a strong presence in Myanmar.

⊘ GENERAL NE WIN

The strongman of Burmese politics for over 30 years, and a powerful force behind the SPDC, Ne Win was born at Pyay in 1910. He took the name Bo Ne Win or "Sun of Glory General" at the time of the formation of the "Thirty Comrades". Educated at Rangoon University, he left without a degree in 1930. He worked for the post office while becoming an early member of the "Our Burma" Association. In 1943 he became commander of the Burma National Army with the rank of Japanese colonel, and in 1945 became commander of the Patriotic Burmese Forces. After the war Ne Win became second in command and later Commanding Officer of the 4th Burma Rifles. He became an MP in 1947, then Commander-in-Chief of the Burmese Army in 1949. In the 1950s he served as Minister for Defence and Home Affairs, before seizing power in a military coup in 1958. In 1960 he was replaced by U Nu in general elections, but in 1962 he seized power again through a military coup. Since that time the military grip on the country has remained strong, and until recently, absolute. Ne Win resigned the presidency in 1981 and stepped down as BSPP chairman seven years later. He retained an influence over the military junta until being placed under house arrest in early 2002 following an alleged plot by his son-in-law and grandsons to overthrow the government. He died the same year.

in which different groups, including the military, should have a say. In spite of the free elections and the clear democratic vote, the military remained in control of the government. In 1994, under pressure from China, the Kachin Independence Organisation (KIO) signed a cease-fire agreement with the Yangon government, thus ending a 30-year war in the north of the country. This was soon followed by agreements with 14 other insurgent groups.

As if to underline these successes, and in a cosmetic bid to improve its overseas image, in

A young protestor at a National League for Democracy demonstration.

1997 the SLORC reconstituted itself as the State Peace and Development Council (SPDC).

THE WAIT FOR DEMOCRACY

Despite the quasi-boycott of Western nations barring Myanmar from World Bank loans and International Monetary Fund assistance, the SPDC managed to speed up the economy by attracting Southeast Asian, Chinese, Japanese and French capital, often in the form of joint ventures channelled through the regime. In the 1990s GDP grew by around 4 to 5 percent a year, but by 2003 the economy was in recession once again.

Meanwhile, the opposition became fractured and weak. Armed resistance lapsed into total disarray, with the Kayin rebels divided into mutually hostile Buddhist and Christian factions. The Thai government – long discreet supporters of the Kayin cause – were angered by the actions of "God's Army". This breakaway Kayin faction led by brothers Johnny and Luther Htoo (who were just ten years old when they launched the movement) seized the Burmese Embassy in Bangkok in 1999, and in 2000 hit international headlines when they took more than 400 Thai nationals hostage at a hospital in Ratchaburi.

The following year, after lengthy negotiations with the UN, NLD leader Aung San Suu Kyi was released from house arrest and permitted to travel around the country. In May 2003, her convoy was attacked by pro-government forces in the north of the country – in which 70 of her supporters were killed – resulting in another period of incarceration lasting seven years.

While the opposition considered its next move, Senior General Than Shwe embarked on one of the barmiest initiatives ever ordered by the regime: the construction of a completely new capital 320km (200 miles) north up the Sittaung Valley from Yangon. Named "Naypyidaw" ("Abode of Kings"), the city cost an estimated $4 billion to build and required the relocation of tens of thousands of government workers.

THE SAFFRON REVOLUTION

Before it was officially completed, however, a decision to remove fuel subsidies, which saw the price of gasoline double, led to one of the worst outbreaks of civil unrest in modern Burmese history. Initially a series of non-violent demonstrations led by students, the campaign escalated in September 2007 to a mass movement spearheaded by Buddhist monks, whence its popular name, "the Saffron Revolution". The demonstrations were put down with characteristic brutality by the junta, which raided monasteries across the country, imprisoning at least 6,000 monks.

Disturbances rumbled on for another year but internal politics took a back seat in May 2008 after Cyclone Nargis wrought devastation across the Ayeyarwady Delta. An estimated 200,000 people were killed and billions of dollars' worth of damage caused in the worst natural disaster ever to afflict the country. The

Burmese government was criticised by inter-national agencies for hampering the emer-gency aid effort.

Armed rebellions intensified in Shan State a year later, when ethnic Chinese, Wa and Kachin minorities took up arms against the Burmese army. Elsewhere in Burma, however, armed groups were fast losing ground in a series of military incursions by the army aimed at subdu-ing the rebel forces once and for all. The crack-down bore fruit in 2010–11 when, in exchange for assurances of representation in a future

Yet the reform process gathered momentum nonetheless, with a relaxation of press censor-ship and the release of hundreds of political prisoners. By-elections in 2012 finally handed Aung San Suu Kyi and 43 other NLD candidates seats in the Burmese parliament, with the mili-tary promising that full parliamentary elections would follow by 2015.

THE NLD IN POWER

Fears that the military would once again renege on its long-standing promise of demo-

Monks marching in Yangon during the Saffron Revolution.

democratic government, insurgent leaders in Mon, Shan and Chin states signed historic accords to end the violence.

THE PATH TO DEMOCRACY

The move was part of a broader initiative by the military to stimulate foreign investment and a relaxation of economic sanctions against Burma. Constitutional reforms were central to the project, led by the new, reformist president Thein Sein, who ordered the release of Aung San Suu Kyi from house arrest in the run-up to national elections held in 2010.

Nominally won by the military-backed Union Solidarity and Development Party, the elections were condemned by the NLD as fraudulent.

cratic elections proved unfounded, leading to the landmark general election of late 2015, the first democratic (or nearly) elections for 55 years. Burmese voters gave a landslide victory to the NLD, as predicted – although the generals reserved a quarter of parliamen-tary seats for themselves, as well as retaining complete control over the armed forces.

Expectations were inevitably high for the new NLD administration, headed by Aung San Suu Kyi in her specially created role as "State Counsellor". Early reform efforts by the new government included the release of politi-cal prisoners and the staging of the United Peace Conference in an attempt to forge last-ing peace with the country's many disaffected minorities – although electoral promises to rein in the military came, not surprisingly, to nothing.

The honeymoon was short-lived, however, with rising communal tensions and anti-Muslims riots in mid-2016 merely a taste of things to come, along with fresh fighting in Kachin and Shan states. Of most concern, however, was the condition of the Rohingya people (see page 66). Tensions, which had been simmering throughout 2012–2014, erupted once again in late 2016. International coverage of

lid on a simmering pot of ethnic unrest and anti-Muslim intolerance (including the 2017 murder of Muslim legal expert Ko Ni, a close advisor to Aung San Suu Kyi – who didn't even attend his funeral). Even state censorship, remarkably, appears to have grown worse since the election of the NLD, while Aung San Suu Kyi is beginning to show worrying signs of the remote and dictatorial governing style employed by her former military adversaries.

The economy, meanwhile, continues to boom, despite political troubles. Tourist fig-

Rohingya refugees crossing the Bangladeshi border.

events showed clear evidence of widespread army atrocities against the Rohingya, including brutal killings, rapes and the burning of villages. Aung San Suu Kyi and other NLD leaders steadfastly refused to address the problem (or simply blamed it on the Rohingya themselves), to the disgust of the international community which had for decades been championing the NLD cause. Throughout late 2016 and 2017 virtually the entire Rohingya population fled Myanmar for Bangladesh and other parts of Southeast Asia, with approaching a million still in refugee camps in Bangladesh at the time of writing.

The removal of military rule, far from bringing peace, in fact appears to have lifted the

ures are rising exponentially and current estimates place Myanmar as the world's seventh-fastest growing economy, even if large parts of the wealth remain in the hands of the military and their business friends, while the average income is well under half that of neighbouring Thailand, and a quarter of all Burmese still live below the poverty line. On the plus side, the NLD have also succeeded in slashing military spending by a quarter, while spending in healthcare has been significantly boosted – although such statistics will mean nothing until the country finally discovers a lasting peace, and can guarantee the basic human rights of its own inhabitants, irrespective of race or creed.

AUNG SAN SUU KYI

Once the world-renowned symbol of peaceful Burmese resistance to military rule, Aung San Suu Kyi's star has fallen spectacularly following the arrival of the democracy she long demanded.

Born in 1945, Aung San Suu Kyi (known to her supporters as "The Lady") is the daughter of the great Burmese nationalist leader, General Aung San. After attending school in Yangon, Suu Kyi lived in India before going to Britain for her higher education, where she met and married her late husband, Michael Aris, an Oxford University professor.

Suu Kyi first came to prominence when she returned home in August 1988 to visit her ailing mother, becoming, almost by accident, the leader of a burgeoning pro-democracy movement in the aftermath of the brutal repression of the uprising. Inspired by the non-violent campaign of Mahatma Gandhi, Suu Kyi organised rallies and travelled the country, calling for peaceful democratic reforms and free elections. The movement quickly grew into a political party, the National League for Democracy (NLD), which went on to win 51 percent of the national vote and 81 percent of seats in parliament, by which time she had already been under house arrest for a year. The military regime, however, refused to relinquish power and stepped up intensified repression of the NLD.

HOUSE ARREST AND RELEASE

Aung San Suu Kyi spent 15 of the next 21 years under house arrest, slandered by the pro-government media as a political opportunist and even a "genocidal prostitute". This last unlikely phrase derived from the military regime's obsession with her marriage to Michael Aris, who died of prostate cancer in Oxford in 1999 at the age of 53. Fearing that she would not be allowed to re-enter the country if she left to visit her dying husband, Suu Kyi remained in Myanmar, separated from her husband and two sons at the time of his death.

Finally, decades of international pressure and sanctions bore fruit on 13 November 2010, when the woman regarded by most of the world as Myanmar's leader-in-waiting was released "for good conduct" from her Yangon home.

For most of the following year, the NLD leader campaigned for her party in the run-up to a key by-election in which her party won 43 of the 45 seats it was allowed to contest. In its wake, Aung San Suu Kyi took her seat in the Pyithu Hluttaw, the lower house of Myanmar's parliament. The inevitable conclusion followed when, in 2015, her NLD party won a landslide electoral victory, although Aung San Suu Kyi herself was barred from becoming president under the Burmese constitution, instead being appointed to the specially created post of "State Counsellor" – leader of the country, in all but name.

Aung San Suu Kyi.

Aung San Suu Kyi's reputation has plummeted since assuming power. Her abject refusal to defend the rights of the horribly oppressed Rohingya has led to widespread calls for her to be stripped of her Nobel Prize. Equally, her government's failure to tackle entrenched military power, to control ever-rising communal tensions (most notably attacks against Muslims) and the flaring up of conflicts in Kachin and Shan states have all cast a lengthening shadow over Myanmar's new democratic credentials. Meanwhile, The Lady herself cuts an increasingly remote and authoritarian figure, growing more detached from the international community and the Burmese people she has for so long claimed to represent.

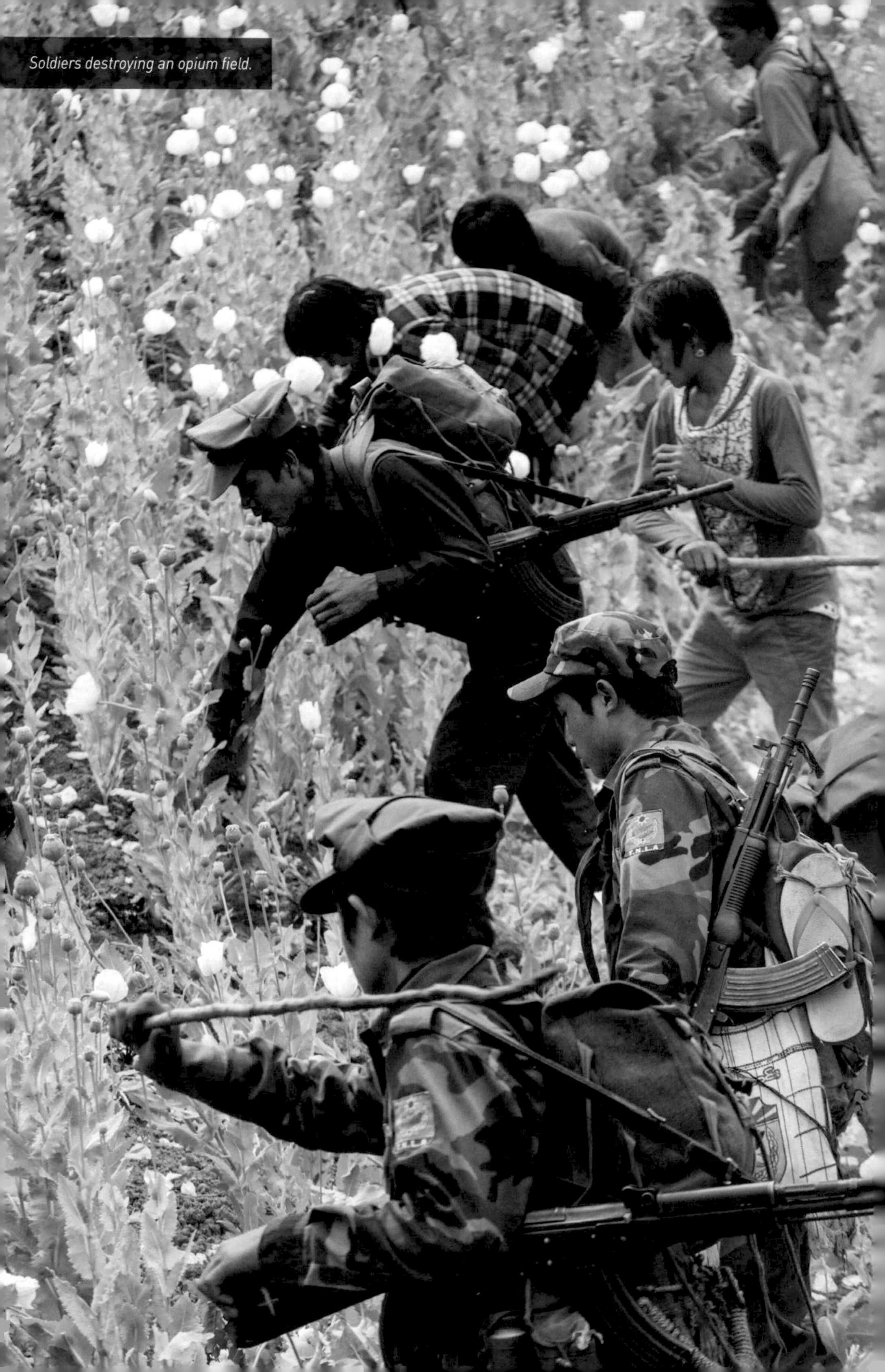

Soldiers destroying an opium field.

THE POPPY TRAIL

In spite of international attempts to curb poppy growing in the region, Myanmar's Golden Triangle remains the hub of Southeast Asia's opium belt.

During the past half century, the remote and often lawless badlands where the borders of Myanmar, Laos and Thailand intersect has become known as the "Golden Triangle". Originally a Western term applied to the area due to its wealth in gems, teak and, above all, opium, this tract of deep, roadless valleys and jungle-covered hills in eastern Shan State is still largely dominated by drug warlords, arms dealers and insurgent armies.

Myanmar is the second-largest producer of opium in the world after Afghanistan, growing around a fifth of the world's opium. Opium production in recent years has been encouraged by a collapse in the price of substitute crops coupled with a dramatic 50 percent rise in the market price for opium, while a major reduction in the amount of opium being produced in neighbouring Thailand has also contributed.

Much of the harvest is grown by poor farmers in far-flung minority villages. Perennially troubled by political instability and food insecurity, smallholders in Shan and Kachin states stand to make five times more per day labouring in poppy fields than cultivating rubber, tea or fruit.

GROWTH OF THE GOLDEN TRIANGLE

The rise of the Golden Triangle as an opium production centre dates back to 1948 when, in the wake of Independence, Burma was swamped by the defeated remnants of China's Nationalist government, the Kuomintang (KMT). Within a few short months, the KMT established itself as a major force in Shan State, attracting to the region a dozen other armed groups – communist, separatist and

Opium poppies are still grown in Myanmar.

By the late 19th century, opium was widely established in Shan State and exported to neighbouring Yunnan, Laos, Vietnam and Siam. Within 50 years the traffic had grown to encompass the world.

warlord – with one thing in common: the need to finance their continued struggle against the authorities, whether Chinese or Burmese. The obvious source of revenue was opium.

Armed with sophisticated weaponry, the KMT soon developed a stranglehold on the trade. Speaking in 1967, General Tuan Shi-wen, commander of the KMT's 5th Army, made no bones about where the money came from. "Necessity knows no law," he informed a visiting journalist. "We have to continue to fight the evil of communism. To fight you must have an army, and an army must have guns, and to buy guns you must have money. In these mountains the only money is opium."

The growing influence of renegade KMT soldiers over the opium business in the Golden Triangle was mirrored by a sustained offensive against drug trafficking and

Khun Sa, dubbed the Opium King.

☉ BAMAR DISAPPROVAL

Despite Myanmar's reputation as a major opium-producing nation, most Bamar have traditionally viewed opiates with strong disapproval. A 19th-century observer noted that "opium use among the better class of Burmese is extremely rare" and that "a respectable Burman would hesitate to be seen around a government liquor shop". This disapproval is based on Buddhist beliefs against taking intoxicants, although nowadays alcohol consumption is on the rise, while local markets for opiates are also growing – in some opium-producing areas of Shan and Kachin states it's thought that over ten percent of the adult male population (perhaps much higher) is now addicted.

manufacture within China. After the founding of the People's Republic in 1949, illicit heroin manufacture in Shanghai or Tianjin became all but impossible. It made sense for the heroin technicians to relocate to Hong Kong, or better yet to KMT-controlled sectors of the Golden Triangle itself.

By manufacturing heroin in the same hills where the opium is grown, costs could be cut appreciably – refined heroin takes up less than 5 percent of the space of raw opium and is therefore easier to both transport and conceal. The trade received another major boost during the Vietnam War, during which large numbers of US troops took hard drugs as a way of blunting the misery and horror of their surroundings. This in turn led to increased demand in Southeast Asia, and especially in the key production areas of Myanmar's Shan State.

A LUCRATIVE INDUSTRY

While long a favoured cash crop of certain hill tribes – notably, the Wa, Hmong, Akha, Mien, Lahu and Lisu – opium has not greatly benefited these peoples; their reward has been government suspicion, widespread addiction and social disruption. Instead, most profits from the drug trade accrue to international syndicates and major traffickers. In the 1950s and 1960s, the KMT controlled the Golden Triangle narcotics business, but during the 1970s and 1980s they were replaced by private warlords such as the notorious Shan-Chinese "freedom fighter" Khun Sa and allies of the Burmese junta such as Lo Hsing Han.

By 1990, Myanmar was producing half of all the world's opium. Production levels then fell steadily to a low point in 2006 in the face of government eradication programmes and the decision, under intense international pressure, by the United Wa State Party, who oversaw the major opium-producing areas, to ban the growing of opium poppies.

Since then, however, poppy production has risen dramatically, fuelled by rising numbers of addicts across the border in China, and also locally – not to mention steady global demand. Production peaked in 2015, and although it has since fallen significantly in Shan State, it has increased in neighbouring

Kachin State following recent fighting, proving again the intimate link between opium production and political instability.

Behind the trend lies the enduring poverty of many ethnic minority farmers. The past few years have seen a marked drop in demand for traditional crops of fruit, tea and rubber from the Chinese; the price of raw opium, meanwhile, has rocketed, tempting many small farmers back into poppy production.

In addition, many of those in Shan State who have given up opium production have simply ended up working in one of the state's hundreds of "meth labs" instead, producing cheap synthetic methamphetamines such as the popular *yaba* (literally "crazy pill"), which is producing further widespread addition throughout the region, often with disastrous social consequences. In Kengtung, it's been estimated that over half of all young people are regular *yaba* users, while over a billion *yaba* tablets are believed to be exported annually to China, Bangladesh, Vietnam and elsewhere.

Myanmar police burning a pile of drugs in Yangon, 2013.

⊘ TRADERS OF THE GOLDEN TRIANGLE

The rugged, indomitable Chinese muleteers known to the Burmese as Panthay were – and to some extent still are – the masters of the Golden Triangle. In the 19th century, they made the remote settlement of Panglong in the Wa region of Shan State their base. From here, their caravans laden with precious stones, jade and guns, but above all opium, traded as far as Mawlamyaing in Burma, Luang Prabang in Laos, Dali and Kunming in Yunnan, and Chiang Mai in northern Thailand.

Wherever they went they were protected with the best weapons money could buy, and they used these to good effect – to ensure the respect of the law-abiding and the fear of the lawless. When the British first arrived in Shan State in 1886, they were amazed to discover the Panthay armed with Remington repeater rifles better, in most cases, than those of their own troops. During World War II, Panglong was looted and burned by marauding Japanese soldiers, but the Panthay – now armed with newer AK47s – survived to help generations of drug-smugglers transport their opium.

Today, most Panthay are respectable and increasingly prosperous, having settled in the larger towns of Shan State and in Mandalay. Their reputation as traders survives, however, and they are still considered to be the hard men of the Golden Triangle.

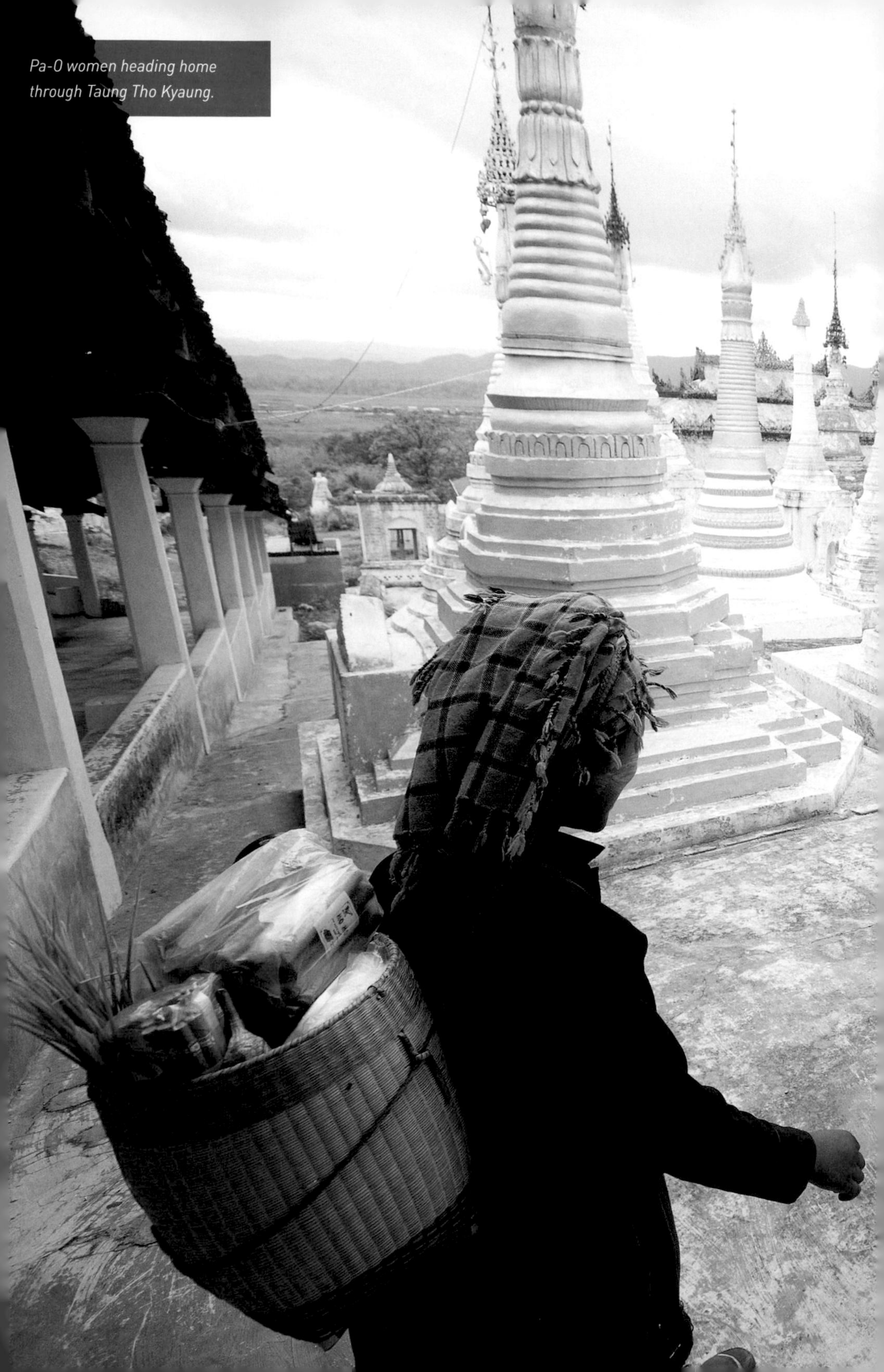

Pa-O women heading home through Taung Tho Kyaung.

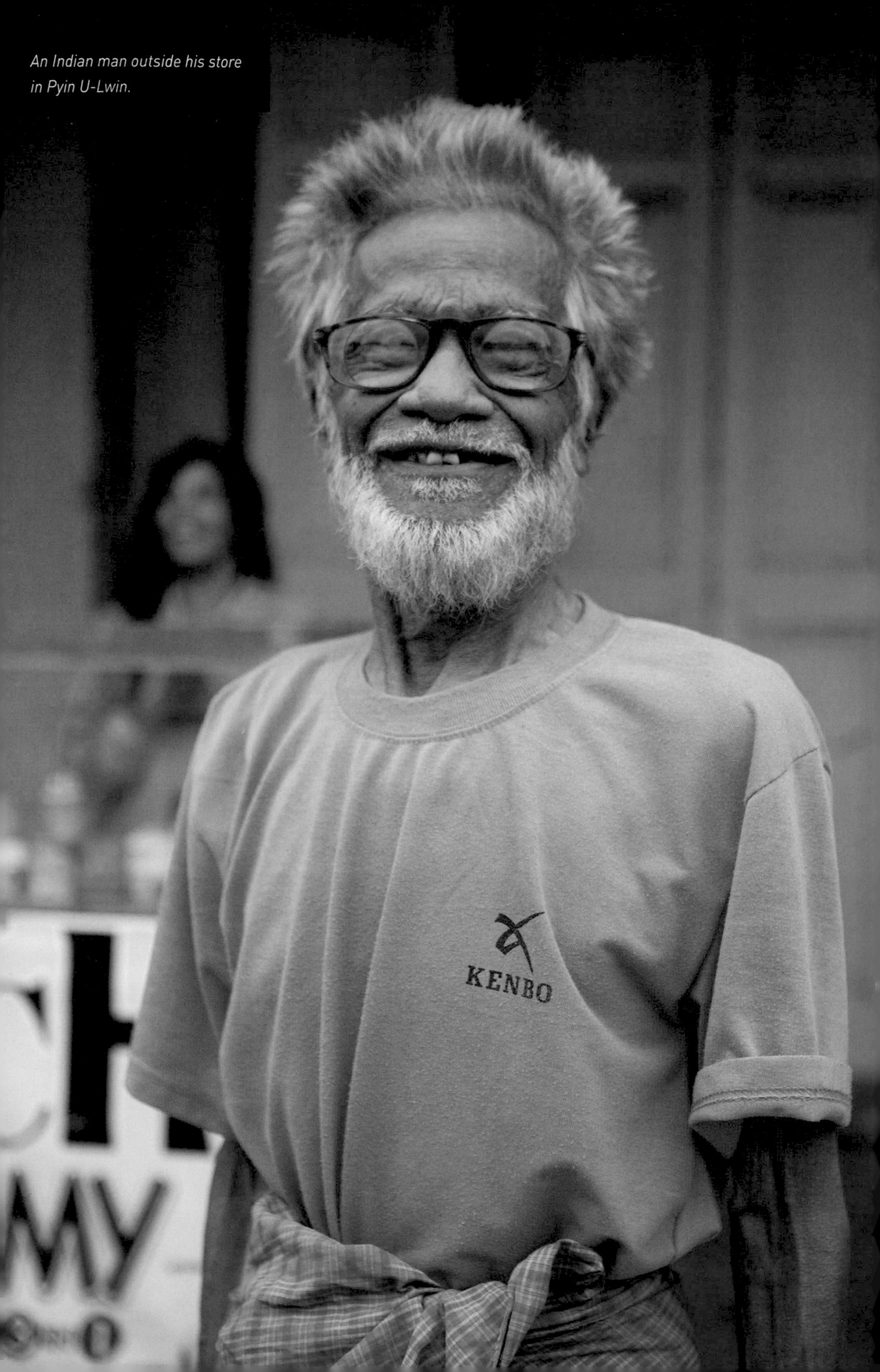

An Indian man outside his store in Pyin U-Lwin.

THE PEOPLE OF MYANMAR

No fewer than 135 indigenous ethnic groups are recognized by the Myanmar government (as well as many others not given official status) speaking around a hundred languages and related dialects.

Ethnically, Myanmar is one of Asia's most diverse nations – a fact which has caused many problems over the years, but which also greatly enriches the country's cultural life and enhances its appeal to visitors. The present population is around 55 million, the majority of whom live in the fertile Ayeyarwady Delta region, in Rakhine, and along the southeastern coastline. The Burmese authorities presently recognise 135 separate ethnic groups living within the union. Of these, the Bamar are easily the largest. The other six main ethnic groups are the Shan, Kachin, Kayin, Rakhine, Chin and Mon, each of which has its own state. These seven main ethnic groups together constitute about 92 percent of the total population, with the remaining 8 percent divided between a fascinating patchwork of minority tribes.

Ethnologists divide Myanmar's indigenous population into four main groups: Tibeto-Burman, Mon-Khmer, Austro-Tai and Karennic. The Tibeto-Burman group, which includes the predominant Bamar, the Rakhine, Kachin and Chin, constitutes around 78 percent of the total. Mon-Khmer peoples include the Mon, the Wa and the Palaung, while the major Austro-Tai group are the Shan. Karennic peoples include the Kayin (Karen) and the closely related Kayah. Major non-indigenous groups, who are predominantly urban-based, are relatively recent migrants (in the past 150 years) from South Asia and China.

THE BAMAR

Myanmar's largest ethnic group (around 40 million people, or two-thirds of the population), the Bamar have traditionally held sway over much of the country, particularly the

The bride at a Pa O wedding ceremony.

fertile central plains and Ayeyarwady valley. Originally migrants from southern China, the Bamar (or "Burmans", as they were known in colonial times) were a wet-rice farming people, Theravada Buddhist by religion, whose tonal, Tibeto-Burman tongue – Burmese – has long been the national language. As the country's largest racial group and main holders of government power, the Bamar are often viewed with suspicion and even hostility by Myanmar's minorities.

Most of the cultural forms described in later sections of this book are broadly representative of the Bamar, who have traditionally lived in thatched dwellings and worked as rice farmers. Perhaps their greatest distinguishing trademark is the pale yellow/white powder, made from *thanaka* bark (see page 237), which Bamar women apply to their faces as protection against the sun. Their traditional dress is the wrap-around *longyi*, similar to the Malaysian sarong.

THE SHAN

At just over 9 percent of the population, Myanmar's 5 million Shan, or Tai Yai as they call themselves, are the second-largest nationality in Myanmar. Close relatives of the Thai,

the Shan mainly inhabit the upland plateaux and rolling hills of northeast Myanmar, work mostly as wet-rice farmers and practise Theravada Buddhism.

From the 15th century – when they were pushed back onto the Shan Plateau after early success in establishing an Ayeyarwady kingdom – until 1959, 34 *sawbwas* (hereditary princes) ruled separate feudal principalities in medieval splendour, with serfs, slaves and concubines. Their alliance of small states was recognised by the 1948 constitution, and

Young men sitting outside a market in Shan State.

⊘ MANNERS AND ETIQUETTE

Burmese society is characterised by *ana or ana-deh*, the all-pervasive avoidance of doing anything that would offend, cause someone to lose face or become embarrassed. This is allied with the concept of *hpon*, "power", used to justify socioeconomic differences between people. *Hpon* is a Buddhist concept, a result of merit (or otherwise) earned in previous lives.

Age is considered synonymous with experience and wisdom, and children are taught from a young age to venerate their elders. It is considered rude to touch a person's head, because it is the "highest" point of the body. It is also considered taboo to touch another's feet, but worse still to point with the foot or sit with feet

pointing at an older person. Shoes are always taken off upon entering homes, monasteries and pagodas.

Photographing meditating monks is considered highly disrespectful. Always ask before taking photos of local people.

Physical demonstrations of affection in public are common between friends of the same gender or between members of the family. It is thus common to see friends walking together holding hands or with arms round each other.

It is considered polite to refer to people by their full title and full name, and there are many different honorific titles in the Burmese language (see page 66).

granted the right to withdraw from the "Union of Burma" after 10 years of membership.

However, in 1959 many of the *sawbwas* sold out, signing an agreement with the Ne Win government to renounce all their hereditary rights and privileges. In exchange, the Shan princes accepted a payment of 25 million kyat, a sum roughly equal to their income over a 15- to 25-year period.

Other *sawbwas* and their followers founded the Shan Independence Army (SIA), and in the ensuing years attempted to wrest territory away from the government. U Nu's inability to deal with this problem was one of the factors which led to Ne Win's military coup of 1962, after which Shan leaders who had remained in Myanmar were imprisoned. Some are now in self-imposed exile, while those who responded to the 1980 amnesty have returned to Shan State.

Shan are recognisable by the turbans worn by men and married women. Men usually dress in baggy, dark-blue trousers rather than in Bamar-style *longyi*. Girls wear trousers and blouses until the age of 14, at which time they don colourful dresses. As they get older, their costumes grow less colourful until, at about the age of 40, the women start to wear sober black clothing for the rest of their lives.

THE KAYIN AND KACHIN

The fiercely independent Kayin (Karen), who constitute about 7 percent of the population (a little under four million people), live scattered throughout central and southern Myanmar, but mainly in their own Kayin State, which they call "Kawthoolei". Many Kayin are Christian, and this – together with the favoured status they enjoyed over the majority Bamar during the British period – has exacerbated their already poor relations with the Bamar-dominated government. Closely related groups include the Kayah and the "long-neck" Padaung of Kayah State.

Comprising around 2 percent of the population (roughly a million people) and the dominant minority of northern Myanmar, the Kachin are skilled dry-rice farmers and hunters. They have been widely Christianised, chiefly by American Baptist missionaries, but retain a complex and wide-reaching kinship system. Like the Kayin, the Kachin were widely employed as soldiers

by the British and have fought a long struggle for independence. Sometimes called the "Gurkhas of Southeast Asia", they are renowned for their military prowess. At war with the military authorities from the early 1960s, the Kachin Independence Organisation (KIO) and its military wing, the Kachin Independence Army (KIA), have proved perhaps the most intractable of Yangon's opponents. In 1994, the Kachin rebels signed a cease-fire agreement with the Burmese government which lasted until June 2011, when fighting broke out once again – and

Padaung woman at a handicraft workshop at Inle Lake.

continues today – in the region between Bhamo and Myitkyina, the capital.

THE RAKHINE AND THE CHIN

Closely related to the Bamar, the Rakhine inhabit Rakhine State (formerly known as Arakan) and constitute about 4 percent of the total population (slightly over 2 million people). Although of the same Tibeto-Burman stock as the Bamar, the Rakhine are sometimes slightly darker in complexion, an indication of the region's 2,000-year history of contact and intermarriage with Indian traders, sailors and settlers. There are several significant differences between the lifestyles of the coastal Rakhine and the Bamar of the Ayeyarwady basin.

The Chin, together with the related Naga people, make up about 1 percent of Myanmar's population, numbering around 0.5 million in total. They live in the far northwest, where they inhabit the dense forest close to the India and Bangladesh borders. Traditionally animist, most Chin have converted to Christianity, having been evangelised by American and Australian missionaries.

Slash-and-burn agriculture has for centuries furnished land for dry-rice growing, though the resulting soil erosion has depleted the amount of cultivable land to less than is required to sustain the population in recent decades. Some Chin along the banks of the Kaladan River, to the north of the ruined former Arakan capital of Mrauk-U, also practise subsistence fishing alongside settled farming. Among these, and throughout the jungle region to the north, may be seen senior women with elaborately tattooed faces, though the custom is rapidly dying out.

Armed insurgent groups, under the umbrella leadership of the Chin National Army (CAN), have been active in the Chin heartland since Independence in 1948. Fighting intensified following the 1988 uprising until the agreement of a ceasefire in 2012. Chin State is officially the poorest in the country, with the least infrastructure: 70 percent of its population live below the poverty line. As a consequence, and to flee the violence perpetrated by the *tatmadaw*, hundreds of thousands of Chin have fled across the Indian frontier to neighbouring Mizoram – a cause of political controversy between the two countries.

THE MON

Possessors of a proud, ancient civilisation even older than that of the Bamar, the Mon – at about 2 percent of the population (a million people) – have their own state centred on Mawlamyine in the southeast of the country. Though largely assimilated into Bamar culture, they continue to use their own distinct language, and have retained their own state within the Burmese union. Traditionally, they have preferred to live in

Young Muslim boy in downtown Yangon.

⊘ THE ROHINGYA

The Rohingya are one of the world's most embattled minorities. Living in Rakhine State, The Rohingya (numbering around 800,000), are Muslims of Bengali descent who arrived in Myanmar during colonial times, or possibly much earlier. They have long been persecuted by the Burmese government, which denies them citizenship and insists they be returned to Bangladesh (a country which doesn't want them either, and in which most of them have never set foot). Their plight, already severe, worsened during 2012 when anti-Rohingya riots spread across Rakhine State, forcing most Rohingya into refugee camps.

Further – and even more catastrophic – violence erupted in 2016, allegedly provoked by Rohingya attacks against the Burmese army, leading in 2017 to a series of "clearance operations" during which thousands of Rohingya were killed and hundreds of villages destroyed. Fleeing Rohingya reported systematic massacres and atrocities perpetrated by the military and roving Buddhist mobs, provoking a global outcry, accusations of genocide and calls for Aung San Suu Kyi to be stripped of her Nobel Prize. A diplomatic stalemate continued into 2018 amidst a backdrop of international outrage, Burmese intransigence and ever-worsening conditions for the displaced refugees. A few Rohingya returned in early 2018, though at present almost a million still languish in refugee camps in Bangladesh, with no end to the crisis in sight.

rainy lowland areas to pursue wet-rice growing. As Buddhists, they observe their own calendar of Theravadin festivals.

THE INDIANS

Myanmar has an influential migrant Indian community, particularly in Yangon and Mandalay. The Indians and their culture have a 2,000-year history in Burma, predating the arrival of the Bamar majority, although it was not until the 19th century, when Burma became a part of the British Raj, that they began to settle in large numbers. At one stage in the early 20th century the population of the capital was almost 60 percent Indian, though this figure has since declined drastically.

Some Indians were well educated and occupied middle and higher levels of administration and business during the colonial era. Those with less education came to Burma as contract labourers for government construction projects, and to work in teak camps. Many of the immigrants were from southern India, and brought with them their beliefs and regional village social structure, which included the caste system, Hindu deities and professional moneylenders (chettyars), who quickly became so entrenched in Burmese society that they bought up more than half of the arable land in the Ayeyarwady Delta region.

Many were forced to return to India during the Japanese occupation. In what would become one of the most desperate and difficult mass evacuations in history, an estimated quarter of a million made the journey on foot via the leech-infested, jungle-covered mountains of the northwest – 4,268 are recorded to have died en route, but the true death toll was probably much higher. Those who remained faced the land reforms of the new government. Large numbers of businessmen who had stayed on after independence then left as a result of Ne Win's nationalisation programme following his 1962 coup.

Besides Hindus, there is a small South Asian Muslim population in major towns, particularly Yangon. Many trace their ancestry back to areas that now form part of Pakistan and Bangladesh. Others, known as *zerbadi*, are the result of unions between migrant Muslim men and Bamar women.

THE CHINESE

The number of Chinese in Myanmar today is estimated at around 1.6 million. In broad terms, there are two groups, with very different histories and lifestyles. The first is mainly rural, comprising the Shan Tayok and the Kokang Chinese. They came across the border of Yunnan during the time when the Shan principalities were under British administration, and are still concentrated in the northeast, close to Yunnan province from where many originate. In the Kokang area of

A priest inside Sri Devi temple, Yangon.

northern Shan State they form more than 80 percent of the population, so that Kokang is known as Myanmar's "Little China".

The urban Chinese, on the other hand, have an entirely different background, being mostly "Overseas Chinese" from the distant coastal provinces of Guangdong, Fujian and Hainan Island. A large number arrived in Yangon to work as merchants or restaurant owners during the colonial era and soon occupied the middle and higher strata of modern society. Despite nationalisation under Ne Win and vicious anti-Chinese riots in Yangon in 1967, the urban Chinese remained strong commercially. In more recent years, large numbers have also settled in Mandalay, which has now supplanted Yangon as the economic and cultural hub of the Chinese community in Myanmar, with Chinese now making up at least thirty percent of the city's total population and dominating much of its trade.

Another Chinese group found in remote parts of Shan State, as well as in large towns like Yangon and Mandalay, are the Panthay. This group is essentially identical with the Hui minority in Yunnan. The descendants of Uzbek soldiery who fought for the Mongol dynasty, their ancestors settled in Yunnan over six centuries ago and intermarried with

Streetside café, downtown Yangon.

local Han Chinese. Today, there is little to distinguish them from other Chinese except for their Muslim faith.

OTHER MINORITIES

Inle Lake, in Shan State, is the adopted homeland of the resourceful Intha minority, whose "one-legged" rowing style, stilted villages, floating gardens and beautiful handicrafts make them one of Myanmar's most distinctive ethnic groups. An immigrant tribe from the southeast coast who left their former homeland in the 18th century to flee wars between the Burmese and Thais, the Intha now number around 70,000, most of whom live in villages clustered around the lush, paddy-filled shores of Inle Lake.

Another of Myanmar's iconic minorities are the Kayan-Lahwi, better known as the Padaung and famous for their "long-necked" women, who wear brass rings around their necks to depress their collar bones and make their necks appear longer. Originally from Kayah State, some have now migrated to villages around Lake Inle, where they can often be seen selling trinkets and handicrafts, and posing for photographs with foreign tourists.

On the northwestern frontier with India, the Naga people inhabit the thick forests sweeping from the Chindwin River. Notorious for their former practice of head hunting, the Naga are today all but completely Christianised, although they continued to resist Burmese rule until 2011, when a peace accord was struck with the government guaranteeing Naga leaders representation in the national parliament. This followed the creation three years earlier of a Naga Self-Administered Zone, formerly part of Sagaing Division. With militancy on the decline, tourism has made its first tentative steps in the region. A handful of Burmese tour operators now run trips to remote Naga towns where the various tribes celebrate their New Year – a great opportunity to see Naga traditional dress and dance in its authentic context. Among the more distinctive elements of Naga attire are the colourful shawl and black kilt worn as everyday garb, and the conical head gear with boars' teeth and feathers donned on ceremonial occasions.

Further north from Naga territory sprawls the most remote, impenetrable region of Myanmar, around the foothills of the Hukaung Valley and Hkakabo Razi massif. As well as harbouring a viable tiger population, the forest here is also home to an array of obscure tribes, including a race of pygmies known as the Taron. The outside world was ignorant of their existence until the American conservationist Alan Rabinowitz, while conducting a wildlife survey in the area in 1996, was introduced to members of the community. Enslaved for generations by the dominant Kachins, the Taron had dwindled to a vestigial population of a dozen individuals who, beset by deformities and other health problems resulting from inbreeding, had made a pact not to have children.

Although not approaching extinction, the Moken of the far south are another ethnic group struggling to survive on the margins of modern Myanmar. Often dubbed "Sea Gypsies" because of their nomadic lifestyle, the Moken spend eight or nine months of the year at sea, rarely touching dry land except to re-provision and trade. For the rest of the year, when the rough conditions of the rainy season make life in their hand-built *kabang* boats too dangerous, they reside in stilted villages at remote sites on the coast of Tan-

fore – something you'll notice from the minute you step off the plane. Traditional dress is ubiquitous, and the Burmese are remarkably polite and deferential towards their elders and strangers. Conventions of hospitality remain strong, as do the beliefs and practices of Theravada Buddhism, fervent adherence to which is a fact of daily life in a country where monks queue in the street each morning to accept alms from lay people and the terraces of huge gilded pagodas throng from sunset to sunrise with pilgrims and worshippers.

Working the silklooms in Phaw Khone weaving village.

intharyi (Tenarassim) Division, particularly in and around the Myeik Archipelago. Diving and beachcombing the shores of these remote islands, the Moken fish and collect sandworms and molluscs to eat, and shells and oysters to trade with the Malay and Chinese market people in the area's ports.

CULTURE AND SOCIETY

Myanmar's decades as a pariah state have ensured that it ranks today among the most staunchly traditional nations in Asia. And it's not just the peripheral, remote and mountainous regions where picturesque, antiquated traditions still hold sway. Even in the cities, adherence to traditional values remains to the

⊘ WOMEN IN MYANMAR

Women, despite their lower status in Buddhist doctrine, have historically enjoyed high levels of social power. Their rights are today almost always equal to those of men, guaranteed by simple divorce laws.

That said, the country's economic difficulties have seen an erosion in the status of women among poorer sectors of society. Burmese women have also been targeted in the nation's ethnic conflicts, recruited as porters and unpaid labourers for the military, and in some cases becoming victims of slavery, murder, torture and systematic rape, as well as being sucked into the country's burgeoning sex-trade industry or being sold on to brothels in Thailand and elsewhere.

Because they comprise by far the largest and most dominant cultural group in Myanmar, the following account refers principally to the Bamar, the overwhelming majority of whom are Buddhists.

DRESS

The Burmese emphasise their national identity through the clothes they wear. Most evident is the *longyi*, introduced by immigrant families from southern India. Similar to the Malaysian sarong, it consists of a kilt-like piece of cloth worn from the waist to the ankle. Together with

Local lady outside Mingun Paya, near Mandalay.

the *eingyi*, a transparent blouse which is worn with a round-collared, long-sleeved jacket, the *longyi* still takes precedence over Western-style garments. For more on *longyis*, see page 236.

The Burmese Premier, General Than Shwe, and other members of the ruling junta caused a stir in February 2011 when they appeared on national television wearing women's acheiks and longbon headscarves – an act political observers were quick to interpret as an example of *yadaya*, something akin to Burmese black magic. Fortune tellers have repeatedly predicted that a woman will rule Myanmar one day, and so the generals' cross-dressing was seen as an attempt to confound the pundits and forestall the rise of NLD leader, Aung San Suu Kyi.

MARRIAGE

By and large, and unlike many of their Indian cousins across the Andaman Sea, the Burmese choose their own life partners. Traditions of romantic love are strong. Couples meet, court and decide to marry themselves, albeit in a style that appears very old-fashioned and demure to Western eyes. Should the parents disapprove of the match there's little they can do about it. Parental opposition to any marriage in Myanmar will typically result in an elopement, followed by a gradual rehabilitation of the couple if the marriage proves a success.

The ceremony itself is considered *lokiya*, or "earthly", in the Buddhist tradition, and as such is not officiated over by a monk or abbot (although to gain merit, monks may well attend the betrothal dinner or wedding reception). Instead, a Brahmin priest presides over the ritual, which begins with the blowing of a conch shell as the couple have the palms of their hands bound together in cloth and placed in a silver bowl (the Burmese for marriage is "*let htat*" or "join palms"). Sanskrit verses are intoned by the Brahmin, who then raises the couple's hands and unties them, to more blasts from the conch shell. Afterwards, there will be entertainment and speeches, and with more affluent families, perhaps a reception dinner at a smart hotel.

Throughout, traditional dress is worn by the participants and those attending, even among more sophisticated urbanites – though with wealthier families the bride's dress tends to be an extravagant modern designer twist on the traditional *htamein* featuring embroidery, pearls, sequins and even on some occasions gold. Upper-class brides will also wear a pearl- and jewel-encrusted tiara, and an opulent necklace.

Burmese get married expecting it to be for life; comparatively few marriages end in divorce, but those that do see the common property divided equally. If the marriage fails, women can return to their parents.

BIRTH AND FAMILY LIFE

One hundred days after the birth of a child, the parents invite family and friends to a naming ceremony at the local monastery, where the baby is given a name by a senior monk based on astrological calculations; it need bear no relation to that of the parents. After the ritual, a grand feast is held at the family home or in a functions venue to mark the event.

Children are sent to school at the age of five. However, despite a system of compulsory education and strenuous efforts by the government since independence to ensure education for all, there are still areas with no state schools. In these places, the local *kyaung* (monastery) takes charge of elementary education.

When a boy is nine years old, his *shin-pyu* takes place (see page 75). This is an initiation ceremony marking the end of childhood and the start of a period of monkhood. Girls of the same age participate in an ear-piercing ceremony called the *nahtwin*, which also symbolises a farewell to the unburdened life of the child.

As two-thirds of the population still work on the arable land, the transition from school to adult life is relatively easy for most young people: during their school years, they help out with the harvest in their parents' fields.

Yangon schoolchildren.

⊘ BURMESE NAMES

Burmse names are a law unto themselves, and a source of considerable confusion to outsiders. Firstly, there are no family surnames in Burmese. Children can be given any name of their parents' devising, often arrived at according to astrological considerations. In addition, women keep their maiden names upon marriage. There's also a tradition of changing one's name according to one's circumstances. The great independence leader Aung San, for example, was actually christened Htein Lin, but adopted his new moniker (meaning "victory") upon entering the independence struggle.

Burmese names are typically made up of between one and three syllables. Names are not divisible. A man called Kau Reng, for example, cannot be called either "Kau" or "Mr Reng." These basic names are often modified by a complex system of added words. Kau Reng, for example, would be called "U Kau Reng" ("U" meaning "mister" or "uncle") by those younger or socially subordinate, or as "Ko Kau Reng" ("Ko" meaning "brother") by those of an equal age or status. "Maung" (also roughly translated as "brother") might be added when talking to someone younger or of an inferior status, or between younger males of similar social status. Similar honorifics apply to female names: "Daw" ("Mrs" or "auntie" when talking to older or socially superior ladies (as in Daw Aung San Suu Kyi, as she's often described) or "Ma", meaning "sister".

BURMESE BUDDHISM

The Buddhist faith permeates every aspect of life in Myanmar, from personal conduct to national politics.

Although Christianity and Islam are practised by some minority communities in Myanmar, the overwhelming majority of the population – just under 90 percent – are Buddhists. Judged by the proportion of monks in society and the amount of money given as alms or donated to other religious causes, Myanmar may fairly be claimed to be the world's most fervently Buddhist country, and the influence of the faith is all pervasive. Moreover, the brand of Buddhism practised is unique, blending the precepts of the ancient Theravada school (which adheres most closely to the Buddha's original teachings) with indigenous forms of spirit, or *nat*, worship, inherited from ancient animistic beliefs.

Burmese Buddhist cosmology has also been shaped by millennia of influences from other cultures, particularly that of India. According to the Burmese, the European-Asian continent is called Jambudvipa. It is the southernmost of four islands situated at the cardinal points surrounding Mount Meru, the centre of the world. This southern island is considered to be a place of misery compared to the other abodes of this universe, and the only place where future Buddhas can be born.

Frieze on the walls of Kaba Aye Pagoda, Yangon.

SIMPLIFYING BUDDHISM

King Anawrahta, founder of the first Burmese empire in the 11th century AD, devoted his attention to simplifying his kingdom's spiritual beliefs. When he introduced Theravada Buddhism into Upper Burma as the national religion, he was unable to eliminate the animistic beliefs of his people. Despite his best efforts, the country's countless folk gods and goddesses, or *nats*, continued to be venerated, serving a similar purpose to the saints of the Catholic Church,

to be called upon in times of need. Rather than directly confront the entrenched beliefs of his subjects, Anawrahta chose to incorporate the *nats* within Burmese Theravada Buddhism, establishing an official pantheon comprising 36 of the most popular *nats* under the leadership of a 37th figure – Thagyamin – Anawrahta's new king of the *nats*. Images of the royally sanctioned 37 Nats were installed around the stupa of his massive new Shwezigon Pagoda in Bagan and their worship tolerated within the overall framework of Burmese Theravada Buddhism. A thousand years later they remain as popular as ever, and images of at least one or two *nats* can be found in every Burmese Buddhist temple right up to the present day.

TEACHINGS OF THE BUDDHA

The division between the Theravada and Mahayana styles, developing for some time, was formalized in 235 BC when King Ashoka convened the Third Synod at Pataliputra, India. The Buddhist elders (Theravada means "the way of the elders") held tight to their literal interpretation of the Master's teaching. They were opposed by a group seeking to understand the personality of the historic Buddha, and its relationship to one's salvation. The Theravada branch of Buddhism is actually a more conservative, orthodox form of Buddhist thought.

The latter group became known as the Mahayana school. It established itself in Tibet, Nepal, China, Korea, Mongolia, Japan and Vietnam. The Theravada school, meanwhile, has thrived in Sri Lanka, Myanmar, Thailand, Laos and Cambodia.

The Buddha denied the existence of a soul. There is no permanence, he explained, for that which one perceives to be "self". Rather, one's essence is forever changing. The idea of rebirth, therefore, is a complicated philosophical question within the structure of Buddhism. When someone is reincarnated, it is neither the person nor the soul which

Inside one of the meditation alcoves at Botataung Pagoda, Yangon.

⊘ SHIN ARAHAN: THE GREAT REFORMER

Legendary in the annals of medieval Burma, Shin Arahan is the missionary monk who, through his influence over four successive Kings of Bagan in the 11th and early 12th centuries, ensured Theravada Buddhism became the state religion at a time when it was fast declining elsewhere in Asia.

Shin Arahan was born in 1034, in the southeastern Mon Kingdom of Thaton. The local rulers had long since embraced Buddhism, but its beliefs and practices were increasingly under threat from Hinduism, which is why Shin Arahan, then a monk in his early 20s, fled north up the Ayeyarwady to meditate in a forest near Bagan.

Bagan in the mid-11th century was the most powerful,

prosperous city in central Burma, but its religious life was a wild mix of *nat* nature spirit worship, Tantricism and Tibetan-influenced Mahayana Buddhism promulgated by an order of forest monks known as the Ari, who were rumoured to engage in debauched rituals strongly disapproved of by Bagan's King Anawrahta.

After meeting the hermit, Anawrahta appointed the 22-year-old monk as his chief spiritual adviser. Shin Arahan's brand of traditional, pure Theravada Buddhism quickly spread across the kingdom, and, by the time of the great reformer's death at the age of 81, had taken root in the neighbouring states of Siam (Thailand), Laos and Cambodia, where it remains the predominant school.

is actually reborn. Rather, it is the sum of one's karma, the balance of good and evil deeds. One is reborn as a result of prior existence. A popular metaphor used to explain this transition is that of a candle. Were a person to light one candle from the flame of another, then extinguish the first, it could not be said that the new flame was the same as the previous one. Rather, in fact, its existence would be due to that of the previous flame. The Noble Eight-fold Path, therefore, does not lead to salvation in the traditional Judeo-Christian sense. By pursuing matters of wisdom, morality and mental discipline, one can hope to make the transition into *nibbana* (nirvana), which can perhaps best be defined as the extinction of suffering, or cessation of desire. It is not heaven, nor is it annihilation – simply a quality of existence.

THE MONK

There are no priests in Theravada Buddhism. But the faithful still need a model to follow on the path to salvation and this is provided by monks. In Myanmar, there are about 500,000 monks (and 50,000 nuns). Most of these are stu-

Nuns collecting alms, Pyin U-Lwin.

⊘ BUDDHIST TERMINOLOGY

Gyo-daing – small Buddha shrines found in temples.
Kyaung – a Buddhist monastery.
Pagoda – the English translation of the term "paya", generally used to describe any Burmese Buddhist temple.
Pahto – another word for a temple.
Pongyi – a Buddhist monk.
Samsara – cycle of birth and death (rebirth).
Sayadaw – Abbot of a Burmese monastery.
Tazaung – a Buddhist shrine.
Thabeik – a monk's bowl.
Thilashin – a Buddhist nun.
Zedi – a stupa.

dents and novices who don the saffron robe only temporarily; nearly all male Burmese devote a period – from just a few weeks to several years – to the monkhood *(sangha)*.

There are three fundamental rules to which the monk must subscribe. First, the renunciation of all possessions, except eight items, including three robes, a needle and an alms bowl. Second, a vow to injure no living thing and to offend no one. Finally, the vow of complete sexual celibacy. The monk must make his livelihood by seeking alms; the food received is the monk's only meal of the day. A young Burmese begins his novitiate at around the age of nine. For the majority of Burmese, this does not last long, and most will have left the monkhood before their 20th birthday.

The most important moment in the life of a young Burmese boy is his *shin-pyu* – the initiation as a novice in the order of monks.

Until a Buddhist has gone through the *shin-pyu* ceremony, he is regarded as being no better than an animal. To become "human", he must for a time withdraw from secular life, following the example set forth by the Buddha when he left his family to seek enlightenment. Unlike his illustrious predecessor, the novice will probably carry his alms bowl for a short period, then return to his normal lifestyle. But his time spent studying scriptures and strictly following the code of discipline makes him a dignified human being.

During the period between his ninth and twelfth birthdays, a boy is deemed ready to don the saffron-coloured robes of the *sangha* and become a "son of the Buddha". If his parents are very pious, they may arrange to have the *shin-pyu* staged on the full moon day of Waso (June/July), the start of the Buddhist Lent. Once the ceremony has been arranged, the boy's sisters announce it to the whole village or neighbourhood. Everyone is invited, and contributions are collected for a festival which will dig deep into the savings of the boy's parents.

FESTIVITIES

The night before a *shin-pyu*, a feast is prepared for all the monks whose company the young boy will join. The following morning, the novitiate's head is shaved in preparation. The boy's mother and eldest sister hold a white cloth to receive the falling hair, and later bury it near a pagoda. This head-shaving is a solemn moment; when completed, the boy looks appropriately like a "son of the Buddha".

In the weeks before the ceremony, the boy would have been familiarised with the language and behaviour befitting a monk. He would have learned how to address a superior; how to walk

with decorum, keeping his eyes fixed on a point 2 metres (6ft) in front of him; and how to respond to the questions put to him at the ceremony. During his novicehood, he will not take any food after noon, sing or play, use cosmetics, sit on any elevated seat, possess any money, interfere in the business of other monks or abuse them. He must

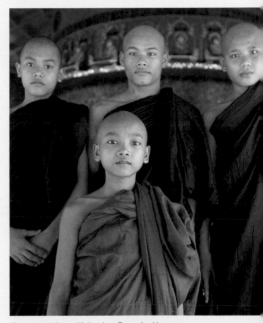

Young monks at Kaba Aye Pagoda, Yangon.

not kill, steal, lie, get drunk or have sex. He must not blaspheme or listen to heretical doctrines.

When the boy's request to enter the monkhood is approved, he prostrates himself three times. He is robed, and now he is ready to walk the path of perfection first trodden by the Buddha. If he is steadfast enough, he might even reach nirvana. Once the *sayadaw* – the abbot who has presided over the ceremony – hangs the novitiate's *thabeit* alms bowl over his shoulder, the boy's childhood is left behind. He has been accepted as a monk. During his time in the monastery, his parents must address him in honorific terms. He will call them "lay sister" and "lay brother", the same names he calls others not in the monkhood.

FESTIVALS

Myanmar's festive events range from solemn Dhammasetkya, marking the beginning of Buddhist Lent, through to the manic Thingyan water festival and the incredible Thadingyut festival of lights.

Myanmar's festival year is based on the Buddhist lunar calendar, which determines the dates of festivals and Buddhist holidays beginning with Thingyan, the Burmese New Year, in April. Whenever the full moon waxes, it's time for a *pwe*, or festival, of one sort or another. Some *pwe* are solemn; others are occasions for fun and frivolity. All are worth experiencing. The festivals below are listed in the order they appear during each year of the Western calendar (January–December), although the Buddhist New Year actually falls in April.

PYATHO

The lunar month of Pyatho (late December/ early January) was formerly the time of the year when Burmese royalty displayed its strength with military parades, although today it's reserved mostly for local pagoda festivals (including the massive Ananda Temple festival in Bagan). These are partly religious, with gifts presented to monks and offerings made for temple upkeep, and partly secular, with impromptu markets set up around temples accompanied by plenty of eating and drinking, performances of music and dance, plus the occasional boxing match.

Held at around the same time, the Kayin New Year (December/January) is marked by vibrant celebrations amongst Kayin communities throughout Myanmar, but especially in Kayin State and the Ayeyarwady Delta. Simultaneously, in Kachin State, the predominantly Christian minority people celebrate their annual Manao Festival with traditional Kachin music and costumed dances around huge, colourfully decorated *manao taing* (totem poles). The festival serves to please Kachin *nat* and ensure peace,

A Buddhist devotee lights a candle at a full moon festival.

plenty and prosperity, and also involves the sacrifice of cattle or buffalo to placate and honour the local *nat*. A *manao* may go on for 24 hours, and a lot of locally brewed alcohol is drunk. It's difficult to predict with any accuracy the exact date on which a *manao* may be held, the decision being taken by the *duwa* (Kachin elders). The biggest *manao* is held in January at Myitkyina, the capital of Kachin State, to celebrate Kachin State Day and bringing together all the various branches of the traditional Kachin tribe for a week of dancing, games and general partying.

TABAUNG

Tabaung (March/April), the last month of the traditional Burmese year, is considered a time of romance and tranquillity. On the full moon day of Tabaung, Burmese travel to lakes or rivers where they play music, sing and recite poetry, often in the company of a loved one.

Tabaung also signals the start of Myanmar's largest temple festival, the Shwedagon Pagoda Festival in Yangon. Thousands of people dress in ceremonial costumes and descend on the shrine for the event, while traditional puppet shows, dance and music recitals, and robe-weaving competitions also take place.

the duration of the festival, government buildings and businesses are closed and pretty much the entire country shuts down.

Pandals – pavilions or stages made from bamboo and beautifully decorated with flowers and papier mâché – are erected in which lines of garlanded girls dressed in identical suits of colourful material perform carefully rehearsed song and dance routines while boys douse them with water. More overtly suggestive versions spring up in the liberal, upper-class neighbourhoods of Yangon, where hot pants, crop tops and

People throw buckets of water onto a car during the Thingyan water festival.

THINGYAN

The beginning of the hot season in April is celebrated with the mammoth Thingyan ("changing over") water festival (April 13–16). Myanmar's biggest party, Thingyan celebrates the Burmese New Year, traditionally held on the full moon day of the lunar month of Tagu (although dates are now fixed according to the Western calendar). The festival goes on for three or four days, the length of the celebration determined by *ponna* or Brahman astrologers. Water is poured from buckets, sprayed from water pistols and hoses, and even blasted from fire hydrants to wash away the old year and welcome the new. The drenching stops each day at 6.30pm, and is followed by an evening of feasting and partying. For

Western-style dancing replace the traditional elegance.

THAGYAMIN

Thingyan also celebrates the descent to earth of Thagyamin, the king of the 37 *nat*, to bring blessings for the new year. He brings two books with him: one bound in gold to record the names of children who have been well behaved in the past year, and one bound in dog skin to record the names of any naughty children. Thagyamin rides a winged golden horse and bears a water jar, symbolic of peace and prosperity. Households greet Thagyamin with flowers and palm leaves at the front door. Guns are fired and music is played in salute. Gaily decorated floats parade up and down the streets of the cities and larger towns. But there are also moments of tranquillity in the midst of this exuberance. Most revellers find time to make offerings at pagodas and at the homes of their elders, and Buddha images are washed by the devout.

KASON AND NAYON

The full moon day of the lunar month of Kason (April/May) sees celebrations for the birthday of Lord Buddha (sometimes known as Vesak). Water is poured over the roots of sacred Banyan trees, beneath the branches of which the Buddha attained enlightenment. At the full moon, the birth, enlightenment and death of the Buddha are celebrated. The devout join a procession of musicians and dancers to the local pagoda.

During the full moon of Nayon (May to June), after the rains have begun and the hot, dry months are at an end, Burmese students are tested on their knowledge of the Tripitaka (the Buddhist scriptures). Abbots lecture before large crowds, schools operated by monasteries are opened to the public, and eminent scholars exhibit their knowledge to public acclaim.

BUDDHIST LENT

The full moon day of the month of Waso (June/July) marks the arrival of Buddhist Lent, celebrated with the festival of Dhammasetkya, a solemn religious occasion, marking the beginning of a period during which all monks go into a period of deep retreat for study and meditation. This is also an auspicious time for young men to have their *shin-pyu* initiation into the monkhood (see page 75). For the next three months the country is soaked in water as the monsoons gain strength. During this time monks are not permitted to travel, and the devout will enter a period of fasting.

WAGAUNG

The month of Wagaung (July/August) is celebrated with the Maha Dok ("Draw-a-Lot") Festival. Since no marriage or other secular celebration is permitted during Buddhist Lent, the full moon day of Wagaung is observed as a festival of merit-making. The name of each member of the local *sangha* is written on a piece of paper, which is then rolled up and deposited into a large basket. A representative from each household of the community draws a slip of paper from the basket, and, the next day,

provides an elaborate feast for the monk named on the piece of paper. One layman will have drawn a paper containing the name of the Gautama Buddha and he has the honour of hosting the Buddha.

> So popular are the Phaung Daw U and Thadingyut festivals held at Inle Lake each September that celebrants often spend all their savings on new clothing.

Procession of villagers during a nat pwe (spirits festival) at Kyaukse.

TAWTHALIN AND THADINGYUT

By mid-September the rainy season is at its height, and Myanmar's waterways, from the mighty Ayeyarwady to the smallest stream, are full. To celebrate this bounty, boat races are held all over the country during the lunar month of Tawthalin, with the most impressive taking place at the Phaung Daw U Festival on Inle Lake.

Heralding the end of Buddhist Lent and the approach of the cool season, a festival of lights is held during the month of Thadingyut (September/October) to celebrate the Buddha's return from heaven to earth after preaching to the gods, ushering a period of weddings and other secular celebrations. To symbolise the radiance of the

Buddha on his return, millions of candles and oil lamps illuminate monasteries, pagodas, houses and trees throughout the land.

TAZAUNGMONE AND NADAW

A nationwide Weaving Festival is held during the month of Tazaungmone (October/November). Under the full moon, unmarried women work at their looms all night to make new robes, which are then presented to the monks at the local temple early the next morning. Hot-air balloons illuminated with candles are also released into the sky,

OTHER FESTIVALS

National holidays of a secular nature are dated according to the Western (international) calendar. Independence Day is held on 4 January and celebrated with week-long festivities. Boat races are staged on Kandawgyi Lake in Yangon and the palace moats in Mandalay.

On 12 February, Union Day marks national unity with flag-bearing and other celebrations. Peasant's Day is celebrated on 2 March, while fireworks and parades mark the annual Armed Forces Day on March 27.

Boatmen racing at the Phaung Daw U Festival.

Some major nat celebrations are also held at other times of the year, including the Mount Popa Festival (Nayon; May/June) and the traditional Shan Festival in Kyaukme (Tabaung; February/March).

most spectacularly at the celebrated "fire-balloon" festival at Taunggyi, near Lake Inle.

The full moon day of the month of Nadaw (November/December) is dedicated to celebrations to the spirit world and is when most *nat* festivals take place, including the raucous Taungbyon Festival, held in the town of Wagaung, north of Mandalay.

The first day of May is Labour Day, and 19 July is Martyr's Day, which commemorates the assassination of Bogyoke Aung San and his comrades in 1947.

Other widely celebrated festivals include Diwali, the Hindu festival of lights, as well as the Muslim celebrations of 'Id al-Fitr to celebrate the end of the fasting month of Ramadan, Maulid al-Nabi to commemorate the Prophet Muhammad's birthday, and 'Id al-Adha to celebrate the conclusion of the annual Haj Pilgrimage to Mecca. The Chinese community mark (discreetly) Chinese New Year, the Festival of Hungry Ghosts and the annual Moon Cake Festival, while Myanmar's Christians celebrate Christmas and Easter.

A FEAST OF FLAVOURS

Incorporating widespread influences from neighbouring China, India and elsewhere, Burmese food remains one of Southeast's Asia least-known but most unusual cuisines.

Sharing borders with two culinary giants, India and China, and with the Southeast Asian nations of Laos and Thailand, Myanmar has inevitably been influenced by the spices, seasonings and cooking styles of its neighbours. Yet it is the way that these shared ingredients are combined which makes the cuisine of Myanmar different.

You'll find Chinese foodstuffs, particularly soybean products such as soy sauce, bean sprouts and bean curd, as well as a distinctive local variation of bean curd made from chickpeas which is popular among the Shan people. Chinese noodles have become a staple, but appear in purely Burmese dishes such as *mohinga*, a rich noodle broth that starts with fish stock and simmered banana stem and finishes with a host of garnishes you'd never find in China. The Chinese wok is used for frying, along with traditional terracotta pots, modern metal saucepans and the ubiquitous banana leaf, used as a wrapper for steaming or grilling everything from rice to meat to fish and cakes.

Indian influence is also noticeable, especially the use of chickpeas – not just whole, but toasted and ground to make a nutty powder which is sprinkled into soups, noodle dishes and over salads. The Burmese use only a few Indian spices, most notably turmeric, cumin and coriander, preferring to flavour their curry-style dishes with huge amounts of crushed onion, garlic and ginger, often slowly cooked to a rich brown. Indian curry leaves, very popular in the south of the subcontinent, are also used in parts of Myanmar, and a number of traditional Indian recipes have been adapted to local tastes.

The food of Myanmar is perhaps most similar to that of its Southeast Asian neighbours. Herbs, such as lemon grass and kaffir lime, pungent fish products and creamy coconut milk are frequently

Deep-fried street food snacks.

used, not forgetting an abundance of fresh, dried and powdered chillies. In the central and southern parts of the country, fish sauce and *ngapi* (dried shrimp paste) are as common as salt in a Western kitchen. Fruity sour tamarind, various types of ginger, including common ginger and fresh turmeric, and butterscotch-sweet palm sugar all add their character to countless dishes.

REGIONAL DIVERSITY

The well-watered Ayeyarwady Delta and Isthmus of Kra, "Lower Myanmar", is the nation's rice bowl. With rivers, estuaries, canals and coastal waters, it's not surprising that fish and other seafood is the main source of protein in this part of the country. Much of it is dried. Small prawns are used in

The Burmese have a pronounced sweet tooth, especially in the afternoons, when they snack on moun – made from coconut, sticky rice, tapioca and fruit. Bein moun, pancakes made from rice flour and palm sugar, are another favourite.

salads, soups, main dishes and spicy side dishes or in condiments such as the indispensable Burmese *balachaung*, a combination of pounded dried prawns, deep-fried garlic and onions, vinegar and chilli powder. Sour, hot, salty and crisp, it can very quickly become addictive to lovers of emphatically flavoured food.

The central plains around Mandalay are the driest part of the country. Being far from the coast, the people of this region rely on freshwater fish. Thanks to irrigation, crops including various beans and lentils are grown, and some of them fermented to make seasonings substituted for the fermented fish products of the south.

The third geographic region encompasses the mountainous regions of the Shan area to the east, the western Chin Hills and Kachin State in the north. Because many of these mountainous areas are poor, the local diet might well include items such as insect larvae, ants and grasshoppers. Parts of the Shan Plateau are a fertile exception, where hill rice, beans and lentils are grown and Lake Inle supports freshwater fish. Lacking the abundant fish and prawns of the southern regions of Myanmar, the Shan have developed fermented bean pastes to replace dried shrimp paste as a seasoning, and also make fermented soybean cakes similar to the Indonesian *tempeh*.

THE STAPLE DIET

Allowing for some regional differences, main meals in Myanmar are typically based on rice, with accompanying dishes chosen to provide contrasting flavours and textures. There will usually be a clear soup *(hingo)*, often slightly sour and with leafy greens floating in it, which is eaten throughout the meal to "help wash down the rice". Then there should be at least one curry of either meat, poultry, fish or even egg; you can tell by the colour roughly what the flavour will be like in advance, with red signifying lashings of chilli, white, a milder coconut gravy, and yellow, plenty of turmeric.

There will also be a cooked vegetable dish, maybe some lentils, a salad, a chilli-hot condiment and almost certainly *balachaung*. When it comes to vegetables, the Burmese living outside the major cities or towns depend on a huge range of wild plants. These include aquatic plants gathered from rivers, canals and lakes, as well as various leaves, tubers, shoots, buds, seeds, and fungi found in the forests or along the edges of the rice fields. The young leaves of many shrubs and fruit trees such as papaya and mango are also edible, as are the leaves of a number of root vegetables.

Mohinga.

⊘ BREAKFAST NOODLES

Myanmar's morning chorus is the sound of slurping as the "national dish" is devoured at food stalls throughout the country. Known as *mohinga*, this starts with pungent fish broth seasoned with lashings of dried shrimp paste, lemon grass, ginger, onion and garlic. This is added to a bowl of rice vermicelli, then topped off with the "small accompaniments" so beloved by the Burmese: crunchy wafers of dried soybean cake, chilli powder, fried garlic, coriander leaf, sliced fish cake, ground roasted chickpeas, egg and spring onions. Forget your breakfast rolls and coffee – *mohinga* is what real men (and women) eat for breakfast.

SALADS AND NOODLE DISHES

The creativity of Burmese cooks is perhaps at its best when it comes to salads and noodle dishes. Salads – called *thoke*, which means "mixed by hand" – begin with raw vegetables, either a single vegetable or a wide range of leaves. For a salty flavour, fish sauce, salt or soy sauce are added, and for greater pungency, some dried shrimp paste or soybean powder.

Sourness comes in the form of tamarind, lime or vinegar, or perhaps some shredded sour fruit. To absorb the moisture of the sour juice, pounded

Tasty street food.

> Chinese-style green tea is served free with meals and snacks in most local cafes. Black tea is also widely available, usually served with condensed milk and sugar, while Indian-style spicy masala chai can also be found in some Muslim establishments.

dried shrimp, peanuts, roasted chickpea powder, sesame seeds or soybeans are added. To blend everything together, vegetable oil and sesame oil are added. The final garnishing comes in the form of crisp fried onion and garlic, roasted chilli and

herbs such as mint, coriander, kaffir lime leaf or lemon grass.

Noodle dishes, too, can be dazzlingly complex in flavour and texture. Take, for example, the popular *mishee* from Mandalay, which begins with rice noodles. These are put into a bowl and topped with some deep-fried pork in batter, deep-fried bean-curd puffs, a pickle made from fermented mustard greens and some crisp bean sprouts. A ladleful of shredded pork in rich stock is added, then a dollop or two of garlic sauce, chilli sauce and a salty sauce made from preserved chilli bean curd. The finishing touch comes in the form of a sprinkle of chopped spring onions.

A more simple but equally tempting noodle dish – and one which has been adopted by northern Thais – is *kyauk shwe*, which consists of chicken simmered in a spicy coconut milk gravy made with plenty of onion, garlic, ginger and chilli. This fragrant mixture is poured over egg noodles, with slices of boiled egg, crisp-fried onions, chilli flakes, fresh coriander and a wedge of lime.

SNACKS AND STIMULANTS

Burmese of all ages love to snack, and along the streets and the markets, *longyi*-clad cooks stand or squat over a single burner holding a wok full of bubbling oil, into which fritters of spiced lentils, dried beans, prawns, and mixtures of pork or chicken and vegetable are plunged. Hawkers offer spiced nuts, salted broad beans, banana chips, pancakes with sweet fillings, brightly coloured squares of sweet jelly, and preserved dried fruits coated in sugar and spiked with chilli powder.

Only in Myanmar can you drink your tea and eat it, too. Be sure to try Myanmar's signature dish, tea-leaf salad (*lahpet*), made with young tea leaves packed into bamboo tubes and left to ferment, widely available both in local cafés and upmarket restaurants alike. The leaves are mixed with salt and sesame oil, then served surrounded by lime juice, chilli and garnishes including fried garlic, dried shrimps, toasted sesame seeds, fried broad beans or dried peas. The secret is to take a pinch of two or three seasonings, together with some tea leaves, and discreetly pop it into your mouth.

Lahpet is supposed to act as a stimulant, as is betel, an addictive snack which you'll also find consumed across South Asia, although its popularity is now steadily diminishing. The preparation of betel involves smearing betel leaf with lime paste, wrapping it around sliced areca nut and spicing it with fennel seeds, cloves or some shredded dried liquorice, and perhaps tobacco. Chew on this mixture for a while and you'll get a modest kick, akin to smoking a cigarette or drinking a very strong cup of coffee, although prolonged long-term use can result in oral cancer and ruined teeth.

TROPICAL FRUITS

Myanmar offers all the luscious fruits of the tropics, many of them available year-round. You'll find juicy mangoes; sweet pineapples; papayas; bananas of different sizes, skin tones and flavours; pomelos (reminiscent of but far superior to grapefruit); giant jackfruit which can weigh up to 25kg (55lbs); and the purple-skinned mangosteen, which has a translucent white flesh with a perfect balance of sweetness and acidity.

And then there is the durian, whose foul-smelling spiky exterior encloses large seeds covered with a buttery flesh that tastes, to the initiated, like heaven. Sir James George Scott, who wrote *The Burman His Life and Notions*, said: "Some Englishmen will tell you that the flavour and the odour of the fruit may be realised by eating a "garlic custard" over a London sewer; others will be no less positive in their perception of blendings of sherry, delicious custards, and the nectar of the gods..."

EATING OUT IN MYANMAR

Finding indigenous Burmese cuisine isn't as easy as you might expect. Particularly in the major cities, the migration of ethnic Chinese and Indians has resulted in many restaurants offering Chinese or Indian food, without a Burmese dish in sight. In Yangon and Mandalay, and tourist centres such as Bagan and Inle Lake, you'll have a choice of the usual five-star restaurants in hotels – which serve Western-style and pan-Asian menus – and more modest pizza-pasta-curry places pitched at independent travellers. However, with the recent increase in tourism, true Burmese cuisine is increasingly available in elegant restaurants in Yangon and in upmarket hotels elsewhere.

Alternatively, if you want to sample real local cuisine, try the simple, semi-open-air restaurants and food stalls, especially those clustered around the markets. And in the more out-of-the-way locations, you're likely to be limited to Burmese eateries. The surroundings are usually basic – with cement floors, Formica tables and dining halls

opening straight onto the street – but the food is invariably fresh and wholesome, though it helps if you've some familiarity with the routine.

First off, order your main-course curries from the hot plates or pots on display. When you sit down, an array of little side dishes and condiments will usually be brought to your table, to be replenished when they're empty: a dhal-style soup or sour broth for dipping; various plates of steamed seasonal veg; *balachaung*; pickled tea leaves; green tea; and lumps of jaggery (unrefined cane sugar). Food is usually eaten with the fingers or by

Mangoes for sale in downtown Yangon.

using a fork and spoon, unless it is a noodle soup when a spoon and pair of chopsticks are used.

The curries forming the centre of the meal will be of fish, chicken, prawn or mutton, or sometimes vegetables; and they'll invariably be swimming in oil. This unctuous covering, intended to help keep the dish fresh and insects at bay, can be spooned off. The sauce beneath, featuring copious amounts of ginger, garlic and tomatoes, will be spicy, but not excessively hot. The Burmese are nowhere near as fond of chillies as their Bangladeshi or Thai neighbours. Curries tend to be mild, but flavoursome.

Out on the streets in the evenings, rows of grab-and-go stalls offer plates of freshly prepared fried and noodle dishes, which you can eat on little plastic chairs with locally brewed Myanmar Beer.

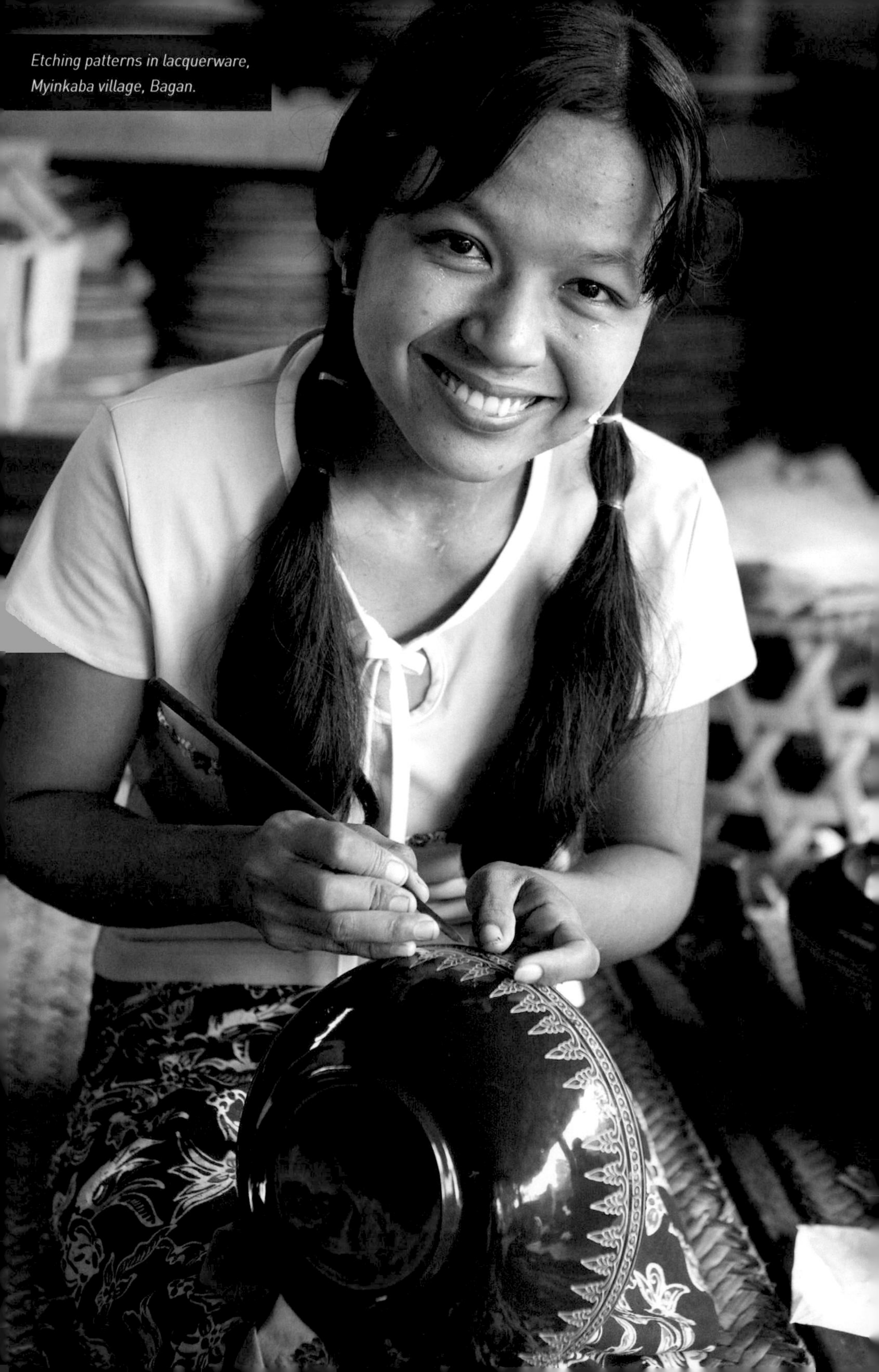

Etching patterns in lacquerware, Myinkaba village, Bagan.

ARTS AND CRAFTS

The time-honoured skills of lacquerware, metalwork, woodcarving and embroidery are still very much in evidence in modern-day Myanmar.

Burmese craftsmen may not have achieved the same international renown as artisans from other parts of Southeast Asia, but they are no less skilled. From Yangon's Bogyoke Aung San Market to Mandalay's Zegyo, and at all local bazaars beyond and between, visitors to Myanmar will find a remarkable variety of native handicrafts, with stalls displaying lacquerware, metalwork, brass and marble sculpture, woodcarvings, embroidered textiles and more.

LACQUERWARE

Burmese lacquerware has developed into one of the country's most refined art forms, tracing Its history back to China's Shang dynasty (18th to 11th century BC). The craft reached Myanmar in the 1st century AD by way of the Nanzhao Empire (modern Yunnan) and is believed to have been carried to Bagan during King Anawrahta's conquest of Thaton in 1057. Today, it thrives in northern Thailand and Laos, as well as in Myanmar.

Raw lacquer is tapped from the thitsi tree (Melanorrhoea usitatissima) in the same way as latex is taken from the rubber tree. As soon as the sticky-grey extract comes in contact with the air, it turns hard and black. In the past, extraordinarily fine lacquerware bowls were produced around inner cores made of a mixture of horsehair and bamboo, or even pure horsehair. This gave such flexibility that one could press opposite sides of the bowl's rim together without the bowl breaking or the lacquer peeling off. Today, two other techniques of manufacture prevail. Cheaper lacquerware comprises a gilded lacquer relief on a wooden base. Better-quality work has a core of light bamboo wickerwork, which assures elasticity and durability.

The finest attention to detail.

This basic structure is coated with a layer of lacquer and clay, then put in a cool place to dry. After three or four days, the vessel is sealed with a paste of lacquer and ash, the fineness of ash determining the quality of the work. It may come from sawdust, paddy husk or even cow dung. After this coating has dried, the object is polished until smooth. Over time, it is given several successive coats of lacquer to eliminate irregularities. At this stage, the lacquerware is still black – ornamental and figurative designs are added later. Cheaper articles are simply painted, while expensive ones are engraved, painted and polished. A similar effect can be produced with coloured reliefs, which are painted and partially polished. Red, yellow, blue and gold are the most frequent colours used. The production of such multi-coloured lacquerware takes about six months, involving 12 or more stages of manufacture.

Generally, the designs represented in lacquerware are of Buddhist origin, derived from the *Jataka* Buddha life-cycle stories, images of the Buddha, and celestial animals from Hindu-Buddhist mythology. Among the most common icons are the *chinthe* or lion, the *hintha* or goose, the *naga* or serpent, the *galoun* or eagle, and – unlikely, perhaps, in such distinguished company – the unassuming *youn* or rabbit.

> Brightly painted paper parasols are a speciality of Pathein. You'll see these exquisitely painted items on sale at souvenir shops in many tourist areas, but they're a lot cheaper in Pathein itself, where you can buy direct from the dozen-odd workshops dotted around the town.

METALWORK

The most frequently seen product of the Burmese metalworking industry is probably the gold leaf, much of it produced in Mandalay, which is pasted by devout Burmese on Buddha images all over the country.

The gold comes from the north of the country in nuggets, which are flattened on a slab of marble until paper-thin. These sheets are then alternately cut and pounded between layers of leather and copper-plate until they are almost transparent. They are then placed between sheets of oiled bamboo paper and neatly packaged in 2cm (1-in) -long stacks of 100 leaves, for sale at pagodas and bazaars. An ounce of gold can produce enough gold leaf for an area of 10 sq metres (12 sq yds).

Burmese silverwork dates back to the 13th century, when palace bowls, vases and betel-nut boxes, as well as daggers and sheaths, were made. Today, the craftsmanship at Ywataung village near Sagaing rivals that of the earlier artisans. While silverwork is not as prominent as it once was, work in copper and brass has never seriously declined in importance and remains a major cottage industry in Mandalay for about 300 families. Bago is another important centre, with the city's

metal-workers producing Buddha images, gongs and bells for pagodas and monasteries.

BRONZE BUDDHA IMAGES

Foundry workers cast bronze Buddhas and ritual implements using the ancient "lost wax process" in the Tampawaddy district of Chanmyathazi, just outside Mandalay (between Mahamuni and the airport). The process is a complex one and requires real skill. The artisan begins by making a mould in three stages. First, a mix is made of dust, manure, ochre clay and rice husks, which is

A woman prepares gold leaf in the Gold Pounders district of Mandalay.

blended with water to make a fine clay-like mixture. The Buddha image-to-be is then moulded from the clay mixture, before being allowed to dry and then covered with layers of wax. Finally, the wax is covered with two further layers of clay, and the whole is fired, allowing the wax to melt and run away – hence the "lost wax process" name.

Cast Buddha images are generally made from bronze (a mixture of copper and tin). Smelting takes place over a large pit filled with coal or charcoal which is fanned to a great heat, causing the metals to melt and blend in a huge clay crucible. The molten metal is then poured into the inverted mould through one of two small holes left there to permit the egress of wax and the ingress of molten bronze. The bronze is poured into one hole, taking the place of the lost wax, until it begins to emerge from the other hole. After a day or two solidifying and cooling, both the outer layers and inner core of clay are removed with a hammer and chisel. Finally the Buddha image is filed, polished and generally made perfect. It may then be decorated, often with a crown or flame-like halo.

Buddha images may be the most obvious and the best-known products of Burmese bronze-making artisans, but they are many others.

These include huge bells – the best example of which is the mighty bell cast on the orders of King Bodawpaya in 1790, and reputedly the second largest in the world after the cracked monster at the Kremlin. Burmese bells cast in this fashion have no hanging central clapper as in Europe, but instead are designed to be hit on the outside with a wooden club.

Also made of bronze, the small "opium weights" that were once used throughout the country are now made as souvenirs. Properly sold in sets of 10, these weights are kept with

At the marble Buddha workshops near Mahamuni Pagoda, Mandalay.

⊘ WHERE TO SHOP

All the major tourist centres in Myanmar have markets selling traditional handicrafts and other souvenirs – these are great places to spend your money, as you can be sure most of it will reach the local people who most need it. In addition, many upscale hotels have souvenir boutiques selling similar merchandise at inflated prices.

For sheer variety, you can't beat the country's two largest markets: Bogyoke Aung San Market in Pabedan, Yangon, and central Mandalay's Zegyo Market. Both offer a vast selection of antiques (both real and fake), arts and handicrafts, bridging all price brackets.

Another good source of unusual souvenirs are the shops lining the stairways in major Buddhist pagodas, specialising in quintessentially Burmese religious paraphernalia, from incense sticks to mini Buddhas and prayer beads. Worth looking out for here too are *kammawa* – traditional "books" of Buddhist manuscripts written on slats of wood, cane or cloth with gilded borders. Beautiful floral motifs and images of birds and animals often embellish the lines of script – rendered in a square style known as "tamarind seed" (*magyi-zi*). In a similar vein are *parabaik* palm-leaf manuscripts, which are bound together concertina fashion.

a set of scales in a specially carved wooden box, usually stained black. The earliest known weights date back to the 14th century, and today's reproductions have changed little. The weights are often in the form of mythical animals or birds from the Hindu-Buddhist pantheon, such as the *hintha* (celestial goose) and the swan-like *karaweik*.

WOODCARVING

Woodcarving is among the oldest of Burmese handicrafts. Most of the country's ancient wood-

Teak carvings at Shwenandaw Kyaung Monastery, Mandalay.

work has been destroyed by the ravages of time, although significant 19th-century work survives in the wood-carved monasteries of Mandalay, Salay and elsewhere. Today, *nat* images are among the most commonly made wooden objects. The artisans first sketch the figures they wish to carve on a solid block of wood, using charcoal and chalk, then shape an outline with chisel and saw. Details are completed with knives and other fine instruments.

Marionettes have traditionally been made for *yok thei pwe* performances and marionette theatres. Often exquisitely carved and colourfully clad, these hinged, wooden figures make excellent souvenirs, and are now manufactured for sale at shops and bazaars all over the country, but especially in Yangon and Mandalay.

Up to a metre (3ft) in height, the marionettes are controlled by as many as 60 strings, although 10 is more usual. The strings allow the puppets to portray basic human movements such as walking, dancing and stylised gesturing. Characters featured in traditional marionette theatre include Thagyamin, the King of the Nats, along with a human king and queen plus their children, ministers, pages, clowns and the obligatory villain.

A typical troupe of marionettes includes 28 such traditional characters. Animals, real and mythological, also feature in the troupe, including horses, elephants, monkeys and *makara* sea serpents.

Marble carvers in Mandalay get their raw materials from a quarry at Sagyin 34km (21 miles) north of Mandalay.

PAINTING

Painting has long been an esteemed art throughout Myanmar, with the subject matter often derived from Buddhist *Jataka* stories and related themes. The temples of Bagan were richly adorned with painted murals, many of which have survived to the present day, albeit in a faded and dilapidated state. In these early examples of temple decoration, Indian influence – and especially that of the Ajanta school – is apparent. Most murals were painted directly onto plaster made from a mix of clay, with sand and rice husks to provide a binding agent.

By the 19th century murals had become more indigenous in style, with the faces, costumes and buildings all taking on a distinctly Burmese quality. Buddhist themes remain predominant, and are almost always drawn from the Theravada tradition, although Mahayana subject matter – for example, representations of Avalokitesvara or Guan Yin – and some Hindu iconography drawn from the *Ramayana* are also found. During the British colonial period, a school of Burmese watercolour painting developed, which combined Western and Burmese artistic traditions and frequently features nationalistic subjects such as the exile of King Thibaw and the perceived uncouth mannerisms of the British. Examples can be found in a few galleries and art shops, especially in Yangon. A speciality of the Bagan area (and sold by hawkers at all the major temples) are sand paintings, richly detailed works often copied from ancient murals in the temples themselves. Excellent souvenirs, these can be rolled up without damaging them, making them a lot more portable than ordinary paintings.

EMBROIDERY

Dress and ornamentation have long been an important part of Burmese life, from the for-

"Golden Land" are the hangings known as *kalaga* or "Indian curtains". These are elaborately sequined and padded wall hangings on black velvet, featuring scenes from the Buddha's life, Hindu-Buddhist mythology and – at least in recent years – more secular subjects such as elephant fights, warriors and princesses, flowers, trees and scenic views. The technique used for making *kalaga* is ancient but adaptable; today's artisans incorporate the art form into clothing, blankets and even gaily coloured bags and caps.

At work in a parasol workshop in Pathein.

mer royal court down to simple *pwe* festivities. The elaborate ornamentation of the Burmese court is mentioned as early as the 9th century AD in Chinese sources, while King Kyanzittha of Bagan felt able to boast in a 12th-century inscription that even his poor subjects were able to adorn themselves with precious gold and fine clothes.

Court dress in ancient periods often featured expensive silks and cloth embroidered with gold and silver threads, and adorned with fine lacework – costumes from the days of kings Mindon and Thibaw were particularly elaborate.

Related to the art of embroidery and popular as souvenir items among visitors to the

⊘ BURMESE SILK

Before the influx of imported textiles during the colonial period, silk was an important product of Henzada and Amarapura. Henzada silks were heavy, brocade-like materials, while Amarapura specialised in shot silks in red, green and yellow, with the weft (the threads that lie across the cloth) colours generally lighter than those of the warp (the threads that run lengthways). Certain colour combinations such as two shades of green were considered unlucky, while rose-pink was deemed lucky and much sought-after. All textiles were traditionally made on simple frame looms. Today, expensive silk *longyi* often display peacock figures or broad belts of floral designs.

THE PERFORMING ARTS

Most musical theatre and dance in Myanmar is inspired by ancient myths and legends, and by Buddhist beliefs.

Music, dance and drama in Myanmar are very much a part of everyday life in the country, performed on makeshift stages by the side of the road rather than in elegant theatres or concert halls, and with an audience of chattering and cheering locals gathered for the occasion. Fairs and festivals are often cultural as much as religious in appeal, with travelling troupes of artists performing *pwe*, a distinctive Burmese blend of theatre, song and dance, mixing slapstick comedy with stories from the great Buddhist and Hindu epics.

Myanmar has a National Theatre with its own company of dancers and musicians, while other troupes are trained in the State Schools of Music and Drama in Yangon and Mandalay. Most theatrical performances, however, are provided by itinerant troupes that travel around villages during pagoda festivals, staging shows throughout the countryside during the dry season. These troupes present their repertoire to throngs of villagers, performing on temporary bamboo stages, under a makeshift awning or (more often than not) in the open air. Large audiences sit on mats spread in front of the stage. Many bring their children, as well as picnics. Performances often last from sunset to sunrise; many spectators doze off for a couple of hours in the middle of the show, hoping to be nudged awake for their favourite dance sequence or story.

UNDERSTANDING PWE

The most characteristic example of the Burmese performing arts is the *pwe*. Most popular is the *zat pwe*, the ultimate mélange of music, dance and dramatics. *Anyein pwe* is a more "folksy" theatrical form presenting episodes from daily life, along with dancing and

Shan traditional dance.

storytelling. *Yein pwe* is pure dance, solos alternating with group numbers. *Yok thei pwe*, or marionette theatre, is a uniquely Burmese theatrical form not so often seen today. *Nat pwe* is ritual spirit-medium dance, only performed in public at animistic festivals.

Among other forms of theatre, *pya zat* is often seen before *zat pwe* performances. A dance-play with mythical themes, it is generally set in a fantasy world where a heroic prince must overcome the evil-doings of demons and sorcerers.

From the mid-18th to the mid-19th centuries, a masked dance-drama called *zat gyi* flourished in royal courts under the patronage of Burmese kings. Today, public performances are rare, although papier-mâché replicas of *zat gyi* dance masks can be purchased at souvenir stalls along the stairs leading to the Shwedagon Pagoda.

DANCE-DRAMA

The history of Burmese dance troupes dates back as far as 1767, when King Hsinbyushin returned to Ava after his conquest of the Thai capital of Ayutthaya. Among his captives were the royal Siamese dancers. It was from these highly trained performers that the Burmese developed the dance movements which still prevail on stage today.

During the Bagan period from the 11th to the 13th centuries, a form of dance resembling that practised in India was popular at pagoda festivals and during royal audiences. This took a back seat to the highly refined Thai classical dance from the late 18th century onwards, but still influenced the shaping of a uniquely Burmese dance form which reached its zenith in Mandalay during the late Konbaung dynasty era.

Although some stylistic leaps and turns of Western ballet were introduced and assimilated during the years of British colonial rule, enthu-

A performance of a traditional Kachin dance.

⊘ PERFORMING PWE

Pwe is a generic Burmese term for theatrical performances and dramatic shows. It embraces all kinds of plays, dramas and musical operas. Dancing is inevitably part of a *pwe*, and performances generally last for at least eight hours, and often right through the night. It's possible to make a loose classification of different types of *pwe*, thus a *zat pwe* is a religious performance based on the various Jataka, or Buddha life-cycle stories, while a *yama zat pwe* is based on the great Hindu epic, Ramayana. *Anyein pwe* are plays without plots, usually accompanied by clowning, ironic repartee and dancing. Finally, *yein pwe* feature group singing and dancing.

siasm for dance went into a period of decline. Efforts have been made to revive the theatrical arts, and while the programme has been quite successful, it's also been very inward-looking.

LEGENDARY TALES

Ancient legends permeate all aspects of theatre in Myanmar. Nearly all performances are based on the Hindu epics (the *Ramayana* in particular), or on the *Jataka* tales recounting the Buddha's 547 prior incarnations. The *Ramayana* is the best-known saga in South and Southeast Asia; it tells the story of the capture of the beautiful Princess Sita by the demon king Ravana, and of her heroic rescue by her husband, Rama. The *Jataka*, meanwhile, are familiar to every

Burmese schoolchild and adult. The tales relate, in a quasi-historical moral fashion, how the Buddha purified his soul before his final rebirth and enlightenment. The tales describing his final ten incarnations immediately preceding Buddhahood are seen as especially important.

As the stories are well known beforehand, it is up to the troupe and its individual dancers to bring them to life for audiences. The highlight of a *zat pwe* performance usually comes in the early hours of the morning at about 2am, when the star dancers show off their finest skills.

public, wooden figures could do without prohibition. And thus the *yok thei pwe* was born.

According to traditional Buddhist doctrine, each organism consists of 28 physical parts. U

Burmese dance emphasises double-jointed suppleness. Wrists, elbows, knees, ankles, fingers and toes are bent in stylised directions with seeming effortlessness.

Wa dancers in Yangon dance in honour of the Karen New Year.

MARIONETTE THEATRE

Quite different from all other forms of Burmese theatre is the *yok thei pwe*, or marionette theatre. Puppet theatre in Burma had its foundation not long after Hsinbyushin's return from Ayutthaya with the Siamese court dancers. The king's son and successor, Singu Min, created a Ministry for Fine Arts, and gave his minister U Thaw the task of developing a new art form.

In 18th-century Burma, and to some extent even today, modesty and etiquette forbade the depiction of intimate scenes on the stage. Further, many actors refused to portray the future Buddha in the *Jataka* tales, considering this to be sacrilegious. U Thaw saw a way around these obstacles. What human beings could not do in

⊘ THE MAHA GITA

The complete body of Burmese classical songs is generally referred to as the *Maha Gita*, meaning "Great Song" or "Royal Song". These are the songs and music of the various Burmese royal courts, which today form the basis of Burmese classical music. The impact of the *Maha Gita* on the performance of Burmese music can hardly be overstated. It forms the basis of both the chamber music ensemble, the *hsaing* ensemble and also of solo musical instrument performances such as the piano. The *Maha Gita* also provides much of the basis for music in the theatre, both that of the puppet tradition and that which employs live actors.

Thaw, seeking to be consistent with this belief, directed that there should be precisely 28 marionettes. Each of these is almost a metre (3ft) tall, faultlessly carved and with costumes designed according to the rules laid down by U Thaw. The two principal characters are a prince and princess – Mintha and Minthami – around whom the romantic plot of the performance revolves.

Burmese master puppeteers are highly skilled performers, manipulating 28 dolls, some with as many as 60 strings, while simultane-

solitary horse, whose heavenly constellation brings order to the primeval chaos, followed by (in order) a parakeet, two elephants, a tiger and a monkey.

These various animals are followed by the appearance of two giants, a dragon and a *zawgyi* (sorcerer), who always flies on stage. These figures prepare onlookers for the magical world of Burmese-Buddhist belief, which provides the plot for almost all puppet plays.

The *yok thei pwe* is fast disappearing in modern Myanmar but can still occasionally be seen

A musician plays the gongs at this show to celebrate the Karen New Year.

> "The girl began to dance... a rhythmic nodding, posturing and twisting of the elbows... like a jointed doll, and yet incredibly sinuous." George Orwell, *Burmese Days*.

ously reciting the show's dialogue – all with the help of just two stage assistants.

Classical *yok thei pwe* begin with a musical overture to create an auspicious mood. Two ritual dancing marionettes subsequently appear, followed by a dance of various animals and mythological beings to depict the first stage in the creation of the universe. Next comes a

at temple festivals, including the Shwedagon Pagoda festival in Yangon, and also at the Marionettes Theatre in Mandalay.

MUSICAL PERFORMANCES

The structure of Burmese music is little known outside the country. There has been little systematic study of it and even today writings by Burmese scholars are extremely rare. It is generally related to the music genres of Southeast Asia and often uses gong and chime instruments similar to those found in neighbouring countries.

Traditional Burmese music (such as that accompanying dance performances) is played by a small group of musicians called the *hsaing waing*, vaguely resembling a Javanese *gamelan* and dominated by percussion instruments. Its centrepiece is a circle of 21 drums, the *pat-waing* (smaller orchestras have only nine drums). Around this groups of small and large gongs (*kyi waing* and *maung hsaing*), a bell and clappar (*si* and *wa*), an oboe-like woodwind instrument (the *hne*) and a bamboo xylophone (*pattala*).

Occasionally, a *hsaing waing* will employ the most delicate of all Burmese instruments, the 13-stringed harp (*saung gauk*), shaped like a toy boat covered in buffalo hide, with silk strings attached to a curved wooden "prow". The *saung gauk* is a solo instrument usually played by a woman, unlike other musical instruments, which are all played by men. When used in a *pwe*, it accompanies solo singing.

Burmese music is based on a series of seven-tone scales referred to as *athan*. There are no chromatic notes, and no harmony in the western sense. Instead, the music is strongly rhythmic and percussive, with a single melodic line played by the *hne* enveloped in virtuoso flourishes and swirls of sounds performed on drums, gongs and xylophone.

Unless you're lucky enough to catch a performance at a venue in Yangon or Mandalay, the place you're most likely to experience traditional Burmese music is at your hotel. Most of the five-stars employ musicians to serenade diners, or as evening entertainment.

THE CONTEMPORARY MUSIC SCENE

While traditional Burmese folk and classical music have been actively promoted by the military regime since the 1960s, with slots on state-controlled TV and radio, the same is not true of the new generation of popular music coming out of Yangon and Mandalay. Heavily influenced by trends in Korea, Europe and the US, Myanmar pop music is dominated by so-called "copy tracks" – covers of foreign hits sung in Burmese, or a mixture of Burmese and English.

Queen of the copy scene is the flamboyant Phyu Phyu Kyaw Thein (sometimes described as Myanmar's answer to Lady Gaga), who belts out chart toppers such as Queen's *I Want to Break Free* and Celine Dion's *The Power of Love* while dressed in peacock-feather hats or figure-hugging pink-lamé jump suits.

Much less acceptable to the authorities are the numerous hip-hop acts which have dominated the country's underground music scene since the early 2000s. More masculine, aggressive and materialistic in tone, they adopt the familiar style of US hip-hop – low-slung jeans, baggy T-shirts and baseball caps – but are just as likely to rap about political and social issues as girls, ganja and good times. Others resort to obscure metaphors to express their anger at oppression and

Punk-inspired musicians on a float, Ka Htain festival.

poverty. The upshot has been heavy censorship, and in some cases imprisonment of artistes, such as rapper (and now politician) Zayar Thaw, who spent six years behind bars. Other well-known hip-hop artists include J-me and Ye Lay.

With YouTube as a platform to bypass state-controlled media, popular music is one of the main ways in which established attitudes to gender and sexuality are being challenged in Myanmar. Short skirts, high heels and dyed hair are nowadays commonplace in the world of girl singers and bands, exemplified by the hugely successful Me N Ma Girls, a kind of Burmese Spice Girls, although their songs also addressed sensitive political issues even during the years of military rule.

📷 THE MANY IMAGES OF BUDDHA

Buddha images have been central to Burmese religious art for almost 1,500 years, reflecting the creative skill of the country's artisans and their deep spiritual beliefs.

Images of the Buddha in Myanmar come in many styles. Experts divide them into various groups, distinguished either by historical period or by region of origin. The earliest major group derives from Bagan and dates from the 11th to 13th centuries. Bagan-style Buddhas, whether of bronze, stone or wood, are usually heavy-set with broad shoulders and large faces. The head, set on a short neck, often tilts slightly forward.

An equally distinguished but separate tradition developed in Rakhine around Mrauk U, characterised by its stout Buddhas with square faces, joined eyebrows and often elaborate crowns. This style is exemplified by the famous Mahamuni image, the most revered in Myanmar, which was taken from Mrauk U in 1784 and is now displayed in the Mahamuni Pagoda in Mandalay – although the lower half of the statue has been coated in so much gold leaf that it is impossible to make out its original shape.

Buddha at Sun U Ponya Shin Pagoda, Sagaing, near Mandalay.

Buddha statues embellish the exterior of Kaba Aye Pagoda in Yangon.

Mon images, by contrast, are often slimmer and more etiolated in design, with fuller faces, downcast eyes and very long ears. Again quite distinct, Shan Buddha images tend to have semi-triangular-shaped faces narrowing towards the chin. A broad forehead arches over narrowed eyes, partly open. Earlobes are long, noses fairly pronounced, and necks shortened. Mandalay-style images are common. Earlier images dating from the Inwa (Ava) period are often carved from alabaster, while later images are made of bronze, gilded wood or lacquer. Eyebrows are slightly raised, and nostrils flared.

The Shweyattaw Buddha statue, Mandalay Hill.

Row upon row of Buddhas at Bodhi Tataung, near Monywa.

Asana and mudra

The Buddha is invariably depicted in one of four traditional basic postures, or *asana*: standing, sitting cross-legged, walking and reclining. In the first three of these postures, the Buddha is perceived as teaching or meditating. In the fourth *asana*, by contrast, the Buddha's death and attainment of *parinirvana* (nirvana beyond death) is celebrated. Equally important and stylised are the various hand positions or *mudra* of the Buddha. In the *bhumisparsa mudra*, or "earth-witness" posture, the right hand of the seated Buddha image touches the ground while the left rests on the lap. In the *dhammachakka mudra* or "turning the wheel of dharma", the thumb and forefinger of the image form a circle while the other fingers fan out to symbolise the preaching of the First Sermon. In the *abhaya mudra*, or "have no fear" posture, the palm of the right hand is raised and turned outwards to show the palm with straight fingers. In the *dhyana mudra* or "meditation" position, the hands rest flat on the lap, one on top of each other, while in the *dana mudra* or "offering" position the right hand is palm up and parallel to the ground.

Big Buddha/little Buddha at Thagyarbone temple, Bagan.

Seated Buddha at Nga Htat Gyi Pagoda, Yangon.

Buddha statues inside the Dhammayangyi temple, Bagan.

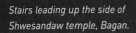
Stairs leading up the side of Shwesandaw temple, Bagan.

TEMPLE ARCHITECTURE

The Burmese landscape is scattered with dazzling pagodas, shrines and stupas – a legacy of the country's Buddhist merit-making traditions.

Burmese Buddhism and Buddhist architecture is unusually eclectic, with the dominant Bamar people borrowing cultural traditions and traits from groups both at home and abroad, ranging from the Theravada-inspired Mon through to the Indian-influenced Rakhine. From the conquest of the Mon Kingdom of Thaton in the 10th century through the long occupation (1564–1774) of Lan Na in what is now Chiang Mai province in northern Thailand and the destruction of the ancient Thai capital of Ayutthaya in 1767, it was common practice for skilled artisans and religious scholars to be taken back to enrich and embellish the Burmese court of the time. In addition, the tendency for new rulers, particularly during the Konbaung era (1752–1885), to move the royal court upon coming to the throne added further to the variety of building styles, as temples were constructed to serve newly established palaces, encouraging a constant updating and evolution of religious architectural practices.

Dhammayazika temple illuminated at sunset, Bagan.

BUDDHIST BUILDERS

The sheer number of Buddhist structures scattered throughout the country leaves a lasting impression on visitors. Many are of exquisite beauty – most famously at the golden Shwedagon Pagoda in Yangon. Their ubiquity is a result of the seemingly endless desire of all Burmese to build temples, shrines and, above all, *stupas*. In spiritual terms, this has everything to do with merit-making, the possibility of an improved rebirth and compensation for transgressions committed in the present life. Raising funds to build *payas* (pagodas) of any sort also brings the sponsor respect and status in the current life, and leaves a fitting memorial for the family to be proud of after the builder has passed on to the next life.

⊘ NORMAN LEWIS'S WORDS

"The special sanctity of the Shwedagon arises from the fact that it is the only pagoda recognised as enshrining relics not only of Gautama, but of the three Buddhas preceding him. Those of the Master consist of eight hairs, four of them original... and four others, miraculous reproductions generated from them in the course of their journey from India. These, according to the account... flew up, when the casket... was opened, to a height of seven palm trees. They emitted rays of variegated hues, which caused the dumb to speak, the deaf to hear, and the lame to walk. Later, a rain of jewels fell, covering the earth to knee's depth." – *Golden Earth: Travels in Burma*, Norman Lewis (1952).

STUPA STYLES

The most common religious structure seen throughout Myanmar is the stupa (*zedi*). There are numerous variations in *stupa* style, but the basic concept and structure remain the same.

The stupa in its present form evolved more than 2,500 years ago in India following the death of Gautama Buddha, when relics of the Enlightened One were taken by his disciples and enshrined within solid structures, usually made of brick and covered in stucco. Stupas are found everywhere in Myanmar, marking passes, raised mounds

View of Hsinbyume Paya from the top of Mingun Paya, near Mandalay.

and hilltops, and sacred places of all kinds. Most commonly, they are found as the centrepiece of temples, typically set upon a raised terrace surrounded by subsidiary shrines (*tazaung*), with perhaps a monastery (*kyaung*) attached.

Generally speaking, most Burmese stupas consist of a bell-shaped dome (*anda*), symbolizing an upturned monk's alm's bowl (*thabeik*), set upon a base comprising a mix of square and octagonal terraces. Above the dome, the stupa narrows to a tall spire supported by concentric rings shaped like lotus petals, rising to a so-called "banana bud".

At the top of the spire rests the *hti*, or umbrella (usually gilded and bejewelled) near the top of

> A *hti* is the elaborate metal "crown" placed on top of the pinnacle of Buddhist stupas, often richly gilded and jewelled, and decorated with small bells.

which is attached a metal, flag-like vane. The topmost part of the *hti* is surmounted by an orb, symbolising enlightenment, release from the cycle of rebirth and the attainment of nirvana.

TEMPLE AND MONASTERY BUILDINGS

Typically, a Burmese monastery forms the spiritual centre of the village or district in which it stands, functioning as a place of worship for monks and lay people alike, as well as a school, social centre and even a hospital.

Temples tend to be built around stupas, but include other buildings such as a *thein* or consecrated assembly hall for the ordination of novices, a *vihara* where the faithful assemble to pray and listen to sermons, living quarters for resident and itinerant monks, a library and a bell tower or gong.

The central stupa is often surrounded by several smaller shrines either housing Buddha images or dedicated to the local *nat* spirit or *bo bo gyi*. There may also be a *zayat*, a hall where lay people may rest by day or sleep overnight during pilgrimages and festivals.

PYU

The oldest surviving remains of religious buildings in Myanmar date from the pre-Bamar Pyu Kingdoms of Beikthano, Thayekhittaya (Sri Ksetra) and Halin (approximately 1st to 11th centuries). Dating from between the 1st and the 5th centuries AD, the brick-built structures at Beikthano, southeast of Bagan, are clearly based on Indian prototypes (the Beikthano Monastery complex, for example, which resembles the monastery at Nagarajunakonda in South India). Later structures at Thayekhittaya (Sri Ksetra), near Pyay, have been dated to the 5th and the 9th centuries and include three bulbous stupas also showing clear Indian influence.

The later (9th to 11th century) stupa-like brick structures at Halin, a short distance southeast of Shwebo, are also attributed to the Pyu.

Skeletons excavated here are aligned to the southeast, commonly considered the direction of the locality spirit or *ein-saung nat*, indicating that the religious beliefs of these early Burmese were probably as much animistic as Buddhist.

MON

Well established in and around Mon State and the Ayeyarwady Delta by the 6th to 9th centuries, the Mon were the amongst the earliest people on the east side of the Bay of Bengal to embrace Buddhism. The early Mon kingdom centred on

court, including architects, painters and artisans. The style of temple which emerged at Bagan was therefore as much Mon as Bamar, and may be described as the first authentically "Burmese" tradition.

BAGAN

Had Bagan been known to classical European antiquity, it would doubtless have been famous as one of the Wonders of the World. In its prime, the city would have bustled with tens of thousands of people, and the greater

The Shwedagon's main stupa at dusk.

Thaton, which according to legend was visited by Buddhist missionaries of the Indian Emperor Ashoka as early as 300 BC.

Today, little of ancient Thaton remains apart from sections of a ruined city wall. Even less remains at another former Mon capital, Bilin, just south of the famous balancing boulder of Kyaikto.

Over the past millennium, the Mon have been substantially absorbed by the dominant Bamar, leaving little evidence of distinct architectural styles. It seems clear, however, that Mon traditions were not destroyed, but rather embraced with enthusiasm by Anawrahta when he conquered Thaton in 1057. The victorious Bamar monarch took back to his capital at Bagan not just the Mon king, but most of his

☉ THE SPELL OF THE PAGODAS

The beauty of Myanmar's pagodas casts a spell over visitors that is hard to break. Ralph Fitch, the first Englishman to visit this part of Asia (in 1586) and leave a record of his impressions, described the golden temple of Shwedagon as "the fairest place, as I suppose, that is in the world". And Somerset Maugham on first seeing Bagan wrote: "A light rain was falling and the sky was dark with heavy clouds when I reached Bagan. In the distance I saw the pagodas for which it is renowned. They loomed, huge, remote and mysterious, out of the mist of the early morning like the vague recollections of a fantastic dream".

The Gentleman in the Parlour (1930).

part of the buildings would have been made of wood and bamboo. These structures have long since disappeared, however, leaving behind the immensity of Bagan's stone-built Buddhist architectural heritage.

The Bagan plain is studded with a plethora of temples and stupas, constructed mainly of brick and decorated with stucco on the outside, and mural paintings within. Archaeologists often distinguish between the earlier, one-storey temples dating from the 10th to 12th centuries, which are sometimes ascribed to the Mon craftsmen captured by King Anawrahta. Many have Mon inscriptions, and are notably smaller and darker than the later temples.

Another common feature of Bagan temples is the Indian-style *pahto*, or "hollow" temple, unlike most Burmese temples in that it substitutes a solid stupa for a cuboid pagoda with interior shrines, built over one storey or (in later examples) over two, with an Indian-style spire atop. When finished, the temples were decorated on the inside with elaborate murals, generally featuring *Jataka* Buddha life-cycle stories.

Shop selling hti outside the Mahamuni pagoda, Mandalay.

⊘ REFINED INWA (AVA)

Inwa – or Ava, as it was formerly known – functioned as the centre of the Shan Kingdom in the 14th to 16th centuries before becoming capital of Burma during the 17th and 18th centuries. As with Bagan, many religious and secular buildings were made of wood, but, unlike Bagan, in Inwa a few wooden pagodas have survived, most notably the *Bagaya Kyaung*, though in its present form this dates from the early 20th century. During its infancy, the religious architecture of Inwa was distinguished by the use of stucco decoration, the refined elegance of its stupas – by now less bulbous and more tapering – as well as very elaborate *pyat-that* or multi-roofed pavilions.

Clear evidence exists that the building of temples was considered an act of merit-making during the Bagan era just as it is now, and that their construction was not limited to the great and the powerful. Bricks were donated by kilns in surrounding villages, sometimes stamped with the name of the village that had given them.

RAKHINE

Isolated from the rest of the country by the coastal Rakhine hills, and enjoying good seaway communications with neighbouring Bengal, Rakhine – formerly known as Arakan – was an independent kingdom until its conquest by King Bodawpaya in the 18th century. Rakhine's architecture is quite distinct from that of the rest of Myanmar, inspired by the temples of Bengal and Bihar, across the Bay of Bengal in India, rather than by the nearby but generally inaccessible Burmese heartlands. It was in Mrauk U, the former capital of Rakhine, that this particular architectural style reached its apogee, with its uniquely fortress-like temples enclosed by massive walls, pierced by narrow corridors and passages often elaborately decorated with painted murals and carvings. Historians suggest that Mrauk U's temples often functioned as places of safe refuge dur-

became apparent for the first time in Burmese history. The murals inside the Kyauktawgyi Pagoda (completed in 1847) are particularly interesting, showing portraits of Western faces amongst groups of Burmese.

Although never a Burmese royal capital, the city of Mingun, on the west bank of the Ayeyarwady River about 11km (7 miles) upstream from Mandalay, was singled out by King Bodawpaya (1782–1819) as the site of the huge Mantara Gyi (Mingun) Pagoda. Work was started in 1816, but Bodawpaya died before the project was com-

Shwenandaw Kyaung Monastery, Mandalay.

ing times of war (which were frequent, in that kingdom's turbulent history).

AMARAPURA AND MINGUN

Amarapura, the "City of Immortality", was founded by King Bodawpaya in 1783 and remained the capital of Burma until 1857, with a hiatus between 1823 and 1841, when the city of Inwa (Ava) was briefly re-established.

The religious architecture of Amarapura is essentially a continuation of the Avan tradition. Marble was increasingly used in temple construction, and the period is also marked by the extravagant use of stucco in temple decoration, notably at the elaborate Nagayon shrine. Various Chinese and European architectural influences

pleted, coming to a halt when the stupa was a "mere" 50 metres (160ft) tall, one-third of the height intended. It was subsequently damaged in the earthquake of 1838.

MANDALAY

The last royal capital of Burma, Mandalay was established by King Mindon in 1857. The architectural style adopted by Mindon was in direct continuation with the Inwa-Amarapura tradition, but if anything it was even more elaborate than the latter. Richly ornamented in stucco and marble, temples also benefited from a wealth of elaborate and highly skilled woodcarving, although most was destroyed during fighting in World War II.

Sunset over pagodas in Bagan.

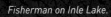
Fisherman on Inle Lake.

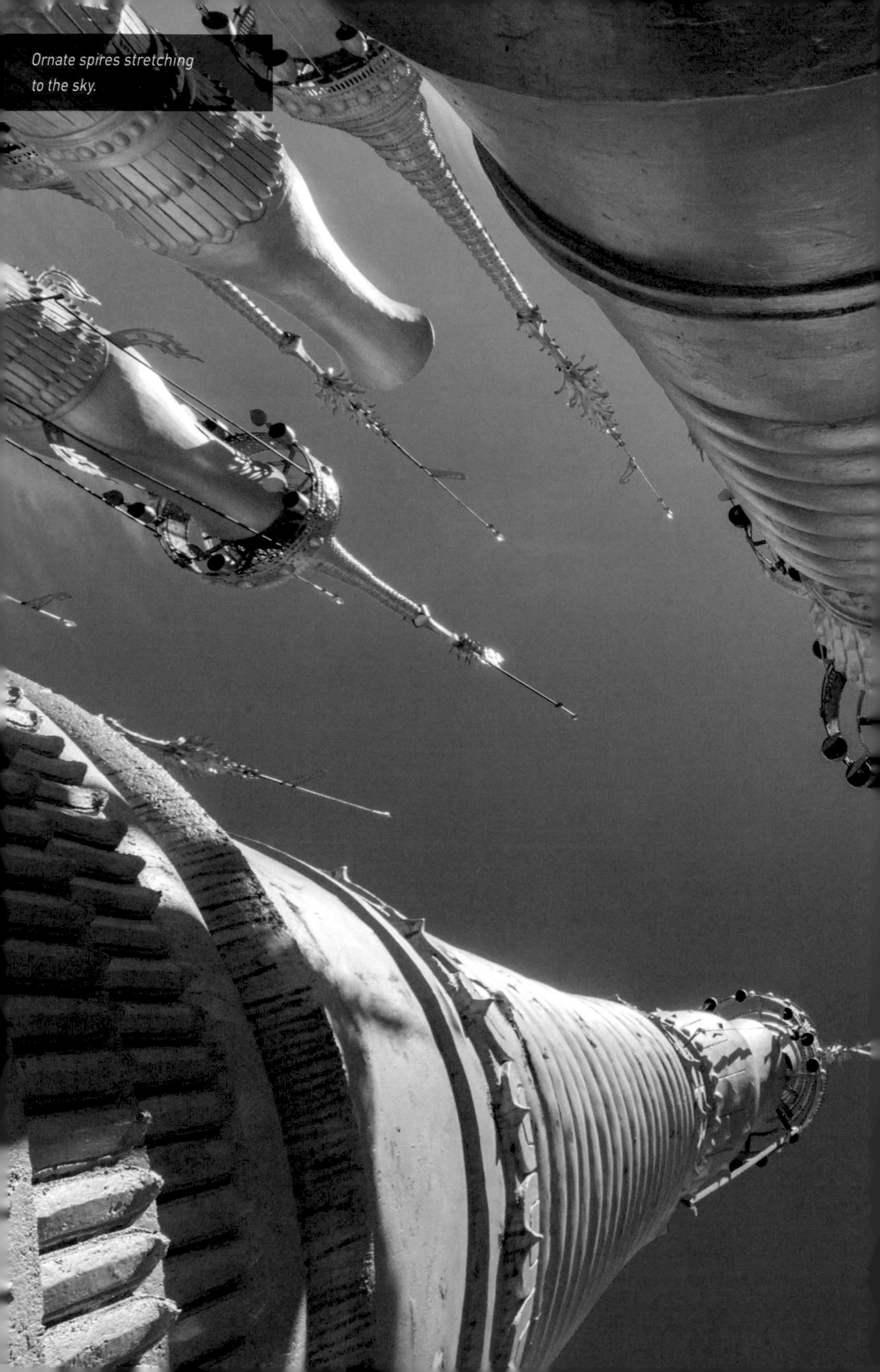

Ornate spires stretching to the sky.

The Ananda Pagoda festival in Bagan.

INTRODUCTION

A detailed guide to the entire country, with principal sights clearly cross-referenced by number to the maps.

Inscribed marble slabs at Kuthodaw Paya, Mandalay.

The standard 28-day tourist visa affords nowhere near enough time to see the whole of Myanmar. By catching planes, however, you can sample its chief highlights and gain a vivid sense of what makes this such a unique country.

Yangon (Rangoon) serves, as it has since colonial times, as Myanmar's principal gateway. Though no longer the capital (an honour now conferred on the city of Naypyidaw, completed in 2012 and 320km/200miles north), it remains a charismatic metropolis whose crowning glory, the gilded Shwedagon Pagoda, ranks among the world's most enthralling religious monuments.

From Yangon, an hour's flight north takes you to Bagan where, between the 11th and 13th centuries, the Bamar kings embellished an arid plain on the banks of the Ayeyarwady River with lavish temples, palaces and monasteries. Bagan can also be reached by cruise boat from Myanmar's second city and cultural hub, Mandalay, whose modern architecture is more than offset by a profusion of Buddhist shrines, crafts workshops and music and dance venues, and by the evocative vestiges of former royal capitals crumbling on its outskirts.

A typical street in Downtown Yangon.

East of Mandalay rises the mighty Shan plateau, a tract of deep river valleys, rocky gorges and denuded hills rippling to the Chinese border. Boat trips to markets, floating gardens and stilt settlements of the local Intha people are the main incentive to make the detour to this region's tourist centre, Inle Lake, along with the serene sunsets, and the chance to trek to nearby hill villages.

With its waterside boutique hotels and souvenir markets, Inle has blossomed into a fully fledged resort in recent years. The same is true of Ngapali beach, in northwest Rakhine State, where you can relax in luxurious beach hideaways under the palms and tuck into succulent seafood.

The rest of the country's great sights, however, require more patience to reach – notably the atmospheric ghost city of Mrauk U further north in Rakhine State, whose weed-infested stupas and monasteries soar above jungle and rice fields, and the relatively little-visited southeast of the country, where the famous "Golden Rock" temple of Kyaiktiyo gleams on a forested mountain-top.

For the majority of visitors, however, the warmth and traditional culture of the Burmese themselves, miraculously intact despite the events of the past fifty years or so, are what tend to make a journey here so memorable.

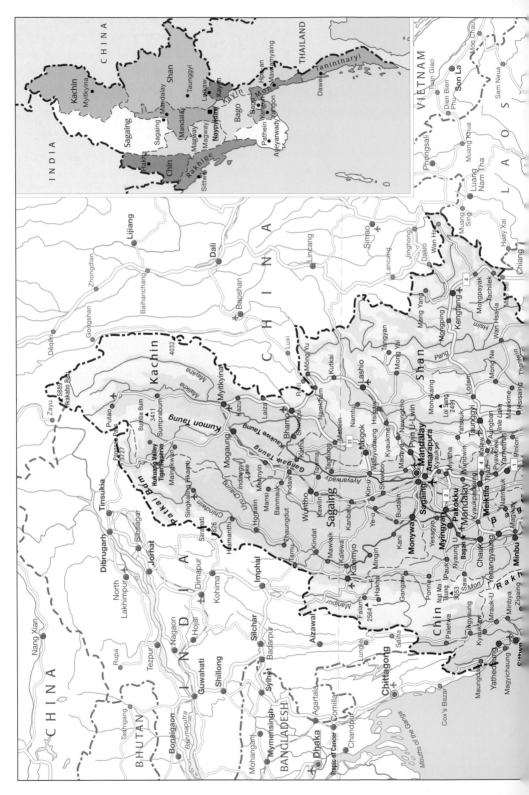

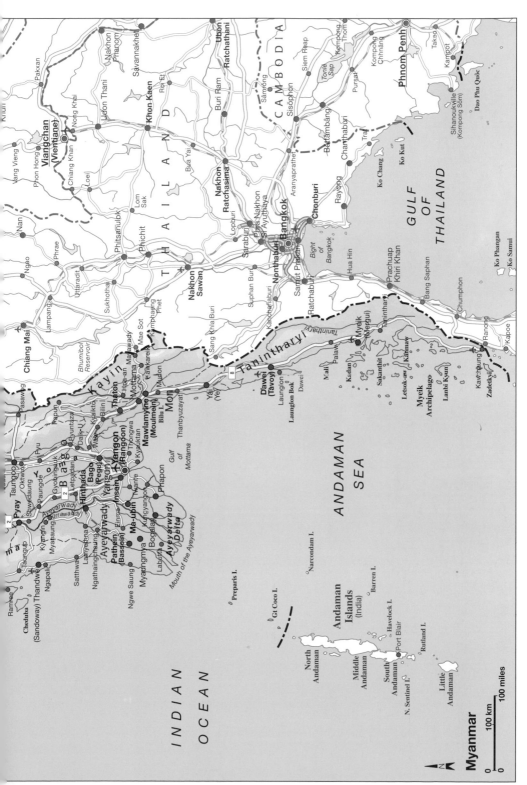

Myanmar

Fabrics for sale at Bogyoke Aung San Market.

YANGON AND THE AYEYARWADY DELTA

Beyond the old-world charms of Myanmar's largest city sprawls the vast Ayeyarwady Delta, a region of winding rivers and lush rice paddies.

Despite having lost its capital status to Naypyidaw in 2005, Yangon remains Myanmar's principal city: with a population of around 6 million it is by far the largest urban area in the country. Few visitors spend more than a couple of nights sampling its distinctive atmosphere, but the faded colonial charm of the downtown district and resplendent Shwedagon Pagoda – just one among a wonderful crop of impressive Buddhist monuments – warrant at least a couple of days' sightseeing.

The Shwedagon Pagoda reflected in Kandawgyi Lake.

For centuries a lowly fishing village, Yangon rose to prominence only in 1755 after King Alaungpaya founded a harbour overlooking the confluence of the Yangon and Bago rivers. Under the British, who annexed the port in 1852, the city, known by its anglicized name of "Rangoon", became for a time one of the most prosperous and cosmopolitan in Southeast Asia. Grand fin-de-siècle administrative buildings were erected along its broad avenues and waterfront, reflecting the booming teak and gem-stone trade.

However, with the economic isolation of the independence era, the city entered a kind of time warp, defined by its dilapidated colonial architecture, dusty streets, vintage Wolseley cars and ageing fleet of trishaws – not to mention the pro-democracy demonstrations, military crackdowns and repeated incarcerations of NLD leader, Aung San Suu Kyi, at her decaying home in the northern suburbs. Signs of modernisation began to appear in the mid-1990s; with the city renamed Yangon, the vintage cars began to give way to shiny Japanese hatchbacks, and a handful of international-chain hotels sprang up in the centre. With the recent political changes, this process is now starting to accelerate, but the old-world charm remains in the city's old-fashioned teashops, sidewalk *mohinga* stalls, shabby old buildings and traditional street markets.

Farming the land in the lush Ayeyarwady Delta.

West of Yangon is the lush Ayeyarwady Delta, Myanmar's "rice bowl" heartland. The inhabitants of these watery lowlands, ravaged in recent years by a succession of devastating cyclones, still travel mainly by boat, through a labyrinth of canals and rivulets. The few foreign visitors who venture into the Delta tend to do so en route to Pathein, the country's fourth city and springboard for the beach resorts of Chaungtha and Ngwe Saung, a favourite weekend escape for Yangon's affluent middle classes.

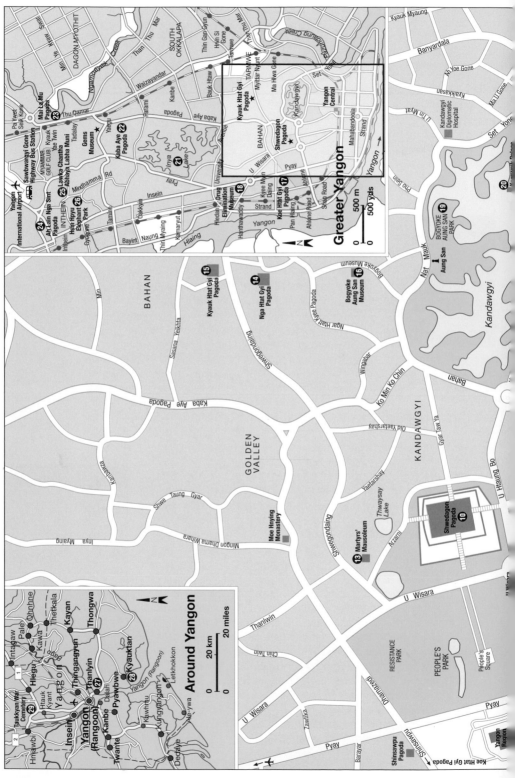

Greater Yangon

- Kyauk Htat Gyi Pagoda
- Myittar Nyunt
- TARMWE
- Ma Hlwa Gine
- Yangon Central
- Mahabandoola
- Strand
- Shwedagon Pagoda
- BAHAN
- U Wisara
- Pyay
- Kyee Myin Daing
- Koe Htat Gyi Pagoda 17
- 18
- Drug Elimination Museum
- Hledan
- Harthawaddy
- Strand
- Ahlone Road
- Shan Road
- Pan Hlaing
- Yangon
- 0   500 m
- 0   500 yds
- N
- SOUTH OKKALAPA
- DAGON MYOTHIT
- Thin Gan Gyun
- Hnin Si Gone
- Tarwe
- Waizayandar
- Thu Qamar
- Mai La Mu Pagoda 23
- Pa Ywet
- Sein Kone
- Kaba Aye Pagoda
- Thu Mar
- Mini Ye
- Swel
- Thitsar
- Thiri
- Bauk Htaw
- Kambe
- Harami
- Yaegu
- Yae Twin
- Kyauk
- Taddalay
- Lawka Chantha Abhaya Labha Muni
- Gems Museum
- Kaba Aye Pagoda 22
- MYANMAR GOLF CLUB
- Sawbwargyi Gone Highway Bus Station
- Yangon International Airport
- Ah Lein Nga Sint 25
- Hsin Hpyu Elephant 26
- Park
- INTHEIN
- 24
- Inya Lake
- 21
- Pyay
- Mindhamma Rd
- Insein
- Oakkyin
- Kamaryut
- Tamwe
- Thit Myaing
- Hlaing
- Bayint Naung

Around Yangon

- 0   20 km
- 0   20 miles
- N
- Taukkyan War Cemetery 29
- Intagaw
- Pale
- Qhohne
- Kawa
- Hlegu
- Thetkala
- Kayan
- Thongwa
- Yangon (Rangoon)
- Thingangyun
- Thanlyin
- 27
- Kyauktan
- 28
- Pyawbwe
- Insein
- Inya Myaing
- Kanbe
- Dalah
- Kungyangon
- Kwhitu
- Letkhokkon
- Twante
- Dedaye
- Ahe-ywa

Kandawgyi

- KANDAWGYI
- Shwedagon Pagoda 10
- Martyrs' Mausoleum 13
- Moe Hnying Monastery
- Mingon Dhama Wihara
- GOLDEN VALLEY
- BAHAN
- Kyauk Htat Gyi Pagoda 15
- Nga Htat Gyi Pagoda 14
- Bogyoke Aung San Museum 16
- Aung San
- BOGYOKE AUNG SAN PARK 19
- Kandawgyi Diplomatic Hospital
- 20
- Banyardala
- Kyauk Myaung
- Kyakkasan
- RESISTANCE PARK
- PEOPLE'S PARK
- People's Square
- Shinsawpu Pagoda
- Yangon Region
- Koe Htat Gyi Pagoda
- U Wisara
- Pyay
- U Htaung Bo
- Kaba Aye Pagoda
- Shwegondaing
- Thwayzay
- Thanlwin
- Chin Twin
- Ngar Htat Kywe Pagoda
- Wingabar
- Ko Min Ko Chin
- Old Yaetarshay
- Gyar Taw Ya
- Bahan
- Sasana Yeiktha
- Kanbawza
- Shwe Taung Gyar
- Inya
- Min
- Pho Sein
- Nat Mauk
- U Tin Myat
- Ma Li Gone
- Nh Yoe Gone
- Azani
- Yaetarshay
- Thwayzay Lake
- Dhamazedi
- Zawtika
- Barayar
- Shinsawpu

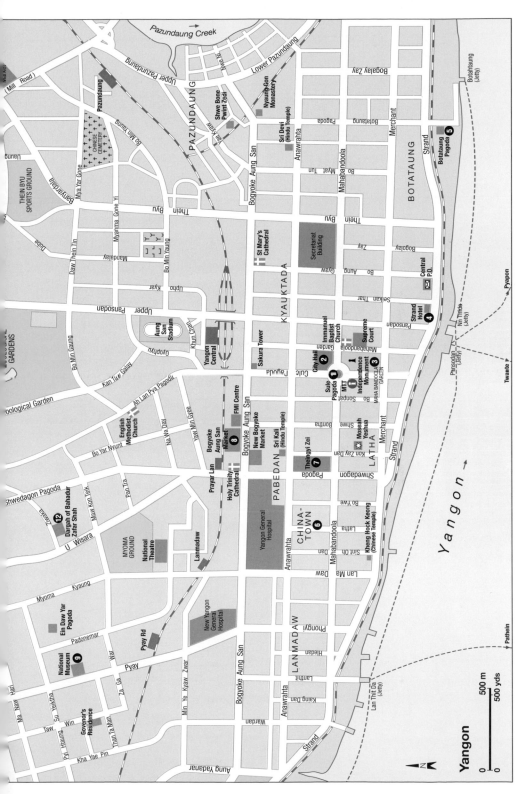

Yangon

Moments of contemplation at the Shwedagon's main stupa.

YANGON

In Yangon, high-rises tower over ancient monuments in a city poised on the brink of sweeping change.

In *Letters From the East* (1889), Rudyard Kipling wrote: "Then, a golden mystery upheaved itself on the horizon – a beautiful, winking wonder that blazed in the sun, of a shape that was neither Muslim dome nor Hindu temple spire. It stood upon a green knoll... 'There's the old Shway Dagon,' said my companion... The golden dome said, 'This is Burma, and it will be quite unlike any land that one knows about'."

It's more than 100 years since Kipling sailed up the Rangoon River to the Burmese capital, but the glistening golden stupa of the Shwedagon continues to dominate the city's skyline. The massive pagoda, said to be around 2,500 years old, is not only a remarkable architectural achievement; it is also the perfect symbol of a country in which Buddhism pervades every aspect of life.

The Shwedagon may be the undisputed show stealer, but Yangon holds plenty of less celebrated attractions. Spend a couple of days here and you'll have time to wander the tree-lined avenues and narrow backstreets of the colonial district downtown, with its court house, city hall and famous Strand Hotel, and to take in a few more pagodas, including the majestic Botataung Pagoda near the riverside. Refuel in a traditional Burmese teahouse before sampling the priceless treasures

Crickets for sale in Bogyoke market.

on show at the National Museum, or mingle with the crowds milling around Bogyoke Aung San market.

The city's vivid street life makes a lasting impression: the street-side *mohinga* stalls, where diners dressed in traditional *longyis* and *htameins* tuck into bowls of steaming noodles; crocodiles of red-robed monks threading their way through the busy traffic with alms bowls aloft; and the open-air markets, whose traders squat beside piles of fresh produce, an outsize cheroot wedged in their

⊙ Main attractions

Shwedagon Pagoda
Botataung Pagoda
The Lion Throne, National Museum
Bogyoke Aung San Market
Kyauk Htat Gyi Pagoda
Thanlyin
Ye Le Pagoda, Kyauktan

⊙ Maps on pages 116, 128

*Colonial buildings,
Downtown Yangon.*

*A trishaw rider takes a
break.*

mouth, and *thanaka* paste smeared over their cheeks.

With the country poised on the brink of rapid economic change, modernity is making its presence felt these days, particularly around the striking Sule Pagoda, whose gilded profile is dwarfed by nearby high-rises. Yet the overriding impression of Yangon remains one of a city that has altered little since the British slow-marched to their waiting steamers in 1948.

Just across the river, the provincial towns of Thanlyin and Kyauktan hold other splendid Buddhist monuments in striking settings, and provide a welcome respite from the headlong rush of downtown Yangon, while the superb medieval stupas at Bago, a daytrip northwest, tempt many travellers to extend their stay.

GETTING YOUR BEARINGS

Home to around 6 million people – the population has increased five-fold in three decades – Yangon is surrounded on three sides by water. The Hlaing or Yangon River flows from the Bago

Yoma (hills) down its western and southern flanks, past the Shwedagon and picturesque artificial lakes created by the British, which today form the focus of some of the city's most affluent residential districts. The river then continues through the Delta to the south before dumping its silt-laden waters in the Gulf of Mottama.

Sri Lankan chronicles indicate that there was a settlement in the area 2,500 years ago – probably a fishing village or a minor Indian trading colony which grew in fame after the building of the Shwedagon Pagoda. For centuries, the history of Dagon, as the village was originally known, was inextricably bound to that of the great Shwedagon Pagoda and the nearby town of Syriam (Thanlyin), across the Bago and Hlaing rivers, which was Myanmar's main port until well into the 18th century.

King Alaungpaya set Dagon on its modern path in 1755, when he captured the village from the Mon, renaming it Yangon (meaning "End of Strife") and destroying Syriam the following year. The British then conquered the

town during the First Anglo-Burmese War in 1824, after which its port began to flourish again. Fire caused devastation in 1841 and, in 1852, Yangon was again almost completely destroyed in the course of the Second Anglo-Burmese War, but thrived after the British annexation of the rest of Burma in 1885, becoming capital of the new colony and growing rich on the back of the lucrative trade in teak and other natural resources procured in the north of the country.

Although the city today lies 30km (20 miles) from the open sea, Yangon's river is easily navigable, and the vast majority of the country's import and export trade is still handled in the docks at nearby Thanlyin. Industrial suburbs have mushroomed to the north and east, providing work for many of the immigrants flocking to the Yangon area. There is a sizeable Indian community – a hangover from the time when Burma was still a part of British India – as well as a large number of people of Chinese descent, and indigenous ethnic minorities.

EXPLORING YANGON

The old heritage district downtown is compact enough to explore on foot, albeit with frequent heat-beating pit stops in teahouses and cafés along the way, and allowing plenty of time to navigate the congested pavements, often gridlocked with crowds of shoppers, hawkers, monks and businessmen threading their way between the endless shops and food stalls. However, quite a few of Yangon's sights lie further afield and are best reached by taxi. Cabs, identifiable by the signs on their roofs, come in a variety of shapes and sizes, but offer great value for money – short trips across downtown cost K1,500–2,000, while you can get from downtown to the northern suburbs for as little as K5,000–6,000. Moreover, the drivers themselves are considerably more courteous and honest than their counterparts in other Asian cities, and many speak at least a few words of English.

SULE PAGODA

The logical place to begin any tour of Yangon is the **Sule Pagoda ❶** (daily;

⊙ Tip

There's no better way to kick-start a day's sightseeing in Yangon than breakfast in a traditional teahouse.

Detail of houses and shops, Downtown Yangon.

⊙ THE CIRCLE LINE

One of the most popular excursions in Yangon is the half-day ride around the city's Circle Line (officially, the Yangon Circular Railway). Looping round the city, a journey on this suburban railway offers entertaining glimpses of Yangon life as the carriages rattle slowly through the margins of the city, and is a great place to chat with local Yangonites going about their daily business. A complete circuit takes three hours; alternatively, go as far as Insein (1 hour) for a taster, and then hop off the train and visit Insein's various sights (including the **Lawka Chantha Abhaya Labha Muni** and **Elephant Park**) before returning to the centre. Trains depart from platforms 6 and 7 at the back of the main railway station, with tickets costing a very modest 200 kyat.

An old jeep in the streets of Yangon.

Sule Pagoda seen from the Sky Bistro at the top of the Sakura tower.

charge), the shining stupa at the city's heart which the British used as the centrepiece of their Victorian grid-plan system in the mid-19th century. For centuries a focus of the city's social and religious activity, the richly gilded monument rises from the middle of a busy intersection, surrounded on all sides by shops, swirling traffic and a proliferating number of high-rise hotels and office blocks – a location that belies the stupa's great antiquity.

The temple is said to be built on the former home of the powerful Sule Nat guardian spirit, and its history is closely connected to the foundation of the Shwedagon Pagoda.

According to legend, shortly after the Buddha's enlightenment, the brothers Taphussa and Bhallika returned from India bearing a sacred hair relic given to them by the Buddha himself (see page 143). Seeking the correct location at which to build a pagoda to enshrine the hair relic, Taphussa and Bhallika are believed to have consulted the Sule Nat (then so old and sleepy, it's said, that his eyelids had to be propped open on tree trunks to keep him awake). Suitably encouraged, the ancient *nat* revealed to them the location on Singuttara Hill where the relics of three previous Buddhas had been buried, and which subsequently became the site of the new Shwedagon Pagoda.

Inside, the pagoda's shrines and images include four colourful Buddhas with neon halos behind their heads. As with all stupas, it's traditional (although not obligatory) for visitors to walk around it in a clockwise direction.

As well as its religious significance, the Sule Pagoda is iconic among the Burmese as the venue for several famous political demonstrations over the past three decades, most notably the rally of 1988 when the military opened fire on unarmed protesters, killing and injuring dozens. The monument also formed the focal point of mass gatherings during the Saffron Revolution of 2007.

DOWNTOWN

The orderly blocks of late 19th- and early 20th-century buildings erected

by the British on the banks of the Yangon River today comprise the largest collection of colonial architecture in Southeast Asia, with most of the streets still largely intact and devoid of modern, high-rise constructions. By turns elegant, pompous and flamboyant, the buildings perfectly epitomise the imperious self-confidence of the Raj at its zenith, and lend to the area as a whole an old-world grandiloquence that's rare for Asian cities of comparable size.

Having been occupied by squatters for decades, many of the structures have lapsed into an advanced state of disrepair, with mildew-streaked walls and peeling plasterwork. Some of the grandest buildings are owned by the Burmese government and were deserted completely when the administration decamped to Naypyidaw in 2005. The establishment in 2012 of the Yangon Heritage Trust by leading historian Thant Myint-U was a major step forward, securing a government moratorium on the demolition of all buildings over fifty years old and the attempt to formulate a citywide plan for the protection and restoration of historically significant buildings – although exactly how much can be saved given the city's current exponential economic growth remains to be seen.

The perfect primer for any tour of Yangon's colonial district is the massive **City Hall** ❷ on the northeast corner of Sule Pagoda Road and Mahabandoola Street. Erected in 1924, it fuses typically British style with Burmese elements, such as traditional tiered roofs and a peacock seal high over the entrance.

Opposite City Hall spread the lawns of **Maha Bandoola Garden** ❸ (daily; charge), named after General Maha Bandoola, leader of the Burmese forces during the First Anglo-Burmese War. In the centre of the park, the 46-metre (150ft) **Independence Monument** comprises an obelisk surrounded by five smaller, 9-metre (30ft) pillars. Formerly known as Fitch Square (after the 16th-century chronicler and trader, Ralph Fitch, who was the first Englishman to visit Burma), the park is popular in the early mornings with t'ai chi

⊙ **Tip**

Sule Pagoda is the point from which all distances to and from the former capital are officially measured.

The red-brick high court and the Independence statue, Mahabandoola Gardens.

⊙ Tip

Relive the old colonial days by propping up the bar at the Strand Hotel. The once-weekly happy hour on Friday evening is one of the city's leading social events.

Monsoon rain at Botataung Pagoda.

practitioners. Facing the square on the east side stands the Queen-Anne-style **Supreme Court**, dating from 1911.

A few blocks east of here stands the most imposing of all Yangon's colonial monuments, the vast, neoclassical **Secretariat building**, sprawling over an entire city block. Dating from 1902, this formerly served as the centre of British power in colonial Burma and also as the national parliament building in post-independence Burma, up until the 1962 military coup. It's perhaps best known, however, as the place where nationalist leader Aung San and six of his ministers were assassinated in 1947. The entire building is now semi-derelict and its future unclear, with various renovation plans being frequently mooted, but yet to bear fruit.

Southeast of the square on Strand Road is the famous **Strand Hotel ④**, patronised by visitors ranging from Rudyard Kipling and Somerset Maugham to Mick Jagger. After decades in the doldrums, the building was comprehensively restored in the mid-1990s, although the lavish makeover and new five-star facilities have rather eroded its original colonial character and charm. Afternoon high tea in the teak-furnished lounge remains a memorable experience, even so, and a lot cheaper than splashing out on one of the hotel's fabulously expensive rooms.

THE BOTATAUNG PAGODA

Heading east on Strand Road for several blocks brings you to the **Botataung Pagoda ⑤**. It is said that when eight Indian monks carried relics of the Buddha here more than 2,000 years ago, 1,000 military officers *(botataung)* formed a guard of honour at the place where the rebuilt pagoda stands today. The original structure was destroyed by an Allied bomb in November 1943, with rebuilding work beginning on the very first day after independence.

During the reconstruction work at the very centre of the stupa, a golden casket was found in which was discovered what was claimed to be a hair and two other relics of the Buddha. In addition, about 700 gold, silver and bronze statues were uncovered, as well as a

number of terracotta tablets, one of which is inscribed both in Pali and in the south Indian Brahmi script, from which the modern Burmese script developed. Some of the finds are displayed in the pagoda, but the relics and more valuable objects are locked away. Among these is a tooth of the Buddha which Alaung-sithu, a king of Bagan, tried unsuccessfully to acquire from Nanzhao (now China's Yunnan province) in 1115. China eventually gave it to Burma in 1960. The 40-metre (130ft) bell-shaped stupa is hollow, and visitors can walk around the interior. Look out for the glass mosaic, and the many small alcoves for private meditation. The small lake outside is home to thousands of terrapin turtles; you can feed them with food sold at nearby stalls, thereby acquiring merit for a future existence.

THE MARKETS

West of the Sule Pagoda are Yangon's main street markets. Before World War II, most of the inhabitants of the city were Indian or Chinese, and their influence is still reflected in this jam-packed district. Take a stroll through **China-town ❻**, stretching from Shwedagon Pagoda Road, west over 24th, Bo Ywe, Latha and Lanmadaw roads, where the cracked sidewalks are piled high with all manner of goods – bamboo baskets, religious images, calligraphy, peanut candy, melon seeds, flowers, dried mushrooms, handmade rice paper, caged songbirds, tropical fish for aquariums and live crabs. In the evening these streets turn into a rambling outdoor restaurant, with stalls offering delicious soups, curries and other local dishes.

A few blocks back towards Sule Pagoda is Yangon's biggest market, the chaotic **Theingyi Zei ❼**. Stretching from Mahabandoola Street up to Anawrahta Road, the market occupies two huge buildings divided by a lane (26th Street) in which one of the city's most colourful vegetable markets is held daily. The southern end of the market is fairly workaday, with hundreds of stalls filled with cheap clothes, textiles, household goods and so on. Further north, towards Anawrahta Road and the Sri Kali Hindu Temple, things take

Afternoon tea is served at the Strand Hotel.

Sugar cane being pressed into juice, Bogyoke market.

Temple offerings for sale outside Botataung Pagoda.

on a much more Indian flavour, with stalls piled high with sacks of aromatic spices, medicinal herbs and mysterious bottled concoctions.

The most interesting of Yangon's bazaars, however, is the **Bogyoke Aung San Market** (formerly the Scott Market) on Bogyoke Aung San Street on the north side of downtown. Stalls sell a wonderful range of Burmese handicrafts, a wide variety of textiles and craft objects, woodcarvings, lacquerware, dolls, musical instruments, colourful *longyis*, Shan bags and wickerware. It's also a good place to shop for jade and gems, with almost all the street-facing shops on the ground floor taken up by jade and jewellery sellers.

THE NATIONAL MUSEUM

A short taxi ride northwest of the market district on Pyay Road, the **National Museum** (Tues–Sun 9.30am–4.30pm; charge) stands in a neighbourhood lined with foreign embassies. The museum's undisputed showpiece is King Thibaw's Lion Throne, originally from Mandalay Palace – one of many valuables carried

Jewellery for sale at Bogyoke market.

off by the British in 1886 after the Third Anglo-Burmese War. Some items on show here were shipped to the Indian Museum in Calcutta; others were kept in London's Victoria and Albert Museum. The artefacts were, however, returned to Myanmar as a gesture of goodwill in 1964 after Ne Win's state visit to Britain. The wooden throne, 8 metres (27ft) tall and inlaid with gold and lacquerwork, is a particularly striking example of the Burmese art of woodcarving. Among the Mandalay Regalia are gem-studded arms, swords, jewellery and serving dishes. Artefacts from Burma's early history in Beikthano, Thayekhittaya and Bagan in the museum's archaeological section include an 18th-century bronze cannon and a crocodile-shaped harp.

THE SHWEDAGON PAGODA

Few religious monuments in the world cast as powerful a spell as Yangon's **Shwedagon Pagoda** (daily 4am–10pm; charge), the gigantic golden stupa rising on the northern fringes of the city. The holiest of holies for Burmese Buddhists, it's also a potent

symbol of national identity, and become a rallying point for the pro-democracy movement during military rule.

Its unique sanctity derives from the belief that the stupa enshrines relics not merely of the historical Buddha, Gautama, but also those of three of his predecessors. No one, however, has been able to confirm whether or not the eight hairs of the Master actually lie sealed deep inside the stupa, as the structure would have to be partly destroyed to reach its solid core – something the shrine's custodians will never permit.

It's tempting when you arrive in Yangon to head straight for the mesmerising gilded spire on the horizon, but resist the urge if you can until early evening, when the warm light of sunset has a transformative effect on the gold-encrusted pagoda and its myriad subsidiary shrines.

The complex can be entered via four different flights of covered steps. Whichever stairway you use, be sure to remove your footwear at the bottom of the steps.

THE STAIRWAYS (ZAUNGDAN)

The passageway most commonly used by visitors to the Shwedagon is the **Southern Stairway** Ⓐ, which ascends from the direction of the city centre. Its 104 steps lead from Shwedagon Pagoda Road to the main platform. The entrance is guarded (as are the northern and western staircases) by a pair of towering *chinthe*, a mythological leogryph, half lion and half-griffin. If you're not up to the climb, note that this stairway also boasts a lift, as do the entrances on the northern and eastern sides.

The **Western Stairway** Ⓑ, which leads up from U Wisara Road, was damaged during the Second Anglo-Burmese War and kept closed by soldiers from the British garrison. In 1931, a stall at the foot of the stairs caught fire. The blaze raced up and around the northern flank of the Shwedagon, causing severe damage to the precincts before being

halted on the eastern stairway, although unfortunately not in time to save many ancient monuments.

The little-used Western Stairway is the longest *zaungdan* with 166 steps (although an escalator running up the middle now removes the effort of walking up). The landing on the platform bears the name **Two Pice Tazaung** because of the contribution of two *pice* (a small copper coin) given daily by Buddhist businessmen and bazaar-stallholders for the stairway's reconstruction.

The **Northern Stairway** Ⓒ was built in 1460 by Queen Shinsawbu, and has 128 steps, with decorative borders shaped like crocodiles. Two water tanks can be seen to the north of the stairway; the one on the right is called *thwezekan*, meaning "blood wash-tank". The name derives from a popular legend recounting how, during King Anawrahta's conquest of the Mon capital Thaton, his commander-in-chief, Kyanzittha, used the tank to clean his blood-stained weapons.

The **Eastern Stairway** Ⓓ is much like an extension of the Bahan bazaar,

Novice monk at the Shwedagon.

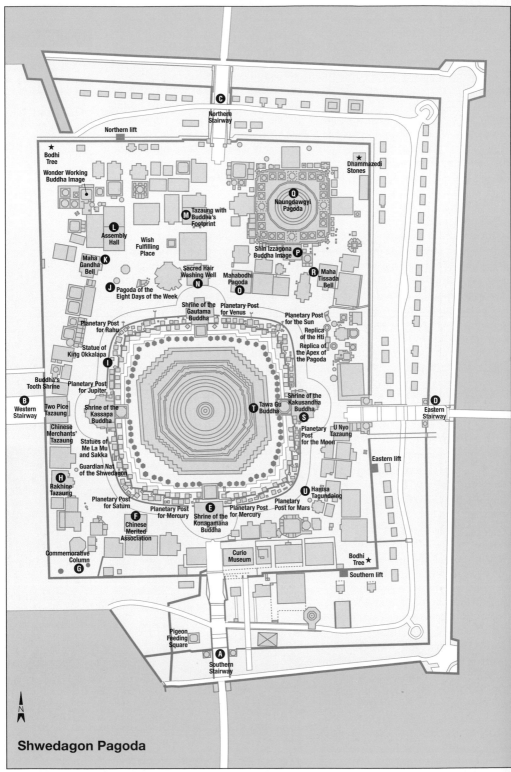

Northern Stairway

Northern lift

★ Bodhi Tree

Wonder Working Buddha Image

Tazaung with Buddha's Footprint

★ Dhammazedi Stones

Naungdawgyi Pagoda

Assembly Hall

Wish Fulfilling Place

Maha Gandha Bell

Shin Izzagona Buddha Image

Sacred Hair Washing Well

Mahabodhi Pagoda

Maha Tissada Bell

Pagoda of the Eight Days of the Week

Shrine of the Gautama Buddha

Planetary Post for Venus

Planetary Post for Rahu

Planetary Post for the Sun

Replica of the Hti

Statue of King Okkalapa

Replica of the Apex of the Pagoda

Buddha's Tooth Shrine

Planetary Post for Jupiter

Western Stairway

Two Pice Tazaung

Shrine of the Kassapa Buddha

Tawa Gu Buddha

Shrine of the Kakusandha Buddha

Eastern Stairway

Chinese Merchants' Tazaung

Statues of Me La Mu and Sakka

Planetary Post for the Moon

U Nyo Tazaung

Eastern lift

Guardian Nat of the Shwedagon

Rakhine Tazaung

Hamsa Tagundaing

Planetary Post for Saturn

Planetary Post for Mercury

Planetary Post for Mercury

Planetary Post for Mars

Chinese Merited Association

Shrine of the Konagamana Buddha

Commemorative Column

Curio Museum

Bodhi Tree ★

Southern lift

Pigeon Feeding Square

Southern Stairway

N

Shwedagon Pagoda

which lies between Kandawgyi Lake and the Shwedagon. This flight of 118 steps suffered particularly heavy damage during the British attack on the pagoda in 1852.

THE TERRACE

A magnificent spectacle greets visitors emerging from the half-darkness of the covered stairways. In Somerset Maugham's words: "At last we reached the great terrace. All about, shrines and pagodas were jumbled pell-mell with the confusion with which trees grow in the jungle. They had been built without design or symmetry, but in the darkness, their gold and marble faintly gleaming, they had a fantastic richness. And then, emerging from among them like a great ship surrounded by lighters, rose dim, severe and splendid, the Shwe Dagon."

The terrace was created in the 15th century when the rulers of Bago levelled off the top of the 58-metre (190ft) -high Singuttara Hill, since when it's been embellished with a fabulous profusion of prayer pavilions (tazaung) and resting places (zayat) topped with innumerable spiky pyatthat roofs layered in tiers of five, seven or nine. The floor of the terrace is inlaid with marble slabs, which can get very hot under bare feet by the middle of the day – a mat pathway is sometimes laid out.

THE STUPA

From the centre of the platform rises the gold-covered stupa itself, the reflected light from which casts an ethereal glow over the forest of subsidiary shrines, temples, pavilions and elaborately roofed halls below. Rising to a height of 99 metres (325ft) and with a circumference of 433 metres (1,421ft), the zedi adheres to traditional Burmese design, divided into distinct sections, each with its particular symbolic significance.

The base, or plinth (paccaya) rising from the main terrace is octagonal and on each of its eight sides rest eight smaller stupas – 64 in all. The four larger stupas opposite the stairways mark the cardinal points. At each of the platform's four corners are manokthiha (sphinxes), each surrounded by several chinthe.

◉ Tip

To experience sailing down the Yangon River, go to the Pansodan Street Jetty, near the Strand Hotel, and board one of the frequent ferries for Dalah. It's about a 10-minute ride costing K5,000/US$4 (for tourists) for the round trip.

The Shwedagon Pagoda.

Tip

Visit Bogyoke Aung San Park, on the shores of Kandawgyi Lake, at night when open-air restaurants offer tasty barbecued food in cool surroundings.

The stepped terraces of the base, which only monks are permitted to access, merge into the stupa's elegantly curved "bell" (khaung laung bon), which is divided from the so-called "inverted alms bowl" (thabeik) by the "turban band" (baungyit). Above the bowl rests one of the most delicately embellished elements, representing 16 lotus petals (kyahlan), which in turn give way to the uppermost section, or conical spire. This begins with a distinctively shaped banana bud (hnget pyaw bu) on which sits the 10-metre (33ft) hti, or umbrella, decorated with 1,485 gold and silver bells, 5,448 diamonds, and 2,317 rubies, sapphires and other precious stones. An enormous emerald sits in its centre to catch the first and last rays of the sun. Finally, crowning the very top of the monument is the golden orb (seinbu), tipped with a single, exquisite 76-carat diamond.

AROUND THE TERRACE

A constant swirl of activity surrounds the great stupa, as worshippers make their ritual circumambulation of the monument, pausing to pray and perform rituals at the numerous shrines and planetary posts along the way. The circuit is always performed in a clockwise direction.

Directly opposite the top of the southern stairway stands the **Shrine of the Konagamana Buddha E** (signed "Kawnagammana"), home to some of the pagoda's oldest Buddha statues. This is one of four shrines attached to the base of the main stupa at the four cardinal points, each dedicated to one of the four Buddhas of the current world cycle – Konagamana, Kakusandha, Kassapa and the historical Buddha, Gautama – whose relics are believed to be enshrined in the pagoda. On either side of the shrine stand **Planetary Posts for Mercury** (Monday), one of eight such planetary posts around the stupa, which worshippers venerate according to the day of the week on which they were born.

On the southwestern side of the stupa is the pavilion of the **Chinese Merited Association F**, home to a single solid jade Buddha decorated with 2.5kg of gold, while immediately behind stands

The Shwedagon at dusk, seen from the Northern exit.

the striking **Sun–Moon Buddha**, flanked with images of a peacock and a hare (symbolizing the sun and moon respectively). Nearby, a **Commemorative Column G**, inscribed in Burmese, English, French and Russian, honours the 1920 student revolt which sparked Burma's drive for independence from Britain.

Continuing down this side of the platform, you'll soon reach the **Rakhine Tazaung H**, beautifully decorated with intricate woodcarvings. Built by two wealthy merchants from Rakhine, the pavilion is home to an 8.5-metre (28ft) reclining Buddha, while pictures on the rear wall depict the legend of the founding of the Kyaiktiyo Pagoda (see page 295).

Just past the top of the western stairs a small pavilion covered in dazzling glass mosaics holds a replica of the **Buddha's Tooth** housed in the Temple of the Tooth in Kandy, Sri Lanka. Behind the Buddha's Tooth pavilion, a museum houses various items gifted to the pagoda over the years, while slightly further on, standing on the base of the main stupa, is a small image of the legendary King Okkalapa **I**, the founder of the Shwedagon, standing beneath a white umbrella, the symbol of royalty.

In an open area to the northwest of the stupa is a small octagonal pagoda known as the **Pagoda of the Eight Days of the Week J**, whose sides hold niches containing small Buddha images, each with the figure of an animal placed above it, corresponding to the eight Burmese days of the week (equivalent to the seven days of the western week, plus an extra day for Wednesday, which is divided into morning and afternoon). Behind it is the huge bronze **Maha Gandha Bell K**, which King Singu had cast in 1779 and which was raised from the Yangon River in 1825 after the British attempted to steal it. The bell weighs 23 tonnes and is 2.2 metres (over 7ft) tall. The **Assembly Hall L** opposite houses a 9-metre (30ft) Buddha image in earth-witness pose.

In the far northwest corner of the terrace is one of the half dozen or so **Bodhi Trees**, decorated with flowers and small flags, which stands around the edge of the enclosure. Some are

The Shwedagon has long dominated the city skyline.

☉ HISTORY OF THE SHWEDAGON

Although the origins of the Shwedagon are shrouded in legend (see page 143), it is known that the site was well-established on the pilgrimage circuit by the 11th century. Queen Shinsawpu (r.1453–72) is revered for giving the pagoda its present shape and form. She established the terraces and walls around the stupa, and donated her weight in gold (40kg/90lbs) to be beaten into gilt leaf and used to plate the pagoda.

King Hsinbyushin of the Konbaung dynasty raised the stupa to its current height of 99 metres (325ft) after a devastating earthquake in 1768 brought down the top of the spire. His son, Singu, had a 23-tonne bronze bell cast; known as Maha Ganda, it can be found today on the northwest side of the main pagoda platform. The British pillaged Shwegadon during their 1824–26 wartime occupation and tried to carry the bell to Calcutta, but the ill-fated object fell into the river. A third bell weighing more than 40 tonnes was donated by King Tharrawaddy in 1841: it sits today on the northeast side of the pagoda enclosure.

In 1931 the pagoda was seriously damaged in a fire, and has suffered from the effects of several earthquakes in recent years. Yet for all the Shwedagon's roller-coaster history, the Burmese are convinced no lasting damage can befall it.

⊙ Tip

Try not to limit yourself to a single visit to the Shwedagon Pagoda, whose appearance and atmosphere changes mysteriously with the shifting light.

said to have been grown from a cutting taken from the holy Bodhi tree in Bodhgaya, India, under which the Gautama Buddha gained enlightenment (or at least from the venerable Sri Maha Bodhi Tree in Anuradhapura, Sri Lanka, which was itself grown from a cutting taken from original Indian tree).

Returning to the main part of the pavilion, you'll notice an especially busy area. This is known as the **Wish Fulfilling Place**, where devotees kneel, facing the great stupa, and earnestly pray that their wishes will come true. Behind here an airy pavilion houses the huge seated **Chanthargyi Buddha**, the largest Buddha image in the entire pagoda. In a nearby cluster of pavilions not far from the north entrance is the **Tazaung with Buddha's Footprint ⓜ** (on the left just before you reach the top of the northern stairway). Life-sized statues of Indian guards stand in front of this hall, while the footprint (*chidawya*) itself is divided into 108 sections, each of which has a special significance.

Between the library and the stupa is the **Sacred Hair Relic Washing Well ⓝ**

(signed "Hsandawtwin"), built in 1879 over the spring in which, according to legend, the Buddha's eight hairs were washed before they were enshrined. The spring is said to be fed by the Ayeyarwady River.

Attached to the base of the main stupa on its northern side is the **Shrine of Gautama Buddha**, dedicated to the current, historical Buddha whose world dominion, it is believed, will last until the 45th century. Across the platform stands the multi-coloured **Mahabodhi Pagoda ⓞ**, a replica of the original pagoda of the same name in Bodhgaya, its distinctive Indian architecture strikingly out of place amongst the Burmese-style monuments which surround it.

Just past here, another pavilion houses the **Shin Izzagona Buddha Image ⓟ**, a Buddha statue with large eyes of different sizes which is said to have been erected by, or for, Shin Izzagona, a *zawgyi* (alchemist) from Bagan's early period. According to legend, Izzagona's obsession with discovering the Philosopher's Stone,

Wooden souvenirs outside the Shwedagon Pagoda.

the mythical substance said to be able to change base metals to gold or silver, plunged the country into poverty. When his final experiment was about to end in failure, he poked out both his eyes to satisfy the king. In his final casting, however, Izzagona did produce the Philosopher's Stone, and immediately sent his assistant to the slaughterhouse to obtain two eyes that would, with the stone's help, allow him to regain his sight. The assistant returned with one eye from a goat and another from a bull; from that time on, Shin Itzagona was known as "Goat-Bull Monk".

Just to the north is the striking **Naungdawgyi Pagoda Q**, looking like a scaled-down version of the main stupas and said to mark the spot where the eight hairs of the Buddha, carried by the merchants Tapussa and Bhallika, were originally kept. Nearby is the **Maha Tissada Bell R**, commissioned by King Tharrawaddy in 1841. It weighs almost 42 tonnes, is 2.55 metres (8ft 4in) tall and has a diameter of 2.3 metres (7ft 6in) at its mouth.

North of here, an open-sided pavilions houses the celebrated **Dhammazedi Stone Inscription,** commissioned in 1485 by King Dhammazedi and recording the history of the pagoda up to that date in Burmese, Mon and Pali three huge stone slabs. South of here is the Eastern Stairway, opposite which stands the **Shrine of the Kakusandha Buddha S**, built by Ma May Gale, the wife of King Tharrawaddy, though later destroyed by the fire of 1931. The temple was rebuilt in its original style in 1940. The Buddha figure in this *tazaung* is unusual in that the palm of its right hand is turned upwards; three of the four smaller Buddha figures in front of the niche are also depicted in this unfamiliar posture. Behind the temple, in a niche on the eastern side of the upper platform, is the **Tawa Gu Buddha T** statue, which is said to be able to work miracles, although from the terrace is rather tricky to see.

Close to the southeast corner of the platform is a **Hamsa Tagundaing U** or prayer pillar. Such columns are said to

One of the many mythical figures surrounding the base of the Shwedagon's main stupa.

Washing the Buddha statue at the planetary post for the moon, Shwedagon.

Gilded spires at the Shwedagon.

Reclining Buddha at Kyauk Htat Gyi Pagoda.

guarantee the health, prosperity and success of their founders.

At the far southeastern corner of the terrace is another of the pagoda's various **Bodhi Trees** which, like its cousin in the northwest corner, is said to be descended from the original at Bodhgaya. On the octagonal base which surrounds it is a huge Buddha statue.

Part of the way down the Southern Stairway you will find a **Pigeon Feeding Square**. Pagoda pilgrims can buy food here to feed the dozens of pigeons, thereby earning merit for a future existence.

AROUND THE SHWEDAGON PAGODA

Numerous sites of religious and cultural interest lie dotted around the Shwedagon Pagoda, an area which after Independence became the spiritual nerve centre of the fledgling Burmese nation.

MAHA WIZAYA PAGODA

A short distance southeast of the Pagoda, on the opposite side of U Htaung Bo Road, the **Maha Wizaya**

Pagoda **⓫** was built in 1980 using public donations to commemorate the unification of all Theravada orders in Burma. The interior of the main stupa is completely hollow, its circular central hall curiously decorated to resemble a forest at night, with mysterious astrological symbols placed in the faux-sky overhead.

DARGAH OF BAHADUR SHAH

One of Yangon's rare Muslim monuments lies on an inconspicuous side street just south of the Shwedagon Pagoda. The **Dargah of Bahadur Zafar Shah ⓬**, at 6 Ziwaka Road, is the final resting place of India's last Mughal emperor, who spent the final four years of his life at a house on the spot. An erudite, religiously tolerant and sensitive polymath with a talent for Islamic calligraphy and poetry, Zafar somewhat reluctantly became a rallying point for the mutinous sepoys in the ill-fated Indian Uprising of 1857 – and paid dearly for backing the wrong side. After the rebellion had been crushed, the British all but destroyed his former capital and palace, executing thousands and

dispatching the king and the few surviving members of his family into permanent exile in Burma, where he died in 1862.

The exact whereabouts of the grave, which the colonial authorities kept secret for fear that it would become a martyr's shrine, was revealed in 1991 when workmen digging foundations for a mausoleum near the site of Zafar's former house came across a brick-covered structure 1.1 metres (3.5ft) beneath the surface. It turned out to be the grave of the last Mughal, alongside that of his wife and grandson. Since his death, the former ruler has come to be regarded as a latter-day saint and his modern tomb is now a place of pilgrimage for Indian Muslims. The three silk-covered tombs on the ground floor are for show; the real ones lie hidden in a tiled crypt below, which the caretaker may unlock on request.

MARTYRS' MAUSOLEUM

Also worth a visit in this area is the **Martyrs' Mausoleum ⑬** (Tues–Sun 8am–5pm; charge), which crowns a low hill to the north of the Shwedagon Pagoda, beyond Arzarni Road. This patriotic monument contains the tombs of Aung San, leader of the Burmese independence movement (and father of Aung San Suu Kyi) along with those of the six ministers who were assassinated alongside Aung San during a cabinet meeting in 1947. Aung San was only 32 at the time. The pre-World War II prime minister, U Saw, was subsequently found to be the instigator of the plot, and was executed the following year, together with the hired assassins. The mausoleum is also notorious as the site of the bombing of October 1983 which killed 21 people, including three South Korean ministers who were accompanying their president on a state visit. Members of the North Korean army were later found to have carried out the attack.

NGA HTAT GYI PAGODA AND KYAUK HTAT GYI PAGODA

From the mausoleum, if you take the northern exit on to Shwegondaing Road, turn right and follow the main road northwest for around 1.5km (1 mile),

Maha Wizaya Pagoda, next to the Shwedagon.

*Souvenirs for sale
outside the Shwedagon
compound.*

*The ornate Karaweik
Palace restaurant,
Kandawgyi Lake.*

you'll reach the spectacular **Nga Htat Gyi Pagoda** , in which a huge sitting Buddha, dating from 1558, resides in an early 20th-century shrine. Called the "five-storey Buddha" because of its size, the figure is unique for the huge, flame-like pieces of gilded armour, or "magites", protruding from his giant head and shoulders.

Five minutes' walk away on the opposite side of Shwegondaing Road, **Kyauk Htat Gyi Pagoda** (aka Chaukhtatgyi Pagoda) is actually a *tazaung* (pavilion) rather than a traditional pagoda, housing a colossal, 70-metre (230ft) reclining Buddha. Although the sculpture is bigger than the reclining Shwethalyaung Buddha of Bago, it is not as well-known or as highly venerated. Elsewhere in the pagoda enclosure is a centre devoted to the study of sacred Buddhist manuscripts. The 600 monks who live in the monastery annex spend their days meditating and studying the old Pali texts.

BOGYOKE AUNG SAN MUSEUM

Around 500 metres (550yds) south of the Nga Htat Gyi Pagoda, the moving

Bogyoke Aung San Museum (Tues–Sun 9.30am–4.30pm) occupies the beautiful old colonial house which was the family home of General Aung San, Myanmar's great independence leader (and also the first childhood home of his daughter, Aung San Suu Kyi). Aung San lived here from 1945 until his assassination in 1947, and the house has been preserved largely as he left it, with just a few modest exhibits including some personal effects, a smattering of original furniture and his signature trench coat, gifted to him by Indian leader Jawaharlal Nehru.

KOE HTAT GYI

You'll need to jump in a cab to visit the last of the major religious sites in the Shwegadon area. The **Koe Htat Gyi Pagoda** (literally "Nine Storey" Pagoda) lies a 10–15-minute drive west on Bargaya Road, a stone's throw from the river. Its centrepiece is a 20-metre (65ft) -high sitting Buddha, with eerily life-like eyes made from blown glass. Inside the figure, a small casket is said to contain relics of the historical Buddha, as well as those of some of his disciples.

In the area surrounding the complex are a great many *kyaung* (monasteries) where early birds can watch the monks emerging onto the streets to fill their alms bowls just after sunrise.

DRUG ELIMINATION MUSEUM

Around 1.5km (1 mile) northwest of the Shwedagon Pagoda, the outlandish **Drug Elimination Museum** ⑱ (Tues–Sun 9am–4pm) on Hanthawaddy Road is one of Yangon's quirkiest mementos of the long years of military rule. Occupying a cavernous three-storey building, the museum serves up an entertaining display of old-school state-sponsored propaganda, showcasing the generals' heroic battle against the pernicious evils of opium, heroin and other banned substances. Numerous didactic displays outline assorted drug-eradication efforts, including one exhibit which allows you to "set fire" to a cache of confiscated narcotics. Elsewhere in the museum, a small, darkened room, filled with a constantly looping soundtrack of random musical fragments and disembodied voices, attempts to give you first-hand experience of the deranged mental state of a hardened drug-user, while the evils of narcotics are further reinforced by assorted pictures of skeletal junkies and jars full of the shrivelled internal organs of expired addicts.

PARKS AND LAKES

Yangon boasts more than a dozen public parks and gardens, and locals take great pleasure in spending the hot hours of the day resting in them, preferably beside a lake. Just east of the Shwedagon Pagoda, the northern shore of **Kandawgyi** ("Royal") **Lake** is given over to **Bogyoke Aung San Park** ⑲, dedicated to the country's most famous martyr, whose children's playgrounds and picnic areas are popular attractions with young families. An attractive, although increasingly dilapidated, boardwalk runs around the southern part of the lake, offering beautiful views over the water.

The park's best-known sight is the surreal **Karaweik Palace** ⑳, on the eastern shore. Constructed in the early 1970s, the structure is modelled on a *pyigyimun*, or royal barge, with a flamboyant, pagoda-roofed building straddling the "deck" and two enormous prows shaped in the form of a pair of mythological *karaweik* birds. The equally sumptuous interior contains some striking lacquerwork embellished with mosaics in glass, marble and mother-of-pearl. It now houses a restaurant which hosts popular buffet dinners every evening at 6.30pm (US$30 per head, payable in dollars) featuring a cultural show including music, classical dance and puppetry.

INYA LAKE AND AROUND

Continuing north from the Shwedagon Pagoda along busy Kaba Aye Pagoda Road you'll arrive at enormous **Inya Lake** ㉑. The lush surrounding area is home to the Yangon University campus as well as some of the city's most prized real estate and most exclusive neighbourhoods, including the

Performing the Aung Mingalar dance.

Old jeeps, Downtown Yangon.

⊙ Tip

The best way to nip between sights uptown is to wave down a cab as and when you need one, rather than book a car and driver for the day. Taxis are cheap and plentiful across the city.

colonial-era home of NLD leader, Aung San Suu Kyi, on University Avenue, while further down the same street is the former home of her old adversary and long-time military ruler, Ne Win. Next to the university, the 15-hectare (37-acre) lakeside park is the most popular place in the city for romantic trysts – images of amorous couples schmoozing on the grassy verges are a cliché of Burmese movies and popular song videos.

The southwest corner of the lake, by contrast, is tainted with much darker associations. During the civil unrest of 1988, an estimated 283 students were beaten to death or drowned by military police on the shore – an event dubbed the "White Bridge Massacre". A further 3,000 or more people are thought to have lost their lives in the brutal crackdown that ensued.

With its prize exhibits now moved to a display in the new Burmese capital, Naypyidaw, the government-run **Myanmar Gems Museum**, at 66 Kaba Aye Pagoda Road (Tues–Sun 9.30am–4pm; charge), just north of Inya Lake, has some interesting exhibits showcasing Myanmar's incredible mineral wealth, as well as a whole floor of jewellery emporia where you can purchase objects fashioned from Burmese jade and precious stones.

THE KABA AYE PAGODA AND MAHAPASANA CAVE

Immediately northeast of Inya Lake is the **Kaba Aye Pagoda** ㉒, which the first prime minister of independent Burma, U Nu, had built in the early 1950s. Legend has it that an old man dressed in white appeared before the monk Saya Htay while the latter was meditating near the town of Pakokku on the Ayeyarwady River, handing him a bamboo pole covered with writing. He then asked Saya Htay to pass the pole on to U Nu, accompanied by a demand that the prime minister actively do more for Buddhism.

U Nu was as well versed in religious affairs as in politics, and not only received the bamboo pole but amazingly complied with the old man's demand. The country's leader built the Kaba Aye Pagoda about 12km (8 miles)

Meditating inside Botataung Pagoda

⊙ MEDITATION COURSES

As a profoundly Buddhist nation, Myanmar attracts individuals from all over the world who wish to study the art of meditation. Residential courses are offered by several monasteries in and around Yangon, lasting anything from a week to several months. The best-known venue is the Mahasi Meditation Centre (http://www.mahasi.org.mm), established by the esteemed Mahasi Sayadaw in 1947. The programme is not for the uncommitted: the day typically begins at 3am and ends at 11pm, and on some courses students are required to remain utterly silent for the duration of their stay. Another well-regarded place is the Dahmma Joti Vipassana Centre, near the Chauk Htat Gyi Pagoda (www.joti.dhamma.org; donation).

north of downtown Yangon in preparation for the Sixth Buddhist Synod of 1954 to 1956, and dedicated it to the cause of world peace.

Although lacking some of the aesthetic appeal of other Yangon pagodas, the Kaba Aye is interesting. It is circular in shape, and contains relics of the two most important disciples of the Buddha. Discovered in 1851 by an English general, these were only returned to their rightful place in the Kaba Aye Pagoda after spending many years at the British Museum in London. Opposite each of the five pagoda entrances stand 2.4-metre (8ft) -high Buddha statues. A platform holds another 28 small gold-plated statues that represent previous Buddhas. Some 500kg (1,100lbs) of silver were required to cast the central Buddha figure in the inner temple.

The temple was the scene of a major attack in December 1996, when five people were killed and dozens injured by a bomb allegedly planted by the military as part of a campaign to provide justification for a crackdown on political opposition.

In the grounds of the Kaba Aye Pagoda is the **Maha Pasana Guha** ("Great Cave"). Built by U Nu for the Sixth Buddhist Synod, the "cave" (actually more like a subterranean conference hall) is big enough to hold 10,000 people and is supposed to resemble India's Satta Panni Cave, where the First Buddhist Synod took place shortly after the death of Gautama. Devout Buddhist volunteers completed the project only three days before the start of the Synod in 1954.

THE NORTHERN OUTSKIRTS

A couple of sights on Yangon's northern outskirts may tempt you to break a journey to or from the city's international airport.

The **Mai La Mu Pagoda** ㉓, in the suburb of Okkalapa, is named after the mother of King Okkalapa, founder of Dagon and original donor of the Shwedagon. According to legend, Mai La Mu – said to have been born from a mango *(me-lu)* tree and raised by a hermit – had this pagoda built to alleviate her grief after the untimely death

⊘ **Fact**

In 2009, an American wellwisher swam across Inya Lake to visit Aung San Suu Kyi while she was under house arrest, resulting in an increase in her sentence.

A walkway filled with souvenirs at the Kaba Aye Pagoda.

⊙ Tip

The most practical means of exploring the sights between Thanlyin and Yangon is to hire a taxi for the day (roughly US$60–80).

of her young grandson. Her statue can still be seen on the southwestern flank of the Shwedagon Pagoda. The complex is a wonderland of gilded spires and vibrantly painted statues including interesting illustrations and figures from the *Jataka* tales, depicting the Buddha in earlier lives and fashioned in a singularly Burmese style. The pagoda also holds a large reclining Buddha.

West of the airport, in the township of Insein, stands the **Ah Lain Nga Sint Pagoda** ㉔ – a centre of worship for adherents of the *weizza* branch of Burmese Buddhism, which places great emphasis on the occult and supernatural phenomena. The grounds contain a five-storey tower, a hall with statues of all kinds of occult figures and a *kyaung* which serves as a residence for monks.

LAWKA CHANTHA ABHAYA LABHA MUNI AND ELEPHANT PARK

A popular visitor destination in the northern suburbs of Yangon is the temple housing the enormous **Lawka Chantha Abhaya Labha Muni** ㉕

statue. Carved from a single block of white marble, the 11-metre (37ft) -tall image was sculpted in 1999–2000 and installed in a lavish new shrine paid for by the military government.

Less than five minutes from the new temple, on Mindhamma Road in Inthein Township, is the site of another prestige-winning initiative by the Burmese junta. The leafy **Hsin Hpyu Daw Elephant Park** ㉖ (daily 9am–5pm; free) is where the government houses a trio of rare white elephants. Such creatures are traditionally regarded as conferring good luck on a country's rulers and have been much sought after by the infamously superstitious military regime. In fact, the elephants aren't so much white as reddish-brown (or pink when they're wet) – technically albinos, hence the importance of shade to keep their fragile skin out of the sun. Pampered they may be with nutritious food and regular baths in a specially built waterfall, but the spectacle of such dignified creatures hobbled with chains in a cramped concrete pagoda is depressing in the extreme.

Taukkyan British war cemetery.

AROUND YANGON

In addition to the pottery town of Twante on the Ayeyarwady Delta (see page 147), a couple of other destinations across the Bago River offer escape from the crowds and noise of Yangon. Foremost among them is the port of **Thanlyin**, overlooked by an attractive hilltop pagoda. Half an hour further south, **Kyauktan** is the site of another pretty Buddhist shrine, this time marooned on an islet. Finally, heading northwest towards Bago and the Sittaung Valley, a recommended stop for anyone interested in the events of World War II is the **Taukkyan War Cemetery**, where thousands of graves and memorial plaques commemorate the fallen of Allied and Commonwealth countries.

THANLYIN AND KYAUKTAN

The city of **Thanlyin** ㉗ (formerly Syriam), on the opposite side of the Bago River from Yangon, has served for centuries as Burma's principal harbour – a role it continues to play thanks to the modern deep-water container port of Thilawa installed on its waterfront. Most of the country's trade passes through here, making this something of an industrial boom city, with a population that quadrupled in the 1980s following the construction of a bridge connecting it with Yangon and which is now nudging the 200,000 mark. The main incentive to make the traverse is to visit the hilltop pagoda of Kyaik-Khauk, on Thanlyin's southern outskirts, and to hop on a ferry to the atmospheric Yele Paya temple at nearby Kyauktan – both of which provide a welcome change of scene from the hectic streets, fumes and traffic of the metropolis.

The seeming absence of ancient monuments in the city belies the fact that it has played a seminal role in Burmese history. A major port since the time of the Hindu Andhran dynasty in the 2nd century BC, it rose to national prominence after being captured by the Kingdom of Arakan in the late 16th century. The invading army was led by the maverick Portuguese soldier of fortune Felipe de Brito y Nicote, who'd

Making a call on the public phones, Downtown Yangon.

Tip

If you're in Yangon in late January, it's worth looking out for evidence of the Thaipusam festival at local Hindu temples, in which Tamil devotees of the Hindu God Murugan stick skewers through their cheeks and walk on hot coals.

left Lisbon decades earlier as a cabin boy (see page 36).

Aside from scant and weed-choked remains of a Catholic church on the roadside, precious little has survived from the Portuguese interlude. The main focus for day-trippers is the much more ancient Kayaik-Khauk Pagoda (free), rising from a low hill on the southern fringes of Thanlyin. Inscriptions suggest a stupa may have been erected on the site as long ago as the third century AD, but the present structure, said to hold hairs of the historical Buddha, is around 700–800 years old. A smaller version of the Shwedagon, it is exquisitely gilded and affords grandiose views across the city and surrounding countryside.

At **Kyauktan** ㉘, about 15km (9 miles) south of Thanlyin on a tributary of the Yangon River, the **Ye Le Pagoda** (charge) is famous for its unusual situation – on an islet in the river. Foreign visitors have to travel to it in a special launch.

With its gilded upturned eaves, seven-tiered roofs and frame of

Lawka Chantha Abhaya Labha Muni.

swaying palm trees, the temple itself is an architectural gem, while locals also visit to feed the huge catfish which hang around the temple waters. Access to the temple is by boat – a one-minute crossing for which foreign tourists are charged a disproportionate $5 return.

TAUKKYAN WAR CEMETERY

Just off the main Yangon–Bago highway, 35km (21miles) north of the city, **Taukkyan** ㉙ (Htauk Kyant; daily 8am–5pm; free) is the largest of Burma's major war cemeteries. It holds the graves of 6,374 Allied and Commonwealth servicemen killed in World War II, as well as memorial plaques listing the names of 27,000 more whose bodies were never found or identified. A large proportion of them were from India and Africa. Maintained by the Commonwealth War Graves Commission, the site is impeccably well kept and a moving tribute to the mainly young men who lost their lives fighting the Japanese in the early 1940s.

AN AUSPICIOUS MOVE

One of the ways in which the kings of ancient Burma expressed their wealth and power – and acquired cosmic merit at the same time – was by creating huge stone Buddhas. In 2000, the country's military generals revived the tradition with the arrival at a purpose-built hilltop temple on the outskirts of Yangon of a giant Buddha carved from a single block of flawless white marble.

The boulder used to make it had been discovered the previous year by master sculptor, U Taw Taw, at the famous quarry of Sangyin, near Mandalay. It took him and his sons twelve months to carve. Recognising the PR potential of sponsoring the project, the generals spared no expense to bring the 600-tonne colossus to Yangon, constructing a special 8-rail train line to transport it to the Ayeyarwady, and a huge golden barge to ship it downriver. The 12-day trip, featuring a flotilla of vessels, was cheered from the banks by vast crowds. Another specially laid rail line conveyed the statue to its new home atop Mindhamma Hill, where the 11-metre (37ft) image – christened Lawka Chantha Abhaya Labha Muni – was enshrined inside a giant glass case. Attracting constant streams of devotees, the mighty white Buddha is today one of Yangon's most popular religious attractions.

THE LEGEND OF SHWEDAGON

Myanmar's most famous sight has a long history, with its origins shrouded in legend.

The legend of the Shwedagon Pagoda is recorded in Myanmar's great historical epic, *The Great Glass Palace Chronicle*, which was compiled in Mandalay during the early 1830s by a royal commission made up of learned monks, brahmins and lay scholars. According to the traditional narrative, the story of the pagoda goes back 2,500 years and centres on Okkalapa, King of Suvannabhumi, who lived near Singuttara Hill in Lower Burma during the time when Siddhartha Gautama was still a young man in northern India. The hill is considered holy because of the relics of three Buddhas enshrined on its summit. Local belief asserts that a new Buddha comes into existence every 5,000 years. As nearly 5,000 years have elapsed since the time of the last Buddha, it was thought that the hill would lose its blessedness unless a new incarnation offered a gift to be enshrined as a relic for the next five millennia. To this end Okkalapa spent many hours on the hill meditating and praying.

In India, meanwhile, Gautama was close to achieving enlightenment under the Bodhi tree in Bodhgaya. Buddhist chronicles assert that he appeared before Okkalapa and promised that the king's wish would be granted. Gautama meditated under the Bodhi tree for 49 days before he accepted his first gift from his disciples: a honey cake offered by Taphussa and Bhallika, two Burmese merchant brothers who had come from the village of Okkala. To express his gratitude, Gautama plucked eight hairs from his head and gave them to the brothers, who then set off on a difficult return journey. First, they were robbed of two of the Buddha's hairs by the King of Ajetta. Then, while crossing the Bay of Bengal, another couple of hairs were taken by the seabed-dwelling King of the Nagas. Despite the losses, the brothers were welcomed by Okkalapa who held a great feast attended by all the native gods and *nat,* who decided a grand stupa should be built to house the relics.

When Okkalapa opened the casket containing the Buddha's hairs, lo and behold, he saw eight hairs in place. As he looked on in astonishment, the strands emitted a brilliant light that rose high above the trees, radiating to all corners of the world. Suddenly, the blind everywhere could see, the deaf could hear, the dumb could speak and the lame could walk. As this miracle took place, the earth shook and bolts of lightning flashed. The trees blossomed and a shower of precious stones rained onto the ground.

ENSHRINING THE RELICS

As a result of the legend of the hairs, the site chosen to enshrine the Buddha's hairs – Singuttara Hill – is considered one of the country's most sacred places, and the golden Shwedagon Pagoda is regarded as the holiest of the country's pagodas. "Shwe" is the Burmese word for "gold", and *"dagon"*, a derivative of *"trihakumba"* (contracted to *"trikumba"*, *"tikun"* and then *"dagon"*), means "three hills".

The Shwedagon Pagoda was later built over the shrine containing the Buddha's relics. Smaller pagodas, constructed with silver, tin, copper, lead, marble and iron brick, were built, one on top of the other, in the golden pagoda to enshrine the relics.

Night descends on the Shwedagon Pagoda.

Putting the finishing touches to pottery in Twante.

THE DELTA REGION

Stretching flat and intensely green for as far as the eye can see, the fertile green Ayeyarwady Delta is one of Myanmar's most distinctive and memorable landscapes.

A giant patchwork of lime-green paddy and twisting waterways, the **Delta Region** west of Yangon is the rice bowl of Myanmar. Its famed fertility derives from the silt deposited by the Ayeyarwady as it reaches the end of its 1,200km (750-mile) journey from Upper Myanmar to the Andaman Sea, fraying like the end of an old rope into hundreds of narrow, sinuous channels.

Although rice cultivation is the mainstay here, the Delta also supports numerous fish farms producing carp, threadfin and giant sea perch, as well as prawns and other shellfish for export. The resulting prosperity has spurred a sharp rise in population since Independence, yet little government money has been invested in sea defences, despite the fact that most of the area lies only 3 metres (10ft) above the high-tide mark.

Just how vulnerable the densely populated towns and villages of the Delta are to the elements became tragically apparent on 2 May 2008, when Cyclone Nargis swept ashore from the Bay of Bengal. One of the most powerful tropical storms ever to hit the country, the cyclone left an estimated 130,000 dead, as well as a million people homeless – the overwhelming majority of them from the Delta. Confronted with a disaster on this unprecedented scale, the Burmese regime singularly failed to

mount any sort of effective relief effort, and also did its best to block the efforts of international NGOs attempting to reach the region's worst-hit areas.

A cause of concern for the future was the damage to the mangroves that fringe many of the Delta's saltwater creeks. These help protect the low-lying land behind them from flooding, but many were wiped out by the cyclone, leaving the alluvial plain behind them more exposed than ever.

Much of the Delta can, with time and determination, be explored by

Main attractions

Twante
Pathein
Shwemokhtaw Pagoda, Pathein
Chaungtha Beach

Maps on pages 146, 148

Working the fields.

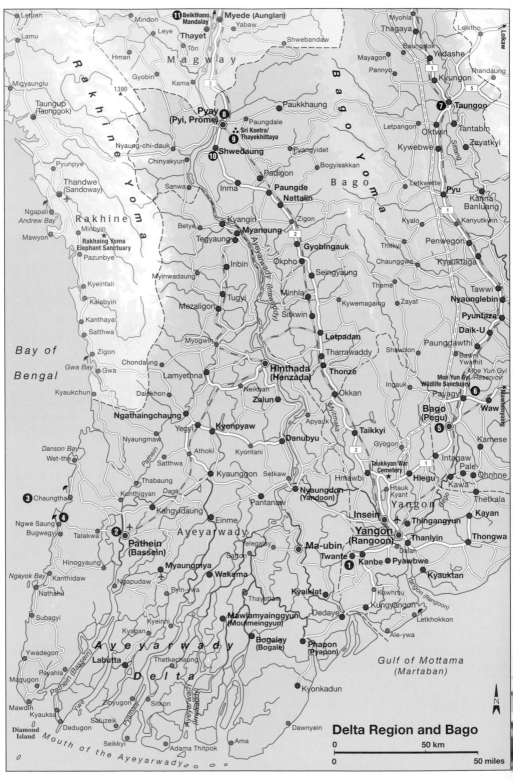

Delta Region and Bago

Letpan
Lamu
Mindon
Leye
Yabaw
Myohla
Thagaya
Myohla
Loikaw
Leiktho
Migyaunglu
Hman
Gyobin
Thayet
Tôn
Shwebandaw
Mayagon
Pannyo
Baunggok
Yedashe
Thandaung
Taungup
(Taunggok)
1390
Kama
Paukkhaung
Letpangon
Kyungon
Tantabin
Pyunpye
Nyaung-chi-dauk
Pyay
(Pyi, Prome)
Paungdale
Sri Ksetra/
Thayekhittaya
Shwedaung
Pyangyidet
Kywebwe
Oktwin
Zayatkyi
Thandwe
(Sandoway)
Chinyakyun
Padigon
Bogyisakkan
Letkwette
Pyu
Kanna
Banluang
Ngapali
Andrew Bay
Mawyon
Minbyin
Rakhaing Yoma
Elephant Sanctuary
Pazunbye
Sanwa
Inma
Paungde
Nattalin
Zigon
Thitkyi
Kyalo
Kanyutkwin
Penwegon
Kyauktaga
Kyeintali
Betye
Kyangin
Myanaung
Gyobingauk
Chaunggwa
Theme
Tawwi
Nyaunglebin
Kalabyin
Tegyaung
Inbin
Okpho
Seingyaung
Kywemagaing
Zayat
Pyuntaza
Daik-U
Kanthaya
Satthwa
Myinwadaung
Tugyi
Minhla
Sitkwin
Paungdawthi
Bawni
Yuamit
Zigon
Mezaligon
Myogwin
Letpadan
Tharrawaddy
Shawdon
Ingauk
Moe Yun Gyi
Reservoir
Moe Yun Gyi
Wildlife Sanctuary
Gwa Bay
Gwa
Chondaung
Lamyethna
Hinthada
(Henzada)
Thonze
Okkan
Payagyi
Bago
(Pegu)
Waw
Mawlamyingaing
Kyaukchun
Dalekhon
Neikban
Zalun
Apyauk
Taikkyi
Gyogon
Kamese
Ngathaingchaung
Yegyi
Kyonpyaw
Danubyu
Taukkyan War
Cemetery
Hmawbi
Hlegu
Intagaw
Pale
Ohnne
Danson Bay
Wet-the
Nyaungmaw
Athoki
Kyontani
Setkaw
Htauk
Kyant
Kawa
Thetkala
Chaungtha
Thabaung
Kyaunggon
Nyaungdon
(Yandoon)
Insein
Thingangyun
Kayan
Kunthigyan
Pantanaw
Yangon
Ngwe Saung
Bugwegyi
Talakwa
Pathein
(Bassein)
Kangyidaung
Einme
Yelegalay
Ma-ubin
Twante
Yangon
(Rangoon)
Thanlyin
Dalah
Thongwa
Hinogyaung
Myaungmya
Satton
Kanbe
Pyawbwe
Kyauktan
Ngayok Bay
Kanthidaw
Nathahu
Pyin-ywa
Wakema
Thayettaw
Kyaiklat
Kawhmu
Kungyangon
Letkhokkon
Subagyi
Kyeinni
Mawlamyainggyun
(Moulmeingyun)
Dedaye
Ale-ywa
Ywadegon
Payahla
Kyagan
Bogalay
(Bogalé)
Phapon
(Pyapon)
Gulf of Mottama
(Martaban)
Magugon
Labutta
Thetkechaung
Mawdin
Kyauksa
Zibyugon
Sitkon
Kyonkadun
Diamond
Island
Dedugon
Saluzeik
Seikkyi
Ama
Dawnyein
Adama Thitpok
Mouth of the Ayeyarwady

Rakhine Yoma
Bago Yoma
Bay of Bengal
Rakhine
Magway
Bago
Ayeyarwady
Ayeyarwady
Delta

0   50 km
0   50 miles

bus, but in practice, travellers tend to head from Yangon to the region's largest city, **Pathein**, via the main road skirting the north of the region, and from there proceed to one or both of the beach resorts on the west coast: **Chaungtha** and **Ngwe Saung**. More conveniently covered in a day trip from Yangon, the town of **Twante** is renowned for its cottage pottery industry and gilded pagoda, the Shwesandaw.

TWANTE

The pottery town of **Twante ❶**, on the Ayeyarwady Delta, makes an interesting day trip west from Yangon, not least because of the enjoyable (if short) ferry trip over the river at the journey's start. Ferries leave from the riverfront in Yangon, taking ten minutes to cross to the village of **Dalah**, on the opposite bank, from where jeeps, pick-up trucks, motorcycle taxis and buses cover the remaining 45 minutes by road. En route, it's well worth stopping at the unusual **Baungdawgyoke Pagoda** snake temple, around 6km

(4 miles) east of Twante, home to a dozen enormous Burmese pythons who have made their home here and who are considered sacred by the temple's nuns.

Twante has one significant pagoda, the spectacular, 76-metre (250ft) **Shwesandaw**, which was built in 1057 to enshrine hairs of the historical Buddha, Gautama. The canal banks around the town are lined with pottery in all shapes and sizes. Visitors can see potters at work and completed pieces being fired in old-fashioned kilns.

PATHEIN

With a population of around 250,000, **Pathein ❷** (also known by its colonial-era name of "Bassein") is the capital of the Delta and Myanmar's sixth-largest city, having grown prosperous as the distribution centre for the bulk of the region's lucrative rice trade. Pathein's other claim to fame is its traditional parasol workshops which, along with a handful of impressive Buddhist monuments, entice a steady stream of travellers

Making offerings outside Shwesandaw Pagoda, Twante.

Pick-up trucks wait to take people home.

to pause here en route to or from the beach resorts further west. Reasonably fast and frequent express buses connect the city with Yangon, 190km (118 miles) east. The overnight ferry between Yangon and Pathein was formerly one of Myanmar's great river journeys, although at present the ferry isn't running, and seems unlikely to restart.

The name "Bassein" is an anglicised version of Pathein, which itself is said to derive from the local word for Muslims: "Pathi". In past centuries, communities of Muslim merchants from India and the east African coast settled here, reflecting the town's importance as a clearing house for goods travelling across the Andaman Sea. Today's inhabitants include Kayin, Rakhine and a small Mon community, most of whom are Christian.

Pathein's resplendently gilded centrepiece is the **Shwemokhtaw Pagoda** Ⓐ ("Stupa of the Half Foot Gold Bar"), whose shimmering, bell-shaped profile soars in spectacular fashion above the city centre,

market area and riverside. According to legend, a Muslim princess named Onmadandi was responsible for its construction, along with two others which she commanded her lovers build in her name. Burmese chronicles, however, identify the 12th- and 13th-century kings Alaungsithu and Samodagossa as the true creators of the 47-metre (132ft) paya, which may have been erected on top of considerably more ancient ruins dating from the time of the Mauryan emperor, Ashoka. Its crowning glory is a priceless *hti* umbrella finial made from more than 6kg (14lbs) of gold, with lower layers of solid silver and bronze, encrusted with hundreds of diamonds, rubies and semi-precious stones.

The pagoda's presiding image, housed in a hall on the south side of the complex, is the Thiho-shin Phondaw-pyi sitting Buddha, believed to have been one of four sculpted in ancient times in Sri Lanka and floated to the Ayeyarwady Delta on a raft.

Spread out around the northeastern edges of town is a colourful cluster

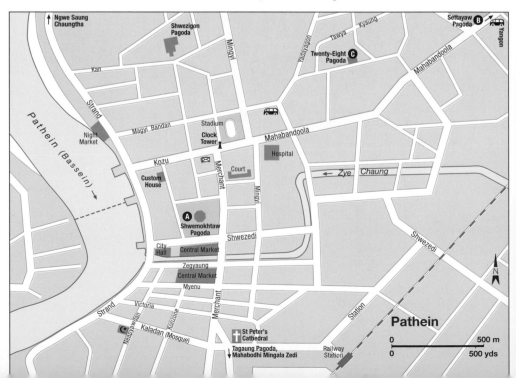

Pathein

0   500 m
0   500 yds

of pagodas and assorted monastic buildings including Pathein's second main temple, the sprawling **Settayaw Pagoda** ⑧. The main shrine is built around a footprint said to have been left by the Buddha during his peregrinations around southeast Asia, now presided over by a bronze Mandalay-style Buddha image.

Between here and the city centre is the **Twenty-Eight Pagoda** ⓒ, so named because it houses 28 sitting and 28 standing images of the Buddha.

Around a couple of dozen traditional **parasol workshops** are dotted around Pathein, several of them in the vicinity of the Twenty-Eight Pagoda, making pleasant detours from the temple trail. They're all unfailingly welcoming, often serving visitors snacks and tea. You can observe the various stages involved in the manufacturing process, from making the bamboo spokes and handles to covering and painting the cotton canopy with pigments derived from various natural resins – a painstaking procedure that can take as long as five days. The workshops produce burgundy-coloured parasols for monks, and hand-painted "summer" versions with flower motifs for lay people. They come in a range of sizes, from child-friendly to extra-large.

DELTA BEACHES: CHAUNGTHA AND NGWE SAUNG

A six-hour bus ride from Yangon (and two hours from Pathein), **Chaungtha Beach** ❸ is a magnet for visiting Yangonites and other monied Burmese who descend here in droves at the weekend to paddle, ride ponies along the beach and consume prodigious quantities of seafood and beer. If you're looking for an idyllic tropical beach then this definitely isn't the place to come. The beach itself is wide but dirty, accommodation is lacklustre and at weekends the whole place is about as peaceful as a funfair – but if

you want to enjoy the unique spectacle of the Burmese middle-classes at play, it can't be beaten.

If you fancy a break from the village itself, local boatmen are on hand to ferry visitors out to nearby **White Sand Island**, just off the southern end of the beach, where the water is a lot clearer.

A short hop down the coast, **Ngwe Saung** ❹ ("Silver Beach") is the Delta's other beach destination. This is the polar opposite of Chaungtha: tranquil bordering on soporific, with a string of stylish, mainly upmarket resorts dotted along the coast north and south of the lively little village and attracting a mix of affluent Yangonites and visiting Westerners. Comprising 14km (9 miles) of gently shelving, golden sand backed by casuarina and palm trees, the beach remains largely unspoilt, despite the burgeoning number of new resorts springing up along it. From the southern end of the beach, a short wade at low tide takes you to Lovers' Island, surrounded by translucent turquoise water.

A nun walks along a typical back road in the Delta.

BAGO REGION

The provincial capital of this rice-growing region, Bago was once a great sea port. Today, its many monuments are a reminder of its glittering past.

The borders of **Bago Region**, the administrative area immediately north of Yangon, encompass a geography as varied as any in the country. To the east stretches the comparatively infertile 420km (260-mile) -long, Sittaung Valley; to the west is the broader, more lush and traditionally prosperous Ayeyarwady Valley, fed by annual deluges of silt from the Himalayas; while between the two sit the eroded slopes and depleted teak forests of the Bago Yoma Range. From the 12th century onwards, this vast expanse of jungle and alluvial plain formed the hinterland of Burma's wealthiest and most powerful city, the port of Pegu, today known as Bago.

Lynchpin of a trade network extending across the Indian Ocean and beyond, Pegu and its rulers, the Mon Kings, amassed wealth that attracted traders from all over the world, and also served as a magnet for rival surrounding kingdoms. Wars with the Burmese Taungoo dynasty, further north up the Sittaung Valley erupted repeatedly between the 16th and 18th centuries, resulting in the capture of Pegu by the rulers of Taungoo (who subsequently made it their own capital) and the eclipse of Mon culture and language throughout southern Burma.

Nowadays, the once-glorious city is little more than a provincial market town on the highway north, though it does retain a hoard of superb Buddhist monuments whose scale and splendour evoke the glory days of the Mon Kingdom. Lying only an hour-and-a-half by road from Yangon, it can easily be visited as a day trip, or as a stopover on the longer haul north to Mandalay via Taungoo, the old Burmese capital, with its splendid pagodas.

To the west, across the Bago Yoma hills, the town of Pyay (or Prome, as it was known in colonial times) on the Ayeyarwady River is the springboard

Main attractions
Bago
Taungoo
Pyay
Sri Ksetra
Shwedaung

Maps on pages 146, 152

The Shwethalyaung reclining Buddha.

for the ancient Pyu capital of Sri Ksetra, whose outlandish conical stupas, rising from the surrounding fields like the helmets of buried giants, are the last vestiges of a civilisation that thrived here between the 5th and 9th centuries.

BAGO

Bago ❺ – or "Pegu" as it was formerly known – retains an amazing concentration of temples, pagodas and giant Buddha statues for a town of its size – a legacy of its former prominence as Myanmar's capital and major port under the Taungoo dynasty during parts of the 16th and 17th centuries. Most of these great religious monuments have been painstakingly maintained or restored, often with coats of vibrant gold leaf and modern paints that make them seem considerably less ancient than they actually are, but they are no less impressive for that. As the majority lie in, or within easy reach of, the town centre, you can comfortably get around them by trishaw or rented cycle. Note that foreigners are obliged to buy combination tickets, on sale at the Shwemawdaw Pagoda, covering all of the sights in a single ticket (K10,000).

Situated around an hour-and-a-half by road (92km/57 miles) from Yangon, Bago makes an easy day trip, but its low-density feel also makes it an ideal first stop if you're heading either north to Taungoo or south to Mawlamyine and beyond.

HISTORY

Local lore suggests Bago dates back to AD 573, but most historians believe the city was founded in 825 by two brothers from Thaton, the then Mon capital. In 1057, King Anawrahta of Bagan conquered Thaton and the whole of southern Myanmar fell under Bamar sovereignty, a situation that continued for the next 250 years. In 1365, the Mon ruler King Byinnya-U transferred the capital to Bago (known originally as Hanthawaddy or Hamsawaddy after its symbol, the *hamsa*, a mythological duck whose mate had to perch on his back).

Thus began the city's golden age, which endured for nearly three

Buddha statues and planetary prayer posts, Shwemawdaw Pagoda.

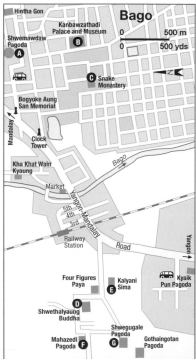

centuries, epitomized by the great building works of the Hanthawaddy dynasty's most famous rulers such as King Razadarit (1385–1425), Queen Shinsawpu (1453–72) and King Dhammazedi (1472–92).

In 1539 Bago was conquered by the ruler of the increasingly powerful Taungoo dynasty, King Tabinshwehti, who promptly selected it as his own new capital. His successor was the bellicose Bayinnaung, who extended the empire's boundaries but drained the treasury with his military campaigns. He conquered Ayutthaya, capital of Siam, but was unable to leave a stable government in the subjugated region. Thus while Bago was one of the most splendid cities in the whole continent during this period, the country itself was reduced to poverty.

Bago remained capital of the Taungoo empire (with a couple of brief interruptions) until 1635, when the Taungoo capital was transferred to Ava (modern Inwa), near Mandalay. By this time Bago was already in decline, with silt deposits choking the harbour and preventing large vessels from docking, slowly strangling the city's trade.

Bago remained under Taungoo rule for a further century until 1740, when the Mon finally cast off Bamar rule and (with Portugese and Dutch help) in 1752 even marched north and overran the old Taungoo capital of Ava. Their success was short-lived, however. Just two years later King Alaungpaya of the newly established Konbaung Dynasty drove Mon forces out of Ava and chased them slowly south all the way back to Bago, which he eventually conquered and sacked in 1757 after a 14-month siege. The city, it is said, was taken at moonrise and the assembled Burmese population of starved men, women and children massacred "without distinction". Alaungpaya then rode into the city on elephant back, and ordered its walls and twenty gates razed to the ground.

Alaugpaya's conquest marked the final end of Bago's spell at the forefront of Burmese history, and also the demise of Myanmar's last independent Mon kingdom. The city's Mon inhabitants either fled to Thailand or intermarried with the victorious Bamar. Though King Bodawpaya (1782–1819) attempted to rebuild the city, partly due to the changing course of the Bago River, it never again approached its former greatness, and today only Bago's many monuments serve as reminders of its glorious past.

SHWEMAWDAW PAGODA AND HINTHA GON

The most outstanding of Bago's attractions is the **Shwemawdaw Pagoda** Ⓐ (Great Golden God Pagoda; daily; entrance with combination ticket), which is to Bago what the Shwedagon is to Yangon. Its stupa can be seen from about 10km (6 miles) outside the city. Richly gilded from base to tip, the pagoda has many similarities to the Shwedagon and is in fact even taller than its more famous cousin, standing at 114 metres (374ft) in height.

A trishaw waiting outside Shwemawdaw Pagoda.

Legend has it that two merchant brothers, Mahasala and Kullasala, returned from India with two hairs given to them by Gautama Buddha. They built a small stupa over the relics, and in the following years, this shrine was enlarged several times, with sacred teeth added to the collection of relics in 982 and 1385. King Dhammazedi installed a bell on the pagoda's main platform, which he had inscribed with runes that can still be seen, indecipherable though they are.

In the 16th century, King Bayinnaung gave the jewels from his crown to make a *hti* (jewelled umbrella) for the pagoda, and in 1796, King Bodawpaya donated a new umbrella and raised the height of the pagoda to 90 metres (295ft). In the 20th century, the Shwemawdaw was hit by three serious earthquakes, the last of which, in 1930, almost completely destroyed it. After World War II, however, the pagoda was rebuilt by unpaid volunteers with the proceeds of popular donations to stand higher than ever. In 1954, it got a new diamond-studded *hti*.

The main stupa and pavilion at Shwemawdaw Pagoda.

As at Yangon's Shwedagon Pagoda, the Shwemawdaw's main terrace can be approached from four directions by covered stairways, each like a miniature bazaar, with shops selling everything from medicinal herbs to monastic offerings for sale. All four stairways are guarded by huge white *chinthe* holding a sitting Buddha in its mouth. Faded murals along the main entrance steps recall the 1930 quake destruction and the pagoda's later reconstruction.

The terrace itself is lined with a string of brightly coloured *tazaung* (pavilions), as well as the usual eight planetary prayer posts found in many larger Burmese pagodas along with statues of various *nat* spirits. It's also worth having a look at the small museum containing some ancient wooden and bronze Buddha figures salvaged from the ruins of the 1930 earthquake.

On a hilltop just to the east, reached via a flight of steps beginning opposite the main entrance to the Shwemawdaw Pagoda, lie the ruins of a more ancient stupa – the **Hintha Gon** (daily 5am–10pm; free). In front of the stupa stands a statue of a pair of *hamsa*, the mythological birds associated with the foundation of Bago. Geologists suspect that the hill was at one time an island in the Gulf of Mottama, and may thus have been the spot where the *hamsa* were believed to have landed (*hamsa* are also known as *hintha* – hence the name, meaning "Hamsa Hill"). A high-roofed platform atop the hill provides a good view of the surrounding countryside.

KANBAWZATHADI PALACE

The area to the south of the Shwemawdaw Pagoda and Hintha Gon is believed to have been the site of the original Mon city of Hanthawady, where Bayinnaung subsequently erected his palace in 1553. Destroyed only fifty years later, the lavish complex of 76 buildings lay forgotten until 1990, when archaeologists uncovered a series of huge post holes and teak pillars beneath half a dozen mounds of brick and soil. Together with 16th-century drawings, these provided the blueprint for a massive restoration programme initiated by the Burmese military government.

At its centre is a shoddily built "replica" of Bayinnaung's **Kanbawzathadi Palace** Ⓑ (daily 9.30am–4pm; entrance with combined ticket), featuring a gilded Lion Throne Room, Settaw Saung and Queen's Bee Hall, complete with spray-stencilled decor. Quite how closely they resemble the originals is anyone's guess, but the buildings do at least hint at the extraordinary wealth and sophistication of the Taungoo dynasty during its heyday. A small museum on the site houses the huge pillars and other artefacts discovered by archaeologists during the excavations of the 1990s.

THE SNAKE MONASTERY

A couple of blocks southwest of the Kanbawzathadi Palace is Bago quirky **Snake Monastery** Ⓒ (Mwei Paya; daily dawn to dusk; free), home to a giant Burmese python which is said to be the reincarnation of a Buddhist abbot from Hsipaw. Pilgrims and tourists file through year round to pay their respects to the snake, which measures a whopping 5 metres (17ft) from head to tail and is now thought to be well over a century old.

THE SHWETHALYAUNG BUDDHA

The rest of Bago's monuments lie on the opposite, western side of town. Foremost among them is the **Shweth-alyaung Buddha** Ⓓ (daily 5am–dusk; entrance with combined ticket), which is said to depict Gautama on the eve of his entering *nibbana* (nirvana). Revered throughout Myanmar as the country's most beautiful reclining Buddha, the statue measures 55 metres (180ft) in length and 16 metres (52ft) in height. It is not quite as large as Yangon's more recent Kyauk Htat Gyi (built in the

1960s) but, as a result of its quality and long history, is much the better-known and loved of the two.

The statue was left to decay for nearly 500 years until it was restored during Dhammazedi's reign. In the centuries that followed, Bago was destroyed twice, and by the 18th century the Shwethalyaung Buddha had become lost beneath countless layers of tropical vegetation. It was only in 1881 that a group of contractors who were building a railway for the British stumbled across it. In 1906, after the undergrowth had been cleared away, an iron *tazaung* was erected over the Buddha, which protects it from the elements, although it does somewhat detract from the view of the statue inside. The Buddha was most recently renovated in 1948, when it was re-gilded and painted.

KALYANI SIMA

To the south of the Shwethalyaung Buddha stands the **Kalyani Sima** Ⓔ (daily 5am–dusk; free) ordination hall, built by King Dhammazedi in 1476 with the aim of rejuvenating the Burmese

Detail of the feet of the giant reclining Buddha, Shwethalyaung.

Admiring Shwemawdaw Pagoda.

Stairway detail, Mahazedi Pagoda.

Kanbawza Thadi Palace.

sangha (monkhood). When the unity of Buddhism in Burma was threatened by schisms following the downfall of the Bagan Empire, Dhammazedi dispatched 22 monks to Sri Lanka, a stronghold of the Theravada Buddhist faith. The monks were ordained next to the Kalyani River (now known as the Kelani River, near present-day Colombo). Upon their return to Burma after surviving a shipwreck, Dhammazedi built the Kalyani Sima, which he named after the Sri Lankan river.

To the west of the hall, 10 tablets provide a detailed history of Buddhism in the region and of the country's 15th-century trade with Sri Lanka and south India. Three of the stones are inscribed in Pali, seven in Mon. Although some of the tablets are shattered and others are illegible in places, the complete text has been preserved on palm-leaf copies.

The Kalyani Sima, which served as a model for nearly 400 other *sima* built by Dhammazedi, did not escape the ravages of the Mon's aggressive politics – or indeed the hostility of other ambitious kingdoms. The Portuguese adventurer de Brito destroyed it in 1599, and Alaungpaya razed the reconstructed hall when he sacked Bago in 1757. The structure collapsed following the earthquake of 1930, but, once rebuilt 24 years later, it was rededicated to its original purpose at a ceremony attended by U Nu. Today, the monks live in lodgings around the *sima*, set today amid peaceful, leafy grounds.

THE MAHAZEDI PAGODA AND AROUND

The **Mahazedi Pagoda** Ⓕ (daily 5am–dusk; free), to the west of the Shwethalyaung Buddha, is famous in Myanmar as the place where King Bayinnaung enshrined a gold- and jewel-encrusted tooth of the Buddha to confirm the divine approval of his reign. He acquired it from the King of Kandy in Sri Lanka on the understanding that it was the original, and much revered, Buddha's Tooth, but the relic turned out to be nothing of the kind.

Undeterred, Bayinnaung locked the tooth away in the Mahazedi Pagoda, where it remained until 1599, when Anaukhpetlun transferred it to his capital, Taungoo. A short time later, King Thalun built the Kaunghmudaw Pagoda in nearby Sagaing to house the relic, where it can still be seen today. The Mahazedi Pagoda was destroyed during Alaungpaya's time, and levelled again by the 1930 earthquake. With the reconstruction work recently completed, the uppermost walkway around the stupa affords a marvellous view of the surrounding plain.

A short distance west of the Mahazedi, on the outskirts of town, stands the **Shwegugale Pagoda** Ⓖ, in which 64 Buddha figures sit in a circle in a gloomy vault around the central stupa. About 1.5km (1 mile) further south, you'll find the **Kyaik Pun Pagoda**. Built by Dhammazedi in 1476, it consists of four Buddha figures, each

30 metres (98ft) tall, seated back to back against a square pillar facing the four cardinal points.

MOE YUN GYI WILDLIFE SANCTUARY

Protecting a serene expanse of lake and wetland some 45 minutes north of Bago by car (or two hours from Yangon), the little visited **Moe Yun Gyi Wildlife Sanctuary** ❻ (charge) is one of Myanmar's premier birding sites. Covering an area of around 40 sq miles (100 sq km), the sanctuary hosts a number of resident species as well as attracting large numbers of migratory aquatic birds between October/November and March, including sarus cranes, pelicans, swamp hens, herons, stilts and cormorants. The sanctuary is best explored by boat – vessels can be hired through the Moe Yun Gyi Resort (www. moeyungyiwetlandsresort.com), next to the lake, who also provide accommodation in houseboats on the waters.

TAUNGOO

Until the construction of Naypyidaw in 2005, **Taungoo** ❼ was the largest city in the Sittaung Valley and still sees a handful of travellers stopping over for a night or two en route between Yangon and Mandalay. It's best known in Myanmar as the home seat of the powerful Taungo dynasty whose rule spanned 150 years and seven kings (although most of the dynasty's later rulers based themselves in Bago, and later in Ava, near Mandalay, rather than in Taungoo itself). Relatively few monuments survive from Taungoo's glory days, however, the royal palace having fallen prey to Japanese bombers during World War II.

The one outstanding historic sight that the town retains is the Shwesandaw Pagoda, which attracts streams of pilgrims year-round, while the town also serves as a springboard for trips into the jungle-covered Bago Yoma Range, to the northwest. Teak and other hardwoods harvested in these ancient forests have formed the mainstay of the local economy for decades; elephants are still extensively used to extract timber. With a little forward planning, it's possible to see tuskers at work at logging camps around Karen villages in the surrounding countryside.

TAUNGOO'S PAGODAS

The focal point of Taungoo's **Shwesandaw Pagoda**, in the centre of the town, is its gilded bell-shaped stupa, built in 1597 on the site of a much more ancient one believed to have contained sacred relics of the Buddha. Statues of the seven Taungoo kings stand in the precinct surrounding the monument; one of the nearby shrines houses a reclining Buddha attended by various devas, while another shelters a sitting Buddha 3.6 metres (11ft) tall. This latter icon was donated by a devotee in 1912, who gave the equivalent of his weight in bronze and silver to cast the statue, and whose ashes have been interred behind it.

Frieze behind the Shwethalyaung reclining Buddha depicting King Migadippa and the making of the statue.

⊙ Tip

All Taungoo's attractions are concentrated in the city centre and are easily explored either on foot or bike, or by hiring a motorbike taxi for a couple of hours.

A two-minute stroll south of the Shwesandaw Pagoda takes you to Taungoo's second pagoda, the Myasigon, a modern structure centred on a gilded stupa. Facing it are two Chinese images of goddesses, one seated on an elephant, the other on a Fu dog, which were gifts from a visiting German Buddhist in 1901. The adjacent museum features a three-headed bronze elephant, the Erawan, believed to have been Indra's mount and rubbed to a brilliant sheen by worshippers, as well as a standing Buddha taken from the Siamese by King Bayinnaung and two 19th-century British cannons.

West of here, the fine Kandawgyi ("Royal") Lake provides another memento of Taungoo's illustrious past, as do the slight remains of a moat and various gateways which can still be made out in various places around the centre of town.

PYAY

Now the seventh largest city in Myanmar, with a population of around a quarter of a million, modern **Pyay** ⑧

– (or "Prome" as it was known to the British) developed in colonial times as a major transhipment port for river traffic travelling between Mandalay and Yangon. The magnificent Shwesandaw Pagoda rising from its midst, however, points to the town's much older roots. These date back to the 5th century or earlier, when the ancient city of Sri Ksetra – or Thayekhittaya as it's now known – was established here, becoming the largest of the ancient Pyu city states which dominated trade along the Ayeyarwady between India and China from the 5th to 9th centuries AD.

While the great gilded pagoda and archaeological site on the outskirts are undeniably Pyay's stand-out attractions, the town itself makes a very pleasant place to break the long journey between Yangon and Mandalay, with lively market squares and a waterfront full of Burmese atmosphere.

SHWESANDAW PAGODA

Crowning a low hill to the southeast of the town centre, Pyay's **Shwesandaw Pagoda** (daily 6am–9pm; free) is one of Myanmar's largest gilded stupas, topping out at a full metre taller than the Shwedagon in Yangon. Its mesmerising form, soaring like a giant rocket above the tin-rooftops and palms below, is reason enough to take time out of the trip to or from Bagan. Come at sunset, when the rich evening light turns the gold leaf a magical colour and the river to the west glows molten orange, for the full effect.

Although its origins are believed to date from 589 BC, the Shwesandaw was enlarged and rebuilt several times by conquering kings, notably Kyanzittha of Bagan in AD 1083, who also commissioned a series of stone inscriptions detailing the pagoda's history. These are now housed in a brick building on the northeast side of the precinct. It was Alaungpaya, however, who gilded the stupa in 1754,

The seated Buddha statues of Kyaikpun Pagoda – close-up of fingers.

and who added a second *hti* to the finial – a feature unique to this *paya*, and which – somewhat ironically – the king hoped would symbolise the "unity of the Burmese people" after his brutal sack of the town.

Looking east from the Shwesandaw, it's impossible to miss the mighty seated Buddha, or Sehtatgyi Paya, whose head rises to almost the same height as the great pagoda. Most visitors content themselves with this view of the giant, but the terrace encircling the statue makes a dramatic spot from which to view the Shwesandaw at sunrise.

SRI KSETRA (THAYEKHITTAYA)

The remains of ancient **Sri Ksetra** ❾ – now better known as Thayekhittaya – are dotted around the village of Hmawza, 8km (5 miles) east of Pyay. Between the 4th and 9th centuries, this was the largest of numerous walled city states founded by the Pyu people, whose kings controlled riverborne trade up and down the Ayeyarwady and out to the open sea to India, from where they drew much of their religious and cultural inspiration.

Three distinct dynasties ruled at Sri Ksetra (from the Sanskrit for "City of Splendour") before their capital fell under the sway of Bagan in the 10th century. Absorbing influences from southwest as well as southeast India, its rulers erected an impressive array of brick-built stupas, palaces and monasteries, encircled by moats and walls whose vestiges are still clearly visible. At its peak twelve centuries ago, the city was the largest and grandest fortified settlement in Asia: 46 sq km (18 sq miles) of land lay behind its ramparts, with most of the buildings grouped on the south side of the site, and fields to the north (ensuring food supplies were protected in times of siege).

Contemporary Chinese chronicles talked of Sri Ksetra's brilliance: "The city wall, faced with green-glazed brick, is 600 lines in circumference and has 12 gates and pagodas at each of the four corners. Within are more than 1,000 monks, all resplendent with gold, silver and cinnabar. The women wear their hair in a top knot ornamented with flowers, pearls and precious stones, and are trained in music and dance."

Whether invasions by the Mons or the silting up of the Ayeyarwady Delta were responsible for Sri Ksetra's gradual decline, no one is absolutely sure, but by the 10th century the capital provided easy pickings for Bagan's army. Today, only the massive, cylindrical brick stupas, now incongruously stranded amidst tranquil fields still give a real sense of the city's former grandeur. None approaches the scale and drama of those at Bagan, but their great antiquity and the site's sleepy, rural feel make for a memorable half day's exploration.

You're permitted to walk around the site, but there's precious little shade and the heat can be infernal. Cycles are forbidden. Foreigners have to

Statue of Aung San on horseback, Pyay.

The four seated Buddha statues of Kyaikpun Pagoda.

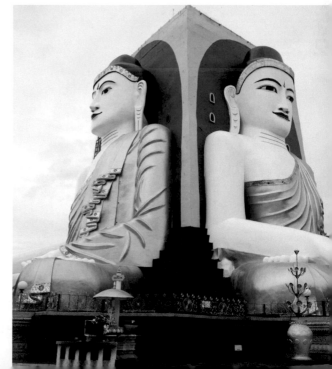

⊙ Tip

The easiest way to get around the sandy tracks threading through the ruins (daily 9am–4pm; charge) is by ox-cart; local drivers appear on arrival at the entrance.

purchase a $5 entry ticket; the warden will also encourage you to buy another $5 ticket for the site museum, but its poorly displayed, desultory collection of votive terracottas, funerary urns and coins doesn't merit the expense, and most of the prize finds dug up here having been taken to London (where many remain on show at the Victoria & Albert Museum) and the National Museum in Yangon.

Approaching via the main road in the north, the first of the large pagodas you pass is the helmet-shaped Payagyi. Dating from the 4th century AD, it's Myanmar's oldest intact stupa – though renovation work has been carried out to its exterior and a golden hti added on top. Further west, just beyond the turning to the site, the equally striking Payamar Pagoda is an exact contemporary of the Payagyi, which local tradition holds enshrines a finger, collar bone and toenail of the Buddha.

Heading further south still from here, through Hmawza village and past its tiny train station, cart drivers make for the vestiges of the Old Palace, scattered over a rectangular enclosure, before striking out across the fields towards the main concentration of monuments beyond the Rahanta Gate. Once clear of the earthworks where the city's south-western entrance, the Rahanda (or Yahanda) Gate, would once have stood, you approach the tiny Rahanda Pagoda, a narrow shrine housing seven sitting Buddhas (there would originally have been eight). Skirting Rahanda Lake, you then come to the site's most famous monument, the 46-metre (150ft) -tall Baw Baw Gyi Pagoda, which dates from the 5th century and served as the prototype for most of Myanmar's ancient stupas. A couple of hundred metres to its east, the Bei Bei Pagoda is a square structure surmounted by three terraces from which an undecorated, round-topped tower rises. Inside it, statues of the Buddha and two of his great disciples peer out of the gloom; look for the ancient Pyu inscriptions on their bases.

Wheeling merchandise through through Pyay market.

SHWEDAUNG

A popular stop on the Ayeyarwady Valley's pilgrimage trail is the **Shwemyetman Pagoda** at **Shwedaung** ⑩, 14km (9 miles) south of Pyay on the main Yangon highway, whose central shrine encloses a laquerware Buddha famous as the only one in Myanmar to wear gold-rimmed spectacles *(myetman)*. Local legend asserts that the original pair were a gift of King Duttabaung in the 4th century AD after the monarch lost his sight – although this seems a little implausible, given that the first historically recorded mention of glasses doesn't appear until the late 13th century, in Italy, almost a thousand years later. A more realistic explanation is that the first pair were donated by a local nobleman sometime during the 17th or 18th centuries, although thieves subsequently stole the sacred specs, and replacement pairs have had to be made on several occasions, including once in the colonial era when the local deputy commissioner, a Mr Hurtno, donated a set of gold-rimmed glasses to the temple to cure his wife's blindness.

BEIKTHANO

Roughly halfway between Pyay and Bagan (and around 65km/40 miles east of the town of Magwe), the remains of the ancient city of **Beikthano** ⑪ are one of Myanmar's most significant, but least known, archaeological sites. Inscribed by Unesco as a World Heritage Site in 2014 (along with the companion sites at Sri Ksetra and Hanlin), Beikthano was the oldest and among the largest of the various Pyu city states which flourished across the Ayeyarwady river basin before the rise of Bagan – and thus quite possibly the oldest of all Burmese cities. Finds excavated here have been dated back to 200 BC, with human occupation of the site lasting at least three centuries, through to the first century AD, if not considerably longer, before being sacked (according to legend) by the army of King Duttabaung, ruler of the younger and more powerful Pyu kingdom of Sri Ksetra.

The city's name translates as "Vishnu City", in honour of the Hindu god, evidence of the strong cultural links which existed between India and the Pyu civilisation in the very earliest days of Burmese history. The ancient city was clearly a place of considerable substance, enclosed by around 8km (5 miles) of 6-metre (20ft) -thick walls and fortifications. The great walls have been significantly eroded, even within living memory, by local villagers carrying off bricks for use elsewhere, and much of the site remains unexcavated, although it's possible to see the remains of a couple of gateways, the royal palace and various monasteries and stupas. There's also a small museum, where it is sometimes possible to pick up a guide to explain the somewhat enigmatic remains. You'll need your own transport to reach the site, which can be visited en route between Pyay and Bagan.

The spectacled Buddha at the Shwemyetman Pagoda in Shwedaung.

📷 GETTING AROUND THE COUNTRY

Travel in Myanmar is seldom boring. The date may be sometime in the 21st century, but some modes of transport hark straight back to colonial times.

Visitors to Myanmar are often amazed at the outmoded and archaic forms of transport in the country. Nevertheless, the clanking old buses, trains and ferries still work, even though they can be frustratingly slow and, in some cases, very polluting. One thing is for sure, however – they add to the fun and charm of travel around the country. With Myanmar largely isolated from the outside world for much of its recent history, practical solutions to getting around had to be found and people had to make do with whatever they had to hand – hence the reliance on animal power and farm equipment such as tractors. So bullock- or ox-carts and horse-drawn carriages – long abandoned in many countries – continue to be seen on the streets today.

A typically overloaded pick-up truck provides a welcome lift to Mount Popa.

RECYCLING CULTURE

The lack of replacement parts also means that where vehicles are available, owners have to be inventive to keep whatever they have on the road. No fuel tank? No problem. Just feed petrol off a plastic tube from a jerry can next to the driver's seat. Vintage cars, including American Jeeps from World War II, and motorbikes are treasured by their owners and no vehicle is considered too old to be of use. With the country opening up to trade, the cars you'll see on the streets are becoming increasingly modern, particularly in the bigger cities. Off the beaten track, however, it's likely to be some time yet before ox-carts, horse-drawn carriages and trishaws disappear completely.

Ox and cart, Inwa, near Mandalay. Some aspects of rural life in Myanmar have barely changed over the centuries.

Cycle rickshaws (trishaws) can still sometimes be seen in Myanmar's towns and cities.

Catching the ferry to Dalah from downtown Yangon.

The evolution of river boats

The classic form of travel in Myanmar is by river. The ancient Burmese kings travelled in resplendent royal barges powered by 30 to 40 oarsmen. Ordinary folk sailed on steamers operated by the Irrawaddy Flotilla Company which started operations in 1865. In its heyday in the 1930s, 602 vessels were ferrying 9 million passengers and tonnes of goods along the river from Yangon as far north as Bhamo. The company's barges and steamers are long gone (many were scuttled into the Ayeyarwady during World War II to prevent them from falling into Japanese hands), replaced by double-decker diesel-powered riverboats. Until recently, tourists could only travel on these boats, sitting on bare floors, crammed in with other passengers and their goods. Despite the lack of comfort, this is still a great way to see the unfolding scenes on the banks of the river. Today, newer vessels and luxury cruise ships are available to foreign visitors (for more on travelling on Myanmar's rivers, see page 309).

Rough-and-ready transport in rural Myanmar.

Horse and carriage transport gives a clue to Pyin U-Lwin's resort status.

Pre-war, rickety, smoke-spewing buses chug along in the major cities replete with wooden gear-sticks and planks for floors.

Boats on Taungthaman Lake at sunset, Amarapura.

A tree-lined road offers welcome shade on the way to Inwa.

MANDALAY AND ENVIRONS

Mandalay is not only Myanmar's cultural heartland,
but also the spiritual hub of Buddhism in the country.

Detail of teak carving,
Shwe In Bin Kyaung,
Mandalay.

Mandalay is the country's second city, a major commercial
centre and the cultural heart of Myanmar. Originally established by King Mindon in 1857 as his new capital, the city
also became a focal point for the teaching of Buddhism and
the preservation of Burmese cultural traditions.

Mandalay did not survive long as the "Golden City" of
Buddhist teachings, but today, despite the pre-eminence of
Yangon, the city maintains its position as Myanmar's main
religious centre, with numerous splendid pagodas and some
two-thirds of all the country's monks still living in the area.

As a result of its proximity to China, Mandalay has benefited
greatly from a recent influx of investment, with the construction of a whole
array of new hotels and commercial buildings – although such development
has done little to enhance the city's character. The upgraded
airport has also made the city more accessible than ever.

U Min Thonze Pagoda, Sagaing.

Despite Mandalay's attractions, the real soul of the place
lies in the various ancient capitals and pagoda complexes
scattered in the surrounding countryside, offering captivating reminders of the region's glorious past. These include the
three former capitals of Amarapura, Inwa (Ava) and Sagaing,
as well as the town of Mingun. All offer abundant evidence of
the power of Upper Burma between the 14th and 19th centuries, between the fall of Bagan and the British occupation.

Sagaing was the capital of Shan-dominated Upper Burma
for a brief period beginning in 1315. In 1364 the seat of government was shifted to Inwa, where it remained for almost 400 years.

Shwebo (Moksobo) was the royal capital from 1760 to 1764, after which the
government returned to Inwa (Ava) before King Bodawpaya moved the capital
once again to the newly built palace of Amarapura. Inwa served as capital of
Upper Burma again between 1823 and 1841, after which it returned to Amarapura for a further 20 years before finally coming to rest in Mandalay during
the rule of King Mindon.

Further afield – in the foothills of the Shan Plateau – the former British hill
station of Pyin U-Lwin (Maymyo) has become one of the north's most popular
tourist destinations. It offers a complete change of scenery, thanks to its mild
climate, manicured gardens, quaint atmosphere and colonial trappings.

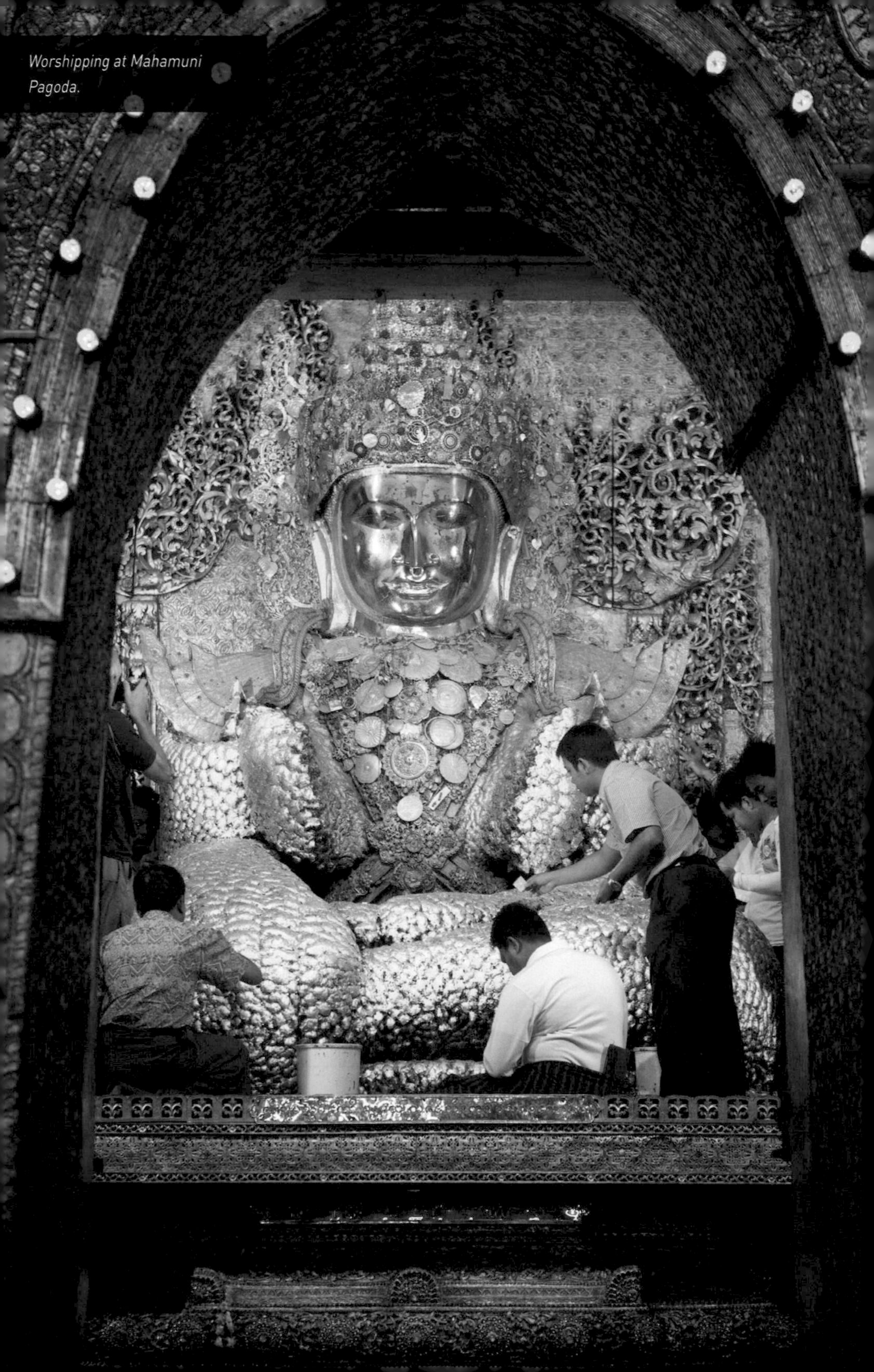

Worshipping at Mahamuni Pagoda.

MANDALAY

The cultural capital of Myanmar, Mandalay is dominated by monument-strewn Mandalay Hill, while the grid of dusty streets below is home to many hidden gems, despite its lack of obvious charms.

Since its creation as a royal capital midway through the 19th century, **Mandalay** has been a byword for everything that's most exotic about Myanmar – from gilded pagodas to secretive walled palaces filled with precious stones and courtiers dressed in elaborate, heavily bejewelled costumes. The modern reality is somewhat more prosaic, with traffic, dust, fumes and bleak concrete architecture dominating most arrivals' first impressions. But give Myanmar's second city some time and its leafier fringes, in particular, can yield up fascinating vestiges of the elaborate courtly culture and arcane religious rituals that all but disappeared following the British invasion of 1885.

The city was founded in 1857 by King Mindon in fulfilment of an ancient Buddhist prophecy. It is said that Gautama Buddha had once visited Mandalay Hill with his disciple, Ananda, proclaiming that on the 2,400th anniversary of his death a metropolis of Buddhist teaching would be founded at its foot. The vision came true when Mindon deposed his half-brother Pagan Min as the Konbaung ruler and moved his capital – with 150,000 people and most of the palace – from Amarapura, 20km (12 miles) away, to establish the fabled "Golden City" foreseen in the Buddhist scriptures.

Mindon's vision, however, was short-lived. On his death in 1878, he was

Shwe In Bin Kyaung.

succeeded by King Thibaw and his imperious wife, Supalayat – Myanmar's own Lady Macbeth, who had many of her friends and relatives killed during King Mindon's last days to ensure that Thibaw would inherit the throne. Their excesses, along with the king's courting of the French, provided just the excuse the British needed to sail up the Ayeyarwady from Rangoon with a fleet of gunboats and army of Indian sepoys to annexe Upper Burma in 1885. Unprepared for the showdown, King Thibaw handed the town over to General Prendergast

⊘ Main attractions
Mandalay Hill
Shwe Nandaw Kyaung
The Royal Palace
Maha Muni Pagoda
Gold Leaf Workshops
Boat to Bagan

Map on page 170

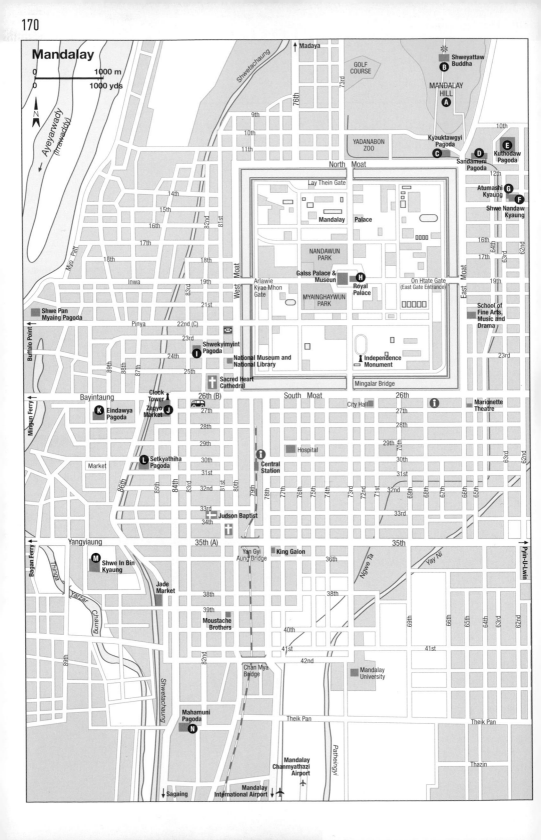

without a shot being fired and meekly went into exile with his queen. The surrounding countryside descended into anarchy, and Mandalay became just another British colonial outpost.

Although its treasures were looted by Prendergast's men, the palace's carved teak buildings survived largely intact – only to be destroyed by Allied bombers in 1945 after the Japanese had commandeered the complex as a supplies store. Mindon's resplendent "Golden City", the last of Asia's great wooden palace complexes, was reduced to ashes by the raid; only its walls and moat, and a couple of minor structures, remained intact.

Another series of devastating fires ripped through the heart of Mandalay in the 1980s. More than 23,000 people were left homeless in the wake of the infernos, and whole districts razed. Many of these newly created urban wastelands were snapped up by Chinese immigrants from Yunnan, heralding a huge influx from across the border; between 30 and 40 percent of Mandalay's million-strong population are now of Chinese origin. Although a source of controversy among native Burmese, their presence has revitalised the local economy, with high-rise buildings and shopping malls erected by Chinese entrepreneurs now punctuating the largely low-rise skyline downtown.

In most respects, though, Mandalay remains, first and foremost, a hub of Burmese cultural traditions. Although Mindon's plan to make his capital a centre of Buddhist teaching was thwarted, more than 700 monasteries survive here, while the city is a bastion of Burmese classical music and dance, as well as other traditional arts and crafts.

The way to get your bearings on arrival is by ascending Mandalay Hill, the sacred, stupa-encrusted hillock overlooking the northeast corner of the royal palace, from where a mesmerising panorama extends over the city and its flat environs of riverine rice fields. Visible immediately below is the giant square of the royal enclosure, with its vast moats and walls. Mandalay's most illustrious pagodas and monasteries are clustered outside the palace's northeast corner. The rest of the sights, including the markets and craftsmen's quarters, lie further south and west towards to river.

NORTH MANDALAY

The area to the north and east of downtown is dominated by the palace and hill overlooking it, around whose base are dotted some of Mandalay's most revered pagodas and monasteries. It's a district best explored on foot, in the relatively cool hours of morning or early evening. The top of Mandalay Hill itself is reached via covered walkways – a walk up of around 45 minutes. The most popular is the southern one, flanked by a pair of colossal, white-painted *chinthe*. Alternatively, you can take a taxi up a long, looping road that climbs to the foot of an escalator near the top.

MANDALAY HILL

Rising 240 metres (790ft) above the city and its surrounding plains, **Mandalay Hill Ⓐ** (daily 24hr; free except for

> **Ⓞ Tip**
>
> Entry for foreigners to Mandalay's principal sights is by means of a $10 combination ticket, valid for five days from its first use. Proceeds go to the Burmese government.

Small stupas line the steps up Mandalay hill.

Atop Mandalay Hill.

uppermost platform) has been an important pilgrimage site for Burmese Buddhists since King Mindon sited his palace at its foot in the mid-19th century. Aside from the meritorious ascent of its sacred stairways to reach the hilltop's richly decorated shrines, the main reason to make the climb is for the spellbinding views from the summit, which extend for many kilometres in every direction.

The most popular route up is from the south (remember to take off your shoes at the bottom), comprising 1,729 steps shaded by a roof that keeps the stone cool and protects visitors from the sun while still allowing fresh air to circulate. Along the way, astrologers and souvenir peddlers ply their trades, while monks, nuns and Burmese pilgrims scale the steps. About halfway up you'll encounter the first large temple, which is said to contain three bones of the Buddha originally unearthed in Peshawar, Pakistan.

The four different stairways converge two-thirds of the way up the hill on the gold-plated **Shweyattaw Buddha** Ⓑ, his outstretched hand pointing to the spot where the Royal Palace was built. This stance is unique in the Theravada world, symbolising Gautama Buddha's prophecy which King Mindon realised in 1857 when he moved his capital to Mandalay.

Further up the steps rests another unusual statue – that of a woman kneeling in front of the Buddha, offering him her two severed breasts. According to legend, Sanda Moke Khit was an ogress who was so overwhelmed by the Master's teachings that she decided to devote the rest of her life to following him. As a sign of humility, she cut off her breasts. When the ogress's brother asked the Buddha why he smiled as he accepted the gift, he replied that Sanda Moke Khit had collected so many merits that in a future life she would be reborn Min Done (Mindon), the King of Mandalay.

The view from the summit is phenomenal. To the west lies the Ayeyarwady and beyond that, crowned with pagodas and temples, the Sagaing and Mingun hills. To the north, the rice-growing plains of the Ayeyarwady valley extend into the distance. The purple Shan Plateau can

be seen in the east. To the south, in the midst of this vast plain, lies the city of Mandalay and the palace complex.

British and Commonwealth troops suffered heavy casualties here in 1945 when they stormed the hill to oust its Japanese defenders, resorting to bitter hand-to-hand fighting that lasted for days. A British regimental insignia is the only visible remains of the battle.

KYAUKTAWGYI PAGODA

Diagonally opposite the South Stairway, with its giant *chinthe*, is the **Kyauktawgyi Pagoda C** (daily 5am–7pm; charge). Work on the temple began in 1853 to a plan modelled on the Ananda Paya at Bagan. Completed in 1878, its focal point is a huge Buddha figure carved from a single block of marble from the Sagyin quarry – an undertaking of Herculean proportions. An estimated 10,000 men took 13 days to transport the rock from the Ayeyarwady to the pagoda site. The 20 figures on each side of the image represent the Buddha's disciples, while a painting of King Mindon hangs inside the pagoda.

SANDAMUNI PAGODA

To the east of the Kyauktawgyi temple, the **Sandamuni Pagoda D** (daily 6am–9pm; free) was built on the site of King Mindon's temporary palace where he resided while the main walled complex was under construction. It was erected over the burial place of Mindon's younger brother, Crown Prince Kanaung, who was assassinated in an unsuccessful palace revolution in 1866. The Pagoda is famous for its commentaries on the *Tripitaka* (Buddhist scriptures), chiselled onto 1,774 stone tablets, with each tablet housed in its own miniature stupa. It's also home to the mighty Sandamuni Buddha, after which the pagoda is named. The largest iron Buddha image in Myanmar, it's fashioned from almost twenty tons of iron, covered in gold leaf.

KUTHODAW PAGODA

Further to the east, at the base of Mandalay Hill's southeast stairway and surrounded by a high wall, is Mindon's **Kuthodaw Pagoda E** (daily 6am–9pm; covered by the Mandalay Combination Ticket). Its central structure, the 30-metre (100ft) -high Maha Lawka Marazein stupa, built in 1857, was modelled on the Shwezigon Paya at Nyaung U in Bagan. The 729 whitewashed pagodas that surround it were erected in 1872 during the Fifth Buddhist Synod to individually house the marble tablets upon which, for the first time, the entire *Tripitaka* was recorded in Pali, veneered with gold leaf. The inscriptions here and at the Sandamuni Pagoda are often collectively described as "the world's largest book" – it took 2,400 monks six months just to recite the Kuthodaw carved texts when they were first unveiled.

The Kuthodaw Pagoda was comprehensively plundered during the annexation of 1885. British looters stripped the *hti* of its precious stones, peeled the gold leaf from the pagoda, carried

Chinthe at the foot of Mandalay hill.

Kuthodaw Paya.

Inscribed slabs of marble, Kuthodaw Paya.

off 6,570 brass bells from the subsidiary stupas, disfigured statues and used the stone tablets of the *Tripitaka* to build a military road. It took over a decade to repair the damage.

SHWE NANDAW KYAUNG

At one time part of the royal palace, the **Shwe Nandaw Kyaung** Ⓕ (daily 9am–5pm; covered by the Mandalay Combination Ticket) is the only building from Mindon's "Golden City" to have come through World War II bombing intact. The building was dismantled and moved, piece by piece, to its present site by Thibaw after his father died inside it. Thibaw initially used the building for private meditation, but later gave it to the monks as a monastery (*kyaung*). The *kyaung*'s miraculous survival amidst the devastation of World War II means that this is now the only place in the city where visitors can get a real idea of the sumptuous interiors of Asia's last great pre-colonial teak palace complex. Intricate woodcarvings of ornamental figures and flowers adorn most of its surfaces, although the gold-plating and

Downtown Mandalay.

glass mosaics which formerly covered the monastery both inside and out have now vanished, bar the gold layered on the imposing ceiling. Thibaw's couch and a replica of the royal throne are displayed inside.

ATUMASHI KYAUNG

Next to the Shwe Nandaw stands the yellow-ochre and white-painted **Atumashi Kyaung** Ⓖ (daily 9am–5pm; covered by the Mandalay Combination Ticket) or the "Incomparable Monastery". A structure of extraordinary splendour, routinely described by European visitors in the 19th century as "one of the most beautiful buildings in all of Mandalay", it burnt down in 1890 but has since been extensively restored and is now said to approximate its former glory. A famous Buddha image – clothed in silk, coated with lacquer and with an enormous diamond set in its forehead – was once the pride of the shrine, but was stolen during the British seizure of Mandalay in 1885 and never returned.

THE ROYAL PALACE

Mindon's **Royal Palace** Ⓗ (daily 8am–5pm; entrance with Mandalay Combination Ticket) was the last in a long line of fortified royal citadels erected on the banks of the Ayeyarwady by successive Burmese rulers. All followed an almost identical ancient Brahmin–Buddhist blueprint, conceived in the form of a giant "mandala", or sacred diagram, representing the Cosmos with Mt Meru – here symbolised by the royal Throne Room – at its heart. Divided into 16 portions by straight roads, the square was enclosed by 8km (5 miles) of outer walls and a 64-metre (210ft) -wide moat. Twelve gates pierced this formidable perimeter, corresponding to the signs of the zodiac. Each is said to have been inaugurated with a human sacrifice: a total of 52 men, women and children (plucked at random from unfortunate passers-by) were buried under teak

posts at each of the entrances to protect the palace's most vulnerable points in the event of attack.

Much of the palace originally comprised buildings from Amarapura, which were dismantled, transported and then re-assembled block by block *in situ in Mandalay*. Centrepiece of the complex was the **Lion Room**, where Myanmar's last two kings held court on a sumptuously carved and gilded throne (now displayed in Yangon's National Museum). From its roof rose a seventiered, 78-metre (250ft) -high *pyathat* canopy, embellished with jewels and gold leaf. With its forest of gleaming finials, upswept eaves and staggeringly elaborate carvings, the teak-built complex must have been an astonishing sight. Sadly, most of its treasures, including the famous library and hoard of rubies and other precious stones kept in the royal treasury, were looted by Prendergast's army in 1885, after which the royal apartments, shrine rooms and assembly halls were commandeered for use as a barracks and the entire complex ignominiously renamed Fort Dufferin. Finally, in 1945, during the battle to retake the city from the Japanese, Allied bombers razed all but a few fragments of Mandalay Palace.

Most of what you see today inside the walls dates from the 1990s, the fruit of a major rebuilding project by the Burmese government. However, rather than employing traditional artisans and materials to replicate the "Golden City" of King Mindon and his son, corrugated iron and concrete were extensively used by the military's architects and the results bear little resemblance to the originals, though they do succeed in at least conveying the scale of the 19th-century campus.

The visitors' entrance is via the **East Gate**, from where a broad central avenue leads to the core of the former palace – the only part open to the public (the rest of the area being in military use). Of the 40 or so reconstructed buildings, the most impressive are the **Throne Room** and (a short distance to the west) the so-called **Glass Palace**, where Thibaw lived amid great pomp and luxury until the British

Details of teak carvings at Shwe Nandaw Kyaung Monastery.

Shwe Nandaw Kyaung Monastery.

⊙ Tip

At the far west end of 22nd Street/Pinya Road (aka C Road), the waterside **Buffalo Point** is a good spot from which to watch water buffalo hauling hardwood logs floated down the Shweli and the Ayeyarwady rivers from the north – especially picturesque at sunset.

occupation. The latter now houses a small **museum** with exhibits including Thibaw's crystal-pillared four-poster bed. You can also scale the curious, spiral-shaped **Watchtower** from which Queen Supalayat is said to have followed the progress of the invading British Expeditionary Force up the Ayeyarwady in 1885.

CENTRAL MANDALAY

The hectic traffic and lacklustre concrete architecture of the downtown area immediately south and west of the palace don't exactly encourage exploration, although there are a handful of temples worth taking in if you have time, as well as a bustling market quarter, while the cooling breezes and intriguing sights of the riverfront area lie only a short ride west.

On 24th Road between 82nd and 83rd streets, the **Shwekyimyint Pagoda ❶** is the oldest Buddhist shrine in Mandalay. Erected in 1167 by Prince Minshinsaw, the exiled son of King Alaungsithu of Bagan, it houses a Buddha image consecrated by the prince himself, along with a collection of further gold and silver Buddha figures collected by later Burmese kings. The images (which were brought here from the Royal Palace during the British occupation for safekeeping) are brought out for public veneration on religious occasions.

In a pavilion at the back of the pagoda precinct is an unusual reclining Buddha depicted on a long throne with an upright torso. Shimmering glass mosaics encrust the walls of the shrine chamber in which the image rests, separated from the remainder of the room by a delicately carved wooden screen.

A couple of blocks southwest, **Zegyo Market ❶**, on 84th Street between 26th and 28th roads, is Mandalay's most important bazaar and a great place for aimless wandering and people-watching, as well as souvenir hunting. The colonial-era buildings that originally stood here burned down long ago and have now been replaced by modern, Chinese-style precincts. As well as fresh produce and flowers, you'll find local handicrafts, clothes, jewellery and furniture shops crammed into the narrow back lanes.

Beating gold with a hammer in the Gold Pounders' district.

⊙ THE MOUSTACHE BROTHERS

The offbeat, slightly surreal comedy show known as the Moustache Brothers is performed every evening in a cramped garage off 39th Street. Rooted in a Burmese brand of vaudeville known as *anyeint*, performances combine clowning with traditional dance, puppetry and satire.

There were originally three "brothers" (Par Par Lay, Lu Maw and their cousin, Lu Zaw); Par Par Lay died in 2013 and Lu Zaw has largely retired from acting, although Lu Maw continues to perform nightly, with assistance from his wife. The trio made international headlines in 1996 after they poked fun at Myanmar's ruling generals. The jokes landed them in dire trouble and two of the brothers received seven years in a hard labour camp. Thanks to a high-profile Amnesty campaign, they were released after five-and-a-half years on the condition they would never do their act in Burmese again. So, at 8.30pm most evenings, you can watch the routine in accented English – a unique way to spend an idle evening in Mandalay.

Apart from earning them a living wage, the Moustache Brothers' international notoriety also brought them some protection from political persecution – although Par Par Lay was imprisoned again for 36 days following the 2007 unrest. The advent of democracy has done little to blunt the edge of Lu Maw's satire, who continues to make fun of everyone from members of the former military junta to Donald Trump.

The **Eindawya Pagoda** , at the western edge of the market district on 27th Road and 89th Street, is one of downtown's most visible landmarks thanks to its brilliantly gilded stupa, with classic bell-shaped dome and octagonal base, built in 1847 by King Pagan Min. The pagoda enshrines an ancient chalcedony Buddha figure brought to Burma in 1839 from Bodhgaya in India, where Gautama achieved enlightenment.

At 31st Road and 85th Street, four blocks south of the Eindawya, stands the **Setkyathiha Pagoda** , which was rebuilt after being badly damaged in World War II. The richly gilded stupa contains a 5-metre (16ft) -high bronze Buddha, cast at Inwa (Ava) by King Bagyidaw in 1823. Overlooking the terrace is a "golden rock" similar to the one at Kaikhthiyo, and a Bodhi tree planted by U Nu, the country's first post-Independence prime minister.

For a break from the mayhem of downtown, head west along 26th Street (Bayintaung Road) to reach the **riverfront**, where you can while away an hour or two watching cargo boats unloading at the jetties. A marvellous view extends across the Ayeyarwady to Sagaing and the Mingun hills, on the river's west bank, studded with pagodas and monasteries.

SOUTH MANDALAY

The trip out to Amarapura and Sagaing leads through the densely packed districts of south Mandalay, where it's worth pausing to admire the city's most important religious complex, the Mahamuni Pagoda, the fascinating craftworkers' quarter surrounding it and the splendidly atmospheric Shwe In Bin monastery.

SHWE IN BIN KYAUNG

One of Mandalay's few surviving antique wooden buildings, the beautiful **Shwe In Bin Kyaung** , situated just south of 35th Road in the heart of the city's monastery district, was donated by a pair of

wealthy Chinese jade merchants at the end of the 19th century. Richly carved with decorative motifs and scenes from the Buddha's life, it retains a delightfully tranquil, off-the-beaten-track feel. Come early in the morning and you'll catch hundreds of monks streaming through its precinct and out into the surrounding tree-lined lanes on their way to collect alms.

One block southeast of the Shwe In Bin Kyaung, Mandalay's bustling **Jade Market** (charge) on 38th Street attracts huge numbers of Chinese businessmen and tourists, with vast quantities of jade stone and assorted artefacts on display at the market's open-air stalls. You can also see stones being crafted at the workshops on the eastern side of the market.

MAHAMUNI PAGODA

The **Mahamuni Pagoda** (charge), 3km (2 miles) south of the city centre on the road to Amarapura, is the most revered Buddhist shrine in Mandalay (and second, in national terms, only to the Shwedagon), thanks to the presence

Jade traders at the Jade Market.

⊘ Tip

Makers of oiled bamboo paper can be found on Mandalay's 37th Road. The oiled paper, used to divide layers of gold leaf, takes three years to make using bamboo which is soaked, beaten flat and then dried.

in its central chamber of a magnificent gold Buddha image – the eponymous "Mahamuni", or "Great Sage" – which Bodawpaya's troops took from Mrauk-U during their pillage of that city of 1784. Revered by pilgrims from all over the world, it is believed to have been one of only five likenesses of the Enlightened One made during his lifetime, although historical evidence suggests the statue was probably cast in AD 146, five or more centuries after the Buddha's death.

A striking feature of the image's body, rising to 3.8 metres (12ft 8ins) in height, is its covering of pounded gold. So many leaves have been pressed on to it as offerings that they now form a 15cm (6in) -thick, lumpy carapace extending all the way around the back. The Buddha's face, however, remains gleaming, as it is lovingly polished twice each day at 4.30am and 4pm by the monks.

The present temple complex is largely modern and undistinguished, its predecessor having been destroyed by fire during Thibaw's reign in the late 19th century. In its northern corner, a cement structure houses six magnificent bronze statues also looted from the former Arakan capital, Mrauk-U (all that remain of the 30 statues originally plundered – the rest having been melted down to make cannonballs by King Thibaw). Representing Hindu deities, the statues are of Khmer origin and once stood in the great temple of Angkor Wat. Pilgrims believe them to possess healing powers, and rub the body parts of the statues corresponding to their own afflictions, which have left them with burnished patches.

CRAFTSMEN'S QUARTER

The streets around the Mahamuni Pagoda are home to Mandalay's craftsmen's quarter. Using the same skills and methods as their forefathers, the main focus of their work is of course religious sculptures – Buddha images, Buddha footprints, lotus-blossom pedestals and even (a throwback to colonial days) the occasional statue of the Virgin Mary. You can see Buddha figures being hewn from alabaster and marble by stonemasons in the streets around the southwest side of the Mahamuni Pagoda.

West of the Mahamuni are the workshops of artisans producing pagoda items, a booming trade given the Burmese propensity to seek merit through the building and renovation of pagodas. Not far away, woodcarvers create more Buddhas, as well as altars for worship at home and in pagodas. Foundry workers, meanwhile, cast replicas of ancient Buddha images and musical instruments.

Gold leaf is produced in a large number of workshops in the southeastern section of Mandalay. This venerable craft is extremely old, and even in the 21st century, the manufacturing process is carried out according to a time-honoured tradition. Further artisans can be seen at work in other locations in and around Mandalay – the skilled silk and cotton weavers of Amarapura are particularly interesting.

⊘ GOLD LEAF MAKING

The making of gold leaves is one of the country's most characteristic cottage industries. To the devout, applying gold leaf to a statue of the Buddha is a sign of reverence, and Burmese visiting a pagoda will often buy a packet of gold leaves at one of the temple bazaars to paste onto a Buddha statue, stupa or other religious object. Mandalay has several workshops engaged solely in the production of these gold leaves. Gold leaf can also be used to make traditional medicines, as well as cosmetics.

Typically, a worker begins with a 2.5cm x 1cm (1in x 0.4in) gold leaf. To get an idea of their delicacy, 200 of these leaves weigh just 12 grams (0.4oz). The leaf is pounded with a wooden mallet for half an hour, resized, then pounded again for about one hour, resized and then again pounded for another five hours.

Workers then take the ultra-thin pieces with which they manufacture individual 2.5 sq cm (0.4 sq inch) gold leaves before packaging them in multiples of 10. The original piece is enough to make about one packet of leaves, which normally sells for around K2,000.

Visitors are welcome to drop in at King Galon at 108, 36th Street between 77th and 78th streets to witness the leaf-making process.

BY BOAT FROM MANDALAY TO BAGAN

The classic way to travel south to the ruins of Bagan is along the Ayeyarwady, the old "Road to Mandalay" as the British dubbed Myanmar's greatest river.

An increasing number of tour operators now offer luxury cruises as part of their package holidays. These vary in price and quality, depending on the vessel used, and can last from anywhere between one to three nights, with stops at places of interest along the route.

Market leaders include Belmond (www.belmond.com) and Pandaw (www.pandaw.com), whose boats are replicas of the old "double-decker" Irrawaddy Flotilla Company steamers. Travellers on more modest budgets, meanwhile, take rather less ritzy ferries from Mandalay to Bagan, run by three local private operators: Malikha River Cruises (www.malikha-rivercruises.com), Myanmar Golden River Group (MGRG; www.mgrg-express.com) and Shwe Keinnery (www.rvshwekeinnery-cruise.com). Tickets cost $42, with daily services leaving at around 7am and taking around 10 hours to get from Mandalay to Bagan.

RIVER SIGHTS

Heading south from Mandalay towards Bagan, the first 36km (20-mile) stretch of the Ayeyarwady passes the densest cluster of religious and historical sites anywhere in Myanmar, including the former capitals of Amarapura and Inwa (Ava), and the bristling hilltop stupas of Sagaing.

Between Inwa and Sagaing, the river flows for a short while towards the west before turning south again. The **Ava** (Inwa) bridge, which runs across the road and railway line to Myitkyina, was the first bridge over the river when it was built in 1934. Destroyed during World War II, it was rebuilt in 1954. Shortly after navigating this part of the river's treacherous shoals, boats pass the confluence with the Mu river that drains from Sagaing province.

Boats travel on to **Yandabo**, where the treaty that ceded Assam, Rakhine and Tanintharyi to the British was signed in 1825. Yandabo, which can only be accessed by river, is well known for its terracotta pottery, which is made with the yellow mud collected from the river bank. Further south is a shallow stretch along the confluence with the Chindwin and its many shifting sandbanks. If travelling on a local slowboat at low water, this is where the boat has the most chance of running aground. When this happens, it can take hours before the boat is ready to be refloated.

Once the boat has turned south again, the heartland of the Bamar people lies to the left. This land south of Mandalay, which has benefited from the irrigation of more than 2,000 years, was the breadbasket that fed the various Burmese kingdoms. Its surplus permitted the development of the advanced civilisation that started with the First Burmese Empire in the 11th century.

Passing **Myingyan** during the dry season, one can feel the dust and heat that bakes this part of the country where rain is scarce. Eventually, boats reach **Pakokku,** worth visiting for its bustling market and workshops producing handwoven cloth and local cigars, while you'll also see the majestic Pakokku bridge, at 3.4km (2 miles) the longest in Myanmar. Past Pakokku, it's another 25km (15.5 miles) to the jetty at **Nyaung U**, the jumping-off point for Bagan.

Deck view from the Road to Mandalay boat (Orient Express).

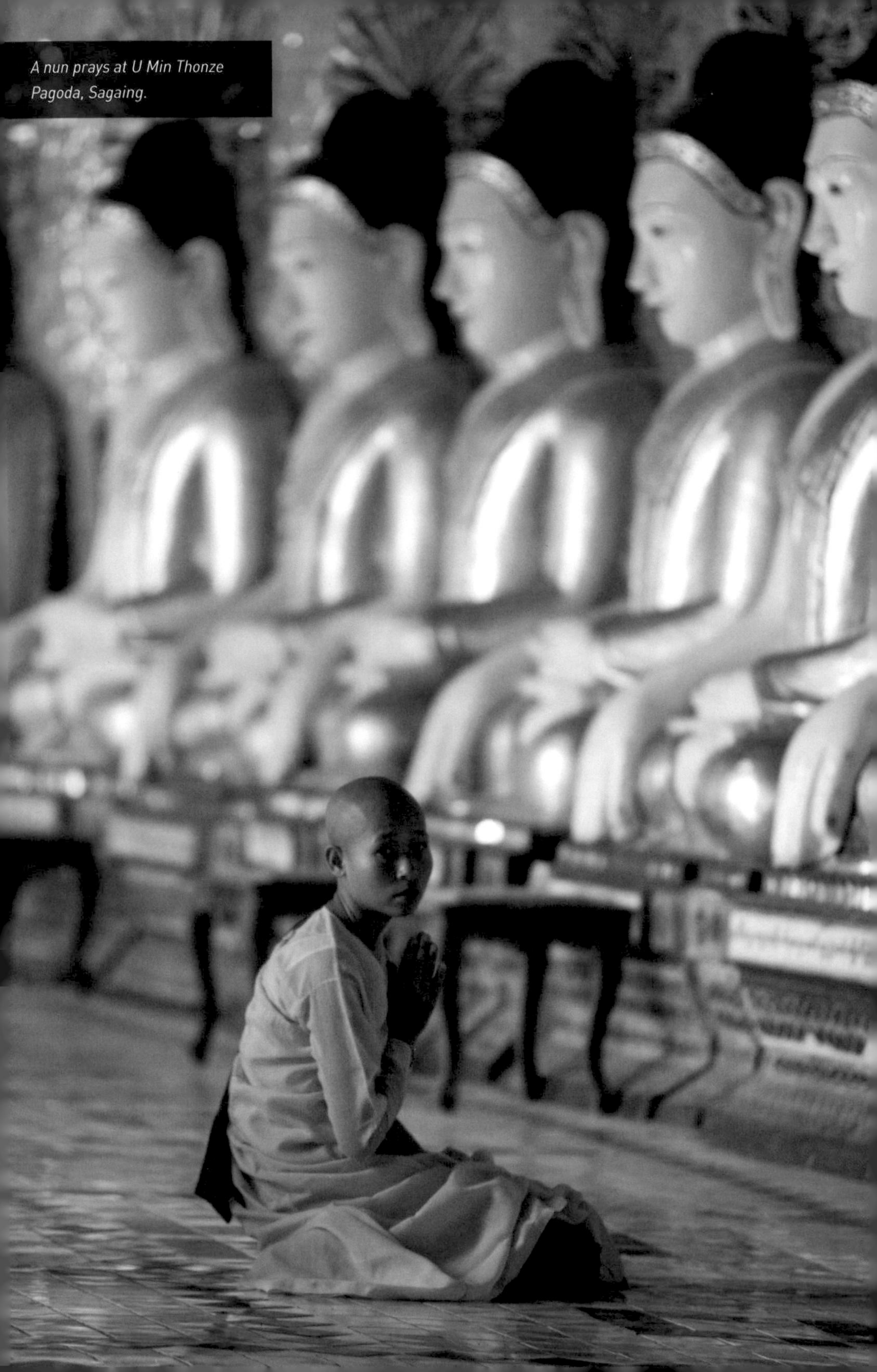

A nun prays at U Min Thonze Pagoda, Sagaing.

AROUND MANDALAY

The area around Mandalay is one of the most varied and interesting in Myanmar, with attractions ranging from the ancient city of Amarapura to the sacred shrines of Sagaing and the colonial hill station of Pyin U-Lwin.

For the majority of visitors to **Mandalay ❶**, the attractions of the modern city pale next to the wonders hidden in the surrounding countryside. Clustered along the banks of the Ayeyarwady amid the vestiges of former capitals and ancient pilgrimage places are some of Myanmar's most iconic sights: the famous U Bein Bridge, a teak causeway along which streams of villagers and red-robed monks file each morning and evening; the exquisitely carved Bagaya Kyaung wooden monastery at Inwa; and the vast, red-brick cube of Bodawpaya's unfinished stupa at Mingun.

These alone hold enough interest to fill two or three days of sightseeing. But with a little more time you could make a foray west to the market town of Monywa, springboard for another crop of amazing Theravada sites: the ornate Thanboddhay Pagoda, where more than half a million Buddha images are enshrined amid a forest of multicoloured stupas; a medieval cave complex hewn from solid rock at Hpo Win Tang; and a pair of gargantuan Buddha images – one standing, one reclining – rising from a hilltop at Bodhi Tataung.

After touring the rivers and bumpy back roads of Mandalay's hinterland, you'll be more than ready for a respite from the heat, and the hill station

of Pyin U-Lwin, on the fringes of the Shan Plateau a day's journey northeast of the city, provides the perfect setting for a recuperative spell away from the plains, just as it did for the British *burra sahibs* who founded the town in the 19th century.

Finally, further highlights await heading south down the highway to Yangon, including the attractive town of Meiktila, with its lakeside temples and shrines, and the sprawling modern capital of Naypyidaw – a bizarre monument to the megalomania and

⊙ Main attractions
Amarapura
Inwa
Sagaing
Mingun
Taungbyon Nat Pwe
Bodhi Tataung
Pyin U-Lwin

Map on page 182

On Taungthaman Lake, Amarapura.

Tip

You can travel across Lake Taungthaman one way by oar-powered gondola to the Kyauktawgyi Pagoda, then return by walking over U Bein's Bridge to get a perspective of the lake's size. Sunset is a good time to cross the bridge for the views.

bombast of the country's former ruling generals.

AMARAPURA

Founded by King Bodawpaya in 1782, **Amarapura** ➋ – "City of Immortality" – is the youngest of the royal capitals near Mandalay. It replaced Inwa (Ava), around 7km (4.5 miles) southwest, on the advice of royal astrologers, who were concerned about the bloody way in which the king had ascended to the throne. In May 1783, the court and entire population duly packed up their belongings and shifted to land allocated to them around a newly built palace, surrounded by a wall 1.6km (1 mile) in circumference, with a pagoda standing at each of its four corners. The site, however, would be occupied for less than 70 years. In 1857, King Mindon dismantled the royal enclave and transported it to a completely new location, 11km (7 miles) further north at the foot of Mandalay Hill.

Today a town of 10,000 inhabitants, the former capital has almost merged with the southern fringes of greater Mandalay, but still preserves a markedly different feel to the big city, with streets draped around the leafy shores of a shallow lake. Many of Amarapura's families are engaged in the silk industry, weaving the exquisite *acheik htamein* (ceremonial *longyis*) worn on special occasions by Burmese women. Every second house seems to hold a weaver's workshop, and the clickety-clack of looms forms a constant soundtrack as you stroll around. Amarapura's other traditional industry is bronze casting: cymbals, gongs and images of the Buddha are made here out of a special alloy of bronze and lead.

Amarapura's major sight, the U Bein Bridge, is at the far southern end of town, while most of the other points of interest are grouped around the north of the lake, meaning you'll need a taxi or bicycle to get around the sights if travelling independently. Come early in the morning or late in the afternoon to avoid the large tour groups: Amarapura and its teak bridge get swamped in peak season.

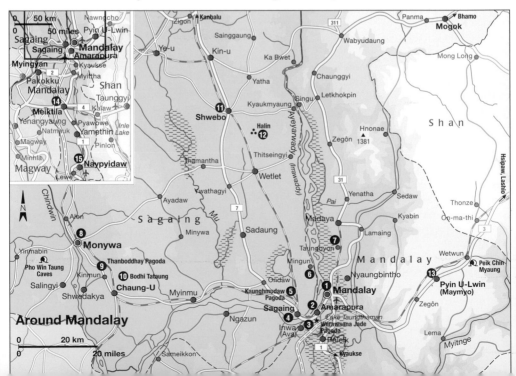

AMARAPURA'S MAIN SIGHTS

Today, virtually nothing remains of the former **Royal Palace**, situated to the east of Amarapura's centre (between a military base and timber yard). Some of the wooden buildings were reconstructed in Mandalay by Mindon, while the walls that were left standing were used by the British as a source of cheap material for roads and railways. The four pagodas which once marked the corners of the city wall, however, can still be seen, as can two stone buildings – the treasury and the old watchtower. The graves of Bodawpaya and Bagyidaw also survive.

In the southern part of town sits the well-preserved **Pahtodawgyi Pagoda**, built by King Bagyidaw in 1820. A bell-shaped stupa, it stands on five terraces which are covered with *Jataka* reliefs. An inscription stone nearby tells the story of the construction of the pagoda.

Amarapura also holds one of the largest monasteries in Myanmar. The presence of up to 1,200 monks (during the Buddhist Lent) in the **Mahagandhayon Monastery** contributes to the religious atmosphere of the city. Visitors are welcome and it is a spectacular sight to witness the hundreds of monks lining up for their one daily meal every morning at 10am – though don't expect to be alone. Busloads of foreigners descend on the refectory to photograph the spectacle.

U BEIN BRIDGE

To the south of Amarapura lies Lake Taungthaman, a seasonal body of water which dries up in the winter, leaving fertile arable land in its wake. The southern side of the lake is spanned by the 1.2km (0.7-mile) -long **U Bein Bridge**, little altered in two centuries, which was constructed using thousands of teak planks salvaged from the buildings of Inwa by King Bodawpaya's mayor U Bein following the move to Amarapura. The best time to view the bridge is early in the morning, when hundreds of locals – from farmers and market stallholders to groups of monks – plod over it, to the delight of the bus parties of

Crossing Taungthaman lake by boat, U Bein bridge in the background.

Maha Gandayon Monastery, Amarapura.

Crossing U Bein bridge.

foreign tourists who turn up in droves at the little boat jetty on the far western side, where they're met by crowds of gee-gaw and postcard sellers. You can, however, bypass the crowds by starting your visit from the far, eastern side.

KYAUKTAWGYI PAGODA

In the middle of a widely scattered village on the east side of U Bein Bridge is the **Kyauktawgyi Pagoda**, built by King Pagan in 1847. Like the Kyauktawgyi in Mandalay, it was designed as an (albeit scaled-down) copy of Bagan's Ananda Temple. Inside, an enormous Buddha made of pale-green Sagyin marble dominates the central shrine.

In the same chamber stand 88 statues of the Buddha's disciples, as well as 12 *manussa*, mythical half-man/half-beast beings. The temple's east and west entrances are decorated with murals depicting the daily life of the Burmese at the time of the pagoda's construction. If you look carefully you may be able to make out European faces among the paintings. The area surrounding the Kyauktawgyi Pagoda is full of smaller pagodas in various stages of decay. These temples have been systematically plundered ever since the prices of ancient Burmese artefacts reached astronomical levels in the antique shops of Bangkok.

On Amarapura's Ayeyarwady bank, 30 minutes' walk from Amarapura's main street, stand two white pagodas – the **Shwe-kyet-yet Pagoda** and the **Shwe-kyet-kya Pagoda** – fronted by a pair of carved lions. Both date from the 12th century. A short distance downriver, King Mindon's **Thanbyedan Fort** was designed in European style by French and Italian advisors. The bastion was intended to stop hostile armies from attacking with warships from the Ayeyarwady. Yet when the British invaded Mandalay in 1885 in exactly this way, not a shot was fired – the Burmese, lacking strong armed forces, had already given up.

WERAWSANA JADE PAGODA

En route between Amarapura and Inwa, it's also worth a detour to visit

the quirky new **Werawsana Jade Pagoda** (around 6km/4 miles southwest of Amarapura), completed amidst much fanfare in 2015. Said to be the world's only Buddhist temple constructed entirely of jade, the pagoda is the creation of a local gem merchant who spent 25 years collecting the vast store of jade (over a thousand tonnes) from which the temple is built. A rather bilious green by day, the temple dazzles after dark, particularly the soaring central stupa, adorned with some thirty thousand tiny jade Buddhas.

PALEIK

Further south (and 8km/5 miles from Amarapura), **Paleik** is famous for its celebrated **Snake Temple** (Hmwe Paya), home to a small menagerie of pythons. The temple's original two pythons were found wrapped around a Buddha statue in an old pagoda here in 1974. The snakes were removed, but continued to return on subsequent days. Eventually, the pythons' persistence persuaded local monks that

they must be holy (perhaps the reincarnated souls of former monks), and the snakes were allowed them to stay unmolested, with a new temple being constructed around their abode.

The original pythons are now dead (although their taxidermied remains can still be seen) but further pampered pythons, donated to the temple by well-wishers, continue to live here. Most people visit at 11am, when the snakes receive their daily wash in a petal-filled bath.

INWA (AVA)

The former city of **Inwa** ❸, known in British times as "Ava" but by its former inhabitants as "Ratnapura" ("City of Gems"), was founded in 1364 by King Thadominbya, and later served as the capital of the Konbaung dynasty. Virtually all the old city has now vanished, although a few vestiges of its old glory survive, including a magnificent teak monastery, the Bagaya Kyaung, marooned amid empty fields on the banks of the Ayeyarwady. It's possible to reach Inwa by car, although most

Kyauktawgyi Pagoda, Amarapura.

Guide at Tojang Paya, Inwa.

visitors arrive by boat via a short crossing of the Myitnge River bounding the east of the site, where you transfer to a horse-cart for the leisurely tour of the ruins – a great way to see the monuments, and a relaxing change after the frenzy of central Mandalay.

Unlike most of Myanmar's other royal cities, Inwa's city wall was not square, but shaped like a sitting lion, such as those found in front of large pagodas. Only a part of the wall still stands; the most complete section is at the north gate (near the horse-cart rank and jetty), known as **Gaung Say Daga**, or "gate of the hair-washing ceremony". Every April during the Thingyan Festival, this ritual hair-washing takes place as a purification rite to welcome the king of the *nat*. Today, the ritual is performed only in homes, but in imperial times even the king washed his hair at this spot.

Tours of the site usually start at the well-preserved **Maha Aungmye Bonzan Monastery**. Also known as the Ok Kyaung, the tall, stucco-decorated brick structure dates from 1818, modelled after a traditional teak *kyaung (monastery)*, although its masonry construction means it has survived far longer than its wooden cousins. In the middle of the monastery is a statue of the Buddha, placed on a pedestal trimmed with glass mosaic. Beside the entrance archway stands an old marble plaque which tells, in English, the story of an American missionary's Burmese wife who was a staunch convert to Christianity until her death during the First Anglo-Burmese War. Next door to the *kyaung* is a seven-tiered prayer hall, which suffered heavy damage in the 1838 earthquake, but was repaired in 1873 by Hsinbyumashin, the daughter of Nanmadaw Me Nu.

A short ride southwest are the ruins of the **Nanmyin Watchtower**, the so-called "leaning tower of Inwa". All that remains of Bagyidaw's palace, this erstwhile 27-metre (89ft) lookout was damaged so heavily by an 1838 earthquake that its upper portion collapsed. Shortly afterwards, the construction began to lean to one side due to

subsidence. Numerous pagodas are scattered around the outlying areas of the site. Among the most interesting is the **Htilaingshin Paya**, built by King Kyanzittha during the Bagan era. Other important shrines include the four-storey **Le-Htat-Gyi Pagoda** and the **Lawkatharaphy Pagoda**, both in the southern part of the former city. Some 1.5km (1 mile) south of the site stands **Inwa Fort**, once considered part of the "unconquerable triangle", which included the Thanbyedan and Sagaing citadels.

BAGAYA KYAUNG

Inwa's single most impressive building, however, is the beautiful **Bagaya Kyaung**, a cavernous, ornately carved teak monastery. Dating from 1593, the monastery once formed the far southern corner of the royal enclave, close to the confluence of the Ayeyarwady and Myitinge rivers. The *kyaung* is famous, above all, for its traditional woodcarving. Doorways, window surrounds, partitions and pillar bases are all richly carved in high Burmese style, combining floral arabesques with reliefs of birds, animals and figures from Buddhist mythology. Enlivening the gloomy and dusty interior, the only splashes of colour are a sumptuously glass-inlaid, lacquered trunk, and the presiding Buddha image itself, which sports a coat of gold leaf. A total of 267 massive pillars support the building, whose seven storeys denote its former royal status. A modern working monastery stands next door.

SAGAING

The sight of **Sagaing Hill** ❹ at sunrise is one of the most serene spectacles in Southeast Asia, with countless stupas, spires and temple towers glowing gold and pale-crimson above the dark, silty water of the Ayeywarwady. Although invisible from the far banks, a maze of stepped walkways and colonnades threads around these other-worldly monuments, swathed in palms, frangipani, tamarind and mango bushes.

Around 5,000 monks live amid Sagaing's Arcadian landscape, in 600 monasteries and a township of private

Nanmyin Watchtower, the so-called "leaning tower of Inwa".

Treelined road on the way to Inwa.

homes scattered over a tangle of valleys and ridgetops. For Burmese Buddhists, this is sacred ground: "the foothill of Mount Meru". Refugees from the city retreat here – for a day or a lifetime – to meditate; devout families bring their young sons to undergo the *shin pyu* ceremony, consigning their loved ones to a period of monastic life. From before dawn until well after dusk, rows of monks file around the lanes, and cymbals, gongs and pagoda bells echo between the whitewashed buildings, as they have for centuries.

Sagaing's unique atmosphere ensures it features prominently on Myanmar's tourist trail, as well as the Buddhist pilgrimage circuit. You can get there by ferry from Inwa, or by road. Jeep taxis and horse-carts are on hand to shuttle visitors from the flat town centre to the monastery-studded hilltop behind, or you can walk, improvising a route up the stepped paths. You technically need a ticket (also valid for Mingun) to visit the temples, although this is rarely asked for.

Teaching novice monks at Bagaya Kyaung, Inwa.

SAGAING'S PAGODAS

Whatever your means of transport, you'll probably be dropped on Sagaing Hill outside Sagaing's most famous landmark, the **Sun U Ponya Shin Pagoda**, an important religious site centred on a huge gilded stupa and a favourite viewpoint for photographers, with superb views across the river to Mandalay from a terrace at the rear. The monument dates from the early 14th century when the city was first established as the seat of the Sagaing kings, one of the dynasties to emerge after the demise of Bagan. After their decline, Sagaing became a fiefdom of the princes of Ava, but rose to be a capital once again in the three-year reign of King Naundawgyi, beginning in 1760.

Also on Sagaing Hill it's worth hunting out the **U Min Thonze Pagoda**, a twenty-minute walk north of the Sun U Ponya Shin, where 45 Buddha images gaze from a crescent-shaped grotto, against a backdrop of superbly elaborate red and turquoise glass mosaic. Among the traditional handicraft stalls at the bottom of the steps leading to it,

look out for ones specialising in bags made from stitched watermelon seeds.

Sagaing's other monuments are scattered over a wide area and, if you're not on a pre-arranged tour, you'll need a taxi to get around the highlights. At the far, south end of town not far from the old Ava Bridge, the **Htupayon Pagoda** – built by King Barapati in 1444 – was destroyed by the 1838 earthquake, and King Pagan, who wanted it rebuilt, was dethroned before repairs were completed. The 30-metre (98ft) -high base is still standing, however, and represents a rare style of temple architecture in Myanmar.

The **Aungmyelawka Pagoda**, built by King Bodawpaya in 1783 on the Ayeyarwady riverfront near the Htupayon Pagoda, is a sandstone replica of the Shwezigon Pagoda in Nyaung U. Bodawpaya had it built to balance the "necessary cruelties" of his reign and improve his merit for future incarnations.

The nearby **Ngadatgyi Pagoda** features an enormous seated Buddha image, installed in 1657 by King Pindale, the ill-fated successor to King Thalun. Pindale was dethroned by his brother in 1661, and a few weeks later was drowned, together with his entire family (this was a common means of putting royalty to death as no blood was spilled on the soil).

Of rather more recent vintage is the **Datpaungzu Pagoda**, which was built upon the completion of the Myitkyina Railway. The monument provided a repository for relics from a number of other stupas which had to be demolished or relocated while clearing the way for the train line across the Ava Bridge.

Probably the most famous of all Sagaing's temples, however, is the **Kaunghmudaw Pagoda** ❺, 10km (6 miles) northwest of the city on the far side of the Sagaing Hills. Built by King Thalun in 1636 to house relics formerly kept in the Mahazedi Pagoda in Bago (Pegu), it is said to contain the Buddha's "Tooth of Kandy" and King Dhammapala's miracle-working alms bowl. The Kaunghmudaw's perfectly hemispherical shape is, according to legend, a copy of the breast of

Pagodas dot the hilltops of Sagaing.

Forty-five Buddhas line the crescent-shaped grotto at U Min Thonze Pagoda, Sagaing.

Mingun Pagoda.

The view across the Ayeyarwady from Sun U Ponya Shin Pagoda, Sagaing.

Thalun's favourite wife. Its huge egg-shaped dome, 46 metres (151ft) high and 274 metres (900ft) in circumference, rises above three rounded terraces. The lowest is decorated with 120 *nats* and *devas*, each in its own niche. A ring of 812 moulded stone pillars, 1.5 metres (5ft) high, surrounds the dome; each one has a hollowed-out head in which an oil lamp is placed during the Thadingyut Light Festival on the occasion of the October full moon. Burmese Buddhists come to the Kaunghmudaw Pagoda from far and wide to celebrate the end of Buddhist Lent at this annual event.

MINGUN

The trip up the Ayeyarwady to **Mingun ⑥**, 10km (6 miles) northwest of Mandalay, deservedly ranks among the most popular half-day excursions from the city, as much for the pleasure of the boat ride as the spectacle of King Bodawpaya's immense, unfinished pagoda looming in surreal fashion above the river bank. The site also holds a couple of other photogenic

buildings, as well as Myanmar's largest bell, and is set amid some bucolic countryside.

A government-run boat service departs from Mandalay at 9am daily, returning at 1pm, while private boats run in both the morning and afternoon. Most people visit on the morning government boat, meaning the site suffers from intense congestion from around 10am. You may prefer to sidestep the crowds by travelling there by road earlier in the day (when the heat is less oppressive and the light more photogenic) or taking the afternoon boat.

Admission to the site is with a combined ticket (also valid for Sagaing).

THE MANTARA GYI PAGODA

From a distance, **the huge Mingun (Mantara Gyi) Pagoda** resembles a medium-sized hill rather than a man-made structure, so vast is the scale of the thing – although what you see today is only the base of an unfinished stupa which, had it ever been completed, would have dwarfed every other on the planet. This insanely

gargantuan project was conceived by King Bodawpaya, fourth son of Alaungpaya, the founder of the Konbaung dynasty. Bodawpaya's forces had conquered Tanintharyi (Tenasserim), the Mon lands, Rakhine. He had underscored his invincibility by carrying off the Mahamuni Buddha statue from Mrauk-U to Amarapura and was at the peak of his power, wanting the world to see it.

In 1790, a Chinese delegation visited Bodawpaya's court, carrying a tooth of the Buddha as a gift. Bodawpaya had the pagoda built to house the tooth – the same one that both Anawrahta and Alaungpaya coveted but had failed to obtain. He then moved his residence to an island in the Ayeyarwady for the next seven years while he supervised construction work on the pagoda. Bodawpaya intended to make his Mantara Gyi Pagoda ascend a full 152 metres (500ft) in height. In order to achieve this, he imported thousands of slaves from his newly conquered southern territories to work on the pagoda.

The lack of available labour in central Burma was irritating to Bodawpaya. Worrying rumours, which had circulated some 500 years earlier during the construction of the Minglazedi Pagoda, had resurfaced, and concerned voices were saying, "When the pagoda is finished, the great country will be ruined." But Bodawpaya, convinced of his destiny as a future Buddha, was not to be dissuaded. He had the pagoda's shrine rooms lined with lead and filled with 1,500 gold figurines, 2,434 silver images and nearly 37,000 other objects and materials, including a soda-water machine – just invented in England, according to the British envoy to Bodawpaya's court, Hiram Cox. Only then were the shrine rooms sealed.

However, the economic ruin which raged at the turn of the 19th century persuaded Bodawpaya to halt construction work on the pagoda. The king died in 1819, aged 75, having ruled for 38 years. He left 122 children and 208 grandchildren – but none of them continued his work on the great pagoda.

Stairs leading to the top of Mingun Pagoda.

Sun U Ponya Shin Pagoda, Sagaing.

Even though it was never completed, the ruins of the Mingun Pagoda are deeply impressive. The upper sections of the pagoda collapsed into the hollow shrine rooms during the 1838 earthquake, but the base of the structure still towers nearly 50 metres (162ft) over the Ayeyarwady. An enormous pair of *chinthe*, also damaged in the quake, guard the riverfront view.

THE MINGUN BELL

The famous **Mingun Bell** stands in an enclosure a short walk north of the main pagoda, just off the main street through the village. Weighing 87 tonnes and standing at 3.7 metres (12ft) high and 5 metres (16.5ft) wide, it was for many years the largest functioning bell in the world until being finally superseded by the 116-tonne Bell of Good Luck at the Foquan Temple, Henan, China, in 2000. King Bodawpaya had it cast in 1790 with the intention of dedicating it to his huge Mingun Pagoda, also intended to be the world's largest. The difficulty of moulding and casting such an enormous clanger using

Mediums dance in one of the numerous shrines dedicated to the nats (spirits) during the Taungbyon Nat festival.

18th century techniques can hardly be underestimated – Bodawpaya himself recognised this fact and rewarded the creator of the bell by having him executed, so as to make sure the feat was never repeated elsewhere.

During the terrible earthquake of 1838, the Mingun Bell and its supports collapsed. Fortunately, there was no damage. Today, the bell is held up by heavy iron rods beneath a shelter. Small Burmese boys who frequent the site encourage visitors to crawl inside it while they strike the metal with a wooden mallet.

MINGUN'S OTHER PAGODAS

Standing on the riverbank at the south side of the souvenir and tea stalls, the unassuming little **Pondaw Pagoda** is actually a scale model of the design for the great Mantara Gyi, yielding a clear idea of what the great stupa would have looked like had it been completed. A stone's throw to the north, the whitewashed **Settawya Pagoda** was built by Bodawpaya in 1811 to hold a marble footprint of the Buddha.

⊘ FESTIVAL OF THE BROTHER LORDS

Each year for eight days before the full moon in August, the village of Taungbyon plays host to a major festival (there are smaller festivals in December and March). Tens of thousands attend the event, held since the 11th century in honour of a pair of *nats* (spirit heroes), known as the "Brother Lords". Thought to have been the sons of a Muslim warrior who recovered the Mon's Buddhist scriptures during Anawrahta's conquest of Thaton, they became part of the labour force coerced by the king into building a pagoda in Taungbyon village, but collapsed from exhaustion and were executed for their frailty.

For reasons that have been lost in the mists of time, the Burmese mourned these two young men's untimely demise with great passion. Their spirits soon became so powerful that a remorseful Anawrahta proclaimed them *nat*, ordering that a shrine be built in their honour in Taungbyon and a summer festival be held to venerate them annually.

The eight-day event, in which the brothers are represented by gilded wooden effigies which are washed and paraded through crowds, now ranks among the most fervent displays of Burmese animism in the religious calendar. It features ritual floral offerings, wild *hsaing waing* music, spirit possession rituals and consultations with transvestite shamans, as well as an enormous bazaar, and lots of eating, gambling and carousing.

Mingun's prettiest stupa, however, stands at the far north of the village. The Hsinbyume or **Myatheindan Pagoda** was built by Bodawpaya's grandson, Bagyidaw, in 1816, three years before he ascended the throne, as a memorial to his favourite wife, Princess Hsinbyume. Severely damaged in the 1838 earthquake, it was rebuilt by King Mindon in 1874. The building's design is a rendition of the Sulamani Pagoda, believed to rest atop Mount Meru in the centre of the universe. The king of the gods, Indra (or Thagyamin as he is known to the Burmese), is depicted on the summit, surrounded by seven additional mountain chains, represented by seven wave-like railings leading to the central stupa. Five kinds of mythical monsters stand guard in niches around the terraces, though most have been defaced or beheaded by temple robbers. In the highest part of the stupa, reachable only by a steep stairway, is the *cella*, containing a single Buddha figure.

The nearby village of **Taungbyon** ❼, on the opposite side of the river some 20km (13 miles) north of Mandalay, is the focus of Myanmar's largest and most intense *nat* festival (see box).

FURTHER AFIELD

The town of **Monywa** ❽, 136km (84 miles) west of Mandalay, sits on the banks of the Chindwin River, the largest tributary of the Ayeyarwady. A bustling, hot, flat market hub, it's visited primarily as a base from which to take in the trio of monuments hidden in its rocky hinterland, as well as by a trickle of adventurous travellers ferry-hopping north or south along the Chindwin.

MONYWA'S SIGHTS

Around 10km (6.2 miles) northeast of Monywa is the flamboyant **Thanboddhay Pagoda** ❾, built in 1939 by the much venerated Burmese abbot, Moehnyin Sayadaw. Guarded by a pair of huge white elephants, the complex consists of a central stupa surrounded by a forest of 845 smaller ones, all painted in a blaze of rainbow colours and encrusted with

> **◎ Tip**
>
> If you're travelling by car between Mandalay and Monywa, Bodhi Tataung and the Thanboddhay Paya can easily be visited en route, as both lie close to the road between the two cities.

Market outside Shwebon Yadana, Shwebo.

Detail of a pavilion at Thanbhodday temple donated by the Aw brothers – from a Chinese family who made their fortune producing Tiger Balm.

The Mingun Bell.

glass mosaic. The prayer hall inside (daily 6am–5pm; charge) is no less astonishing, containing (according to locals) an incredible 582,357 images. Among the myriad Buddha statues look out for others depicting tigers, playful monks and finely dressed ladies with parasols.

While Thanbodday may be famous for its host of tiny Buddhas, **Bodhi Tataung** ⑩, 8km (5 miles) further east, is renowned for its two extremely large ones. The first is a vast, 116-metre (424ft) standing Buddha – the **Laykyun Setkyar** – said to be the second biggest of its kind in the world (just outstripped by China's Spring Garden Buddha, but nearly three times the height of New York's Statue of Liberty). Stairways twist up through twenty-five storeys inside the colossus, climbing through a series of galleries depicting hell at the bottom (with lurid scenes of demons torturing human souls, hammering stakes through hearts and cooking up stews of sinners in big pots) and then climbing up through the various

Buddhist heavens on their way to nirvana at the top of the statue, although unfortunately at present visitors aren't allowed beyond level 16, leaving you stranded slightly over halfway to paradise.

At the foot of the standing giant sprawls an almost equally huge reclining Buddha, measuring 95 metres (312ft) from head to toe. This was the first statue to be completed on the site by its founding father, Sayadaw Bhaddanta Narada, a local abbot who spent the last years of his life touring the world to raise funds for the project. Sadly, he died shortly before the mighty Laykyn Setkyar was finished.

Tens of thousands of smaller Buddha statues rest in neat rows under Bodhi trees radiating from the 131-metre (430ft) **Aung Setykar Pagoda**, on flat ground at the bottom of the complex, inaugurated in 2008.

PHO WIN TAUNG CAVES

A considerably more ancient, neglected feel hangs over the **Pho Win Taung**

ပုံးကျွန်းခေါင်းလောင်းတော်ကြီး

MINGUN BELL

Cast in 1808 A.D. by King Bodawpaya to be dedicated to Mingun Pagoda, which was never completed, and is now in ... Pagoda, Which was never completed, and is the second largest bell ... 90 tons, and is the second largest bell ...

cave complex, a cluster of 492 prayer chambers hewn from three sandstone outcrops 23km (14 miles) west of Monywa. Most were excavated between the 14th and 18th centuries, but with their peeling plaster murals and time-worn Buddha images they feel much older, like an apparition from the Central Asian silk route.

You'll need a decent torch to admire the decoration of the caves' interiors. Some were elaborately painted in geometric designs rendered in earthy reds, browns and blues. Others lead to colonnaded walkways lined with meditating or reclining Buddhas.

The fact that the site lies completely off the beaten track adds to its allure; come prepared for a total absence of facilities – as well as troupes of pilfering monkeys. Getting there under your own steam from Monywa can require some determination. You have to take an open-top ferry across the Chindwin and pick up a jeep from the far side for the remaining 22km (14 miles). Travelling by car, your driver will detour north to cross the Chindwin

via the river bridge, which takes you past the **Shwetaung-U Pagoda** (worth visiting for its panoramic views) and rather more unsightly Ivanhoe open-cast copper mine.

SHWEBO

About 100km (60 miles) north of Mandalay, **Shwebo** ⓫ was the 18th-century capital of the warlike King Alaungpaya, founder of the Konbaung dynasty; it was from here that the reconquest of Burma began after the Mon had seized Inwa in 1752. Alaungpaya didn't much care for its original name – "Moksovo", meaning "the Hunter Chief" – and changed it instead to Shwebo, the "Golden Chief", after which his home village of 300 houses grew to become a prosperous city. "Shwebo-tha!" ("Sons of Shwebo!") was the battle cry of his marauding army, heard across the length and breadth of what is now modern Myanmar during the mid-18th century, in the course of which Alaungpaya's Burmese forces first drove the Mon from Inwa and then

Rows of Buddhas at Bodhi Tataung, near Monywa.

The giant Bodhi Tataung statues, near Monywa.

Gilded pagoda on Kandawgyi Lake, National Kandawgyi Gardens.

A colonial house in Pyin U-Lwin.

rolled south, overrunning Mon territories, sacking their capital at Bago and taking control of what is now the whole of modern Myanmar (although with bits of India and Thailand).

Precious little remains from Alaungpaya's illustrious era, his palace having long since burned to the ground, although the government recently erected replicas of the splendid throne halls, the **Shwebon Yadana** (daily 8am–5pm; charge), whose multi-tiered towers rise from lawned grounds in the centre of the city, overlooking remnants of the old moat. A memorial to the great king marks the spot where his body was cremated in 1760.

Also worth a visit, five minutes' walk south of the old palace grounds, is the **Shwe Daza Pagoda**, which is thought to be five centuries old.

HALIN

A millennium and a half before the rise of Alaungpaya and the Konbaung Dynasty, these same sun-scorched plains between the Ayeywarwady and Mu rivers gave rise to another important regional capital, the Pyu city of **Halin** (Halingyi). Hardly any visitors cover the 18km (11miles) of unsurfaced tracks and back roads separating Shwebo from the **Halin Archaeological Zone** ⑫ (Tues–Sun 9.30am–4.30pm; charge), but the site has a beguilingly forlorn atmosphere, while the adjacent village is dotted with dozens of ancient, crumbling monuments.

Reduced almost to dust and barely visible today, the Pyu settlement was surrounded by rectangular brick walls enclosing an area of roughly 500 hectares (1,250 acres). As at all Pyu cities the walls were pierced by 12 fortified gateways (equivalent to the signs of the zodiac), whose remains have been radiocarbon-dated to between the 2nd and 6th centuries AD. Excavations, conducted in three main waves during the 20th century and still ongoing, pockmark the site and its surrounding area, where numerous graves have been uncovered containing gold ornaments, bronze figures, seals and decorated weapons. In 1999, local farmers also came across a skeleton with gold-inlaid teeth, which they

were in the process of scraping clean when an archaeologist intervened and bought it off them.

PYIN U-LWIN

For anyone with a weak spot for the atmosphere of British colonial times, and others just seeking to escape the dusty misery of Mandalay's hot season, a visit to **Pyin U-Lwin** ⑬ (also often transliterated as Pyin Oo Lwin), in the foothills of the Shan Plateau, is a must. A two-and-a-half-hour drive by jeep takes the traveller to an elevation of 1,070 metres (3,510ft), from where there are breathtaking views of the Mandalay plain.

Formerly known as "Maymyo", or "May Town", Pyin U-Lwin was originally named after one Colonel May, an officer in the Bengal Infantry who was posted to this hill station in 1887 in order to suppress a rebellion that flared up after the annexation of Upper Burma. At a strategically important point on the road from Mandalay to Hsipaw, the town, blessed with a temperate climate,

served as the summer capital for the British administration until the end of the colonial era in 1948.

Pleasant temperatures predominate in Pyin U-Lwin even during the hot season, and in the cold season there is no frost. It's no wonder the British felt at home here. A number of Indian Sikhs and Nepalese gurkhas, whose forebears entered the country with the Indian army, have settled here, retaining many of the old colonial traditions in their work as hoteliers, carriage drivers and gardeners. They also run many of the tea shops in the hill resort.

Pyin U-Lwin's main attraction is its verdant **botanical gardens**, now known as the **National Kandawgyi Gardens** (daily 8am–6pm; charge), surrounding the scenic Kandawgyi Lake (excavated, improbably, by Turkish prisoners of war) and a good spot for a relaxing stroll or picnic, and for a climb up the quirky Nan Myint Tower overlooking the gardens. There is also an 18-hole golf course and three waterfalls in the vicinity for swimming and picnics. Horse-drawn carriages resembling

⊙ **Tip**

For a panoramic view of Pyin U-Lwin, climb to the hilltop Naung Kan Gyi Pagoda, north of the railway station.

The National Kandawgyi Gardens, Pyin U-Lwin.

Wells-Fargo stage coaches are the chief mode of transport.

The resort's cool weather has allowed many flowers and fruits commonly found in milder climes to thrive, including magnolias, chrysanthemums, cherry trees, peaches, strawberries and plums.

Twenty-seven kilometres (15 miles) east of Pyin U-dwin are the **Peik Chin Myaung** caves (also known as Maha Nandamu; daily 6.30am–5pm; free), depicting scenes of Buddha's life in fairy-tale surroundings. Most of the images have been donated by the leaders and family members of the present government to atone for sins previously committed.

Beyond Pyin U-Lwin, the rail line from Mandalay continues as far as the northern Shan administrative centre of Lashio. Further north, the road from Singu along the Ayeyarwady, opposite Kyaukmyaung, leads to the town of **Mogok**, famous for its ruby mines. Independent tourists are barred from visiting the area, although accompanied tours to the city are available through local travel agencies in Yangon and Mandalay.

MEIKTILA

Straddling a major crossroads at the head of the Sittaung Valley, the lakeside town of **Meiktila** ⑭ is infamous as the site of one of the fiercest Burmese battles in World War II. In late February 1944, Allied forces took the town from its poorly equipped Japanese defenders, only to find themselves under siege soon after. The ensuing fight dragged on for two months, until the fall of Rangoon sealed defeat for the Japanese – although not before virtually every Japanese soldier in Meiktila had been killed and the town itself reduced to rubble. A legacy of these events, and of Meiktila's strategic position in the country's heartland, is that today the town serves as the home of Myanmar's largest air-force base.

More recently, in March 2013, the town hit the international headlines thanks to a series of anti-Muslim riots during which forty Muslims were killed and an estimated 12,000 others driven

A horse-drawn carriage speeds through Pyin U-Lwin.

from their homes (while local police, it's said, stood by and watched). The burnt-out and bulldozed remains of some of the affected houses, plus a pair of mosques, can still be seen in the former Muslim district east along the road from the clocktower.

Despite recent troubles, Meiktila remains an enjoyable place to overnight at the crossroads on road and railway routes between Mandalay, Bagan and Inle Lake. There are few specific sights, but it's a good place to soak up the atmosphere of life in small-town, provincial Myanmar, and the lively night market is one of the best in the region.

Centrepiece of the town is the beautiful Meiktila Lake, surrounded by assorted colourful temples and shrines including the eye-catching **Phaung Daw U Pagoda**, a floating temple built in the shape of a golden Karaweik bird. A scattering of stately old wooden mansions on the opposite, western shore, recalls the colonial era. Aung San Suu Kyi and her late British husband, Michael Aris, spent their honeymoon in one of the largest of them.

NAYPYIDAW

There can be few capital cities in the world visited by virtually no tourists, but **Naypyidaw** ⑮ – also spelt "Nay Pyi Daw", "Nay Pyi Taw" or "Naypyitaw" (literally "Abode of Kings") – is one of them. Built from scratch, at vast expense and with considerable haste, the project was the brainchild of Senior General Than Shwe. No one is quite sure why, in 2002, the former Commander-in-Chief of the Myanmar armed forces decided to move the Burmese seat of government 320km (200 miles) north from Yangon: the official reason was "lack of space". It was, however, widely rumoured at the time that Than Shwe's personal astrologer had foreseen some kind of foreign invasion by sea, and that the general preferred this much more easily defensible site in the centre of the country.

Whatever its inspiration, Naypyidaw, 252km (157 miles) south of Mandalay, is here to stay. A sprawling, soulless, white-elephant city of empty 8-lane highways and giant

> ### ⊙ Tip
> Be careful where you point your camera in Naypyidaw. Photographing military or government buildings, soldiers, police and officials is strictly forbidden.

One of Naypyidaw's extraordinarily spacious roads.

concrete buildings, it cost an estimated $4 billion to create and required the relocation of hundreds of thousands of government employees (many of whose families still reside in Yangon).

Much of the new construction consists of sprawling, Lego-like suburbs whose roofs are colour-coded to denote the rank or job of their inhabitants. Widely spaced so as to minimise the potential impact of air raids, these are already showing signs of age, with peeling plaster and mildew-streaks staining their walls. The top military brass, meanwhile, live in swanky mansions and Orange-County-style villas in the suburbs and surrounding hills, complete with secret bunkers and tunnels.

Naypyidaw is decidedly not somewhere you come for sightseeing, so much as for its strange, slightly sinister, atmosphere. But the city does boast one stand-out monument: the huge, gold-covered **Uppatasanti Pagoda**. An almost exact replica of Yangon's Shwedagon Pagoda, the

White elephant at the Hsin Hpyu Daw park.

giant stupa was donated by General Than Shwe and his wife and is hollow, containing dioramas illustrating scenes from the life of the Buddha. On the east side of the stupa, look out for the shelter where the general's much-prized quintet of **white elephants** are housed.

Visits to the government enclave, with its 31-building Parliament complex, are not allowed. Also off limits is the military zone in **Pyinmana** to the east, which is a pity as the latter holds the most outlandish of all the follies erected in the new capital by the regime – a vast square overlooked by three colossal statues of Burma's great kings: Anawrahta, Bayinnaung and Alaungpaya. The space serves mainly as a venue for displays of military might.

The only other major sight of note in Naypyidaw is the city's showpiece **Zoological Gardens and Safari Park** (Tues–Sun 8.30am–4.30pm; charge), a forty-minute taxi ride northeast of the centre, where you can see everything from alpacas to zebras.

⊘ WHITE ELEPHANTS

A party was thrown in the Burmese capital, Naypyidaw, in November 2011 to welcome a pair of white elephants into captivity after they'd been captured in the jungles of Rakhine State. Symbols of power and good fortune, white (or albino) elephants are normally a light reddish brown, and are regarded as auspicious in Myanmar. So seriously do Myanmar's generals take the old dictum that these rare animals confer blessings on heads of state that they even name their personal aircrafts "White Elephant 1" and "White Elephant 2". Myanmar today boasts a total of eight such animals, with three of them housed in a pavilion on the northern outskirts of Yangon, in a park close to the airport, and the other five in Naypyidaw.

FROM PYIN U-LWIN TO LASHIO BY TRAIN

The train journey from Pyin U-Lwin to Lashio is Myanmar's most picturesque rail route, taking in the magnificent Gokteik Viaduct.

Although the train from Pyin U-Lwin to Lashio originates in Mandalay, many travellers prefer to board it at the hill station, given that the journey from Mandalay to Pyin U-Lwin takes four hours by train (leaving at the ungodly hour of 4am), but just two by bus – besides which the most interesting part of the journey is from Pyin U-Lwin to Lashio.

PYIN U-LWIN TO THE VIADUCT

The rail journey starts in Mandalay Region, but most of the towns it passes through are in northern Shan State.

Until 1995, these towns were largely unknown to foreign tourists, as the route from Mandalay to Lashio was considered a haven for bandits. When this problem was eliminated, restrictions on train travel for foreigners were also lifted. Although it is possible to go by road, the train provides a more comfortable ride, albeit in carriages that have seen better days. The journey covering the 220km (146 miles) between Pyin U-Lwin and Lashio takes about 11 hours and is a great way to get a glimpse of northern Shan State.

After Pyin U-Lwin, the train passes gardens full of cabbages and strawberries which soon open out into broad valleys dotted with hamlets. Mist-covered mountains loom in the distance as **Wetwun**, the first stop, after 90 minutes, approaches. As soon as the train stops, vendors hop on board to sell snacks.

The highlight of the journey is the **Gokteik Viaduct**, a magnificent steel bridge spanning a 300-metre (990ft) -deep river gorge, which the train passes after Wetwun. The approach is stunning – the giant steel girders stand out from the dense jungle like silver latticework, set against a craggy, ochre mountain face. The steel viaduct was something of an engineering marvel when it was completed in 1903. In his book, *The Great Railway Bazaar*, Paul Theroux, who travelled this way in 1973, described it as "a monster

of silver geometry in all the ragged rock and jungle... Its presence there was bizarre, this man-made thing in so remote a place, competing with the grandeur of the enormous gorge and yet seemingly more grand than its surroundings, which were hardly negligible – the water rushing through the girder legs and falling on the tops of trees, the flight of birds through the swirling clouds and the blackness of the tunnels beyond the viaduct."

BEYOND THE VIADUCT

After crossing the viaduct, the train passes through lush valleys surrounded by green mountains. The following stop, **Kyaukme**, is deep in Shan territory and dotted with Shan hill-tribe villages. Green valleys soon give way to rice fields, banana plantations, bamboo groves and orange orchards on the approach to the next station, **Hsipaw**. The train then snakes through jungle-clad valleys cut through by the rapid-strewn, emerald-coloured Namby River, which flows all the way to **Lashio**. By twilight, the panorama fades and darkness envelopes the rest of the ride until Lashio is reached at about 7.30pm.

The mighty steel girders of the Gokteik Viaduct.

The temple-strewn skyline of
Bagan Archaeological Zone.

Buddha statue inside Sulamani
temple, Bagan.

THE PLAINS OF BAGAN

Bagan's glory days are over, but what remains is the most beautiful collection of ruined stupas and temples in Myanmar.

Sulamani temple, stupa detail.

Providing a direct trade corridor between southwest China and the Indian Ocean, the Ayeyarwady River always offered rich pickings for any dynasty powerful enough to control traffic along it. Not until the early 11th century, however, did one emerge with sufficient strength to unify the warring regions of Lower Burma: the Bamars. The result was vast wealth and a capital of unparalleled splendour, founded on a flat, arid bend in the river roughly midway along its course. In classical Pali, the city was known as "Arimaddanapura", "City That Tramples on Enemies", and in Old Burmese as "Pukam" or "Bagan".

Over a period of around 250 years, a succession of rulers erected an astonishing crop of religious monuments on the site to glorify their reign and assure merit for the afterlife. Travellers and pilgrims from across the Buddhist world were amazed by the brilliance of the capital at its zenith, recording with wonder the spectacle of 13,000 temples, monasteries and gilded stupas that rose from Bagan's dusty plains.

The decline of the Bagan Empire's fortunes, coupled with the unforgiving Burmese climate and frequent earthquakes (the most recent of which struck in 2016, measuring 6.9 on the Richter scale and causing widespread damage), has taken its toll. All the city's secular buildings have long since disappeared, being made of wood, bamboo and thatch. However, more than 2,000 religious monuments survive, forming a spectacle no less mesmerising for modern eyes than it must have been for medieval pilgrims 700 or more years ago, when the now crumbling brick and stucco towers were smothered in gold and silver.

A Sulamani temple fresco.

Bagan today is far and away Myanmar's most important visitor attraction. As a result of some heavy-handed restoration work carried out by the military government over the past decade, the site has been denied coveted Unesco World Heritage status. But with the tourism boycott now lifted, the wider world is fast rediscovering these amazing ruins, whose impressive scale and exquisite setting in the rain shadow of the Rakhine mountains assure it a place alongside the likes of Angkor Wat, Sigiriya and the Taj Mahal as one of the undisputed wonders of medieval Asia.

Exquisite Bagan temples.

BAGAN ARCHAEOLOGICAL ZONE

The great plain of Bagan is the site of thousands of ancient Buddhist pagodas, temples and monasteries.

The ruins of medieval **Bagan** – nowadays officially known as the "**Bagan Archaeological Zone**" – are scattered over an area of roughly 50 sq km (26 sq miles), 290km (180 miles) southwest of Mandalay on the east bank of the Ayeyarwady River. Formerly inhabited by between 50,000 and 200,000 people, the ruined city is now largely deserted, with most of the local population and tourist-related businesses confined to settlements on the peripheries, leaving the monuments rising in a state of charismatic isolation inland.

An estimated 2,200 temples, pagodas, monasteries (*kyaung*) and other religious structures rise above the plains here – survivors from the 13,000 or so erected between Anawrahta's conquest of Thaton in 1057 and Kublai Khan's invasion of the Bamar Empire in 1287. The spectacle of their towers and finials bristling from the table of flat scrubland is hypnotic at any time of year, but especially so on mid-winter mornings, when river mist and cooking-fire smoke often enfolds the brick and stucco structures, glowing red in the first rays of daylight.

At the height of the tourist season, between mid-December and late January, droves of visitors converge via a maze of dusty footpaths and cart tracks on the more famous

viewpoints to savour this exotic spectacle. But you can easily sidestep the crowds by venturing a short way off-piste. Indeed, aimless explorations of Bagan's fringes are just as likely to yield memorable visions as the dozen or so "must-sees" that dominate tourists' tick-lists. Wherever you wander, though, glimpses of exquisitely proportioned stupas and temple towers are guaranteed, along with swirling *Jataka* murals in beautiful earthy red hues and meditating Buddhas in dimly lit shrine chambers.

Main attractions
Balloon Flights
Ananda Temple
Upali Thein
Shwezigon Pagoda
Abeyadana Temple
Shwesandaw Pagoda
Dhammayangyi Temple

Map on page 208

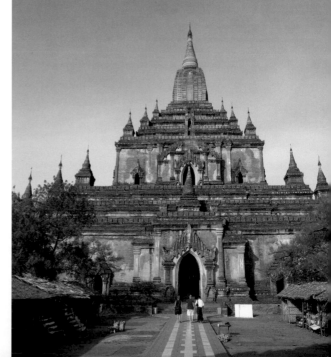

Sulamani temple.

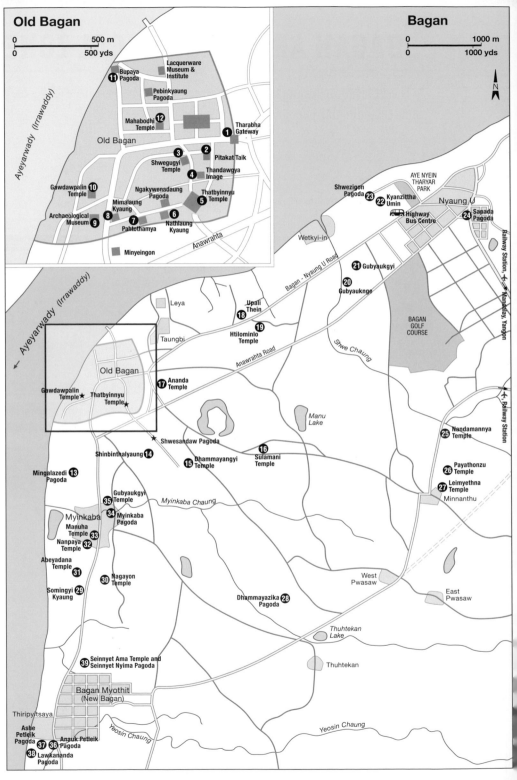

Old Bagan

0 — 500 m
0 — 500 yds

11 Bupaya Pagoda
Lacquerware Museum & Institute
Pebinkyaung Pagoda
Mahabodhi Temple **12**
Old Bagan
1 Tharabha Gateway
3 Shwegugyi Temple
2 Pitakat Taik
4 Thandawgya Image
Ngakywenadaung Pagoda
Gawdawpalin Temple **10**
Mimalaung Kyaung
5 Thatbyinnyu Temple
Archaeological Museum **9** **8**
7 **6**
Pahtothamya
Nathlaung Kyaung
Minyeingon

Ayeyarwady (Irrawaddy)

Bagan

0 — 1000 m
0 — 1000 yds

N

AYE NYEIN THARYAR PARK

Nyaung U

Shwezigon Pagoda **23** **22** Kyanzittha Umin
24 Sapada Pagoda
Highway Bus Centre

Wetkyi-in

Bagan - Nyaung U Road

21 Gubyaukgyi
20 Gubyauknge

Railway Station, Mandalay, Yangon

BAGAN GOLF COURSE

Ayeyarwady (Irrawaddy)

Leya
Taungbi
Old Bagan
Gawdawpalin Temple ★
Thatbyinnyu Temple ★

18 Upali Thein
19 Htilominlo Temple

Anawrahta Road

Shwe Chaung

17 Ananda Temple

Manu Lake

Shwesandaw Pagoda

Railway Station

25 Nandamannya Temple

Shinbinthalyaung **14**
15 Dhammayangyi Temple
16 Sulamani Temple

26 Payathonzu Temple
27 Leimyethna Temple
Minnanthu

Mingalazedi Pagoda **13**

Gubyaukgyi Temple **35**
Myinkaba
Manuha Temple **33**
34 Myinkaba Pagoda
Nanpaya Temple **32**

Myinkaba Chaung

Abeyadana Temple **31**
30 Nagayon Temple
Somingyi Kyaung **29**

West Pwasaw

East Pwasaw

28 Dhammayazika Pagoda

Thuhtekan Lake

Thuhtekan

39 Seinnyet Ama Temple and Seinnyet Nyima Pagoda

Bagan Myothit (New Bagan)

Thiripyitsaya

Ashe Petleik Pagoda
38 **37** **36** Anauk Petleik Pagoda
Lawkananda Pagoda

Yeosin Chaung

Yeosin Chaung

The majority of visitors spend at least two days and three nights at Bagan, but you could conceivably spend double that here without re-tracing your own footsteps. Begin at Old Bagan, the walled city enclosing the largest concentration of monuments, and work your way clockwise around the Archaeological Zone from there through highlights picked out in our account. Unmissable locations include the enigmatic **Dhammayangyi Temple**, the delicately shaped **Ananda Temple**, with its four teak Buddhas, the classic **Sulamani Temple**, arguably the most perfect of all Bagan's temples, and the colourful **Shwezigon Temple** in Nyaung-U, still (unlike most of Bagan's temples) a living place of worship and pilgrimage. Due to a ban on climbing the temples, it's no longer possible to scale most of them for sunset views; the main exception is the Shwesandaw Pagoda, although there are several other places from which to admire the last rays of the day.

The riverside villages dotted around the Archaeological Zone, where most of the hotels, restaurants and shops are located, are where you're most likely to kill time between temple tours. A handful of waterfront cafés offer breezy spots from which to admire views of the distant Rakhine hills, while sunset cruises on the river provide a relaxing perspective on the site and its environs. The ultimate way to see Bagan, however, has to be from the air, from one of the hot-air balloons that drift over the ruins each morning and evening.

SITE PRACTICALITIES

The Burmese government levy a $25 admission fee, collected on arrival at the airport or boat jetty and valid for one week. You'll be issued with an individually numbered ticket card, normally retained by your tour operator if you're on a pre-booked holiday.

Guides and transport around the **monuments** are also taken care of by holiday companies, but independent travellers will have to organise their own transport given that most of the Archaeological Zone is far too big to explore on foot. Hiring a bike or e-bike is a good way to get around, while

Balloon over Bagan.

SHIN ARAHAN: THE GREAT REFORMER

Legendary in the annals of medieval Burma, Shin Arahan was the missionary monk who consolidated Buddhism's hold on the country.

Through his influence over four successive kings of Bagan in the 11th and early 12th centuries, Shin Arahan ensured Theravada Buddhism became the state religion of Myanmar at a time when it was fast declining elsewhere in Asia.

He was born in AD 1034, in the southeastern Mon Kingdom of Thaton. The local rulers had long since embraced Buddhism, although the faith was coming under increasing threat from Hinduism. Dissatisfied with the falling religious standards of the Mon, Shin Arahan, then a monk in his early 20s, fled north up the Ayeyarwady to meditate in a forest near the capital of Bagan.

Bagan was the most powerful, prosperous city in central Burma in the mid-11th century, but its religious life was a wild mix of *nat* nature spirit worship,

Gotama, the west-facing standing Buddha at the Ananda temple.

Tantricism and Tibetan-influenced Mahayana Buddhism, promulgated by an order of forest monks known as the Ari, who were rumoured to engage in debauched rituals strongly disapproved of by Bagan's King Anawrahta.

SHIN ARAHAN'S RISE

According to the Burmese chronicles, when reports reached Anawrahta that a yellow-robed monk "of pure heart and mind" was living alone in woods near his palace, he summoned the young ascetic to his court. But rather than perform the usual prostrations, Shin Arahan simply sat on the King's throne – an act normally punishable with summary execution. The monk, however, claimed merely to be demonstrating his belief that "the only True Law was the teachings of the Buddha".

The ruse worked. Anawrahta appointed the 22-year-old monk as his chief spiritual adviser, and Shin Arahan became the vanguard in Bagan's battle with *nat* worship and the Ari order. At his behest, an army was dispatched south in 1057 to conquer Thaton, his homeland, whose king owned a coveted set of Buddhist scriptures known as the *Tripitaka*, setting out the Buddha's Three Sermons.

Bagan triumphed and its forces returned with thousands of Mon prisoners, among them architects, skilled craftsmen and scholars learned in Pali texts whose talents would be deployed over the coming decades building magnificent pagodas, temples and libraries – the splendid ruins of which still litter the Bagan Plains to this day. Their ranks were swollen by many eminent monks from the great Buddhist universities of northern India, at that time suffering repeated attacks by Muslim raiders.

Espoused by four generations of Bagan kings, Shin Arahan's brand of pure Theravada Buddhism quickly spread across the kingdom and, by the time of the great reformer's death at the age of 81, had taken root in the neighbouring states of Siam (Thailand), Laos and Cambodia, where it remains the predominant school.

The monastery built for Shin Arahan by his first royal patron, Anawrahta, where the sage gave his first sermons in Bagan, is the principal memorial to the much venerated monk. It stands to the west of Hnget Pyit Taung Compound on the outskirts of Nyaung U.

horse-carts (charged by the day or half day) are another popular, if rather uncomfortable, option. The cart drivers, most of whom speak rudimentary English, know the ground well, and where to find the key warden for a monument if it is locked (a precaution for those temples whose wall paintings or stone-carved *Jataka* panels are at risk from vandals). Although admission to the locked temples is technically covered by your entrance ticket, the warden will generally expect a small gratuity for his trouble.

In the evenings, **sunset boat trips** from the jetty at Old Bagan are a popular way to experience the atmosphere of the river. Most of the boats tend to be booked by holiday companies in high season, but you can usually find one with a spare space or two by asking around.

Pressure for tickets is even more intense for the **balloon flights** over the site. Flights are run by three operators: Balloons over Bagan (www.balloonsoverbagan.com), Oriental Ballooning (www.orientalballooning.com) and Golden Eagle Balloon (www.bagan-balloon.com). The 45-minute to 1-hour trips offer a truly magical perspective on the ruins. The experience begins with a pre-dawn hotel pick-up (Balloons over Bagan use vintage teak Chevrolet buses), which takes you to the river bank to watch the balloon being inflated. After the flight, horse-carts collect you from wherever the balloon lands following a light champagne breakfast. Flights cost a hefty $350 per person and up – and they're like gold dust over the Christmas–New Year period. All three firms fly around five balloons every morning between October and March.

HISTORY

There has been a settlement in the region of Bagan since early in the 2nd century AD, when Thamuddarit, a Pyu king, led his followers here. The city walls were erected by King Pyinbya in 849, but it was left to King Anawrahta, 42nd ruler of the Bagan dynasty, to usher in the city's golden age.

Anawrahta ascended to the Bagan throne in 1044, and his victory over the Mon following the conquest of their capital of Thaton in 1057 marked a turning .point in Bagan's history. Religious change came too, following the arrival of a young monk from Thaton, a Brahman priest's son named Shin Arahan, who was so successful in converting Anawrahta to the Theravada Buddhist school that the king became consumed with spreading the doctrine.

Following Anawrahta's death in 1077, his son Sawlu succeeded to the throne only to be faced with major rebellions among the Mon to the south. Hundreds of monuments were erected during the 28-year reign of his half-brother and successor Kyanzittha, when Bagan became known as "city of the four million pagodas". Mon Buddhist culture became paramount – not surprisingly, given that the 30,000 Mon captives who had been brought north after the conquest of Thaton had

Tip

Bagan is huge. Don't underestimate the size of the site or the heat of the central plains. It's better to see some temples in detail and slowly than to rush through too many and exhaust yourself.

The "Mr Handsome" nat shrine at the Tharabha gate, Old Bagan.

> Tip

It's usually cheaper to hire a taxi in Nyaung U than in New Bagan (around $40 per day as against $60 or more).

Thatbyinnya temple.

already significantly altered the lifestyle of the Pyu and Bamar.

Kyanzittha's grandson Alaungsithu succeeded him as ruler of Bagan and held the throne for another 45 years. A highly developed irrigation system supported the production of rice and provided the economic backbone of the empire.

Bagan's power slowly weakened in the 13th century under the threat of growing Shan influence and the menacing Mongol army of Kublai Khan, which had already overwhelmed China. When King Narathihapate refused to pay a tribute to the Khan, his armies were defeated on the battlefield, and the Mongols took control.

Following the empire's decline, Bagan slipped into relative obscurity, hastened by the numerous earthquakes that have repeatedly devastated the area. One major tremor in 1975 (measuring 6.2 on the Richter scale) reduced many of the monuments to rubble, prompting Unesco to launch a multi-million-dollar restoration project. Their efforts were, however,

subsequently eclipsed by those of the Burmese government who, using funds donated by merit-seeking religious sponsors at home and abroad, embarked on its own ambitious reconstruction programme, heavily criticised by Unesco, which claimed the restoration work was at best "speculative" and refused to confer on the site World Heritage status (though the site has since been restored to the Tentative List). The government, meanwhile, continued its work undeterred by international criticism, erecting a ersatz new Bamar-style palace and massive viewing tower inside the Archaeological Zone. Further controversy attended the government's decision in 1990 to forcibly re-locate villagers from Old Bagan, the walled area on the riverside, to a newly built town 4km (2.5 miles) further south at New Bagan.

OLD BAGAN

The walled enclave overlooking a bend in the Ayeyarwady river, now known as **Old Bagan**, was formerly the centre of the medieval city and still boasts the

greatest density of monuments. The area can easily be covered on foot, though an early start, sun hat and plenty of drinking water are recommended. Beginning at the main east entrance, the route outlined below proceeds in a clockwise direction.

THARABHA GATEWAY

The principal entrance to Old Bagan is via the **Tharabha** (aka "Sarabar") **Gateway ❶**, the only section of King Pyinbya's 9th-century city wall still intact, originally forming the eastern entrance to the heart of the city. The gateway also houses prayer niches to Bagan's two guardian spirits – the so-called Mahagiri *nat* – Nga Tin De ("Mr Handsome") and his sister Shwemyethna ("Golden Face"). Both *nats* are believed to reside on nearby Mount Popa – hence the name Mahagiri, meaning "Lords of the Great Mountain".

PITAKAT TAIK

One of the few surviving secular buildings in Bagan is the **Pitakat Taik ❷**, King Anawrahta's **library**, reached by taking the first left turn immediately after passing through the Tharabha Gate. Anawrahta had it built close to the city's east gate to house the 30 elephant-loads of scriptures he brought back to Bagan after his conquest of Thaton. The building gives an idea of what the wooden buildings of Bagan might have looked like during the city's golden age. Its original appearance, however, was altered in 1783, when King Bodawpaya had finials added to the corners of the five multiple roofs.

SHWEGUGYI TEMPLE

A block west of the old library, the **Shwegugyi ❸** ("Great Golden Cave") was built by King Alaungsithu in 1131, taking just seven months to erect according to a carved inscription inside. Ironically, King Alaungsithu was later murdered here by his own son, the patricidal Narathu, at the age

of 81. Unlike most Buddhist monuments, which face east, the Shwegugyi stands on a high platform facing north, towards the royal palace. Its hall and inner corridor are well lit by large windows and doorways, one of the main features distinguishing Bagan's later Bamar architectural style from the older Mon- and Pyu-influenced style.

THANDAWGYA IMAGE

In a small brick temple just down the lane from the Shwegugyi sits the **Thandawgya Image ❹** – a great seated Buddha figure measuring six metres (19.7ft) in height. It was erected by Narathihapate in 1284 and shows the master with hands in earth-witness (*bhumisparsa*) *mudra*. The plaster has crumbled away over the centuries, leaving only greenish sandstone blocks, which give the statue an entrancing, mystical appearance.

THATBYINNYU TEMPLE

The centre of Old Bagan is dominated by the **Thatbyinnyu** ("Omniscience") **Temple ❺**, just inside the old walls south of

The "Golden face" nat shrine at the Tharabha Gate, Old Bagan.

Gawdawpalin temple.

*Stupa near
Shwesandaw temple.*

Bupaya Pagoda.

the Thandawgya image. At 61 metres (201ft), this is the tallest building in Bagan, and also a good example of the transition between the earlier Mon and the later Bamar architectural styles.

Built by Alaungsithu in the mid-12th century during one of the high points of the dynasty's political power, the Thatbyinnyu is similar in shape to the Ananda, although it does not form a symmetrical cross since the eastern vestibule projects out of the main structure. The construction of this temple introduced the idea of placing a smaller "hollow" cube on top of a larger Bamar-style structure, whereas the previous Mon-style shrines were of one storey. The centre of the lower cube is solid, serving as a foundation for the upper temple, which houses an eastward-looking Buddha figure.

There are two tiers of windows in each storey of the Thatbyinnyu, as well as huge arches inlaid with flamboyant pediments, making the interior bright and allowing a breeze to flow through. The first two storeys were once the residence of monks. The third level housed images, and the fourth, a library. At the top was a stupa containing holy relics.

NGAKYWENADAUNG PAGODA AND NATHLAUNG KYAUNG

Immediately west of the Thatbyinnyu, on the right (north) side of the lane, stands the **Ngakywenadaung Pagoda**, a small, bulbous stupa (very similar to the Bupaya) standing on a circular base.

Diagonally opposite, the **Nathlaung Kyaung ⑥** is the last surviving Hindu temple at Bagan and a perfect example of the religious tolerance that prevailed here in the early 10th century. It is thought to have been constructed by Taungthugyi in 931 – well before Theravada Buddhism was introduced from Thaton – and was dedicated to Vishnu. The Nathlaung Kyaung remained Bagan's greatest Hindu temple throughout its golden age, a time when Theravada and Mahayana Buddhism, and *nat* and *naga* worship, were followed, and the Tantric practices of the Ari monks were tolerated.

The main hall and superstructure of the Nathlaung Kyaung still stand today,

although the entrance hall and outer structures have crumbled and disappeared. The 10 *avatar* (past and future incarnations) of Vishnu were once housed in niches on the outer walls of the main hall. Seven can still be seen today. Remains of the Nathlaung Kyaung's central relic sanctuary indicate that it once contained a large Vishnu figure, which sat on the mythical Garuda with spread wings. Stolen by a German oil engineer in the late 1800s, this now resides in the Dahlem Museum, Berlin.

PAHTOTHAMYA TEMPLE

Dating from the 11th century, when Theravada Buddhism was in the ascendant at Bagan, the **Pahtothamya Temple 7**, on the left (south) side of the lane just beyond the Nathlaung Kyaung, is a classic example of Bagan's earlier, Mon-influenced architecture, built over a single storey, and with a central shine surrounded by an ambulatory. The small windows ensure that the interior remains plunged in a mysterious gloom even in the middle of the day, while the walls are covered in a profusion of murals – amongst the oldest in Bagan, although you'll need a torch to see any of them.

MIMALAUNG KYAUNG

A stone's throw west of the Pahtothamya, the **Mimalaung Kyaung 8**, near the old city's south gate, was erected in 1174. The small, square shrine stands on a massive 4-metre (13ft) -high base, intended to protect it from destruction by fire and floods (the name Mimalaung Kyaung – meaning "The Temple Which Fire Cannot Burn" – is said to have been bestowed after the building survived a devastating conflagration in 1225). The design of the shrine itself is equally unusual, with a three-tiered, heavily decorated stone roof topped by a slender spire. The views from the terrace are amongst the best in Bagan.

The temple's creator, Narapatisithu, is noted in Bagan's history for the way in which he became king in 1173: his brother, King Naratheinka, had stolen his wife and made her queen while Narapatisithu was on a foreign campaign. The wronged sibling returned to

The Bupaya Pagoda is used as a navigation aid by boats due to its prominent location.

Buddha statues around Mahabodhi temple.

☉ Tip

Nearly all hotels in Bagan have cycles for hire, and these can be a great way of exploring the ruins – early morning or late afternoon is best, when the heat is bearable.

Bagan with 80 trusted men, murdered his brother and re-took the throne. His wife, Veluvati, remained queen.

ARCHAEOLOGICAL MUSEUM

Opposite the Mimalaung Kyaung stands the government-run **Archaeological Museum ❾** (Tues–Sun 9.30am–4.30pm; charge), containing rather lacklustre displays of Bagan's varied architecture, iconography and religious history. Its prize exhibit is the **Myazedi Inscription** (AD 1113) – Myanmar's own Rosetta Stone, which tell the story of King Kyangsittha and Prince Yazakumar in four ancient languages (a second, identical copy of the inscription can be see nearby at the Myazedi temple in Myinkaba village). The translations enabled scholars to decipher the script of the ancient Pyu, the first civilisation of the Ayeyarwady Valley.

GAWDAWPALIN TEMPLE

One of the most majestic buildings in Bagan, the 12th-century **Gawdawpalin Temple ❿** rests on the opposite side of the lane from the museum. Built by King

Narapatisithu, the temple's lofty dimensions and "double cube" design (like a pair of cubes, one set on top of the other) are typical of Bagan's later Bamar style. The Gawdawpalin suffered particularly badly in the 1975 earthquake, during which the *sikhara* and stupa collapsed, and a wide crack opened through the middle of the central structure. Renovation work since, however, has remedied most of the damage. Square in plan with porticoes on all four sides, the shrine is one of the largest in Bagan, featuring a vaulted corridor inside which reside four gilded Buddhas.

BUPAYA PAGODA

From the Gawdawpalin, turn left on to the main lane running north and follow it to the far, northern perimeter of the old walled city, where the **Bupaya Pagoda ⓫** enjoys a prime site overlooking the river. According to tradition, the stupa was built by the third king of Bagan, Pyusawti (AD 162–243), who found a way to get rid of a gourd-like climbing plant *(bu)* that infested the river banks. As a reward, Thamuddarit,

The Mingalazedi pagoda covered in scaffolding.

the founder-king of Bagan, gave him the hand of his daughter in marriage – and the Bamar throne. Pyusawti had the Bupaya Pagoda built to commemorate his stroke of good luck. The oldest stupa in the city (although what you see now is actually a reconstruction, the original having been toppled during the 1975 earthquake), the Bupaya looks quite different from most of Bagan's other stupas, with a distinctively bulbous shape, similar in some ways to the Tibetan *chorte*, and supported by rows of crenellated walls. Because of its prominent position on the river bank, it is used as a navigation aid by boats. An altar to Mondaing, *nat* of storms, sits beneath a pavilion with a nine-gabled roof in the pagoda grounds.

MAHABODHI TEMPLE

Across the road from the Pebhinkyaung stands the **Mahabodhi Temple ⑫**, a replica of a 6th-century structure of the same name built at Bodhgaya in India, where the Buddha achieved Enlightenment. The pyramidal shape of the temple tower is of a kind favoured during India's Gupta Period, quite different from the bell-shaped monuments common elsewhere in Burma.

Constructed during the reign of Nantaungmya (1210–34), it followed a long-standing fascination among Bagan's kings with Indian architecture. More than a century earlier, Kyanzittha had sent men and materials to India to carry out some renovation work on the Bodhgaya Temple, and in the mid-12th century, Alaungsithu made the king of Rakhine (Arakan) do the same.

The lower section of the Mahabodhi is a quadrangular block supporting the pyramidal structure, which in turn is crowned by a small stupa. The pyramid is completely covered with niches containing seated Buddha figures. Apart from a copy erected on the terrace of the Shwedagon in Yangon, the Mahabodhi is the only temple in Burma built with such profuse exterior decoration.

CENTRAL PLAIN

The belt of central plain running east from Myinkaba in parallel with the road to Nyaung U features some of Bagan's

Stupa detail, Mahabodhi temple.

View of Shwesandaw temple.

A sign reminds visitors to remove their shoes at Dhammayangyi temple.

Leaving Dhammayangyi temple.

largest and most visited temples, among them the mighty Shwesandaw Pagoda.

MINGALAZEDI PAGODA

Close to the left bank of the Ayeyarwady, between Myinkaba and Old Bagan, the **Mingalazedi Pagoda** was the last of the great stupas erected during the Era of the Temple Builders and represents the pinnacle of Bamar stupa architecture, towering 40 metres (131ft) above the surrounding plains. Six years in the making, it was completed in 1287, just ten years before the Mongol invasion, by Narathihapate, the last king to reign over a unified Bagan Empire.

Steep flights of steps lead up to the main platform from the middle of each side. Miniature stupas in the shape of Indian *kalasa* (nectar pots) stand at the corners of each of the terraces, whose walls are adorned with large glazed tiles depicting scenes from the *Jataka* stories. These were considered great luxuries in their time, and the fact that over a thousand such pieces were commissioned is indicative of the wealth and extravagance that prevailed

in the twilight of the empire. Many have been stolen, but 561 survive *in situ*.

SHWESANDAW PAGODA

The **Shwesandaw Pagoda** and adjacent **Shinbinthalyaung** , with its reclining Buddha, comprise one of only four religious structures Anawrahta built in Bagan. Erected in 1057 upon his victorious return from Thaton to enshrine hairs of the Buddha (sent by the king of Bago as a token of thanks for Bamar military support against the Khmers), the Shwesandaw is sometimes called the Ganesh Temple, after the elephant-headed Hindu god whose image once stood at the corners of its five successively diminishing terraces. The cylindrical stupa, nowadays sporting a spectacular coat of gold leaf, stands on an octagonal platform atop these terraces, which, like the nearby Mingalazedi, was originally adorned with glazed ceramic *Jataka* plaques. The original *hti*, which collapsed along with the rest of the central spire in the 1975 earthquake, can still be seen lying near the pagoda. Affording spectacular panoramic views across the temple-strewn

plains, it's the most popular sunset-viewing spot in Bagan and attracts crowds of visitors and postcard sellers towards the end of the day, during which the narrow terraces can become impossibly crowded.

The long flat building within the walls of the Shwesandaw enclosure contains the **Shinbinthalyaung Reclining Buddha**. Over 18 metres (60ft) in length, this 11th-century image lies with its head facing south and therefore depicts the sleeping Buddha (only the dying Buddha faces north).

DHAMMAYANGYI TEMPLE

Despite occupying the throne for only a short time, Narathu is remembered as the creator of Bagan's largest temple, the **Dhammayangyi ⑮**, which rises from the scrub a short walk southeast of the Shwesandaw. Deeply concerned about his karma for future lives after having murdered his father and brother, Narathu built the Dhammayangyi intending to atone for his misdeeds. It remains one of Bagan's most memorable buildings, with a layout similar to that of the Ananda but lacking the delicate, harmonious touch of its prototype. The brickwork and masonry, however, are without equal.

Local legend asserts that Narathu oversaw the construction himself and that masons were executed if a needle could be pushed between the bricks they had laid. The building, however, was never completed. Before work could be finished, Narathu himself was assassinated by an Indian hit squad dispatched by the father of one of his wives, whom he'd had executed because he disliked her Hindu rituals. Disguised as Brahmin priests, the assassins drew swords as soon as they'd been received by the king, then killed themselves when surrounded by the palace guard.

SULAMANI

Marooned in the middle of Bagan's central plain, well off the site's surfaced roads, the **Sulamani Temple ⑯** is one of Bagan's greatest two-storey monuments and the classic example of the fully developed Bamar architectural style. Built by Narapatisithu in 1183, the temple is named after the legendary palace of the god Indra, crowning the peak of Mount Meru. The plan of the temple may have been modelled on that of the Thatbyinnyu, and was later copied by the builders of other temples including the Gawdawpalin and Htilominlo. None, however, quite matches the perfect proportions of the Sulamani. Each of the two storeys is of an equal height, with three terraces on top of each one, lending the entire structure a classic simplicity and grace and striking the perfect balance between vertical and horizontal elements – Bagan architecture at its finest. The original tower collapsed during the 1975 earthquake and was subsequently rebuilt – although it's only close up that the difference becomes apparent.

Inside, the upper storey rests on a huge central pillar that occupies the middle of the ground floor. The lower level has seated Buddha images on

There are dozens of temples in the Bagan Archaeological Zone.

The Ananda temple and surrounding pagodas.

all four sides. Porches face the four cardinal points on each storey, with those oriented eastwards being larger than the others. The remains of some 18th-century murals can also be seen, with various Buddhas and other figures painted in an engagingly naïve, almost child-like manner.

NORTHERN PLAIN

Half a dozen noteworthy monuments lie on the plain dividing Old Bagan from Nyaung U. Though relatively close to both Old Bagan and Nyaung U, you'll need some form of transport to reach them. The following account works from west to east, starting at the area's most distinctive landmark, the white-washed Ananda Temple.

ANANDA TEMPLE

Just to the east of the old city walls, the **Ananda Temple** ⑰ is considered the masterpiece of Bagan's Mon architecture. Completed in 1091, it was, according to *The Glass Palace Chronicle*, inspired by a visit to Kyanzittha's palace by eight Indian monks, who arrived one

day begging for alms. They told the king they had once lived in a legendary Himalayan cave temple and, using meditative powers, made the mythical mountain landscape appear before Kyanzittha's eyes. Overwhelmed by the beauty of the vision, the king immediately decided to build a replica of this snowy abode at Bagan and is said to have been so awe-struck by the result that he personally executed the architect to ensure the temple could not be duplicated.

The entire enclosure, 53 metres (174ft) on each side, is in the shape of a perfect Greek cross. The roof above the central superstructure consists of five terraces, covered with 389 terracotta-glazed tiles illustrating *Jataka* tales. Together with those inside the temple and at its base, they represent the largest collection of such tiles in Bagan.

Capped by a golden stupa rising 51 metres (168ft) above the ground, Ananda's beehive sanctuary tower *(sikhara)* rises from the tiered roof. Smaller pagodas, copies of the central spire, stand at each of its four corners,

creating the impression of a mountainous Himalayan landscape.

The labyrinthine interior is one of the most interesting in Bagan. Each of the four entrances is protected by a pair of guardians seated in niches and by a huge teak door, while inside, rather than the customary single ambulatory, the Ananda has two (one enclosed inside the other).

Four huge, 9.5-metre (31ft) -tall teak Buddha images, dimly lit from the slits in the sanctuary roof, stand on each side of the temple's central core. The north- and south-facing statues are originals; those facing east and west are later copies. The two lacquer figures sitting at the feet of the Buddha on the western side are said to depict the temple's creator, King Kyanzittha, and his spiritual advisor Shin Arahan. The eastern Buddha is unusual in that it doesn't conform to any recognised Buddhist mudra, holding a small object said to be a herbal pill and perhaps symbolising the relief from suffering provided by the Buddha's teachings. Strangest of all, however, is the southern Buddha, whose face changes from a pensive frown to a clownish smile as you walk away from it.

UPALI THEIN

About 1.5km (1 mile) down the main road from the Ananda Temple towards Nyaung U, the 13th-century **Upali Thein** ⑱ or hall of ordination, was named after the monk Upali. Although of brick construction, it is said to resemble many of the wooden buildings of the Bagan Era which have long since disappeared. The roof has two rows of battlements and a pagoda at its centre. The Konbaung dynasty undertook extensive renovations at the end of the 18th century, re-painting the beautiful frescoes of Buddhas and *Jataka* stories that adorn the walls.

HTILOMINLO TEMPLE

Across the road from the Upali Thein stands the last major Bamar-style temple built in Bagan, the **Htilominlo** ⑲. The building was constructed in 1211 under the orders of King Nantaungmya who, according to *The Glass Palace Chronicle*, was the son of one of King

Buddha statue at Upali Thein temple.

Fresco at the Upali Thein.

Narapatisithu's concubines. He chose this spot to site the shrine because it was where the white umbrella used to identify future rulers tilted in his direction.

The soaring temple reaches a height of 46 metres (150ft) – not the tallest temple in Bagan, but certainly one of the most graceful. Finely executed stucco carving showing lines of ogre-like *kirtimukhas* decorate the exterior walls, their fang-filled mouths linked with chains of garlands. Inside some of the temple's old murals can still be seen along with some old horoscopes, painted on the walls to protect the building from damage.

GUBYAUKNGE AND GUBYAUKGYI

Half a kilometre further up the main road towards Nyaung U, near the village of Wetkyi-in, the **Gubyaukgne** ⑳ is notable for the fine stucco work on its exterior walls. Standing next to it is the **Gubyaukgyi** ㉑, which dates from the early 13th century and has a pyramidal spire similar to that of the Mahabodhi. Inside are some of Bagan's finest *Jataka* murals. Unfortunately, many of these were removed by a German enthusiast in the late 19th century and spirited out of the country – the gaping holes he left in his wake are still sadly obvious.

NYAUNG U

The principal hub for the Archaeological Zone is **Nyaung U**, a busy little riverside market town, 5km (3 miles) north of the walled village of Old Bagan. This is where you'll find the largest concentrations of budget hotels, restaurants and souvenir shops, as well as transport connections. The town also holds its own small collection of historic monuments, notably the huge and resplendently gilded Shwezigon Pagoda, one of Bagan's most iconic landmarks.

KYANZITTHA UMIN

On the southwestern outskirts of Nyaung U, close to the Shwezigon Pagoda, is the **Kyanzittha Umin** ㉒, a cave shrine that also once served as a place of lodging for monks. Although its name suggests it was created by King Kyanzittha, in all probability it dates from Anawrahta's reign. The long, dark corridors are embellished with frescoes

Feeding pigeons outside the Shwezigon Pagoda, Nyaung U.

from the 11th, 12th and 13th centuries; some of the later paintings even depict the Mongols who occupied Bagan after 1287. The resident caretaker may have a torch to lend you for a small gratuity if you don't have your own.

SHWEZIGON PAGODA

The **Shwezigon Pagoda** ㉓, a short walk north of the cave temple, ranks among Myanmar's most revered Buddhist shrines. The prototype for all Burmese stupas, the Shwezigon was begun during the reign of Anawrahta at a spot designated by a white elephant to house the empire's most sacred relics: a replica of the Tooth of Kandy; frontal and collar bones of the Master; and an emerald Buddha image from China. Only the pagoda's three terraces had been finished when Anawrahta was killed by a rampaging buffalo in 1077. His son, Kyanzittha, completed the structure in 1089.

The stupa sits on top of the three terraces, reached by stairways from the cardinal directions. The pagoda spire, crowned by a *hti*, rises above the bell in a series of concentric mouldings. Smaller stupas can be seen at the corners of the terraces, each decorated with glazed plaques illustrating the *Jataka* tales. Small square temples on each side of the central stupa contain standing Buddhas in the Indian Gupta style. To the left and right of the eastern entrance are two stone pillars, each inscribed on all four sides, recording the establishment of the pagoda during Kyanzittha's reign.

During the second week of the Burmese month of *Nadaw* (November and December), Buddhist pilgrims from throughout the country converge on the Shwezigon for the temple's annual festival. The event is one of the nation's most popular, largely because it was at the Shwezigon that *nat* worship was first combined with Buddhism. Anawrahta had the images of the 37 of the most important *nats* carved in wood and placed on the lower terraces, believing

that "men will not come for the sake of the new faith. Let them come for their old gods and gradually they will be won over." The *nat* are no longer on the terraces, but are housed in a small hall to the southeast of the pagoda, where they are still venerated today.

SAPADA PAGODA

An example of a stricter adherence to orthodox Theravada Buddhism can be seen at the **Sapada Pagoda** ㉔, at the eastern end of Nyaung U on the airport road. Built in the 12th century by the monk Shin Sapada, it bears witness to one of the great schisms in Burmese Buddhism. Sapada (or Chapata, as his name is also spelt) was one of the monks sent to Sri Lanka in the latter part of the 12th century, accompanying the king's own spiritual advisor, Shin Uttarajiva. Uttarajiva came back to Myanmar soon afterwards, but Sapada remained in Sri Lanka for a decade before eventually returning. When he did so it was to expound a significantly different, and much more orthodox, version of Theravada Buddhism, based

Bagan's expansive temple site.

Dhammayazika temple detail.

Dhammayazika temple aglow at sunset.

on the doctrines of the conservative Mahavihara School of Sri Lanka. This differed markedly from the Mon-style of Theravada Buddhism preached by Shin Arahan, which had remained the dominant form of the religion in Bagan up to that time. A major schism ensued until King Narapatisithu threw his weight behind Sapada, after which the Sri Lankan version of Theravada rapidly ousted that inherited from the Mon.

SOUTHERN PLAIN

The plains immediately south of Nyaung U are home to a huge number of temple ruins, most easily be reached via the main road running from the airport to New Bagan, past the villages of **Minnanthu** and **Pwasaw** – though the majority of horse-cart drivers prefer to reach it via the sandy tracks of the central plain. Being so far from Old Bagan and the tourist enclave, this is among the least frequented corners of the Archaeological Zone, and one that's received less attention from the restorers over the past couple of decades, which makes it all the more atmospheric.

NANDAMANNYA TEMPLE

The **Nandamannya Temple** ㉕ lies a ten-minute walk north of Minnanthu village. Dating from the 13th century, the temple was originally called Ananta Panna ("Endless Wisdom") until its name was changed to Nandamannya to avoid confusion with the Ananda Temple. This is one of the few monuments in this far-flung southern group to attract much attention – a fact attributable to the erotic murals adorning its interior walls. Unusual for the normally austere Theravada tradition, these depict the famous "Temptation of Mara" during which the demon Mara attempted to distract the meditating Buddha with visions of beautiful maidens. There's also a seated Buddha image in a state of advanced decay.

PAYATHONZU TEMPLE

The **Payathonzu Temple** ㉖, the next but one temple south, contains more fine frescoes which archaeologists think were probably painted by the same artist responsible for those at the nearby Nandamannya, although they're somewhat

less sensuous. Unusually, the structure consists of three interconnected buildings – hence the name Payathonzu, meaning "Three Shrines" – joined by narrow vaulted passages and crowned with a *sikhara*. Three empty pedestals stand inside, their Buddha images having long since disappeared. The frescoes fascinate art historians due to their signs of both Mahayana and Tantric influences. As the Payathonzu was erected in the late 13th century, this suggests that some form of Mahayana Buddhism, albeit as a minority faith, was practised throughout the later years of the Bagan Empire. It has also been suggested that the triple nature of this temple harks back to the *trimurti* of Indian religion, the Hindu holy trinity of Vishnu, Shiva and Brahma – though Buddhists might argue that the triple nature of Buddha, *sangha* and *dhamma* would provide an equally valid interpretation.

LEIMYETHNA TEMPLE

On the northern fringes of Minnanthu village, just beyond the Payathonzu, is the whitewashed **Leimyethna Temple ㉗**. Topped by a gilded spire in the same style as that of the Ananda, it was built in 1222 by Ananthasuriya, Naratheinhka's minister-in-chief, in commemoration of a verse written by his predecessor and close namesake, Ananthathurya. Sentenced to death by King Narapatisithu, this man penned a poem that is still regarded as a Burmese literary treasure. "If... I were to be released and freed from execution I would not escape Death," he wrote. "Inseparable am I from Karma." The king was reportedly so moved he reconsidered and decided to pardon the poet, but was too late – the unfortunate minister had already been executed. The temple, which faces east, contains some still vibrant murals.

DHAMMAYAZIKA PAGODA

Located midway between Minnanthu and Myinkaba is the **Dhammayazika**

Pagoda ㉘, built in 1196 by King Narapatisithu. The temple is highly unusual on account of its pentagonal layout, with five gateways leading into a five-sided central enclosure, and five shrines attached to the central stupa (rather than the usual four). The five-sided layout is the result, it's believed, of the desire to accommodate an additional shrine to the future Buddha, Maitreya, alongside the usual four Buddhas (Kakusandha, Konagamana, Kassapa and Gautama) of the current world cycle who are commonly shown at the cardinal points of Burmese Buddhist temples. The shrines themselves are unusually impressive, topped by statues of lions and guardian figures, and with traces of Konbaung-era murals within, while delicate stucco carving and glazed *Jataka* panels can be seen around the pentagonal terraces supporting the main stupa itself.

MYINKABA

When King Anawrahta returned to Bagan in 1057 with the Mon royalty in tow, he exiled King Manuha and his

⊘ Tip

Myinkaba is nowadays the centre of a thriving lacquerware industry, with around a dozen family workshops and showrooms where you can observe the various stages of the production process and see some outstanding antique pieces.

Abeyadana temple details.

family to Myinkaba (Myinpagan), 2km (1.2 miles) south of the city walls. With royalty present, the settlement became the site of the most splendid Mon-style architecture on the Bagan plain. Many of these monuments still stand.

SOMINGYI KYAUNG

Almost halfway between Myinkaba and New Bagan is the **Somingyi Kyaung** ㉙, one of the few brick monasteries (*kyaung*) on the Bagan plain. It's a good example of the myriad monasteries that once dotted this arid tableland; most were built of wood and have now disappeared without trace. A lobby surrounds the raised platform of the *kyaung* to the east, with monks' cells to the north and south, and a two-storey shrine, which houses an image of the Buddha, to the west. It is thought to have been built around 1204 and is named after the woman who sponsored its construction.

NAGAYON TEMPLE

Reclining Buddha inside the Manuha temple.

The **Nagayon Temple** ㉚, where Kyanzittha is said to have hidden during his flight from Anawrahta, stands on the opposite side of the road from the Somingyi. Legend has it that a *naga* offered the fugitive protection here, much as the Naga Muchalinda shielded the meditating Buddha from a storm. The temple's markedly Mon style is typical of the buildings constructed during Kyanzittha's reign, although this one also shows influences from India's Orissa region – a major trading partner.

In the interior of the Nagayon are stone reliefs depicting scenes from the life of the Buddha plus a large gilded standing Buddha, with the hood of a naga-king providing shelter above.

ABEYADANA TEMPLE

A short distance north of the Somingyi, on the river-side of the road, the **Abeyadana Temple** ㉛ was named after Kyanzittha's first wife. Local legend claims the temple is situated at the place where she waited for him during his flight from Anawrahta. Abeyadana, originally from Bengal, was probably a follower of Mahayana Buddhism: the frescoes on the outer walls of the corridor represent Bodhisattva, or future Buddhas, and on the inner walls are images of Brahma, Vishnu, Shiva, Indra, and other gods of the Hindu pantheon paying homage to the Master, along with wonderful *Jataka* murals.

NANPAYA TEMPLE

The **Nanpaya Temple** ㉜, just north of the Abeyadana, is said to have once been Manuha's residence. Its interior, which holds some of Bagan's most accomplished sculptural detail, shows the influence of Hinduism on Mon Theravada Buddhism. Four huge central pillars stand in the middle of the shrine, each decorated with various friezes plus a large image of the god Brahma holding a lotus. On the outside walls of the temple are friezes of the mythological *hamsa* bird, which, besides being the heraldic crest of Mon royalty, was also the vehicle on which Brahma was usually depicted riding.

MANUHA TEMPLE

A short stroll further north, bang in the middle of Myinkaba village, the **Manuha Temple** ⓼ was built (according to tradition) by Manuha, the captive king of Thaton, in 1059. Fearing he would be reincarnated as a temple slave, Manuha sold some of his jewels in order to finance the construction of this shrine, thereby hoping to improve his karma for future lives. One reclining and three seated Buddha images cramped within the narrow confines of the building are said to symbolise the distressed soul of the defeated king.

In contrast to most other Mon-style temples, the Manuha has an upper storey. This collapsed during the 1975 earthquake and buried the Buddhas beneath it, but renovation work was completed in 1981. A corner of the temple compound is dedicated to the *nats* of Mount Popa.

MYINKABA PAGODA

On the banks of a small stream at the north side of the village, the diminutive **Myinkaba Pagoda** ⓽ allegedly marks the spot where Anawrahta slew his predecessor and half-brother, Sokkate, in a duel for the kingship in 1044. Sokkate and his elder brother Kyiso had wrested the Bagan throne from Anawrahta's father, Kunhsaw Kyaunghpyu, himself a usurper, in AD 986; but Anawrahta's victory over Sokkate with his mythical spear "Areindama" put an end to over a century of court intrigues. This shrine's bulbous form and round terraces mark it clearly as predating the establishment of Mon Buddhist influence in the Bagan region.

GUBYAUKGYI TEMPLE

Close to the roadside at the northern edge of Myinkaba village, the **Gubyaukgyi Temple** ⓾ (not to be confused with the identically named temple near Nyaung U) is famous above all for the **Myazedi Stones** originally discovered inside it in 1887. These two pillar inscriptions are inscribed in a different language on each of their four sides – Burmese, Mon, Pali and Pyu – a kind of Burmese Rosetta Stone which allowed philologists finally to decipher the ancient Pyu language. One of the two pillar inscriptions is now housed in a small concrete pavilion in the modern Myazedi temple, right next to the Gubyaukgyi; the other can be found inside the Archaeological Museum in Old Bagan (see page 216).

The temple also boasts some well-preserved murals inside its (very dark) shrine and ambulatory. These include a set of the 547 *Jataka* tales, believed to date back to 1113, when Rajakumar built the temple upon the death of his father, Kyanzittha. The east-facing vestibule contains a representation of a 10-armed Bodhisattva typical of Mahayana Buddhism.

NEW BAGAN AND THIRIPYITSAYA

South of the major ruins at the southwest corner of the Archaeological Zone lies the modern settlement of **New Bagan (Bagan Myothit)**, comprising a neat grid of streets laid out in the 1990s to accommodate people forcibly

Crafting lacquerware in Myinkaba village.

re-located by the government from the walled city of Old Bagan. With trees and shrubs planted by the locals now well established, Bagan Myothit is no longer the barren place it was a decade ago and makes a relaxing base if you're staying in one of its numerous hotels or guesthouses.

On its southwest corner, tiny **Thiripyitsaya Village**, where King Thinlikyaung's 4th-century palace was situated, was the site of Bagan's main port during its glory years, where foreign ships plying the Ayeyarwady from lands as far away as Sri Lanka dropped anchor. Today, the chief attractions are a trio of well-preserved pagodas. Two of them, known as the **Anauk ("Eastern") Petleik** 🅰 and **Ashe ("Western") Petleik** 🅱 were built in the 11th century, but collapsed in 1905. The unglazed terracotta plaques originally housed in the vaulted corridors are now preserved under replicas of the original roofs. Of the two temples, the Anauk is the better preserved. The numbered plaques depict 550 *Jataka* tales including the only known representations of three particular stories, as

On the way to Dhammayangyi temple.

only 547 *Jataka* tales are officially recognised by the Theravada Buddhist *sangha*.

At the south end of Thiripyitsaya is the **Lawkananda Pagoda** 🅲, raised in 1059 as one of only four stupas known to have been built by Anawrahta in the Bagan area (the others being the Shwezigon, Shwesandaw and Myinkaba). Brilliantly gilded, and with fine river views, the stupa has an unusual cylindrical body (rather than the usual bell-shaped construction) and stands on three octagonal terraces. The pagoda still functions as an everyday place of worship and houses what is believed to be a replica of the Buddha's tooth.

The **Seinnyet Ama Temple and Seinnyet Nyima Pagoda** 🅳, on the main road a short distance to the north of New Bagan, are traditionally attributed to the 11th-century Queen Seinnyet, although the style is more typical of the 13th. The pagoda in particular is notable for its design, incorporating Buddhas in niches at each of the cardinal points on the bell-shaped dome, and lions guarding miniature stupas in the corners of the second terrace.

RESPONSIBLE TOURISM

After many decades, foreign visitors are no longer being asked to boycott visiting Myanmar on ethical grounds, but challenges still exist.

In 2010, after the military government embarked on a process of democratic reform in Myanmar, Aung San Suu Kyi's National League for Democracy (NLD) declared an end to the longstanding tourism boycott of the country. Foreigners had long been discouraged from visiting on the grounds that their presence legitimised and generated income for the repressive regime and its cronies – while thousands of political prisoners languished in jail, and ethnic minorities were subject to torture, forced labour and other forms of abuse perpetrated by the Burmese army (Tatmadaw)

Things have moved on rapidly since the NLD's announcement and their subsequent victory in the elections of 2015, while tourism is booming as never before. Many of the issues that confronted visitors to Myanmar pre-2015 have now become significantly less pressing. Equally, new concerns have emerged, particularly the NLD government's lack of interest in halting the mass murder and displacement of the horribly oppressed Rohingya community (see page 54) – an act of state-sponsored barbarity which has led to calls for Aung San Suu Kyi to be stripped of her Nobel prize and which might in itself be seen as sufficient reason to avoid the country.

ETHICAL PRACTICE

The following points should ensure that your visit to Myanmar has the greatest benefit for your hosts.

Although the generals no longer rule Myanmar, they and their cronies still control significant sectors of the economy, including many hotels and tourist-related services. You may wish to avoid staying in resorts owned by or connected to high-ranking members of the former junta – although identifying such places can be difficult, and they also employ thousands of blameless civilians whose livelihoods rely on tourism.

In addition, all the country's domestic airlines are owned by companies linked to the former junta, so every time you fly you contribute money to their coffers. The same applies to the country's banks – every time you use an ATM the local withdrawal fee you pay goes into crony pockets.

Despite the huge recent increase in tourist numbers, the vast majority of visitors still only travel to the big four attractions: Yangon, Mandalay, Bagan and Lake Inle. Much of the country still sees little benefit from tourism. By stepping off the beaten track at least once in your journey you help ensure that the benefits of tourism are spread at least a little more equitably. Travel independently rather than as part of a large organised tour, using locally owned accommodation.

If you do book a tour, avoid large foreign-owned operators in favour of smaller, independently run ones with a clear policy on benefiting local economies.

Spread your money around as widely as possible. Patronise different taxi drivers, eat in family-run restaurants and buy souvenirs from local shops.

Interact at every opportunity with Burmese people you meet – though be cautious when discussing politics.

Don't take photographs of people without first seeking their permission.

Wear appropriate clothing and behave respectfully when visiting religious sites.

Rather than giving money to individuals, make donations to social projects where your gift may contribute to ongoing work.

Selling sand paintings outside Abeyadana temple.

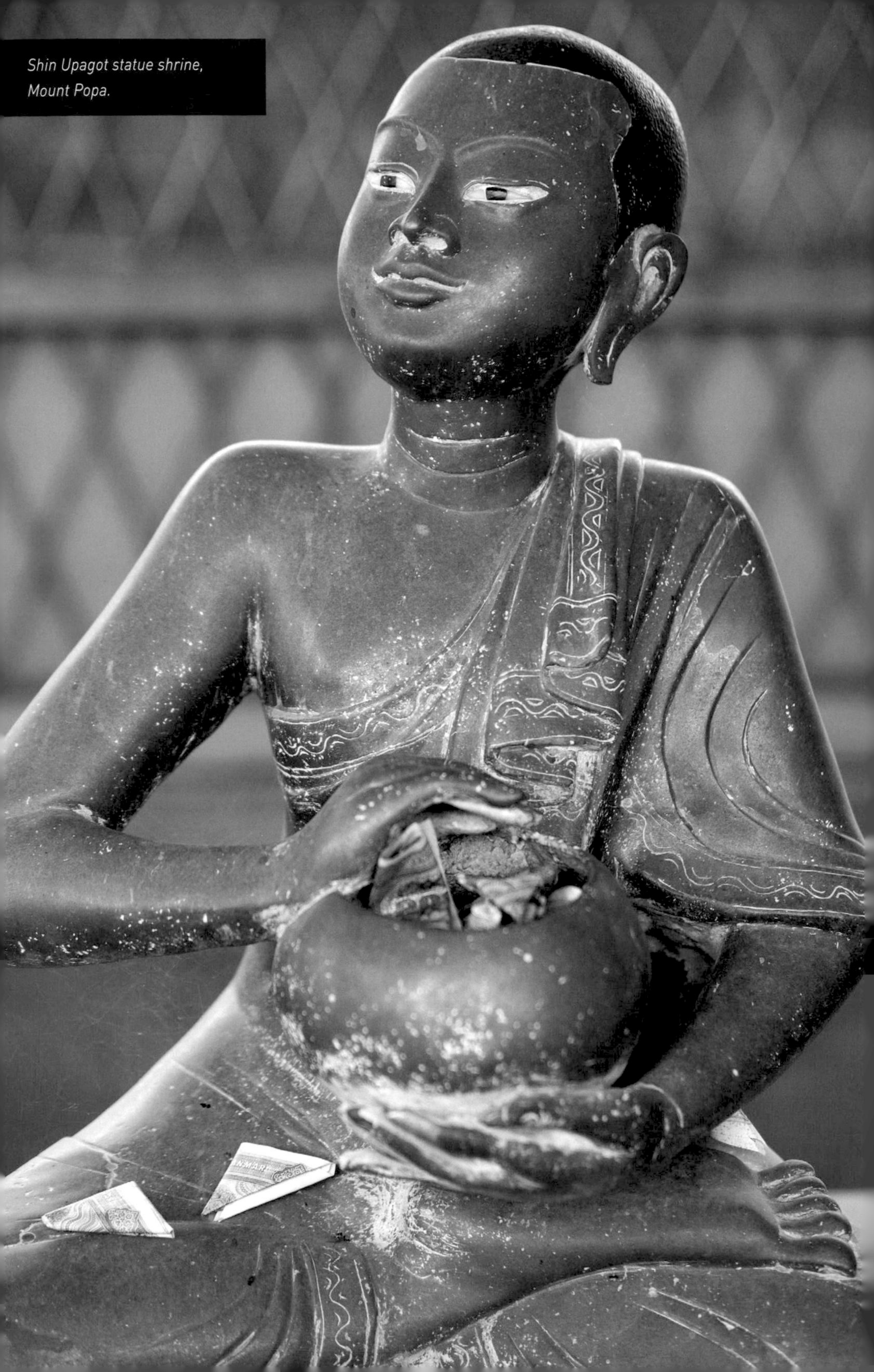

Shin Upagot statue shrine, Mount Popa.

AROUND BAGAN

Dominated by the magnificent Mount Popa, the otherwise flat plains around Bagan are scattered with ancient temples and bustling market towns.

The arid plains around Bagan are dotted with a number of rewarding sights which make for interesting half- or full-day trips. The most popular excursion is to **Mount Popa**, an extinct volcano 90-minutes' drive southeast, whose dramatic profile can be seen on the horizon from Bagan in clear weather. Poking up from the flanks of the mountain is the craggy basalt plug of **Popa Taung Talat**, a geological curiosity which has become the country's principal centre for *nat* worship. It's worth making the trip just for the views from the top of Taung Talat, which surveys an awesome sweep of mountainous landscape. The surrounding village is usually busy with local worshippers, with huge numbers descending during the two annual temple festivals. There's even a decent hotel should you be tempted to stay the night for the trek up Mount Popa itself early the following morning.

Closer to **Bagan ❶**, a cluster of off-track ancient temples lies upriver, reachable by boat from the jetty at Nyaung U, while the region's market towns provide a splash of local atmosphere. Elsewhere, the bustling town of **Pakkoku** and the superb wooden monastery at **Salay** attract a sprinkling of visitors looking to get a little further off the beaten track.

This wood will be used as fuel to heat palm sugar and turn it into jaggery.

TEMPLES UPRIVER FROM NYAUNG U

Boats can be chartered throughout the day from Nyaung U's little jetty for trips to a trio of small temples upstream – an excursion of around three or four hours including stops at the monuments.

The first site you come to, 1km (0.6 miles) north, is the 13th-century **Thatkyamuni Temple ❷**, in which panels of murals depicting Ashoka, the great Mauryan Emperor who ruled in India during the 3rd century BC, adorn

◎ Main attractions
Boat trips from Bagan
Pakhangyi
Popa Taung Kalat
Mount Popa

Map on page 234

⊙ **Tip**

Come prepared if you plan to climb Popa Taung Kalat. The ascent takes less than half an hour but is a fairly stiff climb. Bring a hat or parasol, and ensure that you have plenty of water with you.

the walls. Other scenes record the introduction of the Buddhist faith to Sri Lanka. On a low hill close by, the **Kondawgyi Temple** was a contemporary of the Thatkyamuni, and also holds some paintings, this time of *Jataka* scenes and floral patterns.

Boats continue for 3km (2 miles) until they reach a clay escarpment overlooking the Ayeyarwady, from which the **Kyaukgu Umin cave temple ❸** surveys the river. A maze of passages leads into the caves behind: the stone-and-brick-built chamber is in fact an enlargement of the natural hollow. A large Buddha sits opposite the entrance, and the walls are embellished with stone reliefs. The Kyaukgu Umin's ground floor dates from the 11th century; the upper two storeys have been ascribed to the reign of Narapatisithu (1174–1211).

POPA

The most popular excursion from Bagan is to the *nat* temple at **Popa Taung Kalat**, 50km (30 miles) southeast. Confusingly, this spectacular

The Pandaw III takes to the water.

pilgrimage place, which centres on an eerie outcrop of rock rising sheer from the plains, is often referred to as **"Mount Popa"**, although strictly speaking this is the name of the much larger mountain rising immediately to the east. While the former can be reached in an easy day trip from Bagan, the latter massif requires a dawn start and a full day of leg work to ascend, for which you'll need to stay in the area.

The name *"popa"*, Sanskrit for "flower", is believed to derive from the profusion of blooms nourished by the famously fertile soil of the mountain. Local legend asserts that the volcano first appeared in 442 BC after a great earthquake forced it out of the Myingyan plains. Volcanic ash gradually coalesced into rich soil, and the great peak was soon festooned with flowers. For the inhabitants of the surrounding regions this seemed a true miracle and Popa soon became legendary as a home of the gods – the "Mount Olympus" of Burma. Alchemists and occultists settled on its slopes, and people generally became convinced that mythical beings, the *nat*, inhabited its woods.

POPA TAUNG KALAT

The plug of an extinct volcano, the weirdly shaped hill of **Popa Taung Kalat** is a major centre of *nat* worship in Myanmar, particularly associated with the four "Mahagiri" ("Great Mountain") *nats* who are believed to reside on nearby Mount Popa, as well as the many other *nat* spirits of the Burmese supernatural pantheon. Worshippers from all over Burma come here to propitiate the assorted spirit deities installed both in the *nat* temple at the base of the hill (with its impressive, slightly spooky gallery of *nat* mannequins) and in the various shrines which dot the steps up the hill.

From the *nat* temple, a covered walkway lined with stalls selling religious souvenirs winds steeply up the hill itself. It's around a 20-minute walk to the top, where you'll find a small terrace crammed with a gleaming profusion of Buddhist and *nat* shrines and magnificent views across the plains to the Rakhine hills, rising from the dust haze on the horizon. Look out for the voracious macaques that patrol the steps and are not averse to snatching titbits from pilgrims' hands.

MOUNT POPA

Technically a spur of the **Bago Yoma** range, **Mount Popa ❹** is an extinct volcano rising due east of Taung Kalat to a height of 1,518 metres (4,981ft). Numerous trails lead through the lush forests wrapped around the mountain's flanks to the spectacular, 610-metre (2000ft) caldera marking its summit. Far-reaching views are guaranteed from the very start of the strenuous four-hour trek, for which guides can be arranged through the Popa Mountain Resort (http://popamountain.htophospitality.com). Bird-spotters will also enjoy the hike through Popa's pristine jungle, home to 176 species, including two endemics (the Burmese bushlark and

hooded treepie), as well as 65 different kinds of orchid.

THE LEGEND OF THE MAHAGIRI NAT

A trip to the shrine of the **Mahagiri Nat**, situated about halfway up the mountain, is an essential part of a visit to Mount Popa. For seven centuries preceding the reign of Anawrahta, all kings of central Burma were required to make a pilgrimage here to consult with the two powerful *nat* about their reign.

The legend begins with a young blacksmith, Nga Tin De, and his beautiful sister who lived outside the northern city of Tagaung in the mid-4th century, when King Thinlikyaung ruled in the Bagan area. Perceived by the king as a threat, Nga Tin De was forced to flee into the woods. The king then became enchanted with the blacksmith's sister, and married her, after which he convinced her that Nga Tin De was no longer his rival, asking her to call her brother back from the forest. But when Nga Tin De emerged, he was seized by the king's guards, tied to a tree and set alight.

Monkeys climb the steps to Mount Popa.

Nat deities inside the nat temple at the base of Mount Popa.

⊘ NAT WORSHIP

The veneration of spirit heroes known as *nat* is particular to Myanmar, where it runs in parallel and seeming harmony with the rituals of Theravada Buddhism. *Nat* shrines often appear next to, or frequently inside, Buddhist temples, and Burmese worshippers tend to see no contradiction in this, even though numerous kings tried to stamp out the tradition. After failing spectacularly in the 11th century, King Anawrahta chose to incorporate *nat* worship into local Buddhist mythology.

It was Anawrahta who first fixed the *nat* pantheon, incorporating 37 of the most popular *nat* spirits and naming them the "Great Nats" – although many other *nats* not included in Anawrahta's selection continue to be venerated. Numerous temples are dedicated to the flamboyant 37 Great Nats, all of whom have their own peculiar origin myths and personalities. All died violent deaths except Thagyamin, the King of the *Nats*, usually portrayed riding a three-headed white elephant and carrying a conch shell.

Believers propitiate different *nat* depending on what they need, visiting a local shrine or, perhaps, a temple of national importance. However, *nat* worship is practised in its most fervent form at *nat pwes*, annual festivals where special oracles called *natkadaws* dominate proceedings. After a serious drinking session, the *natkadaws* enter trances during which they're possessed by the presiding *nat* and appeased with offerings.

Nuns collecting alms.

As the fire lapped at her brother's body, Shwemyethna broke free from her escorts and threw herself into the blaze. Their physical bodies gone, the siblings became mischievous *nat* living in the tree. To stop them from causing him harm, the king had the tree chopped down and thrown into the Ayeyarwady. The story of their deaths spread rapidly throughout Burma. Thinlikyaung, who had wanted to unite the country in *nat* worship, learned that the tree was floating downstream through his kingdom. He ordered the tree fished out of the river and had two figures carved from it. The *nat* images were then carried to the top of Mount Popa and given a shrine where they reside to this day. Every king crowned in Bagan between the 4th and 11th centuries would make a pilgrimage to the brother and sister *nat*, who would supposedly appear before the ruler to counsel him.

Two other nats also subsequently became closely associated with Mount Popa. The story begins with Mai Wunna ("Miss Gold" – aka Popa Mai Daw, or the "Queen Mother of Popa"),

A local scoops her kid goat into her arms.

a flower-eating ogress who is said to rule over the mountain. According to legend, Mai Wunna fell in love with a certain Byatta, an Indian Muslim in the service of King Anawrahta. Byatta was subsequently executed for neglecting his duties, after which Mai Wunna died of a broken heart. Their two sons, Min Gyi and Min Lay, were also later executed by Anawrahta, becoming *nats* in their turn – the *nat pwe* festival celebrated in the sons' honour at Taungbyone, near Mandalay, remains to this day one of the country's most popular and riotous religious events.

SALAY

Around 55km (35 miles) south of Bagan, just past the small town of Chauk, the small riverside settlement of **Salay** ⑤ developed as an adjunct of Bagan during the 12th and 13th centuries. It's now an increasingly popular half-day trip from Bagan (or full day in combination with Mount Popa), with a cluster of still active Buddhist temples and monasteries, some fascinating colonial architecture and a number of little-visited

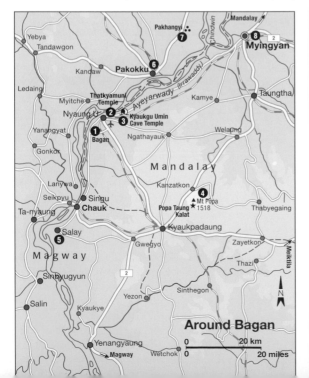

Around Bagan

0   20 km
0   20 miles

ruins. Particularly interesting is the magnificent **Yoke Sone Kyaung** (daily 9am–4pm; charge). Built in 1882, this is one of Myanmar's most impressive surviving 19th-century wooden buildings, decorated with flamboyant *Jataka* carvings outside and full of intricately carved shrines within.

PAKOKKU

To the north of Bagan, the town of **Pakokku** ❻, on the right bank of the Ayeyarwady, made international headlines during the so-called "Saffron Revolution" of 2007, when local monks spearheaded a protest against a sudden rise in petrol prices. The protest subsequently went national and led to a massive military clampdown on pro-democracy campaigners.

There's little to see in the town beyond the local market, which specialises in tobacco and *thanaka* wood. If you have a little time on your hands an enjoyable side trip can be made to the 19th-century ruins of **Pakhangyi** ❼, 20km (12 miles) northeast. The site includes old city walls, an archaeological museum and an imposing wooden temple – one of the oldest in Myanmar – supported by more than 250 teak pillars.

MYINGYAN AND THE CHINDWIN RIVER

Roughly equidistant between Mandalay and Bagan, on the left bank of the Ayeyarwady, the Bamar market town of **Myingyan** ❽ is both an important river port and cotton-trading centre, forming a junction between a branch railway to Thazi and the main line between Yangon and Mandalay. There isn't much of historical interest on offer, the central market is thriving and the almost complete lack of western visitors offers a real taste of life well off the tourist trail.

Myingyan is located just downstream from the mighty **Chindwin River**, the main tributary of the Ayeyarwady. The Chindwin is formed in the Patkai and Kumon ranges of the Indo-Myanmar

border by a network of headstreams including the Tanai, Tawan and Taron. It drains northwest through the Hukawng valley and then begins its 840km (520-mile) main course. The Chindwin flows south through the Naga Hills and past the towns of Singkaling Hkamti, Homalin, Thaungdut, Mawlaik, Kalewa and Monywa. Below the jade-rich Hukawng valley, falls and reefs interrupt it at several places. At Haka, goods must be transferred from large boats to canoes.

The Uyu and the Myittha are the main tributaries of the system, which drains around 114,000 sq km (44,000 sq miles) of northwestern Myanmar. During part of the rainy season (June–November), the Chindwin is navigable by river steamer for more than 640km (400 miles) upstream to Singkaling Hkamti. The Chindwin's outlets into the Ayeyarwady are interrupted by a succession of long, low, partially populated islands. According to tradition, the most southerly of these outlets is an artificial channel cut by one of the kings of Bagan. Choked up for many centuries, it was reopened by an exceptional flood in 1824.

Collecting palm sugar, destined for the manufacture of jaggery.

Pressing peanuts to extract the oil.

📷 THANAKA AND LONGYI: BURMESE TRADITIONS

The sarong-like *longyi* is worn by the vast majority of Myanmar's people, while *thanaka* is the cosmetic of choice.

A Burmese, it is often said, never feels comfortable in anything but a *longyi*. Since the 19th century, when it was introduced by immigrants from southern India, this simple panel of cloth (equivalent to the Malaysian sarong or the Indian lungi) wrapped around the waist has been the mode of dress for all Burmese, from commoners to members of the royal court.

Traditional *longyis* comprise rectangular lengths of printed or embroidered cloth, around 2 metres (6ft) long, which are sewn into a tube shape. When worn by men it is known as a *pasoe*, by women a *htamein*.

Both look similar but are wrapped differently: men tie a knot in front, while women tie to the side, with the knot tucked into a waistband called a *htet sint*.

Simple, checked or striped patterns in subdued colours are used for men; ladies don flowery designs and bright hues. Men finish with a Western-style shirt. Women wear a short blouse or matching top.

For special occasions such as weddings, more elegant silk *longyis* – or *acheiks* – are usually worn, accompanied by jackets and turbans for men, or in the case of women, a more elaborate, tailored top to create a suit-style outfit, with velvet-thong slippers.

The Burmese Premier, General Than Shwe, and other members of the ruling *junta* caused a stir in February 2011 when they appeared on national television wearing women's *acheiks* and *longbon* headscarves – an act political observers were quick to interpret as superstition, or *yadaya*. Fortune-tellers have repeatedly predicted that a woman will rule Myanmar one day, and so the generals' cross-dressing was seen as an attempt to confound the pundits and forestall the rise of NLD leader, Aung San Suu Kyi.

Turning thanaka wood into a paste for applying as sunscreen.

A young souvenir-seller in Inwa sporting thanaka on her cheeks.

A woman protects her face with thanaka as she chops bamboo to be used in the making of mats and as the walls of houses.

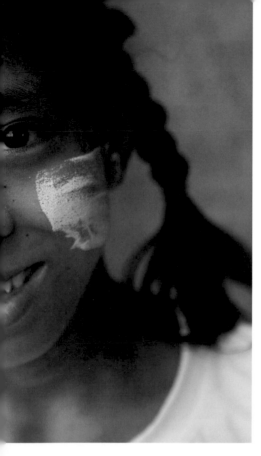

Men and women alike wearing longyi for some shopping at Nampam market.

Thanaka – the face of Myanmar

Thanaka is the yellowish-white paste that most Burmese women and girls daub over their faces (boys also often wear it, as do a few men) in various patterns ranging from a simple circular patch on each cheek to more complicated patterns painted using intricate leaf stencils. The cream is made from the ground bark of several trees, and is worn to protect fragile complexions from the darkening, dehydrating effects of strong sunlight. With a fragrance close to that of sandalwood, the cream has been used for at least 2,000 years.

Apart from its cosmetic and sun-blocking properties, *thanaka* is believed to cure acne and act as an antiseptic, which perhaps goes some way explaining why this most Burmese of traditions has so resolutely stood the test of time.

A thanaka-daubed aubergine-seller on the platform at Aungban train station.

n army of sweepers at Shwedagon Pagoda presents a olourful array of longyi.

extiles for sale in Bogyoke Market, Yangon, the flowery esigns and bright shades aimed at female customers.

Canoeing around Nampam village, Inle Lake region.

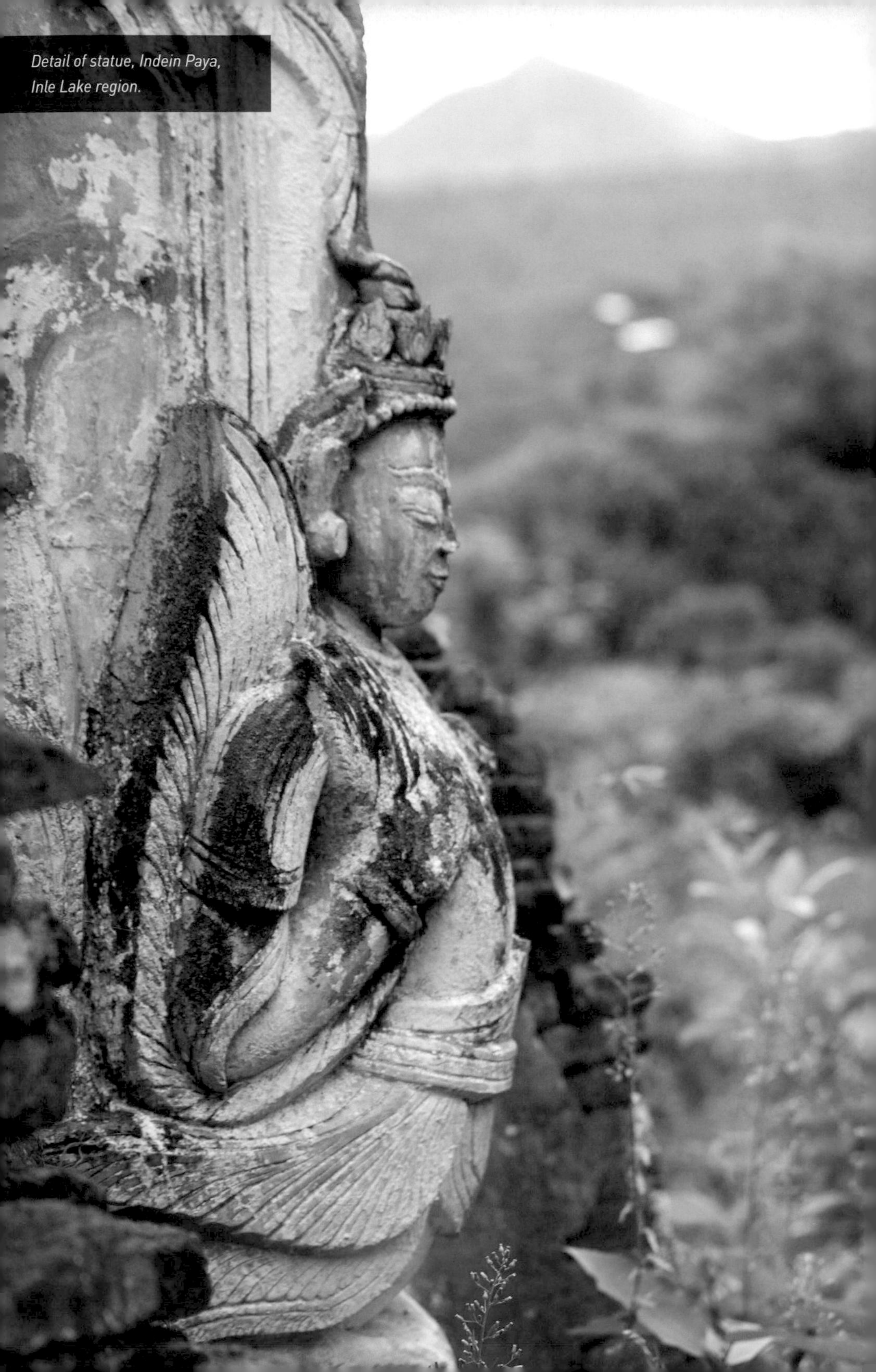

Detail of statue, Indein Paya, Inle Lake region.

NORTHEASTERN MYANMAR

The hills of Shan State extend north to China, east to Thailand and Laos, and south to Kayah. In the far north, Kachin State reaches into the Himalayas. For visitors, these far-flung regions are some of the most rewarding in Myanmar.

A novice monk cradles a kitten at Shweyan Pyay Monastery.

The image of an Intha fisherman standing on a flat-bottomed canoe, rowing with one leg past a backdrop of mist-shrouded mountains on shimmering Inle Lake, is one of Myanmar's most iconic. With its stilted villages, ancient temple complexes and green hills, Inle is the top attraction of Shan State, in Myanmar's hilly northeast. But the region holds plenty of other compelling destinations, many only recently opened to tourists.

Shan State is Myanmar's largest, extending east from its administrative capital, Taunggyi, for 350km (220 miles) to Laos and the notorious, opium-rich "Golden Triangle"; north to the Chinese border; and south to the tribal states of the Kayah and Kayin. This is a region of high, roadless peaks, of rugged river gorges and fiercely independent tribes-people who remain locked in conflict with the Burmese government, with large areas off-limits to foreigners as a result.

The overwhelming majority of foreign visitors to Shan see just the tiny corner of the state around Lake Inle, one of Myanmar's most popular, and most memorable, tourist destinations. Nearby Kalaw, a former British hill station, is visited primarily by trekkers heading into the surrounding tribal areas. The most popular routes wind east to the lake, through pine forests and a fertile belt that's intensively farmed by a variety of colourfully dressed minority groups. Another popular trail works its way 110km (70 miles) northwest to the fabulous Pindaya Cave, with its thousands of carved Buddha images. An alternative trekking hub is the market town of Hsipaw in the Nam Tu Valley. The choice of accommodation is more limited here, but the tribal villages nestled in the surrounding countryside see correspondingly fewer visitors.

Eyes down over the goods at Nampam market.

North of Shan is Kachin State – again, largely off-limits to foreigners thanks to ongoing clashes between local separatists and the military. The main draw here is the week-long trip up or down the Ayeyarwady to (or from) the towns of Myitkyina or Bhamo, which can be covered on occasional government ferries or on one of the handful of luxury cruises that operate on this relatively unfrequented stretch. West of Myitkyina, Kachin State's Indawgyi Lake is the largest in Myanmar, home to colourful tribal groups and surrounded by breathtaking scenery, while at the northermost tip of the country spectacular snowcapped mountain ranges extend around the town of Putao, near the border with India.

Young residents of the stilt
houses of Nampam village.

SHAN AND KAYAH STATES

The former lands of the Shan princes are home to gilded Buddhas and hot sulphur springs, as well as serene Inle Lake, heartland of the Intha people.

Yangon

Shan State, in eastern Burma, encompasses a beautiful plateau of rolling highlands, lakes and forests that extend all the way from the central plains to the borders of China, Laos and Thailand. This vast hill tract, which accounts for around a quarter of the country's total surface area, has always been something of a land apart – geographically remote, culturally separate, difficult to govern and perennially vulnerable to invasion. For most of the past four decades armed conflicts of one kind or another have rendered much of it off limits to foreign tourists. Ceasefires signed by the Burmese government with more than a dozen insurgent groups have significantly improved the situation, although low-level fighting between the government and the Shan State Army flared up again in 2016. The main tourist destinations, however, are now at peace, with a corresponding rise in visitor numbers – not just in the popular destination of Inle Lake, in the west of Shan, but also the much less explored frontier districts of the state's far east around Kengtung, which is attracting growing numbers of Western trekkers.

HISTORY

The present-day population of Shan State is mostly descended from Mongol soldiers who accompanied Kublai Khan

in the late 13th century and never left. Since then, the region has been dominated by a mosaic of petty princedoms ruled by *saopha* or *sawbwa*, chiefs who were allowed to retain their regalia and privileges after the Konbaung Dynasty annexed the area in the 18th century. In return, the chiefs paid tribute to Mandalay and provided troops for the Burmese army. Shan soldiers were at the forefront of the Konbaung's wars of conquest in the south of Burma and played a seminal role in the First Anglo-Burmese War of 1824–26.

Main attractions

Boat trips, Inle Lake
Hill-tribe trekking from Kalaw
Kakku
Pindaya Caves
Kengtung
Trekking from Hsipaw

Maps on pages 244, 245

Sampling the goods in Kalaw market.

In order to ensure the good behaviour of the Shan Chiefs, the Burmese kings kept their sons as de facto hostages at court. The British did something similar after they took the region in the late 1880s, only instead of holding the Shan boys in the capital, they sent them to public schools in the hill town of Taunggyi, and later to universities in Britain. The result was a generation of anglophile local rulers who were more sympathetic to British rule than that of their former Burmese overlords. When the latter came to dominate the nation's political life following independence, many of the Shan chiefs began agitating for self-rule, leading to the formation of an embryonic insurgent army on the Thai border.

The political situation became even more unstable in 1950, after 20,000 troops of the Chinese People's Liberation Army swarmed across the frontier to oust Kuomintang (KMT) forces that had settled in the area. While the Chinese communists fought from the east, the Burmese battled from the west. In the end, the KMT were defeated and the People's Liberation Army headed home triumphant, but large numbers of Chinese troops chose to stay behind in Shan – the first of several waves of immigration from neighbouring China that has totally changed the ethnic complexion of the state's eastern flank.

A full-blown Shan insurgency erupted in 1964 after General Ne Win's military coup. Fuelled by income from the

Golden Triangle's booming opium trade and illegally mined rubies, this rumbled on for nearly four decades until the government and various strands of the Shan State Army (SSA) signed a ceasefire agreement in 2011–2012, although fighting resumed in 2016.

Armed rebellion has also dogged neighbouring Kayah State, homeland of the Karen people, which has seen some of the worst atrocities committed by the Burmese government and their insurgent adversaries in the modern era. A ceasefire agreement of 2012 finally brought peace to the region, however, and parts of the state have now opened to independent travellers.

WHAT TO SEE

The strife of the recent civil wars feels a world away from serene Inle Lake, the region's main attraction, whose glassy waters are cradled by verdant hills on the placid, western rim of the Shan plateau. While you're in the area it's well worth making a detour up to the former British hill station of Kalaw, a genteel Raj-era town whose colonial architecture and mild climate make it an ideal springboard for treks into the neighbouring hills, home to a colourful array of ethnic minority groups.

East of Shan's administrative capital and main market town, Taunggyi, the landscape grows more rugged as you approach the so-called "Golden Triangle", where the Burmese border meets those of Thailand, Laos and China. Fought over for much of the 20th century by rival states and drug lords, this backwater region is nowadays stable and accessible again. A strong Thai influence pervades the streets of its attractively old-fashioned capital, Kengtung, home to assorted Buddhist monasteries and temples, while the hilly hinterland is populated by minority groups whose way of life has changed little since the Konbaung Dynasty ruled more than a century ago. Overland travel to Kengtung is, however, currently forbidden, and the town can be only be reached by air (from Mandalay, Yangon or Heho near Inle Lake) – although it is possible to continue overland from Kengtung to

One legged rowing technique and floating gardens, Inle lake.

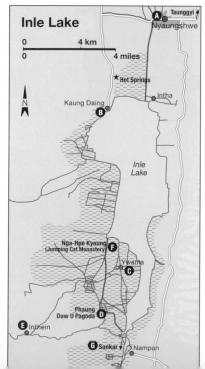

Inle Lake

0 ___ 4 km

0 ___ 4 miles

N

A Taunggyi
Nyaungshwe

★ Hot Springs

● Intha

Kaung Daing
B

*Inle
Lake*

Nga-Hpe Kyaung
(Jumping Cat Monastery) **F**

Ywama
C

Phaung
Daw U-Pagoda **D**

E Inthein

G Sankar
Nampan

*Frying snacks at a
roadside teashop in
Nyaungshwe, Inle Lake.*

*Canoeing around
Nampam village
on Inle Lake.*

the town of Tachilek, on the Thai border, and then on into Thailand.

INLE LAKE

Thanks to its cooler climate and picturesque setting in the lap of the Shan Hills, **Inle Lake** ❶ these days attracts serious numbers of visitors during the winter tourist season, thanks to the beautiful lake itself and the varied attractions dotted around its shores, including ruined *stupas*, hot springs and the stilted villages of the local Intha people. The Intha are responsible for Inle's defining image – that of the local "leg-rowing" fishermen, who propel themselves across the lake by wrapping one leg around oars fixed to the stern of their flat-bottomed canoes, their hands free to handle the nets with which they scoop fish out of the lake.

Around 70,000 Intha live in the various towns and villages scattered around the shores of the lake, which measures approximately 21km (13 miles) from top to bottom, and 11km (7 miles) across. An immigrant tribe from Dawei in Myanmar's far south, the Intha left their former homeland in the 18th century to escape the perpetual conflicts between the Burmese and Thais. As well as their distinctive rowing technique they are also skilled metalworkers, carpenters and fishermen – local men setting long conical traps, which are used to catch Inle's metre-long carp, giant catfish and eels, are a common sight.

You will probably also see the Intha's ingenious "floating gardens", or *kyunpaw*, created by collecting weeds from the surface and lashing them together to form metre-thick strips. These are then anchored to the bed of the lake with bamboo poles, and heaped with mud scooped from the bottom. One advantage of the method is that it can be used regardless of fluctuating water levels. Crops – including cauliflower, tomatoes, cucumbers, cabbage, peas, beans and aubergine – are grown year-round.

Surplus produce is taken by boat to the local markets, which are held each day in different villages around the lake (rotating between villages on a five-day

cycle). These also provide a popular day-trip destination for visitors, attracting minority people dressed in their finest traditional garb, and are a great source of authentic souvenirs, such as locally handwoven Shan shoulder bags and *longyis* made from lotus silk.

With regular connections to Heho airport (40km/25 miles northwest) from Yangon, Mandalay and Bagan, getting to Inle is easy if you fly. Overland it's a longer but straightforward ride by bus or taxi along mountain roads via Kalaw and Shwenyaung to the lake's principal town and transport hub, **Nyaungshwe**.

NYAUNGSHWE

Nyaungshwe Ⓐ, the oldest of the 200 or so Intha settlements around Inle Lake, stands on a 5km (3-mile) -wide belt of silt and tangled water hyacinth on the north side of Inle Lake. The town has grown considerably thanks to the ongoing tourism boom and now holds the lion's share of the area's accommodation, restaurants and other visitor facilities. Lake trips by motorised boat,

canoe or bicycle are the main focus here, but you could spend an enjoyable morning looking around the **Yadana Man Taung Pagoda**, the town's principal Buddhist shrine, whose centrepiece is a towering, gilded *stupa* made to a unique seven-stepped design.

The largest monastery in Nyaungshwe is the **Kan Gyi Kyaung**, a couple of blocks east of the Yadana Man Taung on Myawady Road, which boasts a resident population of around 250 monks. Photographers, however, tend to make a beeline for the **Shwe Yaunghwe Kyaung**, a couple of kilometres north of the centre, whose teak-built ordination hall is lined with picturesque oval windows – the young novices know the drill and pose cheerfully in them for visitors as soon as any turn up.

For something a bit different, the **Red Mountain Winery** (www.redmountain-estate.com; daily 9am–6pm; free), a short drive (or longer bike ride) southeast of Nyaungshwe off the road to Maing Thauk, is worth a visit. The main engine behind Myanmar's fledgling viticulture industry, Red Mountain's

A barge carrying the Buddha images of Phaung Daw U Pagoda during the festival of the same name.

⊙ THE PHAUNG DAW U FESTIVAL

The Phaung Daw U Pagoda's annual festival, celebrated during the Buddhist month of Thadingyut (September/October) to mark the beginning of Buddhist Lent, is Shan State's principal religious celebration, attracting devotees from across the region and beyond. Its focal point is the parade of the temple's amorphous Buddha statues around Inle's 18 largest settlements aboard a re-created royal barge with a huge gilded *karaweik* bird at its prow. Celebrations, lasting around 20 days, are a reminder of the pomp that once attended the Buddhist courts.

Only four of the temple's five sacred images are used in the parade. Legend has it that all five were at first employed in the procession, but that in 1965, a storm capsized the barge carrying the images, and it sank to the bottom of the lake. Only four images were recovered and these were taken back to the Phaung Daw U Pagoda, where, lo and behold, the fifth one was also found, still covered with weeds. Since then, this fifth image has never left the pagoda. Today, the spot on the lake where the barge capsized is marked by a pole crowned by the sacred mythological *hintha* bird. The Phaung Daw U festival draws crowds from all over Myanmar, arriving in boatloads carrying elaborate offerings. They come not only for the "royal" procession, but also for the famed leg-rowing competitions, where crews of Inle oarsmen race each other in sprints around the lake.

⊙ Tip

Find out the name of the village where the Phaung Daw U festival will take place on the day that you wish to see it and hire a boat the night before. Be sure to start out early (preferably before 5am) as festivities kick off before dawn.

French winemaker and team turn out some surprisingly good vintages, including reds, whites, plus a rosé and port. Sampling one of the winery's inexpensive four-glass taster sets on the terrace of their beautiful outdoor pavilion is a nice way to pass an hour.

KAUNG DAING

Kaung Daing B, southwest of Nyaung-shwe on the lakeshore, is the site of a couple of large upscale resort hotels. The village also has some enjoyable hot sulphur springs (daily 8am–6pm; charge) and is a popular destination for day-tripping tourists wishing to see the local Padaung tribeswomen, with their fantastically elongated necks clad in brass coils. The small community, who live on a reserve near the village, are originally from Loikaw in Kayah State.

YWAMA

About 12km (7.5 miles) from Kaung Daing on the southwest side of Inle, the village of **Ywama C** is about as touristy as the lake gets, with a clutch of hotels, restaurants and lanes lined

Crumbling stupas at Inthein Pagoda.

with souvenir stalls, as well as a fleet of water-borne trinket sellers hassling any visitors who venture out on boats. Every tour group in the region comes here once every five days for the village's famous "floating market", which started out as a purely authentic local bazaar but is now largely a tourist event.

The nearby **Phaung Daw U Pagoda D** is the venue for one of the country's most important festivals, centred around a waterborne procession of four sacred images enshrined in the temple. These were carried back to Burma by the widely travelled 12th-century King Alaungsithu upon his return from the Malay Peninsula, and then deposited in a cave near the lake. They were not rediscovered until centuries later, since when they've been covered with so many layers of gold leaf that they now look more like little shiny orbs than Buddha figures.

INTHEIN

Among the most popular day-trip destinations on Inle Lake is the village of **Inthein E**, which sits at the end of two

long, winding rivulets running inland just southwest of Ywama and the Phaung Daw U Pagoda. Lined by reed beds and open fields, the channels narrow as they approach the village, which is famous for its collection of crumbling Shan *stupas*. The most accessible of these is **Nyaung Oak**, a short stroll south across a foot-bridge from the village proper. While some have been restored with fresh coats of limewash and gold leaf, many more are half-collapsed and overgrown with weeds. Stucco reliefs of guardian deities and mythical creatures flank the ornately carved fronts of the older monuments. From Nyaung Oak, you can follow a long covered walkway lined with souvenir stalls uphill to the **Shwe Inthein Pagoda**, a much larger complex of 17th-century *stupas* arranged around a central shrine, and with magnificent views over the lake.

The largest numbers of visitors descend on Inthein when it hosts one of the lake's famous five-day markets, which fills a dusty market square in the centre of the village. To escape the melee, follow the lane running from the northwest corner of the square and take the footpath striking left off it shortly after to the stupa crowning the hilltop above, from whose base another stupendous panorama over Inle and its mountain backdrop is revealed.

NGA HPE KYAUNG

Inle's **Nga Hpe Kyaung** ⑥ was formerly one of Myanmar's wackier visitor attractions and is still known as the **"Jumping Cat Monastery"**, thanks to the resident felines who were once trained to leap through hoops in exchange for titbits. The cats are still in situ, although the resident monks have now abandoned the practice of urging them into displays of feline acrobatics, fearing it was exhausting the animals, who now simply lounge around, doing what cats generally do. The monastery remains worth a visit, even so, thanks to its fine old teak architecture, the

superb collection of antique Buddhas in its meditation hall and the sweeping views outside – while the presence of the occasional (albeit non-jumping) cat adds its own particular charm.

SOUTH OF INLE LAKE TO SANKAR

A good way of escaping the tourist crowds around Inle Lake is by making a long but absorbing day-trip by boat along the canal running off the south end of the lake. First stop is the village of **Taung Tho** (one of the least touristed locations of the lake's itinerant five-day market), beyond which the canal runs past assorted Shan and Pa-O settlements to reach serene **Moebye Lake**. Bordering the lake, the village of **Sankar** ⑥ boasts the usual picturesque medley of buildings both on land and rising on stilts from the lake, while opposite stands the **Tharkong Pagoda**, with its marvellously photogenic cluster of crumbling stupas, sometimes (depending on water levels), rising directly from the waters of the lake itself.

One adventurous possibility from here is to continue directly southwards

Buddha image and Pa-O deities, Kakku pagoda.

Nga Hpe Kyaung monastery.

Tip

Hotel and guesthouses in Nyaungshwe can arrange a car for trips to Kakku. The round-trip fare costs around US$40–60 in a vehicle seating four to six people.

to **Loikaw** (see page 255), the capital of Kayah State, some 3–4 hours distant. Travel agents in Nyaungshwe should be able to arrange the trip, given a couple of days' notice.

TAUNGGYI

Seat of the Shan Council of Chiefs during the British colonial period and now the capital of Shan State, **Taunggyi** ❷ also serves as the administrative centre and main market hub for the Inle Lake region. The town was founded by Sir James George Scott, one of the most respected colonial officers in the history of British Burma. A devoted student of Burmese history and culture, Scott, under the pseudonym Shway Yoe, wrote the book *The Burman, His Life and Notions* – generally regarded as the 19th century's finest work on Burma, and one which remains frequently consulted to this day.

Despite its altitude, Taunggyi no longer enjoys as mild a climate as it did in the past and lacks the traditional atmosphere of settlements around the lake itself. Few tourists venture here

Pa-O guide at Kakku Pagoda.

except when the lake's itinerant five-day market comes to town or during the spectacular "Fire Balloon" festival, lasting a week in November, when huge, intricately decorated hot-air balloons are released into the sky amidst great flourishes of fireworks.

South of the centre, the small **Shan State Cultural Museum** (Mon–Fri 10am–4pm; charge) is worth a look if you're interested in the region's hill tribes, with displays of 30 or so costumes from Shan minorities.

KAKKU

The archaeological site of **Kakku** ❸, 42km (26 miles) south of Taunggyi, comprises a forest of ancient stupas rising in spectacular fashion from a valley on the far side of the mountains from Inle Lake. There are said to be 5,257 individual pagodas here, arrayed in rows. Some date from the Bagan period (11th to 13th centuries), but others may even have their origins in the distant Mauryan Empire of the Indian ruler, Ashoka (304–232 BC). Little else is known about them but closer examination reveals a remarkable wealth of decorative detail.

Kakku lies on land belonging to the Pa-O people, who consider themselves guardians of the site. The Pa-O also supply guides offering insightful tours of the stupas, dressed in their traditional red turban-like head-dresses.

KALAW

Perched on the western rim of the Shan Plateau, **Kalaw** ❹, 70km (44 miles) west of Taunggyi, was once a favourite hill-station retreat for British officials and their families during the hot season – little wonder, considering its beautiful setting amid bamboo groves, orange orchards and pine woods. In common with mountain retreats in the Himalayan foothills of India, the town retains a faded colonial atmosphere, with some attractive gardens and Victorian buildings as well as a noticeably cosmopolitan mix of people descended from the Sikhs, Tamils, Nepalis and Indian Muslims who were drafted in as a labour force in the late 19th century. Despite its undoubted attractions, most visitors come here principally to walk in the surroundings hills, with trekking operators all over town offering myriad hikes, as well as an increasing number of cycling tours. Kalaw also hosts one of the region's most vibrant five-day markets, for which minority people descend en masse from the hills dressed in traditional costume.

Also worth a visit is the magical **Shwe Oo Min Pagoda** (daily 6.30am–5.30pm; free), a couple of kilometres south of town and resembling – if not quite rivalling – the similarly named cave temple in Pindaya. A forest of slender gilded pagodas leads to the entrance to the cave, inside which hundreds of Buddhas have been crammed into every available space, gleaming enigmatically in the half-light.

TREKKING FROM KALAW

Innumerable trails thread through the green, forested hills around Kalaw, but the ones most commonly followed by foreign visitors are those leading to Inle Lake. Passing numerous Buddhist pagodas and villages of the Palaung, Danu, Pa-O and Taungyo tribes, the routes take between two and three days to cover and usually wind up at the ruined stupa complexes of Inthein, from where you'll be transferred to your hotel by motorboat. The trails are not all that physically demanding, but standards of comfort vary greatly in the village houses and monasteries where you'll overnight along the way. Bring a torch and plenty of insect repellent. Treks can follow stretches of surfaced road, winding over ridges into lush valleys, across patchworks of tea plantations, *tanaq-hpeq* bushes (whose leaves are used for rolling cheroots), orange groves and rice

paddies, so you'll need footwear that can cope with a variety of terrain, as well as warm clothes for those chilly evenings in the hills. If you don't fancy the full walk to Inle, there are also numerous one-day walks available in the surrounding hills, while the two- to three-day trek to Pindaya is also growing in popularity as visitors seek to escape the increasingly touristy trails to Inle.

HILL-TRIBE ETIQUETTE

Trekkers should follow certain guidelines to protect hill-tribe sensibilities and promote good relations. Always ask permission before entering any building or before taking a photo. Avoid photographing old people, pregnant women and babies, as well as touching, photographing or sitting beneath village shrines, or stepping or sitting on doorsills (which brings bad luck, according to village custom). Don't change clothes in public and always dress modestly, and avoid public displays of overt affection and excessive wealth. A friendly smile

Ingredients for paan (a stimulating betel leaf snack) in Kalaw market.

Kalaw street scene.

always helps, as does speaking calmly and quietly at all times.

GREEN HILL VALLEY ELEPHANT CAMP

A worthwhile excursion from Kalaw, especially if you're travelling with children, is the delightful **Green Hill Valley Elephant Camp** (www.ghvelephant. com). This privately run centre, set in a beautiful conservation area a 45-minute drive out of town, cares for sick and retired forestry elephants, using profits from tourist visits to protect traditional local lifestyles and some 60 hectares (150 acres) of woodland. Visitors can undertake treks through the surrounding countryside, as well as getting the chance to feed and bathe the resident pachyderms under the watchful eye of their mahouts.

PINDAYA

A spider at the entrance to the Pindaya caves references a local legend.

Pindaya, a three-hour drive northwest of Nyaungshwe, is famous across Myanmar as the site of the extraordinary **Shwe U Min Cave Temple** ❺ (daily 6am–6pm; charge), a huge, convoluted complex of limestone grottoes crammed with around 9,000 Buddha images. Varying in size and style, the figures were mostly installed between the 16th and 18th centuries, and are made of gold, silver, marble, lacquer, teak and ivory.

The caves honeycomb a steep hillside rising above **Pone Taloke Lake**, accessed via a network of covered stairways and lifts leading to ornately gilded and decorated entrance pavilions. It's obvious from the start that the Buddha statues are very much objects of active veneration: worshippers young and old bow before them, offering flowers and incense in clasped hands to honour the principles of kindness, compassion and tolerance which the images embody. The rear section of the main cave, aptly christened "The Maze", is particularly stunning, with a disorienting network of tiny paths between myriad stacked-up Buddhas and, from the very back, stunning views down over the thousands of statues gleaming softly in the darkness below.

EASTERN SHAN: KENGTUNG AND BEYOND

The far east of Shan State is one of the most remote corners of Myanmar open to foreigners. Separated from the rest of the country by a convoluted mountain range, it has retained strong cultural affinities with neighbouring Thailand and Laos, from where its original settlers migrated with the Chiang Mai Dynasty in the 13th century. Opium has long been the region's principal cash crop, and protracted armed struggles for control of the narcotics trade have kept much of the area off limits to outsiders.

At present the only part of the region open to visitors is the small area around the town of Kengtung – although the road from Taunggyi to Kengtung is closed, meaning that the only way of getting there is by plane.

Foreigners are, however, allowed to continue by road east of Kengtung to Tachilek, and then continue on into Thailand (although you can only travel in the opposite direction with a pre-booked, government-approved guide – a convoluted and costly business).

KENGTUNG

The capital of eastern Shan State, **Kengtung ➏**, the "Walled City of Tung" (also known as "Kyaingtong", although this Burmanised version of the name is little used locally), can seem rather unprepossessing at first acquaintance but improves rapidly on closer inspection. Laid out around **Nawng Tung Lake**, the town preserves a taste of old Asia, with a wealth of striking temples (some showing distinct Thai influence) and markets frequented by the many hill tribes who inhabit the town's rugged hinterland, including the Akha, Palaung, Kachin, Lahu, Pa-O, Shan and Wa.

A cluster of impressive 19th-century Buddhist sites can be found in and around the town centre, including the **Maha Myat Muni** ("Wat Phra Jao Lung" in Shan/Thai), boasting an interior richly decorated with gold paintings on a red background. Even more spectacular is **Zom Kham** (Wat Jom Kham), with a tall, gilded *stupa* topped by a golden *hti* inlaid with precious stones.

If you're in Kengtung on its weekly market day, you'll be treated to a feast of traditional costume. The Kung, who make up around 80 percent of the town's population, wear horizontally striped green *longyi*, while women of the Lahu tribe wear black dresses with wavy patterns. The Lu are noted for their silver elbow and wrist bangles, but the most colourful are the Shan-gyi (Big Shan) women, in their yellow blouses, *longyi*, and green-striped headdresses. Local specialities on sale at the market include dried frogs and gingered quail eggs. If you want a closer look at the fascinating patch-work of ethnic groups living in the

countryside around town, Kengtung is also emerging as a popular trekking destination, with a number of opera-tors offering day-trips to local Lahu, Akha, Loi and Eng villages.

NORTHERN SHAN

While Inle Lake and its environs in the southwest are the main lure for travellers to Shan State, its northern region has attractions, too – although the area between the two is off-limits to foreigners so you'll have to back-track to Mandalay in order to reach it. The most frequented route is by rail from Mandalay via Pyin U-Lwin to Hsipaw and Lashio (see page 201) via the **Gokteik Viaduct**.

Heading north, **Kyaukme** is the first town of significance on the Pyin U-Lwin–Lashio road. Located 85km (56 miles) from the ruby, sapphire and jade mines of the restricted town of **Mogok** in the northwest and the sil-ver mines of **Namtu** in the northeast, Kyaukme is an active trading town for gem stones and jewellery and a good place to shop for them. There are also

A parasol workshop's dainty creations, Pindaya.

a couple of operators in town offering motorbike tours along with day-treks and longer walks through local Palaung and Shan villages.

HSIPAW

Hsipaw ❼, an old mountain valley town on the sinuous Tu River, was once the administrative centre for the state of the same name, one of nine formerly ruled by Shan princes. The town is noted for its *haw*, or European-style palace (not open to visitors), where the last *sawbwa*, Sao Kya Seng, and his Austrian-born wife, Inge Sargent, lived until the military coup of 1962, when the chief disappeared. He was later found to have been murdered by the regime – events described in vivid detail in Sargent's bestselling biography, *Twilight Over Burma*.

The majority of travellers who make it as far northeast as Hsipaw tend to come in order to trek to **hill-tribe villages** in the area, which are far less frequented and accustomed to foreigners than the country around Kalaw (although if you really want to get away from other foreigners you're better off trekking from Kyaukme). For those travelling independently, trips of varying lengths, from day hikes to full-on expeditions lasting a week or more, may be arranged through local hotels and guesthouses.

Hsipaw's main pagoda is the **Maha-myatmuni Paya** on Namtu Road, a much more modest complex than its name-sakes further south but which is worth a visit for its immaculately painted stupas and gleaming brass Buddha statue, backed by a halo of flashing red and purple UV lights. Of more traditional interest is the old quarter just north of the centre where, among numerous antique wooden buildings, stands the **Maha Nanda Kantha Kyaung**, home to a Buddha made entirely from strips of woven bamboo.

For a great panoramic view over the town, head 1km (0.6 miles) south to Five Buddha Hill, where the terrace fronting the **Thein Daung Pagoda** offers a popular spot for a late-afternoon stroll, hence its local nickname, "Sunset Hill".

BAWGYO PAGODA

A good time to be in Hsipaw is the full moon in March when the **Bawgyo Pagoda**, 8km (5miles) west of town, hosts its annual festival. Focus of the event is a spectacular stupa encased in a pavilion whose pillars, walls and domes are adorned in elaborate, multicoloured mirror mosaic – an amazing spectacle at night, when the complex is brightly lit.

During the festival, the temple's four Buddha images are paraded around the precinct for pilgrims to make offerings of gold leaves. Members of the tea-growing Palaung minority people attend the Bawgyo festival in great numbers. Ox-carts trundle in with pottery, lacquerware, baskets and other handicrafts to sell, while vendors set up stalls offering food and games of chance. Lively *pwe* (shows) are held in the evening.

Washing off water buffalo near Kalaw.

LASHIO

The end of the Mandalay rail line is **Lashio ⑧**, 100km (66 miles) away from the Chinese border. The last large town before the start of the historic **Burma Road** to China, which supplied the nationalist Kuomintang forces in World War II, it retains a frontier atmosphere, with a mostly Han-Chinese population. Devastated by a fire in 1988 and largely rebuilt in concrete and corrugated iron, the town is far from the prettiest in Myanmar. If you come here at all it will probably be en route to or from the airport – the nearest to Hsipaw. With time to kill, the most worthwhile option is the ornately gilded **Thatana 2500-Year Pagoda**, nestling amid the forest on a ridge top overlooking the centre. The town centre markets are also worth a browse, including the covered market between Lanmadaw and Samkaung streets and the night market on Bogyoke and Thiri roads. Just south of the centre look out too for the town's attractive main mosque, rebuilt after the previous mosque was burnt to the ground during anti-Muslim riots in 2013.

KAYAH STATE

Southwest of Shan, the diamond-shaped state of **Kayah** is the smallest in Myanmar. As in many other areas of the country, travel restrictions have been steadily lifted since 2013 and some parts of the state can now be visited by independent travellers. Most people head for the pleasantly laid-back state capital of **Loikaw ⑨**, reachable from Kalaw/Nyaungshwe, or with a licenced guide direct from Taunggyi. From Loikaw it's possible to organise day trips to various local villages inhabited by some of the colourful array of ethnic groups living in the state. It's a particularly good place to visit the famously long-necked Padaung (see page 68) in their native homelands (rather than amidst the tourist crowds and souvenir stalls of Inle Lake, where they're most commonly seen by foreigners), centred on a cluster of villages around **Pan Pet**, a 90-minute drive south of Loilkaw.

⊙ Tip

Outside town, on the twin-peak summit of Taungkwe, is the Taungkwe Zedi, which offers great views of Loikaw. You can also visit the Lawpita Falls, which drive a large hydroelectric power plant.

Buddha statues in the Pindaya caves.

⊙ THE BAWGYO PAGODA IMAGES

According to local legend, the four sacred Buddha images of the Bawgyo Pagoda were carved from a piece of wood given by a celestial to the 11th-century Bagan king, Narapatisithu. The Bawgyo Pagoda was subsequently built to house the images while the rest of the wood was planted in the courtyard, whereupon it miraculously took root, growing into a sacred tree which survives, and indeed thrives, to this day.

The four Buddha images, meanwhile, are enshrined in the inner sanctum of the Bawgyo Pagoda and brought out just once a year during the February/March full-moon pagoda festival (Bawgyo Paya Pwe) to allow devotees to venerate them and adorn them with gold leaves.

During the reign of the *sawbwa*, fear of potential robbery meant that the images were for many years kept in the *haw* in Hsipaw for safekeeping, and accompanied back to the Bawgyo Pagoda at festival time amidst a grand ceremonial procession, including a parade of elephants. The festival was the only time when gambling was allowed; it was also an important social event that brought together the Shan, as well as ethnic minorities from all over Burma, to display and sell their goods.

At Namti, a passenger leans out of the window of the train to Myitkyina to buy some food.

KACHIN STATE AND THE UPPER AYEYARWADY

In the far north of the country, gold mines spread out along the banks of the Ayeyarwady, while Myanmar's largest lake, Indawgyi, rests among high hills and teak forests.

Comparatively few travellers venture beyond Mandalay into Myanmar's northernmost state, Kachin. The handful that do nearly all stick closely to the Ayeyarwady, flying first to the capital, Myitkyina, or the market town of Bhamo, a couple of days' journey downstream, and make the trip in a southwards direction, following the flow of the river. Whether you're chugging on an old government ferry or being pampered in a luxury cruiser, traversing this stretch yields an experience of Myanmar in the raw. Don't expect to encounter many other tourists along the way. Development in the region has been painfully slow since independence, frustrated by repeated outbreaks of civil war between the Burmese government and Kachin rebel armies, who have since the 1960s maintained control of the region's trade in jade, precious stones, narcotics and smuggled goods. Although they account for only two percent of the country's total population, the predominantly Christian Kachin form the majority in their homeland, and beyond the main train lines, trading posts and towns, the regime holds only token power.

The rule of the state weakens the further north you travel, which explains why overland trips to Myanmar's northernmost town, Putao, are forbidden to foreigners. If you want to explore the rugged hills and jungles of the border valleys, where the frontiers of China, India and Myanmar intersect, and where the country's highest peaks, Hkakabo Razi (5,881m/19,295ft) Gamlang Razi (5870m/19,258ft), bring the country to a suitably spectacular climax, you'll have to fly there and travel as part of a pre-arranged tour.

The long-running conflict between the Kachin Independence Army (KIA)

Map on page 258

◎ Main attractions

Indawgyi Lake
Welatha Cliff (Second Defile)
Cruising the Ayeyarwady
Kyundaw Island
Hkakabo Razi

Spinning a potter's wheel with the foot at a pottery workshop in Kyaukmyaung.

Kachin State and the Upper Ayeyarwady

0   200 km
0   200 miles

and government forces first erupted following the imposition of military rule in 1962 and rumbled on until 1994, when a ceasefire was agreed. This held until 2011, when fighting erupted around the town of Laiza, the KIA's headquarters on the Chinese border between the capital, Myitkyina, and Bhamo. Clashes continue to the present day, with the early months of 2018 seeing renewed fighting during which thousands of civilians fled their homes in the face of repeated government artillery and aerial bombardments, alongside accusations that aid supplies to refugees were being deliberately blocked. Not surprisingly, given the current situation, the long-standing ban on travel overland and by river between the state capital Myitkyina and Bhamo remains in force, with access to the capital only permitted by air, or on the horrendously slow train from Mandalay (a journey of at least 16 hours, and often considerably more).

MYITKYINA

Myitkyina ❶, the state capital, is located 144 metres (476ft) above sea level below the foothills of the Himalayas. Following the completion of the Yangon–Mandalay–Myitkyina rail link in 1898, the town became the commercial hub of the north and is today the largest settlement in the region.

Myitkyina was levelled by fierce fighting in World War II, during which it changed hands several times between the Allies and Japanese. Veterans of the Japanese army, who lost 3,200 soldiers in the battle for Myitkyina, paid for the renovation of the town's principal Buddhist shrine, the gilded **Hsu Taung Pye Pagoda**, near the riverfront at the north end of Strand Road, which also holds a huge reclining Buddha.

Due to the proximity of the jade mines, there has been an influx of

Chinese money, which has helped to modernise the town. Myitkyina holds little in the way of sights, but its early morning fresh produce market is particularly picturesque thanks to the stalls piled with mandarin oranges, apples, grapefruit and kumquats, all of which grow abundantly in the north.

INDAWGYI LAKE

One of the principal attractions of Kachin State is **Indawgyi Lake ②**, the largest body of fresh water in Myanmar. Around 24km (16 miles) from north to south and 12km (8 miles) across, it is sustained by a dozen streams feeding into a depression. Large gold deposits are held in the surrounding hills, as well as extensive teak forests worked by three major logging camps.

A chain of picturesque Shan villages dots the lake shore, comprising clusters of wooden stilted houses. From an island in the middle of the lake rises the dazzling white and gilded **Shwe Myitzu Pagoda** where relics of the Buddha are said to be enshrined. It sits on a two-tier platform consisting of a central golden *stupa* surrounded by scores of smaller white *stupas*. Panels depicting scenes from the Buddha's life decorate the ceilings covering the lower tier of the platform, which is also adorned by statues of *nat*, said to still roam the Indawgyi area. Access is via a narrow sand causeway that gets partially submerged in the wet season. Visitors can take in the various villages, wooden monasteries, Kachin churches and *manao* totem poles, and it may also be possible to arrange a trip to a local logging camp to see elephants at work. The huge jade mines of Hpakant, to the north of Indawgyi, are strictly off limits to tourists.

Travelling to the lake from Myikyinta by train, the jumping-off point is **Hopin**, a sleepy town with a large ethnic Chinese population, some five hours from the capital. Pick-up trucks are available to ferry travellers from the station over the remaining 45km (28 miles) of bumpy, sinuous mountain roads. A couple of basic guesthouses offer accommodation for visitors.

> **⊘ Tip**
>
> Train tickets to Hopin should be booked on the eve of departure. Arrive at Myitkyina railway station early as there is almost always a long queue.

The natural causeway to Shwe Myitzu Pagoda, which appears at festival time.

⊘ THE LEGEND OF INDAWGYI LAKE

According to local legend, Indawgyi was once the capital of the Htamanthy tribe. Two dragon brothers were looking for a place to call home and chanced upon Indawgyi. They found the people there living wicked lives and, as punishment, flooded the city and turned it into a lake for themselves.

Until about 240 years ago, Indawgyi Lake remained uninhabited as it was believed to be guarded by fierce spirits. It was only when the Shwe Myitzu Pagoda was built by a monk, U Thawbita, during the reign of King Mindon, that people's fears were sufficiently allayed and they started to settle in the area.

The pagoda has since been built over three times until it gained its current height of 15 metres (50ft). Shwe Myitzu is the most important pagoda in Kachin State and is the focus of a 10-day festival held each year in March.

According to tradition, just before the start of the festival two sandbanks emerge from the lake. One of these stretches all the way from the shore to the Shwe Myitzu Pagoda, allowing pilgrims to walk the entire distance. The other is broken in parts and is believed to be a passage for the gods. Strangely, both sandbanks disappear into the water as soon as the festival is over.

⊙ Tip

The Ayeyarwady boats usually have tiny cabins better suited to single than double occupancy. If you are travelling with a companion, you may prefer separate cabins as the fare is per person, not per cabin.

BHAMO AND BEYOND

The largest town on the Ayeyarwady between Myitkyina and Mandalay, **Bhamo ③** is currently open to foreign travellers either by plane or boat, though not by road. The town marks the closest and most accessible point on the river to China (the border is only 65km/40 miles west), and was, as such, always a site of huge strategic and commercial importance, attracting Western colonialists since the 16th century. The British may not have admitted it at the time, but control of the land route running north into Yunnan was one of the principal goals of the Anglo-Burmese Wars in the 19th century, and although not yet surfaced, the old caravan route up the Daying Jiang Valley, which Marco Polo followed in the 13th century, is still in use.

Some 5km (3 miles) north of the centre (ask your driver to take you to "Bhamo Myo Haung", or "Old Bhamo"), the remnants of the ancient but now very decayed Shan capital of **Sampanago** comprise an overgrown wall and gateway, along with a pair of pagodas

A group of Kachin tribal girls at the Manao Festival.

– the Eikkhawtaw and the Shwekyaynar – two gold-tipped *stupas* thought to date from the 5th century.

The centre of Bhamo was rebuilt after a devastating fire in the 1990s and so attractions are thin on the ground, though the spacious modern **marketplace**, frequented by minority people from the surrounding hills, deserves an early morning browse. Also in the town centre, the Thai-style **Theindawgyi Paya** is said to have been built by King Ashoka in the 3rd century BC to house a tooth relic, and has a precious ruby-encrusted *seinbu* (golden orb).

Photographers shouldn't miss the pretty **ceramics market**, at the south end of the riverfront area, where each morning hundreds of pots in a bewildering range of sizes are set on the banks of the Ayeyarwady for sale – a delightful scene against the comings and goings of freighters and other boats on the water behind.

SECOND DEFILE

After leaving Bhamo, the Ayeyarwady crosses a fertile plain as it

⊙ THE MANAO FESTIVAL

If you're anywhere near Myitkyina around 10 January, don't miss the colourful Manao Festival. Celebrated in the town stadium, the event brings together all seven Kachin tribal groups in dance, fun and games centred around four totem (*manao*) poles. Some of the headgear on display includes tassels, beads, horns, feathers and even stuffed birds. The rhythms of the drums and chants resemble the Pow Wow gatherings of Native American Indians. Since most Kachin have converted to Christianity, this originally animist festival has now become a mixture of religion and culture.

The festival features dances performed around the *manao* totems, led by tribal chieftains honouring various *nat* (spirits) to ensure a bumper harvest or to celebrate good fortune. Meaning "centre" or "summit", the Manao Festival was referred to by the ancient Kachin as a "meeting of gods" and was formerly hosted by rich and noble chieftains.

Similar Kachin dances and festivities are often held to celebrate a special occasion (the Ninghtan Manao is a wedding feast, for instance, and the Hting Hkring Manao is performed when moving to a new house), with the whole neighbourhood invited, and celebrations sometimes lasting for days.

approaches the **Second Defile**. Flanked by steep cliffs cloaked in dense vegetation, the 13.5km (7.5-mile) passage is the most scenic along the entire length of the river. During the rainy season the water's depth can reach an amazing 61 metres (180ft), and when the water is low, elephants haul huge teak logs from the jungle to the river's shore.

At the narrowest point of the defile rises a spectacular 300-metre (985ft) cliff, the **Nat-Myet-Hna-Taung** ("Face of the Nat Mountain"), also called the **Welatha cliff**. Not far away is the famous **Parrot's Beak**, a painted rock that acts as a marker for river traffic: if the water reaches the parrot's red beak, the current is deemed too strong for boats to pass.

SHWEGU

The first stop after the defile, where the river widens again and flows through a series of sun-bleached sand banks, is **Shwegu** ❹. Elephants still roam the jungle in the hills behind the town, but the main reason you might wish to jump ship here is to explore the island of **Kyundaw**, in the river opposite, where 7,000 or more *stupas* are dotted around the monastery of **Shwe Baw Kyaung**. The monuments range from crumbling 10th-century piles choked in creepers and weeds to immaculately whitewashed and gilded modern *zedis*.

KATHA

On a bluff overlooking the west bank of the Ayeyarwady, **Katha** ❺ stands in the shadow of the Gangaw Taung hills, presiding over a fertile plain where kidney beans are the principal cash crop. This quiet provincial town, shaded by ranks of beautiful trees, is the main administrative hub of the district, and an obligatory stop if you're travelling by riverboat. A branch of the mainline railway also serves the town, allowing you a fast option to Mandalay if the slow ferry is starting to lose its allure.

Katha's one and only claim to fame is that it served as the inspiration for George Orwell's fictional town

A cheerful resident of Shwebo.

Monks from Shwe Daza Paya collecting alms, Shwebo.

of Kyauktada in his novel *Burmese Days*. Orwell, or Eric Blair as he was christened, was stationed here as a police officer in 1926–27, and a handful of colonial-era buildings featured in the book survive, including the town jail and British Club. For more on Katha's Orwell connection, track down a copy of Emma Larkin's entertaining travelogue, *Finding George Orwell in Burma*.

SHWELI SANDBARS

South of Katha the boat passes the estuary of the **Shweli**, Myanmar's main logging river, which enters the country from China after crossing the jungles of the northern Shan State – although the great rafts of teak and other hardwoods which were once floated south from here have been significantly diminished following recent logging bans. As well as timber, its waters have also swept vast quantities of silt downriver which has, over the years, coalesced into a sandbar off **Inywa**, at the mouth of the estuary. This prohibits the entry

Boatman on the Irrawaddy.

of larger boats from the main channel, and as a consequence, the large government ferries have to anchor midstream off Inywa until daylight, since even local pilots cannot steer boats safely through the shifting sandbars in the dark.

MYADAUNG AND TIGYAING

The next port of call south on the Ayeyarwady is **Myadaung** ⑥, a market town facing the southern end of the beautiful **Gangaw Taung**, the densely forested ridge stretching south from Myitkyina. The range has a mystical quality, especially when the white pagodas on the hilltop above the town appear through the early morning fog. Wide landscapes and high river banks form the typical setting of the fertile Upper Burma plain. Each of the docking stations is fairly similar to the one just passed, with locals getting on and off with huge sacks, cartons and baskets on their heads.

From Myadaung the boat crosses the river to call at **Tigyaing** ⑦, another atmospheric thatched town with an

old pagoda on its hilltop. A stroll through this little community provides a real window on everyday life in Upper Myanmar. Small stalls and tea shops line the narrow lanes, which are for the most part calm and peaceful. Only when the Ayeyarwady boat arrives does the town erupt into a frenzy of activity. Regardless of the time of day, the entire population assembles on the steep shore, joined by those from regions further inland for whom Tigyaing is the vital gateway to the rest of the world.

Both the *stupas* at Myadaung and Tigyaing are said to have been built by King Alaungsithu back in the 12th century.

TAGAUNG AND THE THIRD DEFILE

Tagaung ❽, the next major stop on the river route to Mandalay, is believed to have been one of Burma's ancient capitals. There is some debate as to whether or not it was established as long ago as 850 BC by an Indian dynasty, the Satkyas, but the town was definitely a major Pyu settlement between the 6th and 9th centuries. The ruins of at least two lost cities have been discovered in the vicinity by archaeologists, though the remnants are none too impressive. The only surviving monument to speak of today is a huge golden *nat* shrine said to represent the founder of the ancient centre.

Beyond Tagaung, the river runs in a straight north–south direction to enter the **Third Defile** 45km (26 miles) before reaching Kyaukmyaung. During the low-water season, hundreds of boats can be seen panning for gold in the river sand at **Ka Bwet**, midway along the passage.

KYAUKMYAUNG

The town of **Kyaukmyaung** ❾, at the southern end of the Third Defile, lies 17km (10 miles) east of Shwebo and 46km (28 miles) north of Mandalay. Long a minor port of call on the Ayeyarwady, it is famous today principally for its pottery industry, centred on the clay-rich river bank known as Ngwe Ngein to the south of town, where you can see scores of

CRUISING THE AYEYARWADY: MYITKYINA/BHAMO TO MANDALAY

One of the most enjoyable activities for visitors to Myanmar, a cruise along the mighty Ayeyarwady is not to be missed.

Myanmar's greatest river, the Ayeyarwady, has its source in Kachin State, just north of the capital, Myitkyina, from where it flows south in a sweeping "S" bend through the Kawkwe Taung Hills and out on to the plains at Bhamo. A mighty slick of yellow-brown, silty water, it makes another arc before plunging definitively south towards Mandalay.

The northern stretch of the Ayeyarwady sees far fewer foreign tourists than the area between Mandalay and Bagan, and offers a chance to experience Myanmar very much off the beaten track, whether travelling by luxury cruiser or local ferry. Travel along the river is permitted up to Bhamo, but foreigners are not permitted to continue north of Bhamo towards Myitkyina due to ongoing clashes between the government and Kachin rebel forces. .

The cheapest way to enjoy a trip along the northern Ayeyarwady – referred to for obvious reasons as "the slow boat" – is on the double-decker IWT ferries that chug three times per week between Bhamo and Mandalay. These take at least 30 hours to cover the

Passengers ride on the roof of this boat on the Ayeyarwady River at Bhamo.

distance (sometimes considerably longer), depending on water levels and the state of the vessel's engine. A few cabins are available, but most passengers sleep on deck, eating and drinking whatever the itinerant vendors happen to be hawking.

Quicker, smaller, private boats, carrying between 40 and 80 people, also operate along various stretches of the river including Shwe Irra (daily between Bhamo, Shwegu and Katha) and Katha Irra (between Katha and Mandalay). They're faster and depart much more regularly, but don't run at night, so you have to break the journey at towns en route. The fast boats also tend to be more uncomfortable, with passengers wedged tightly together on wooden seats for the duration of the journey.

THE RIVER SCENE

As the landscape is largely flat and monotonous for most of the route, life on the river itself, and on board the ferry, provides the main interest. Calling at 47 different stops along the way, the ferry boats are a lifeline to communities in the Upper Ayeyarwady, carrying farm produce and essential supplies as well as people. During the harvest season, huge drums of molasses and sacks filled with sesame seeds, fruit, beans or rice are regularly hauled on board, while vendors line up on the deck to sell fruits, cookies and a variety of other small luxuries, from flowers and cheroots to candles, tobacco leaves, Mandalay beer, rum and soft drinks. You'll even come across towers of woven cane hats and live chickens in cane cages for sale.

Karom is a popular pastime among the male passengers, and crowds form around the best players. Monks have their own platform on which they sit in full lotus position, puffing one cheroot after another while running their prayer beads through their fingers. In the rear of the upper deck is the kitchen where, on an open fire, tea, coffee and a variety of foods are prepared.

The sunsets on the Ayeyarwady are glorious and are best seen from the bridge. Often, during the night, the boat docks somewhere along the high, sandy embankment and the air is filled with the shouting of villagers carrying barrel after barrel of goods on board. Just remember to bring plenty of insect repellent – the Ayeyarwady's bugs can be voracious.

ceramic items drying picturesquely in the sun. Most striking among them are the massive 50-gallon vessels known since early colonial times as "Martaban jars" or "Ali Baba pots". They were first made here in the mid-18th century by captive potters from Bago, brought to the town by the Konbaung king, Alaungpaya, after his defeat of the Mons. The jars, which could hold two hogshead of palm liquor, *ngapi* fish paste, *ngapy-ayei* fish sauce or peanut oil, were the main vessel used in the Mons' international maritime trade. Shards of them have been found across China and the Middle East. This is now one of the few places in Myanmar where they are still made according to the traditional process. The shape and ochre-glazed rosette motifs adorning the upper portion of the jars has altered little in centuries, but the rich earthy red brown colour is an innovation, achieved by using a mix of clay from Shan State and battery acid powder. The potters are happy for you to browse and photograph, and will show you the massive brick-and-earth-floor kilns where their work is fired for a week.

Kyaukmyaung is also the epicentre of a Protection Zone set up in 2005 to protect the rare Irrawaddy dolphin, for whom this stretch of the river is something of a stronghold.

THE FAR NORTH

Sandwiched between Arunachal Pradesh in India and the Chinese province of Yunnan, the far north of Myanmar contains some of the last true wilderness in Southeast Asia – a spectacular amphitheatre of jungle-covered foothills ringed by the eternal snows of the Himalayas. Unfortunately, access to this formidable cul-de-sac remains problematic. The KIA maintains control of all but a few outposts, and infrastructure of any kind is minimal

outside the region's main hub, **Putao (Fort Hertz)**. Overland travel via the dilapidated Myitkyina–Putao road is strictly forbidden. With the necessary permits, tourists can, however, fly into the region, but only as part of a pre-arranged tour with an accredited operator – and even then, route options are limited.

That said, given sufficient time, money and determination, it is possible to penetrate the leech-infested rainforest north of Putao and press on through wild, beautiful mountain valleys inhabited by minority people for a close encounter with Southeast Asia's highest peaks, **Hkakabo Razi**, which rises to 5,881 metres (19,295ft), and Gamlang Razi (5870 metres/19,258ft).

MYITSONE

The official source of the Ayeyarwady is the confluence of the Maykha and Malikha rivers, near the town of **Myitsone ⑩**, 42km (21 miles) north of Myitkyina. In the 1990s, the Burmese government attempted to develop the

⊘ IRRAWADDY DOLPHINS

In many countries of the world, dolphins are regarded by fishermen as competitors, but at several places along the Ayeyarwady in central Myanmar, a unique bond has evolved between local cast-net fishers and pods of Irrawaddy dolphins – a rare species of cetacean distinguished by its beluga-like high, round forehead. When attracted by the knocking of oars against the side of a wooden canoe, the dolphins round up shoals of fish and drive them into the waiting nets – a service for which they're rewarded with a share of the catch.

This form of cooperative fishing has been handed down from father to son for generations on the river, although not surprisingly this ancient symbiosis has come under increasing threat. Gill net fishing, mercury poisoning from gold-mine run-off and increasing numbers of dams all caused dolphin populations to fall rapidly for a time – by 2003 it was estimated there were only 37 dolphins left in the entire river. This perilous decline now appears to have been reversed following the creation of a protected zone (and a ban on long gill nets) along a 74km (46-mile) stretch of the Ayeyarwady between the pottery town of Kyaukmyaung and Mingun, just north of Mandalay. As of 2018, some 80 dolphins were estimated to be living in the protected zone, with sightings from ferry and cruise boats commonly reported.

⊙ Fact

It was the Tibetans who gave the mountain Hkakabo Razi its name, derived from the original Tibetan "Ka Karpo Ri", which means "peak of white snow".

area around the spot where the rivers merge as a visitor attraction, but what natural splendour there may have been is these days comprehensively eclipsed by the mud slicks and dirt scars of the open-cast gold mining fields lining the riverbanks. An environmental disaster potentially even more devastating than this, however, threatens to engulf the entire valley if work on Myitsone's controversial **mega-dam** is ever completed. Funded by the Chinese, the $3.6bn project will see the construction of a 140-metre (466ft) -high, 1,310-metre (4,297ft) -long barrage across the river. Some 770 sq km (300 sq miles) of agricultural land is scheduled to be flooded – an area the size of Singapore – which will force the relocation of 13,000 people from 47 villages. This, along with fact that the electricity generated will go to China, has proved a lightning rod for anti-Chinese sentiment in Kachin. Popular opposition, however, has for once made some impact on the normally recalcitrant ruling generals. Bowing

to public pressure in late 2011, President Thein Sein ordered that work on the dam be stopped – though whether or not the bulldozer ban can hold out against ongoing political opposition to the halt from the Chinese remains to be seen, while it's claimed locally that construction work continues in secret, using imported Chinese labour. Aung San Suu Kyi's NLD government has yet to make a final ruling on the future of the project, apparently stalling for time and perhaps aware than whatever decision she makes will be deeply unpopular, either with the Kachin or the Chinese.

PUTAO

Myanmar's northernmost town, **Putao** ⓫ (population: 10,000), was known by its original Shan inhabitants as "Hkamti Long" – "Great Place of Gold", but later renamed **Fort Hertz** by the British after the district commissioner William Axel Hertz, who first explored and mapped this remote corner of the country in 1888. Some 354km (220 miles) north

Oxen and cart on the road to Kyaukmyaung.

of Myitkyina, the outpost became legendary in the annals of the Burma campaign of World War II for remaining out of Japanese hands throughout the conflict. For most of 1942, until the parachute regiment dropped in with fresh supplies, the airfield also remained out of radio contact with Allied command. But once the runway had been upgraded, it served as an emergency landing strip for planes making the notorious flight over the "Hump" of the eastern Himalayas to re-supply Chinese forces.

Although the road from Myitkyina is these days open during the dry season, sporadic flights from Yangon are the only way foreign nationals are permitted to travel to Putao, which sits in a valley encircled on all sides by mountains, with the snow-capped ridges of Hkakabo Razi dominating the northern horizon. The few visitors who come here each winter generally do so on three- or four-day tour extensions, staying at the luxurious and beautifully sited Malikha Lodge on the outskirts of town, from where guests make day trips to Putao's Myoma market, local picnic sites, suspension bridges, tribal villages and logging camps in the area, or else recuperate after treks into the nearby ranges.

A memorable but challenging route is the ten- to twelve-day round trip to the summit of **Mount Phonkan Razi** (3,630 metres/11,909ft), offering a superb vantage point over the valley.

HKAKABO RAZI

Foreigners are also permitted to trek to the base camp of **Hkakabo Razi** (5,881 metres/19,295ft), a ten-day round-trip from Putao. First climbed by a Japanese expedition in 1996, the mountain was traditionally believed to be the tallest in Myanmar (and indeed the whole of Southeast Asia), although an alternative school of thought suggests that its height has been slightly over-estimated, and that the adjacent Gamlang Razi (5870 metres/19,258ft), first summited in 2013, is actually the taller of the two – a question which

A potter stops for a smoke.

is unlikely to be definitively resolved until another team equipped with suitable equipment reaches the top of Hkakabo Razi.

Both mountains lie within the Hkakabo National Park, a 2,414 sq km (1,500 sq mile) tract of protected rainforest and high valleys whose flora and fauna were first surveyed by the American conservationist Alan Rabinowitz in 1996. As well as rare stone martens, blue sheep and an endemic species of deer, Rabinowitz came across a community of indigenous forest-dwelling pygmy people in his reconnaissance work. Known as the Taron, they had for generations been enslaved by the local Kachins and were fast approaching the point of extinction. Frail from inbreeding, the twelve surviving individuals had apparently made a pact not to have children.

HUKAWNG VALLEY TIGER RESERVE

A pottery workshop's wares in Kyaukmyaung.

Alan Rabinowitz also played a leading role in the creation of another national park in Myanmar's far-flung north: the **Hukawng Valley Tiger Reserve** . The sanctuary, close to the old Ledo Road north of Myitkyina, extends over a sprawling 13,602 sq km (8,452 sq miles) of swampy jungle to the southwest of Putao, cradled by the hills lining the Indian border. Critics argue that the creation of the park was merely a ruse to wrest control of the region from the Kachin Independence Army (KIA), citing the increase in government-sponsored logging, and the granting of oil exploration and uranium mining rights to foreign companies by the Burmese government. Irrespective of the motives behind its creation, the reserve has been a resounding failure. Around 100 tigers were estimated to inhabit the park in 2003, though as of 2012 some local observers were suggesting that there was not a single big cat left in the reserve thanks to the effects of rampant poaching, gold-mining and illegal logging. Although the government's forestry department estimated tiger numbers rose in 2015–16, there is no survey data to confirm this.

THE NAGA HILLS

Remote and unknown, the Naga Hills comprise a formidable geographical barrier along the Indian border in far northwestern Myanmar.

The Naga Hills of Myanmar, in the far north of Sagaing State a short distance west from the Kachin border, are as isolated as anywhere in Asia. Centred on the mountainous Angpawng Bum range, Burmese Nagaland comprises the eastern third of the Naga-inhabited hills straddling the Myanmar–India frontier

The term "Naga" is loosely applied to a group of more than 20 tribes inhabiting the border area. The many Naga languages belong to the Tibeto-Burman group of the Sino-Tibetan language family. Almost every village has its own dialect; different groups of Naga communicate in broken Burmese, Assamese, or sometimes in English and Hindi.

Most Naga live in villages strategically placed on hillsides close to water. Shifting cultivation (jhum) is commonly practised, although some tribes farm terraces where rice and millet are the staples. Weaving and woodcarving are also highly developed art forms, while Naga fishermen are noted for the use of intoxicants to kill or incapacitate fish.

Tribal organisation ranges from autocracy to democracy, and power may reside in a council of elders or tribal council. Descent is through the paternal line; clan and kindred are fundamental to social organisation. Due to missionary efforts in the 19th century, a sizeable majority of Indian Naga became Christians, although in Myanmar, animism remains predominant.

POLITICAL STRUGGLES

In the 1970s, Burmese Nagaland became a base for rebels fighting for independence in neighbouring Indian Nagaland. The National Socialist Council of Nagaland (NSCN), led by Indian Naga Isak Chishi Swu and Thuingaleng Muivah, together with the Burmese-born Naga S.S. Khaplang, who ruled the Burmese Naga Hills, preached a strange blend of nationalism and born-again Christianity under the slogan "Nagaland for Christ".

In 1988, Khaplang rebelled against the Indian leadership of the NSCN and took over the rebel movement on the Burmese side of the border. He maintained a base in a remote area north of the town of Hkamti, on the Chindwin River, but in 2011, after securing autonomous status for the Nagas in Myanmar as well as top cabinet jobs for Naga leaders in the National Assembly, he signed a bilateral cease-fire.

One of the consequences of the truce is that foreigners can now undertake trips to the Naga homeland to experience the tribe's flamboyant New Year celebrations, held in mid-January. Government-accredited tour operators can arrange the necessary permits for the trip, which take in colourful festivals during which totem poles are raised and Naga men don their finest traditional headdresses and jewellery, as well as soft treks to Naga villages.

Naga tribesmen.

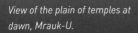
View of the plain of temples at dawn, Mrauk-U.

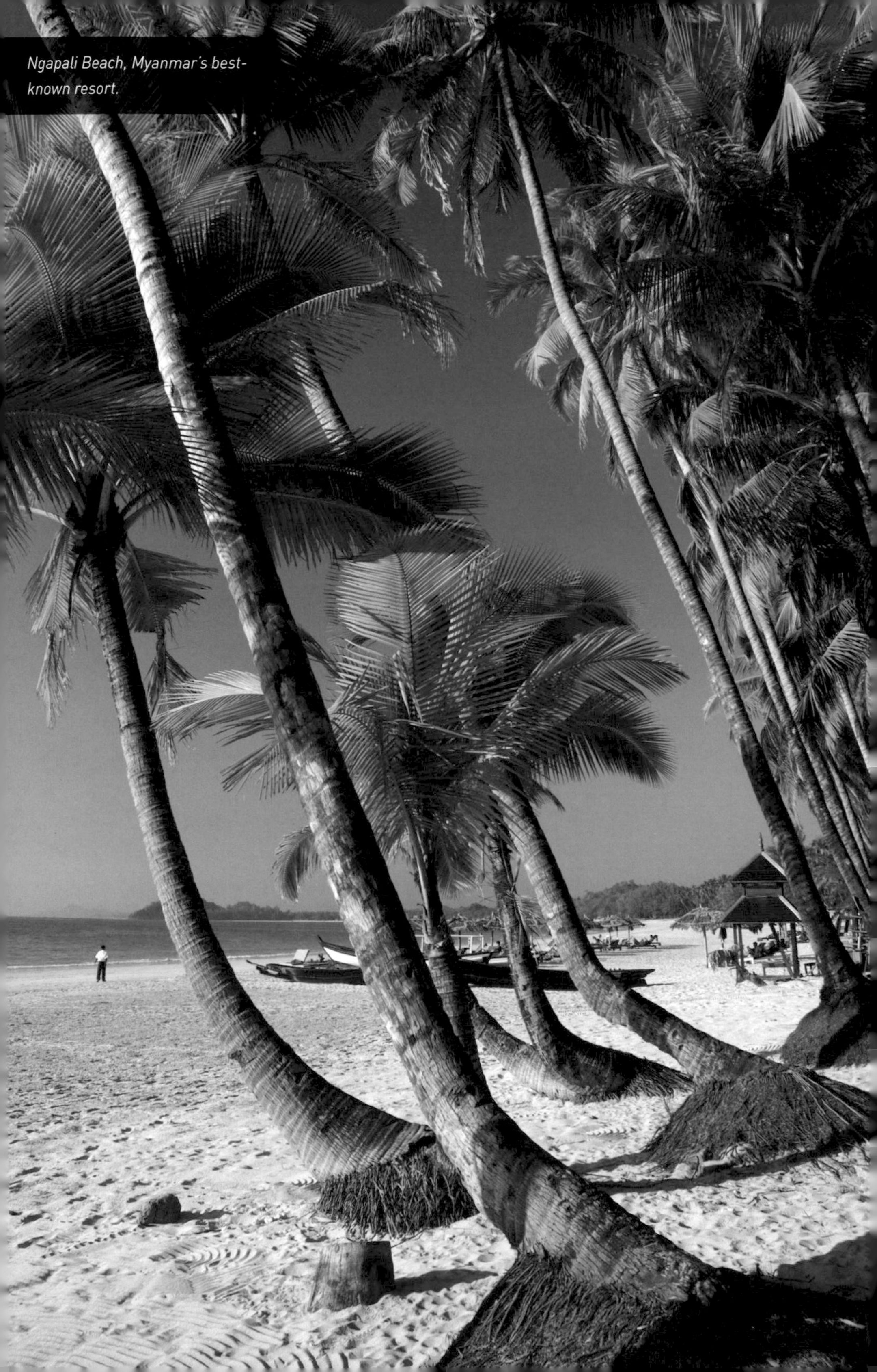

Ngapali Beach, Myanmar's best-known resort.

WESTERN MYANMAR

Now a relative backwater, western Myanmar preserves many relics from its glory days as the major meeting point between Southeast Asian and Indian culture and history.

Wracked for many years by ethnic conflict and political unrest, western Myanmar is still very much off the beaten track. It's an extensive region of placid, sandy beaches, slow-moving broad rivers, jungle and impenetrable hills. From the beaches of Rakhine in the south, to the Indian border in the north, it is isolated from central Myanmar by a series of hardy mountain ranges. To the southwest, the region is washed by the Indian Ocean, then the land frontier marches north by Bangladesh and India.

A fisherman with his nets.

This is where the historically independent Kingdom of Arakan once flourished, a Buddhist state whose kings traditionally also carried a Muslim title, and where Southeast Asian Buddhism met and intermingled with Bengali Islam. In historical terms, western Myanmar is a peripheral land, neither Burmese nor Indian – particularly given the continual, merciless oppression of the region's Indian-descended Rohingya people, once a major feature of Rakhine's towns and villages, most of whom have now been driven abroad or internally displaced into refugee camps.

North of Rakhine the unexplored hill tracts of Chin State remain one of the least-known parts of Myanmar – not just largely unvisited by foreigners, but unfamiliar to all but a handful of Bamar, most of them military men or frontier police. In the south of Chin State, unmarried Chin women still don traditional dress. Further north, the Chin have been Christianised and mainly wear Western dress.

The elegant Ratanabon Pagoda at Mrauk-U.

Rakhine's attractions at present boil down to just a handful of stand-out highlights. The idyllic resort of Ngapali is the biggest draw, with its pristine sands, gorgeous (if pricey) resorts and idyllic, miles-from-anywhere ambience. Further north lies the interesting Rakhine capital of Sittwe, from where the memorable boat trip up the Kaladan River brings you to the remote and magical city of Mrauk-U, the temple-studded capital of Old Arakan.

Chin State, meanwhile, remains largely off the tourist itinerary, although it's now possible to visit parts of the state with a permit and travel with a licensed guide. Most visitors head for the spectacular Nat Ma Taung (Victoria Peak).

Western Myanmar is not the easiest part of the country to visit. While access by sea or by road is possible, these are slow and unreliable options. Most people fly in from Yangon or Mandalay to either Sittwe or Ngapali.

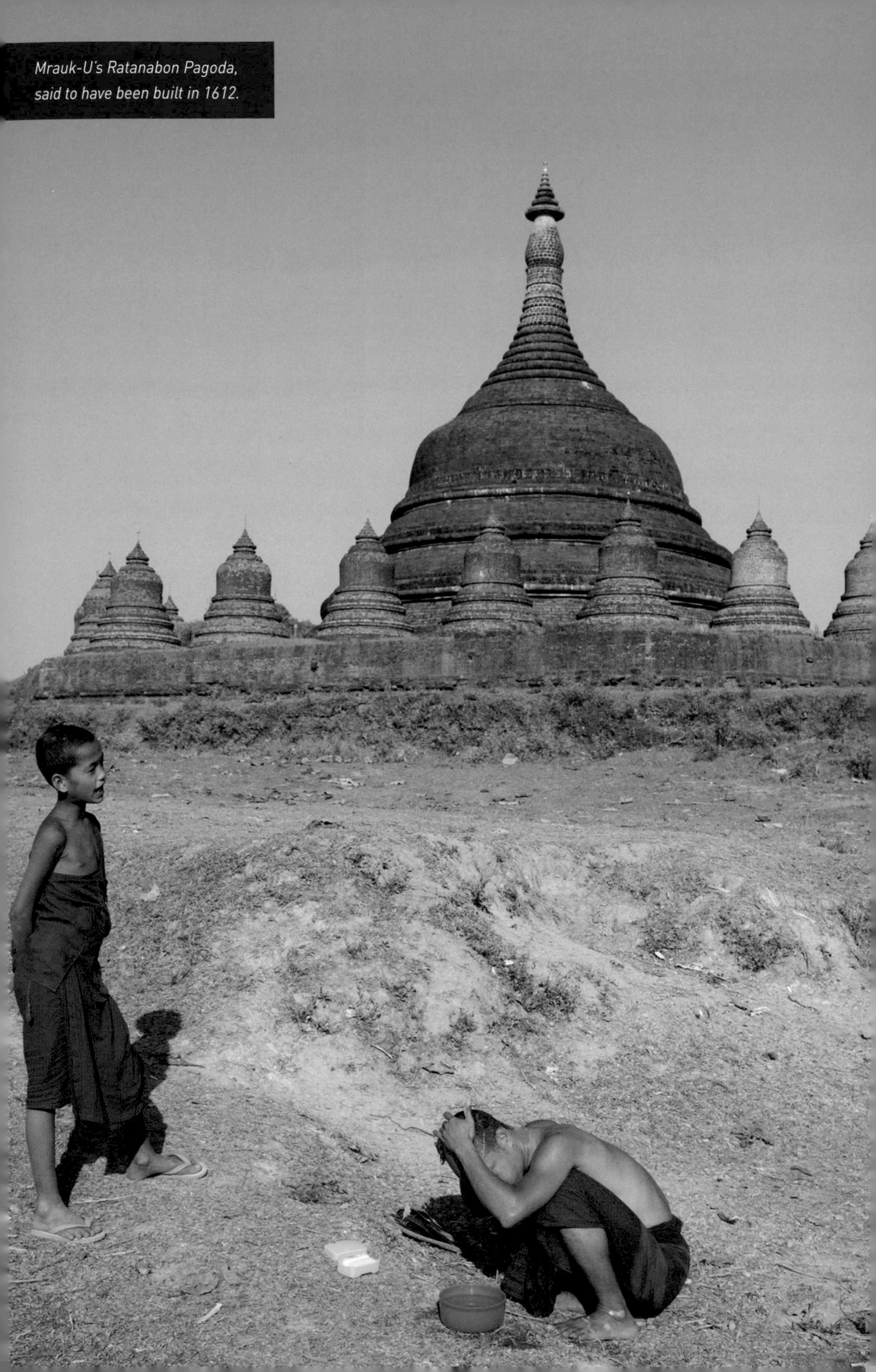

Mrauk-U's Ratanabon Pagoda, said to have been built in 1612.

MRAUK-U, NGAPALI AND CHIN STATE

On an isolated plateau in western Myanmar stand the charismatic ruins of an ancient royal city, while further south, Ngapali Beach is fast blossoming as an international resort.

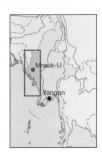

Screened from the Ayeyarwady Valley by a long wall of jungle-covered mountains, Rakhine (formerly known as "Arakan") State in the west of Myanmar is today one of the most remote and under-developed parts of the country. Yet 350 years ago, its coastal strip formed the heartland of a powerful, prosperous kingdom presided over by one of the most cosmopolitan courts in the history of Southeast Asia.

Its capital was Mrauk-U, a port founded in 1430 by King Narameikhla (aka Min Saw Mon), who had spent 25 years in exile fleeing attacks from his Burmese enemies in the Bengali city of Gaur. Although himself a Buddhist, Narameikhla was seduced by the hybrid, Indo-Muslim sophistication of Bengali high culture, and on his return encouraged a similarly inclusive ethos in his own court. The result was a highly advanced brand of royalty, with a monumental architecture to match. At the empire's height in the mid-16th century, when Arakan territory extended all the way from Dhaka to the mouth of the Ayeyarwady, the splendour of Mrauk-U's temples, monasteries, palaces and libraries was legendary across Asia.

The glory days lasted until 1784. Arakan first lost Chittagong to the Mughals and subsequently descended into a bloody civil war, after which the

Burmese army of King Bodawpaya invaded, leaving in its wake devastation from which Mrauk-U never recovered. Today, the ruins of Narameikhla's great city stand smothered in creepers and weeds, its brickwork crumbling into the fields and forests, priceless Buddhas peering from the undergrowth.

Although nowhere near as extensive as the remains of Bagan, Mrauk-U is all the more atmospheric for its neglected state. Moreover, getting to the site is a real adventure. It's now possible to reach the town via an

Main attractions
Mrauk-U
Dhanyawadi
Ngapali Beach
Nat Ma Taung (Mt Victoria)

Maps on pages 276, 281

Restaurant overlooking Ngapali Beach.

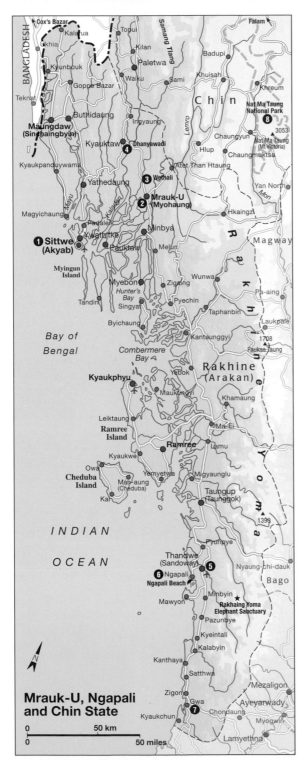

Mrauk-U, Ngapali and Chin State

```
0        50 km
0        50 miles
```

epic and gruelling journey overland (although the route is sometimes closed due to security concerns), but almost all visitors fly to the Rakhine capital of Sittwe, from where boats travel daily to Mrauk-U.

A very different, but equally stellar, attraction can be found in the far south of Rakhine State, where the burgeoning beach resort of Ngapali is attracting ever greater numbers of foreign visitors. With multiple daily flights to and from Yangon and Mandalay, the resort is easily accessible but relatively unspoilt for the time being, its pristine white sands and turquoise water backed by low-rise luxury hotels.

At the diametric opposite end of Myanmar's economic and cultural spectrum, landlocked Chin State, to the northeast of Rakhine, is the country's most disadvantaged region. Members of the persecuted Chin minority group, who live from hunting, fishing and slash-and-burn cultivation in remote jungles and hills, comprise the majority of its population. A long-standing insurgency, coupled with the virtual absence of infrastructure, means that large parts of this far-flung corner of Myanmar remain off limits to tourists, although foreigners are granted permission to scale its highest peak, Nat Ma Taung (aka "Mt Victoria"; 3,053 metres/10,016ft), reached from the Bagan-Ayeyarwady Valley side of the Rakhine Yoma range.

SITTWE

Occupying a breezy site at the mouth of the estuary where the Kaladan, Mayu and Lemro rivers converge, **Sittwe** ❶, capital of Rakhine State, was founded in 1826 by the British, who moved their barracks from Mrauk-U to escape the inland humidity during the First Anglo-Burmese War. Daily steamers from Calcutta (Kolkata) used to dock here in the hey-day of the Raj, whose Anglo-Indian legacy can still be traced in the architecture of the grid-planned centre.

These days, however, Sittwe (formerly known by its Bengali name, "Akyab") remains somewhat remote from the mainstream of Burmese life and looks a little down on its luck, though the city's fortunes may well improve when the new $120 million harbour, funded jointly by the Burmese and Indian governments, is completed in 2019 (according to latest estimates). The city has also been wracked by intermittent political and ethnic unrest – the Muslim Rohingya, who once formed a sizeable minority here, are now conspicuous by their total absence.

Most visitors to Sittwe are just passing through en route for Mrauk-U, served by daily boats which leave early each morning for the four- to seven-hour trip upriver.

The town's handful of sites serve to kill a few hours; the main **market** district, on the riverfront at the northeastern edge of the centre, is lively and colourful throughout the day. Close by, as a primer for a visit to Mrauk-U, it's worth having a look around the **Rakhine State Cultural Museum** on Main Road (Tue–Sat 10am–4pm; charge), for its collection of stone inscriptions, carvings and Buddha images. An exhibition devoted to Arakanese culture occupies the upper floor.

Next to the museum, between Strand Road and Main Road No. 1, is the pretty little South Asian-style Jama' Masjid, which once marked the centre of Sittwe's main Rohingya Quarter, although following riots in 2013 and subsequent clashes all Sittwe's former Rohingya inhabitants have now fled. The mosque itself has been blocked off behind barbed wire, with police on guard outside.

A 3km (1-mile) trishaw ride south, the so-called **View Point** ("Point" for short) is a popular local beauty spot, with a spit of land jutting into the estuary, crowned by an old lighthouse that's been converted into a lookout tower. Beer stations and cafés offer relaxing vantage points from which to admire the sunset vistas over the water on both sides.

Also worth a visit is the huge **Lokananda Pagoda**, 2km (1.2 miles)

Evening mist and smoke from village cooking fires swirl around Ratanabon Pagoda, Mrauk U.

northwest of the Point near the airport, where a massive gilded stupa donated by General Than Shwe dominates the city's fringes. In a building next to it, reached from the stupa terrace's western side, a modest pavilion holds a contrastingly small but greatly venerated bronze Gautama, its surface teeming with thousands of mini Buddhas.

MRAUK-U

The ruins of the Arakan Dynasty's former capital, **Mrauk-U ❷** (Myohaung), are strewn over a plateau between the Kaladan and the Lomro rivers, 65km (40 miles) upriver from Sittwe. Comparisons with Bagan are inevitable: the houses and other secular buildings that would once have lined the city's streets have long since disappeared, leaving in their wake dozens of religious structures marooned amid the bleached grass, tropical foliage and fields. Yet the site doesn't nearly approach the scale or grandeur of its older counterpart on the Ayeyarwady; many of the monuments languish in a somewhat tumbledown state, often

literally in cultivated land where buffalo graze and villagers tend their radish patches – all of which, of course, add considerably to Mrauk-U's allure. Choked with weeds and creepers, the brick stupas and temple complexes exude a feeling of tantalising remoteness that more than repays the time and trouble required to reach the site.

Pending the completion of a controversial new rail line being bulldozed through the edges of Mrauk-U, the only way foreigners can access the ruins is by catching a plane to Sittwe and picking up a boat for the remaining leg – a delightful river journey that heightens the overall sense of anticipation. If you're on a pre-arranged tour you'll be transported in a comfortable, fast motorboat. Independent travellers have three options: a slow, double-decker ITW ferry (departs Tue and Fri, returns Wed and Sat; K7000), which takes around 7 hours to cover the route; the faster and more expensive privately run Aung Kyaw Moe ferry (departs Mon, Thur and Sat, returns Tue, Fri and Sun, around 5 hours; K10,000); or the express **Shwe Pyi Tan** (departs Wed, Fri and Sun, returns Thur, Sat and Mon; K25,000), which takes around 2.5 hours. All boats leave Sittwe and Mrauk U at 7am. Whichever boat you come on, after following a broad river and then narrower tributaries, you'll be dropped at Mrauk-U's jetty, a bumpy five- to ten-minute jeep ride from most of the hotels.

"CITY OF THE MONKEY EGG"

At the peak of its power in the mid-17th century, Mrauk-U – literally "Monkey Egg" – harboured a population of around 160,000. The city's prosperity – founded on the export of rice and slaves to the Dutch colony of Batavia (present-day Jakarta), and by tax income from its Bengali possessions, including the city of Chittagong – attracted not only settlers from the Burmese hinterland, but also Bengalis,

⊘ THE MAHAMUNI IMAGE

Maurice Collis wrote of the Mahamuni image, "The Yattara bell was not sounded as a warning, but as an occult offensive. The notes, provided the particularities of the tables were complied with, would operate to put the invaders to flight by deranging their astrological chart and so placing them in jeopardy. In the exact centre of the top of this enclosure was the shrine (of the Maha Muni image). The original had been destroyed at the time of the Mongolian or Arakanese invasion of 957 and... rebuilt during the period when the country was a feudatory of the Pagan kings of Burma. In Manrique's time it must have resembled a small pagoda of the Pagan Dynasty type, a structure with massive brick or stone walls enclosing a chamber and surmounted by a spire. In the chamber was the famous image, a bronze over 10 feet high representing the Buddha...seated on a throne, his legs folded under him, his left hand opened on his lap, the right touching the earth with the tips of his fingers, a symbolic gesture denoting active compassion for mankind. The image was removed in 1784 to Mandalay... it has been plastered so thickly with gold leaf that its antique beauty has been smothered... you would never guess that it belonged to the first centuries of Indian colonisation eastwards, a classical bronze perhaps 1,800 years old."

Afghans, Persians, Thais, Abyssinians, Japanese Christians and Portuguese freebooters. The king even boasted a personal bodyguard of Samurai warriors. Art and literature – both Arakanese and Bengali – received passionate royal patronage.

The accommodating spirit of the Arakan court, however, would prove its downfall. In 1660, the Mughal prince Shah Shuja, son of the recently deceased Emperor Shah Jahan and a former governor of Bengal, took refuge in Mrauk-U after a failed bid to seize his father's throne. The royal fugitive and his entourage were at first generously received by Sanda Thumadha, the Arakanese king. But after a year of effective house arrest, it became increasingly clear to the prince that the Arakanese were intent on killing him in order to seize the treasure he'd brought with him. Shah Shuja duly fled to the countryside, while some of his Bengali followers mounted a rebellion among the local population, which ended with the burning of Mrauk-U. Shah Shuja managed to escape to neighbouring Tripura in the ensuing melee, but his sons were captured and beheaded by a furious Sanda Thumadha, and their wives incorporated into the royal harem.

The executions enraged Shah Shuja's brother, the new Mughal Emperor Aurangzeb, who promptly dispatched a punitive army to annexe Chittagong and the eastern portions of Bengal occupied by the Arakans, effectively cutting them off from their main source of prosperity.

The loss was the beginning of the end of Mrauk-U. Soon, the state sank into civil war and the countryside into poverty and disorder, encouraging the forces of the Konbaung king Bodawpaya to invade in 1784. Hundreds of thousands of Arakanese men, women and children were massacred or taken prisoner by the Burmese, and the very symbol of their sovereignty, the majestic, gold-covered Mahamuni image, was carried off across the hills to the Ayeyarwady plains, leaving the former capital to be reclaimed by the jungle.

Today, more than two centuries after the conquests of Bodawpaya, the Arakanese still regard themselves as a separate entity, protesting against discrimination and persecution by the central government. Their situation, however, is as nothing compared to the plight of the region's Rohingya Muslims, descendants of Bengali settlers who arrived in Burma during colonial times (or perhaps much earlier) and who have been systematically persecuted since independence. The Rohingya's plight, already desperate, plumbed new depths in 2016 when state-wide clashes and a string of military atrocities (see page 66) drove virtually the entire Rohingya population into refugee camps in Bangladesh, where many of them remain to this day. Once a major and very visible feature of life in Rakhine's towns and villages, the Rohingya have now effectively been removed en masse.

Eat

Food and accommodation options are available in most price brackets at Mrauk-U, and more or less keep track with demand, although advance booking is strongly recommended in peak season from December–January.

Koethaung Pagoda, one of the Mrauk-U temples.

VISITING MRAUK-U

Encircled by fragments of a 30km (19-mile) fortified wall, Mrauk-U's surviving monuments are spread over a 5 sq km (3 sq mile) area, extending north and east from the village centre and the remains of the former royal palace. A K5000 entry fee covering admission to all the temples is charged at the Shittaung Temple, while bicycles are widely available and offer the best way of exploring the site (which is a little too spread out to be comfortably covered on foot) – if you don't mind the horribly pot-holed roads. A couple of full days is sufficient to take in the highlights, although you could profitably spend two or three times as long pottering around more remote locations. Come armed with a strong torch – essential for viewing carved reliefs and murals in dimly lit corridors.

THE NORTHERN GROUP

The cluster of pagodas lying to the north of the village includes some of the most spectacular on the entire site; most are within easy walking distance of one another.

Leymyathna Temple, Mrauk U.

Begin at the **Shittaung Temple Ⓐ**, erected by the most formidable of all the Arakan rulers, King Minbin, to celebrate his conquest of Bengal in 1535. The 3-metre (10ft) **Shittaung Pillar** next to the temple's northern entrance enumerates in eroded Sanskrit script the history of the Arakan dynasties from the 5th until the 8th centuries. One of the grandest of all Mrauk-U's monuments, the pagoda centres on a large bell-shaped stupa surrounded by myriad smaller ones. On entering the central **prayer hall** inside you'll see why the shrine was dubbed as the "Temple of 80,000 Images". Encircling the central chamber and its presiding Buddha statue are two inner passageways containing scores of meditating Buddhas and superb bas-reliefs of *Jataka* scenes, many of them revealing vivid glimpses into life in 16th-century Arakan. The stone corridors are well lit: notice the clumsy grey cement work liberally applied by Archaeology Department workers to stop water from leaching inside the building and spoiling its treasures.

Numerous sitting Buddha figures are also found in the early 16th-century **Andaw-thein** ❸ ordination hall, northeast of the Shittaung Temple. The name means "Tooth Shrine" and the temple is believed to enshrine yet another of the master's molars, originally brought here in the 8th century. It's similar to the Shittaung in layout, though much smaller, and with fourteen stupas rising from an octagonal base. Two concentric passages surround the central hall inside, where a brick Buddha provides the centrepiece.

Dating from 1612, the **Ratanabon Pagoda** ❸, just north of the Andawthein, is as elegant an example of a brick-built stupa as you'll see in Myanmar, with its central, bell-shaped *zedi*, encircled by 24 smaller *stupas,* looking like a piece of exquisitely lathe-turned wood. It received a direct hit from Japanese bombers in World War II but has been completely restored since.

Standing on a hillock to the west, the **Dukkan-thein (Htukkanthein)** ❹ ordination hall consists of another large, bell-shaped stupa, only this time surmounting two raised terraces. A stepped entrance on the east side leads to vaulted passageways that spiral to a central chamber. These are lined with stone images, including some of Mrauk-U's best-known sculptures, showing seated ladies (thought to be the wives of Arakan noblemen) offering lotus buds to the Buddha. Each of the 64 figures sports a different hairstyle. Niches in the side walls contain more Buddha statues.

Immediately northwest of the Dukkan-thein, the **Lemyethna Temple** ❺ was built by King Min Saw Mon in 1430. The exterior is a good example of Mrauk-U's fortress-like temple architecture, lacking any windows and as seemingly impregnable as a bomb shelter. Inside, eight seated Buddhas sit in a circle, with their backs against an octagonal central column and a fine vaulted ceiling above.

ROYAL PALACE

Looming above the centre of the city like a Southeast Asian Acropolis, the **Royal Palace** ❻ was Mrauk-U's nerve centre

> **◉ Tip**
>
> En route to or returning from Mrauk-U, especially near dusk, watch out for mosquitoes – wear long-sleeved tops and trousers and always carry a spray repellent to apply liberally.

Sakyamanaung Paya, Mrauk-U temples.

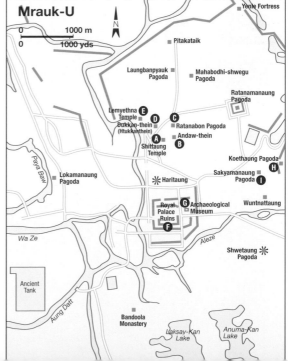

A red-robed Buddha statue in one of the temples at Mrauk-U.

Stone Buddha statues seated in rows, Mrauk-U.

and most splendid building. Sadly little remains to hint at its former glory other than the old sandstone walls – the outermost of three concentric ramparts that once surrounded the royal abode. A stone platform on the site of the former reception rooms and private chambers provides a vantage point from which to view the surrounding monuments and their backdrop of wooded hills.

The **Archaeological Museum** ⓖ (Tues–Sun 9.30am–4.30pm; charge), just inside the palace's western wall, gathers together artefacts found around the site, including stone inscriptions, ceramics, gold and silver ware, weapons, coins and numerous Buddha statues, along with a scale model of Mrauk-U.

The best viewpoint for admiring the palace area itself is the **Haridaung Pagoda**, a diminutive whitewashed temple crowning a hilltop just to the north of the old palace walls.

EASTERN GROUP

Scattered over flat paddy fields and marshland east of the Palace is another significant group of monuments, dominated by the profile of the splendid **Koethaung Pagoda** ⓗ, Mrauk-U's largest surviving temple. The building was said to have been intended by its creator, King Minbin's son, Dikkha, as an attempt to trump the Shittaung erected by his father – hence its superior number of Buddha images and name ("Koethaung" means "90,000"). For a perfect view of the complex, climb up to the fragmentary ruins of the **Peisidaung Pagoda** which crowns a hilltop immediately to the south.

The other outstanding monument in this area is the graceful **Sakyamanaung Pagoda** ⓘ, a kilometre northeast of the palace walls, whose *hti* soars to an impressive 82 metres (280ft).

AROUND MRAUK-U

The lush rice fields that patchwork the alluvial land dividing the Kaladan and Lemro rivers underpinned the rise not merely of Mrauk-U, but a succession of much older city-states, the scant

remains of which litter the country-side north of the archaeological site. At Wethali, a half-hour jeep ride north, you can see the vestiges of ancient walls and a palace dating from the 4th century AD. Further north at **Dhanyawadi** is the Buddhist temple from where the famous **Mahamuni Buddha** image was stolen by Bodawpaya's army in 1784. By far the most popular excursion from Mrauk-U, however, is the trip up the Lemro River to visit villages of the Chin minority, where you can still see a few older women with their faces tattooed in traditional style.

WETHALI

Founded in AD 327 by King Dvan Sandra, the ancient city of **Wethali** ❸ lies 8km (5 miles) north of Mrauk-U, on the road to Dhanyawadi. Fragments of the old walls can still be traced, along with the ground plans of Buddhist temples and ordination halls excavated in the 1980s, but the site's principal vestige is the **Great Wethali Payagyi**, a 5-metre (17ft) Buddha image carved from a single boulder during the reign of Dvan Sandra. It's one of the oldest Buddha images found in Myanmar, though its original features have been lost to more recent renovation work.

Occupation of the walled site, also known as Vesali, spanned from the 4th until the mid-11th century AD, a period coinciding with Pyu townships such as Sri Kshetra in the Ayeyarwady Valley, whose overall shape and plan this settlement closely resembles. The inscribed pillar now displayed in Mrauk-U's Shittaung Temple was originally found here and recalls the names of the twenty kings who ruled ancient Wethali. The rest of the coins, sculptural pieces and other artefacts unearthed on the site are displayed at Mrauk-U's palace museum.

DHANYAWADI

Arakanese chronicles assert that Lord Buddha himself visited the city of **Dhanyawadi** ❹ ("Grain Blessed"), 40km (25 miles) northwest of Mrauk-U, in 554 BC – an event commemorated by the casting of Myanmar's most revered Buddha image, which was made from precious metals donated by the local nobility. Worshipped for centuries by the Arakan kings, the Mahamuni Buddha was the country's most powerful protector deity and attracted streams of devotees until King Bodawpaya took the statue back to Mandalay as war booty in 1784. It's now enshrined in Mandalay, but the temple survives, albeit in a heavily modernised form, and its three presiding stone images, housed on the topmost level, still command great adoration among the Buddhist population of Arakan and beyond. A small museum adjacent to the shrine (free) houses a modest array of sculpture fragments and Sanskrit inscriptions.

The temple is the most visible remnant of a city that thrived here between the 4th and 6th centuries AD. Encircled by a 10km (6-mile) oval of perimeter walls, remains of a square palace

Within the walls of Koethaung Pagoda, one of the Mrauk-U highlights.

⊘ A 17TH-CENTURY METROPOLIS

Father Sebastiao Manrique, a Portuguese missionary and traveller writing in the 17th century, left a vivid description of Mrauk-U's formidable appearance. Surrounded on all sides by high rocky mountains, its thoroughfares were waterways navigable by large and small vessels alike. "The greater number of houses in the city are made of bamboo... much ingenuity and labour are spent on making the houses' mats of the finest material and of many colours, which are very neat and handsome."

His description of Mrauk-U's market at the time of the king's coronation is a portrait of a true metropolis: "So numerous were the different classes of dress and language, such the varied customs at that capital, that the eye was kept busy trying to distinguish the different nationalities by their apparel."

The town also had a vibrant and rich trading community: "In the shops were being sold in abundance, diamonds, rubies, sapphires, emeralds, topazes, gold and silver in plates and bars, tin and zinc. Besides these articles, there was much copper, fine brass ambergris, musk, civet scent, fragrant resin, essence of almonds, incense, camphor, red lead, indigo, borax, quicksilver, saltpeter, opium, tobacco..."

⏲ Tip

Visitors unhappy with the human zoo aspect of tribal tourism may admire a selection of Chin facial tattoos online, at the website of German photographer Jens Uwe Parkitny (www.bloodfaces. com), who has been visiting Rakhine to record this dying tradition since the 1990s.

compound and other stone structures can be discerned in the fields immediately south of the Mahamuni shrine and adjacent village, though you get a much more vivid sense of the site's scale from satellite imagery.

CHIN VILLAGES

Mrauk-U is the starting point for boat rides up the bucolic Lemro River to visit villages inhabited by Chin subsistence farmers and fishing communities. One of Myanmar's most marginalised and poorest minorities, the Chin are famous above all for the facial tattoos traditionally worn by their women. The practice, however, was banned by the socialist regime in the 1960s and discouraged by the American missionaries who evangelised most of the Chin population during the colonial era. Only older women in more remote settlements today sport the inky, blue-green spider's-web patterns on their faces, and those in a couple of villages two hours' upriver from Mrauk-U are cashing in on their tattoos to supplement their families' meagre incomes.

Chin woman with facial spider-web tattoo.

The skin art was not, as is often claimed, done to protect them from the unwanted attentions of local noblemen, but to beautify their faces. All-inclusive trips can be arranged through hotels and guesthouses in Mrauk-U, costing around $80 for a boat seating four people and including transport and guide. Expect an early start.

SOUTHERN RAKHINE

The southern coastal strip of Rakhine State, home to Myanmar's principal beach resort, **Ngapali**, is unreachable overland from Sittwe and the north of the state (although it can be reached on an arduous bus journey via Pyay). Most people fly from Mandalay or Yangon to the town of **Thandwe**, a short taxi ride north of Ngapali. Flights also operate between **Sittwe** and **Thandwe**, and government ferries ply the coast between Sittwe and Taungup (Tuanggok; an hour's drive north of Thandwe).

THANDWE

Thandwe ❺ is southern Rakhine's largest town and the springboard

for visits to nearby Ngapali Beach. In ancient times, when it was known as Dvaravati, the harbour served as a port of call for Indian seafarers en route to or from the Malay Peninsula. The Buddha is said to have lived three of his 547 previous lives here. Local pagodas enshrine various animal relics from the era: the tooth of a cobra in the Andaw Pagoda, just across the river; the rib of a partridge in the Nandaw Pagoda, 1.6km (1 mile) west of the centre; and a yak hair in the Sandaw Pagoda, west of the centre. Other than the temples, there's little to see in this former garrison town, known in British times as "Sandoway", although it's worth taking a look at the local market, housed in a Raj-era prison and full of intense local sights and smells.

NGAPALI

Myanmar's only fully fledged beach resort, **Ngapali** ❻, 10km (6 miles) southwest of Thandwe, centres on a tranquil, palm-lined bay in the south of Rakhine. Its soft white sand, translucent water and wonderful seafood offer a welcome respite from the dust and humidity of travel inland. Visitors on luxury tours comprise the majority of the clientele here, served by a string of small-scale hotels dotted around the bay. Plans are afoot to extend the runway of nearby Thandwe airport to accommodate long-haul flights from Bangkok and Singapore, while increasing numbers of swish five-stars are already rising up in the surrounding palm forests in expectation of the coming bonanza. For the time being, however, the atmosphere remains peaceful, with oodles of space on the sand. Fishermen from the nearby villages still easily outnumber tourists, and their boats bob around offshore unmolested by jet-skis and powerboats.

Snorkelling and fishing trips offer alternatives to lounging on the sand in one of the string of breezy bars dotted along the bay. Most of the hotels are clustered at the north end of the beach, but it's worth taking a walk south around the headland to the picturesque fishing village of **Gyeiktaw**, strewn behind a south-facing cove.

South of Ngapali, it's possible to travel by car (or by bus from Thandwe) to the bustling town of **Gwa** ❼, jumping-off point for a number of idyllic beaches still visited by only a handful of Western travellers, including the secluded palm-fringed white sands of **Zik Hone** beach and the slightly livelier **Kanthaya**, popular with a local crowd.

CHIN STATE

The shadowy hills visible to the north of Mrauk-U mark the southern limits of Chin State, a region the size of Belgium tapering northwards along the frontier of the Indian state of Mizoram. Penetrated by few roads, this is Myanmar's poorest and least developed province, a vast, remote area covered with lush, densely forested valleys and soaring mountains. Almost the entire state was formerly off-limits, although there has

⊙ Tip

For superb views of Ngapali and the coast from above, Oriental Ballooning (www.orientalballooing.com) runs sunrise flights offering a peerless perspective of sea, sand and jungle-swathed hills.

Palm-fringed Ngapali Beach.

been a partial easing of travel restrictions in recent years, with a sprinkling of adventurous travellers now making it to the state capital of **Hakha** and the hill station of **Falam**.

The main attraction for most visitors, however, remains the memorable trek up the state's highest peak, **Nat Ma Taung**  (aka "Mt Victoria"; 3,053 metres/10,016ft) – but allow plenty of time for advance planning and the services of a government-accredited travel agent.

The overwhelming majority of this state's 500,000-strong population are members of the Chin minority, most of whom live from shifting "slash-and-burn" agriculture in far-flung, roadless valleys. It took the British more than a decade to subdue the infamously fierce Chins at the end of the 19th century, since when a combination of American Christian missionaries and persecution by the Burmese military junta has had a devastating effect on the area's traditional culture.

Selling fruit.

Attempts to resist the systematic "Burmanisation" of the Chins by the Yangon government coalesced in the late 1980s into a fully fledged insurgency, spearheaded by the Chin National Front (CNF) and its armed wing, the Chin National Army (CNA). The backlash was predictably brutal. Throughout the 1990s, human rights groups reported the extensive use by the Burmese military of forced labour, arbitrary arrest and religious suppression, as well as widespread rape of Chin women by soldiers.

A wave of mass emigration resulted, mostly into neighbouring Mizoram. Then, in 2007, famine broke out in many parts of the state after the once-in-fifty-year flowering of the Chin bamboo forest – the "Mawta" – which caused a surge in the local rat population, and a subsequent decimation of grain stocks by the suddenly increased rodent population.

Other reasons the Myanmar government is still cagey about allowing foreigners access to the whole of Chin State include the thriving cross-border narcotics trade, and fears that the Burmese Chin will join forces with their even more rebellious brethren over the frontier in Mizoram.

NAT MA TAUNG (MT VICTORIA)

For the time being, the only place in Chin State that registers on Myanmar's tourist map is the mountain soaring majestically above the Ayeyarwady Valley 80km (49 miles) west of Bagan. Rising to 3,053 metres (10,016ft), Nat Ma Taung (Mt Victoria) stands proud of the rest of the Chin Hills range, forming a so-called "sky island" with its own distinct micro-climate, flora and fauna. From Bagan, the round trip to the summit and back takes a minimum of six days (four of trekking and two of jeep travel). Government-accredited tour agents can help negotiate the necessary permits, but allow at least one month to be sure of getting your paperwork in time.

MYANMAR'S ELEPHANTS

Myanmar is richly endowed with teak forests, and the lucrative logging industry still relies on elephant power.

Elephants are most readily found in upcountry logging camps, but they also exist in the wild – roaming the slopes of remote mountain ranges from the borders of Shan and Kachin State in the east, to the Rakhine Yoma in the west. Estimates put the total number at around 8,000–10,000 (about half of which are in captivity), or about one-third of all those in Asia. The majority of captive elephants are thought to be engaged in timber extraction, making Myanmar home to by far the largest herd of working pachyderms in the world.

The Burmese authorities have now established a sanctuary for wild elephants in the southern Rakhine Yoma, not far from Minbyin on the upper waters of the Thandwe River. Encompassing 175,000 hectares (432,400 acres) of forested hills to the southeast of Ngapali, the Rakhine Yoma Elephant Sanctuary is currently closed to tourists, but as development gathers pace on the nearby coast, it may well open up.

ELEPHANTS AT WORK

Working elephants until recently extracted over a million tonnes of fine teakwood and other hardwoods from the Burmese forests each year, although bans on logging and the export of raw teak wood enacted by the government since 2014 – albeit made with the best environmental intentions – have had the unwanted side effect of putting many elephants out of work, placing the future of thousands of elephants in doubt.

Traditionally, the extraction of timber involves the use of powerful bull elephants, who haul cut pieces of timber with harness and drag trains to the encouragement of shouts from their handlers, known as *uzi*. Trained elephants are amazingly adept. Using their heads, trunks, tusks and feet, they push, pull and otherwise manoeuvre logs of up to five tonnes to the banks of Myanmar's fast-flowing rivers. From here, the timber can be floated out of the forests and down to the sawmills.

Properly managed – as in Myanmar and in India's Andaman Islands – teak forestry can be a self-sustaining industry in which elephants play a major role. They can haul and manoeuvre without damaging the environment in much smaller spaces than bulldozers or cranes. These skills have ensured that Myanmar remains one of the last places in Asia with a thriving elephant culture.

While many working elephants are bred in captivity, some are captured in the wild and trained. Each year, the Burmese Forestry Department determines how many of such elephants are to be taken from the forest under the Elephant Control Scheme. Capture is a dangerous process involving specially trained elephants called *kunkee*. In times past it was even more risky as elephants had to be lassoed; today, tranquiliser darts are used. A wild calf can usually be trained to basic levels in only a few months using a combination of "carrot" (tasty morsels of food, hypnotic singing and small kindnesses) and "stick" (sleep deprivation, confinement, limited food intake), but it takes around 20 years before an elephant is fully trained.

Mahout and his elephant clearing logs.

Relaxing and swimming in the Thanlwin River at the end of a long day.

A boy rides a buffalo during heavy monsoon rain.

SOUTHERN MYANMAR

Myanmar's lush south holds a diverse range of attractions, from idyllic beaches and limestone caves through to the spectacularly precarious Golden Rock of Kyaiktiyo.

A backpacker naps on the bow of a boat travelling upstream on the Thanlwin River.

Tapering down the western side of the Gulf of Mottama to the Isthmus of Kra, southern Myanmar comprises a long, narrow finger of land extending from Kayin and Mon State, through Tanintharyi, almost to the Thai island of Phuket. In historical terms, this was a marginal land, until recently always peripheral to the Bamar centre, with distinct cultural, ethnic and historical ties to neighbouring Thailand and the Malay–Indonesian world further to the south.

Age-old antipathies between its predominantly Kayin (Karen) population and the Burmese have for decades meant that the region has been blighted by one of Asia's longest-running civil wars, meaning that large parts of the area were until recently inaccessible to visitors. However, following the 2011 peace accord between the government and Kayin insurgent armies, the area has now fully opened to foreign visitors, although permits are still required to visit parts of Myeik archipelago in the far south.

Foremost among the region's many unique attractions is the extraordinary Golden Rock Pagoda of Mount Kyaiktiyo in Mon State, which can be reached in a day from Yangon. Further south, the Mon capital, Mawlamyine (Moulmein), retains a distinct colonial-era charm and serves as the start, or end, point of cruises by old double-decker ferries on the Thanlwin (Salween) River into neighbouring Kayin State, where the striking limestone hills, caves and mountaintop monasteries around the town of Hpa-an entice increasing numbers of travellers.

Kyaiktiyo's Golden Rock.

Still more isolated is the exquisite coast of Tanintharyi in the far south, now increasingly accessible to foreign travellers following decades of isolation. At present, the entire region is a delightful tropical backwater, perhaps fifty years removed from the relative affluence and openness of neighbouring Thailand. A more pristine, more beautiful part of mainland Southeast Asia would be hard to find.

With care, the Tanintharyi Coast – particularly the totally undeveloped Myeik Archipelago of 800 coral-fringed offshore islets – might become one of Myanmar's major destinations, although for the time being the almost complete lack of development means that it is still largely off the beaten track.

MON AND KAYIN STATES

Myanmar's laid-back southeast is home to numerous attractions including stunning natural landscapes and an eclectic array of religious and colonial landmarks.

Bordered along its western flank by the Andaman Sea and on its eastern side by Kayin State, **Mon State** is home to the Mon people, the ethnic group that formerly dominated southern Myanmar. Squeezed gradually southwards by the Bamars, the Mon were ousted from their capital, Bago, in the mid-18th century by King Alaungpaya and retreated southwards along the coast to their former heartland, where they survived the turbulence of succeeding centuries thanks to the fertility of the region's rice fields.

The Mon martial tradition, however, weathered defeat by the Bamars to re-surface in World War II, when Mon regiments fought bravely alongside Allied forces, in recognition of which the British promised them their own autonomous state. But self-rule never materialised – even after a decades-long war against the Burmese-dominated government fought by Mon guerrillas in the hills of the Tenghyo range, to the south.

The lengthy insurgency explains why Mon State remains something of a tourist backwater, although growing numbers of foreign visitors are now discovering the region's diverse charms. The spellbinding **"Golden Rock Pagoda"**, remains the region's

leading attraction, while a day's journey further south, **Mawlamyine** (or Moulmein, as it was known by the British), the state capital, offers a superbly atmospheric relic of colonial rule with heaps of old-world atmosphere and a bumper crop of monuments, including the world's largest reclining Buddha at nearby Win Sein Taw Ya.

En route to Mawlamyine, it's worth pausing in neighbouring **Kayin State** to experience the otherworldly karst landscapes of **Hpa-an** and its hinterland, where you can hike up

⊙ Main attractions
Kyaiktiyo: "Golden Rock
  Pagoda"
Mawlamyine (Moulmein)
Mount Zwegabin
Saddar Cave
Hpa-an–Mawlamyine river
  trip

Maps on pages
294, 299

A girl waits for customers outside her family's shop.

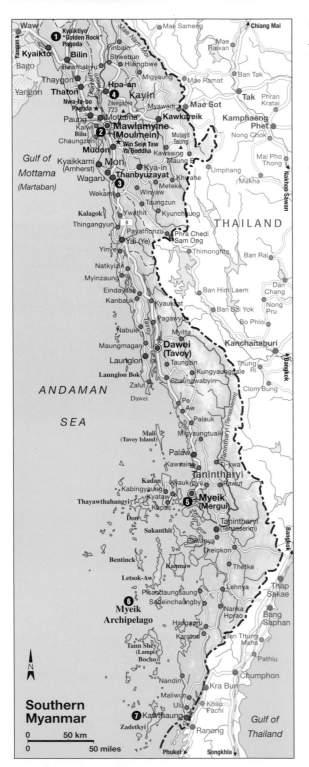

Southern Myanmar

sheer-sided limestone hills swathed in jungle to summits crowned by sacred stupas and monasteries, explore remote Buddhist cave complexes and catch old-style double-decker ferries up the Thanlwin (Salween) River.

MON STATE

Mon State occupies a thin sliver of the Tanintharyi coastal belt south-west of Yangon, on the opposite bank of the Gulf of Mottama. Backed by the Tenghyo hills, this region was the crucible of the early Mon king-dom. Local historians assert this was the "Suwanabhumi" ("Land of Gold") referred to in ancient Bud-dhist chronicles, to which the Mau-ryan emperor Ashoka dispatched the missionaries Sona and Uttara from India in the 3rd century BC. Recent archaeological and genetic evidence, however, suggests that the Mon, who are of Tibeto-Burman origin, had not even begun their migration across Himalayas by this date. More certain is that they were among the first set-tlers in lowland Burma to espouse

Theravada Buddhism, absorbing considerable Indian influences along the way.

From their capitals at Bago and Thaton, the Mon dominated lower Burma until the rise of Bagan and military defeat at the hands of King Anawrahta in 1057. Thereafter, their power waned, though Mon influence on Burmese culture has always been considerable. Only after King Alaungpaya's brutal attack on Bago exactly seven centuries later, when the Mon who survived the invasion were either massacred or driven across the border into Siam, did they disappear from the mainstream of Burmese life.

Today, Mon State is emerging from decades of fighting between the military regime and the Mon National Liberation Army (MNLA), which has struggled since the 1970s for greater self-determination. Human rights abuses have been rife in the region, although with the exception of a few remote hill areas, the conflict has subsided since the signing of an accord with the government in 2012. Rice, rubber, fishing and betel nut farming are the mainstays of the local economy, with tourism virtually non-existent beyond Maylamyine and the Golden Rock temple at Kyaiktiyo – at least for the time being.

MOUNT KYAIKTIYO: THE "GOLDEN ROCK" PAGODA

Forming one of the most ethereal spectacles in Southeast Asia, the **Kyaiktiyo "Golden Rock" Pagoda ❶** crowns a ridge of forested hills in the far north of Mon State, 210km (130 miles) east of Yangon around the Gulf of Mottama. During the pilgrimage season between November and March, tens of thousands of devotees climb daily to the shrine, regarded as the third most sacred in the country after the Shwedagon Pagoda and Mahamuni image in Mandalay, for a glimpse of a modest, 7.3-metre (24ft) stupa mounted atop a lavishly gilded boulder. According to the faithful, only the presence inside the reliquary spire of a hair of the Buddha prevents the rock from toppling into the sheer-sided ravine below.

Packaged gold leaf for sale which the devout will stick onto the already heavily gilded Golden Rock Pagoda.

A Burmese Buddhist prays beside the Golden Rock Pagoda.

⊘ Fact

Although theoretically Kyaiktiyo can be rocked by a gentle push, don't try, even in jest! It's a highly venerated pagoda, and should be treated as such.

The hour-long climb to the hilltop temple can be arduous in the heat, and the journey to and from the starting point of the walk in an open-topped truck is less than comfortable. But the effort is rewarded with the chance to see the magical boulder bathed in the delicate, rose-coloured light of dawn or the afterglow of sunset, when crowds of ecstatic pilgrims and monks illuminate flickering candles and incense sticks as offerings.

VISITING THE KYAIKTIYO PAGODA

The turning off the coastal highway for the pagoda is at the town of **Kyaikto**, but the starting point for the pilgrimage proper lies another 10km (6 miles) further northeast at the village of **Kinpun**. While devout Buddhists disembark here to begin the 4-hour, 11km (7-mile) trek to the temple, the majority of locals – and virtually all foreigners – transfer to an open-topped truck fitted with wooden slats for the bumpy, 45-minute ride to the road end at **Yatetaung**.

From here, a paved path, lined with refreshment and souvenir stalls, zigzags steeply uphill to the main shrine – an hour-long climb that can be tough in the heat. Teams of blue-shirted porters are on hand to carry in sedan chairs those unwilling or unable to make the ascent under their own steam. A government entrance ticket has to be paid for at the temple entrance.

Only men are allowed to cross the footbridge over the chasm separating the golden rock from the temple terrace, which devotees do in order to be able to press a propitious gold leaf on to the boulder. To be at the temple for the pre-dawn rituals, pilgrims sleep on the adjacent terrace or in the nearby monastery. Foreign tourists, however, are obliged to spend the night in one the hotels recently built near the top of the hill, or down in Kinpun.

MAWLAMYINE (MOULMEIN)

"By the old Moulmein Pagoda
Lookin' lazy to the sea,
There's a Burmese girl a-settin'
And I know she thinks o' me."

The Golden Rock Pagoda is built around a huge boulder on the rim of a cliff in the Kalasa Hills.

⊘ KYAIKTIYO LEGEND

According to legend, the Kyaiktiyo pagoda was founded in the 11th century by King Tissa to enshrine a hair of the Buddha he had been given by a holy man, on the condition that he install it on a rock the shape of his head. This the king was able to do thanks to his supernatural powers, along with the help of Thagyamin, king of the *nat*, who directed him to a suitable rock on the sea bed. This was then transferred by boat to the foot of a holy mountain. The legendary boat used to carry the boulder eventually turned into stone, and can now be found a few hundred metres away from the golden rock.

Thanks to its fleeting mention in the famous poem *Mandalay* (1890), the former capital of British Burma, Moulmein – or **Mawlamyine ❷** as it's now known – will forever be associated in the foreign imagination with Rudyard Kipling, which is ironic considering the writer only spent a few fleeting hours here. Yet the town, or more accurately the beauty of its women, made a lasting impression on the 24-year-old, who was travelling to England for the first time from Calcutta via the US.

The pagoda in question (actually the Kyaikthanlan Pagoda) is one of several still encrusting a prominent ridge inland from the city, today home to around half a million people, making it the fourth largest in the country. Strategically sited 28km (18 miles) inland from the mouth of the Thanlwin River, Mawlamyine was ceded to the British by the Kingdom of Ava in the Treaty of Yandabo at the end of the First Anglo-Burmese War in 1826, whereupon it was transformed into a thriving teak and rubber port. Few

of the once sizeable Anglo-Burmese community that formerly dominated colonial Moulmein remain, the majority having left for more prosperous corners of the empire after independence, but plenty of mildewing Raj-era buildings attest to its 19th-century prominence. However, it's the considerably more ancient Buddhist monuments crowning the ridge inland that tend to draw the eye.

Foremost among them, at the far northern end of the ridgetop, is the **Mahamuni Pagoda ❶** a traditional Mon-style complex whose presiding image is a beautiful replica of Mandalay's Mahamuni. Housed in a shrine lined with sparkling precious stones and mirrorwork, the statue was commissioned by a homesick queen, Mibaya-gyi, one of King Mindon's consorts, during her exile following the British annexation of Mandalay in 1885.

For the best views of the city, head further south to the splendid, and much older, **Kyaikthanlan Pagoda ❸**, erected in the late 9th century to house a hair relic, Tripitaka manuscripts and

An old Morris truck in downtown Mawlamyine.

Thanlwin Bridge, Mawlamyine.

A mosque in Mawlamyine.

Buddhist monks at the Water Lake Monastery in Hpa-An.

gold images of the Buddha. Successive rulers raised the height of the central stupa, which is now magnificently gilded and the tallest in the area. You can either walk to the upper terrace via a covered staircase, or ascend in an elaborately roofed elevator.

At the southern end of the ridge, **U Zina Pagoda** Ⓒ houses four life-sized statues of the images that inspired young Siddhartha Gautama to take up the life of a wandering ascetic: an old man leaning on a staff; a sick man suffering from a terrible disease; a corpse; and a yellow-robed monk blissfully free of worldly worries.

AROUND MAWLAMYINE

Burma's second longest bridge, the 6.6km (4.1-mile) **Thanlwin Bridge**, carries the coastal highway and its adjacent rail line north across the river towards Thaton. Crowning the hills overlooking the estuary is a local pilgrimage site, the **Nwa-la-bo Pagoda**, renowned as the seat of another sacred golden boulder shrine, although far less visited than

the one at Kyaiktiyo. There are, in fact, not one but three separate rocks here, balanced precariously on top of each other to create a phantasmagorical monument that perfectly complements the astounding view over the bamboo forest and jungle-covered valleys below it.

A much more easily accessible option is the gigantic reclining Buddha at **Win Sein Taw Ya**, 20km (12 miles) south of Mawlamyine just off the main road to Mudon. Measuring 180 metres (600ft) in length, the statue is the largest of its kind in the world and, like the one at Bodhi Tataung near Monywa (see page 194), holds diorama galleries illustrating the teachings of the Buddha. The statue's not entirely finished however, while some of the stairwells inside the statue (marked with chalk crosses) are structurally unsound.

While you're in the area, don't miss the striking **Kyauktalon Kyaung**, a peculiar, jungle-draped outcrop of rock rising sheer from the paddy fields a short way further south.

⊘ THE DEATH RAILWAY

The Siam–Burma rail line, better known as the "Death Railway", was built to supply Japan's advancing army in the run-up to the invasion of India, when Japanese shipping was vulnerable to attack by Allied submarines. A slave labour force of around 180,000 Asian and 60,000 Allied POWs captured at the fall of Singapore was used to carry out the work, which involved the laying of 415km (258 miles) of track, bridges, embankments and cuttings through dense jungle. Disease, starvation, exhaustion and brutal treatment at the hands of the Japanese cost the lives of an estimated 106,000 men, including 16,000 British, Commonwealth and European servicemen, during the 14 gruelling months it took to complete the project.

The most notorious stretch, due to its remoteness and extreme terrain, was the one crossing the Tenasserim Hills via the "Hell Fire Pass", where 69 labourers were beaten to death or crucified on trees using barbed wire over a period of just six weeks. When the two opposing sections of the line finally met in October 1943, most of the POWs were transferred to Japan. Those that stayed behind to maintain the railway experienced horrific conditions, as Allied bombing attacks gradually destroyed the line during the final months of the war.

Formed from limestone, the flat top of the vertical-sided hillock holds a Buddhist temple, reached via a flight of ancient steps. The Hindu temple at the foot of the rock is patrolled by troops of voracious macaques, so keep any food you may have brought well wrapped up.

A further 65km (40 miles) down the highway from Mawlamyine is the town of **Thanbyuzayat** ❸ where the infamous Japanese **"Death Railway"** (see box) formerly joined up with the existing British-built one to Yangon. On the outskirts of town, a large **war cemetery** (daily dawn to dusk; free) holds the bodies of 3,617 of the 16,000 or more POWs who perished during the construction of the Burmese portion of the route. Many more were interred where they expired in camp burial grounds or at remote sites alongside the railway; dog tags removed from thousands of such bodies were incorporated into memorial plaques on the site, which is impeccably maintained by the Commonwealth War Graves Commission.

KAYIN STATE

Kayin State – formerly known as Karen State – comprises one of Myanmar's most perennially troubled regions. Since Independence in 1948 it saw near-continuous fighting between the Burmese army and various factions of Karen insurgents, particularly the Karen National Union (KNU) and its armed wing, the KNLA. The conflict, often dubbed the world's longest-running civil war, saw a dramatic escalation in 2010, when the Burmese generals ordered a major offensive in the region. Having wiped out all but a few pockets of Karen resistance, this led in 2011–2012 to the signing of a peace accord with the rebels, guaranteeing representation in parliament in exchange for a cessation of hostilities.

Plans were announced the following year to restore the overgrown **Death Railway** line that formerly ran through the interior hills of Kayin to the Thai border at Three Pagodas Pass – a move which, it is hoped, will encourage tourism and trade in this

⊘ **Tip**

Unfortunately, getting to the Nwa-la-bo Pagoda can be difficult without your own transport as the trucks waiting at the foot of the approach path only leave with a minimum of forty-odd passengers. The walk takes around three hours.

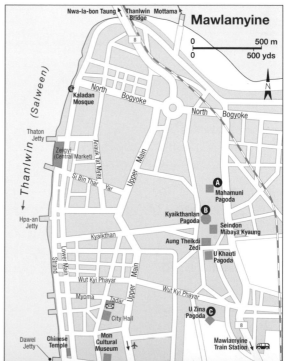

A Burmese woman carries a boy on her back up Mount Kyaiktiyo.

Mawlamyine

Tip

Also worth a visit at the foot of Mount Zwegabin is **Lumini Park** (free), a collection of one thousand life-sized Buddhas seated on pedestals in recently planted woodland.

impoverished area. In the meantime, the only part of the state you're likely to want to explore is the capital, **Hpa-an**, with its pretty hinterland of karst hills, sugar-cane and rice fields, where several fascinating Buddhist monuments nestle amid some of the country's most photogenic landscapes. The other worthwhile trip, and a great way to experience backwater Myanmar, is the journey by government ferry from Hpa-an to Mawlamyine via the Thanlwin River.

HPA-AN AND AROUND

Although holding few sights of note, **Hpa-an ❹** is an easy-going, uncongested state capital with a lively riverfront and market area, and a mostly Karen population of 50,000. Increasing numbers of foreigners are now beginning to visit, attracted by the surrounding landscapes of the countryside, with its outcrops of towering, jungle-draped limestone similar to those of Guilin in southern China.

The highest of these spectacular massifs is **Mount Zwegabin** (732

metres/2,373ft), whose unmistakable profile rises 13km (8 miles) south of Hpa-an, soaring out of the paddy fields like a vision from a lost world. If you've the legs for it, consider the hike to the top, via a flight of steep, winding stone steps. The main incentive to brave the two-hour slog, and troupes of aggressive monkeys who patrol the route, is the chance to watch the sunset from the summit of the mountain, where a lonely Buddhist monastery enjoys a fabulous panorama over the beautiful Thanlwin Valley to the distant Andaman Sea. There's very basic accommodation (K5,000) in the monastery in two twin rooms, allocated on a first-come first-served basis, but the privations are worth enduring for the chance to admire the wondrous sunrise the following morning – although note that the local immigration authorities occasionally clamp down on the practice, since foreigners are technically not allowed to spend the night anywhere except officially licensed guesthouses or hotels.

The world's largest reclining Buddha statue at Win Sein Taw Ya.

Considerably older Buddha statues lie hidden in the many **caves** riddling the limestone hills around Hpa-an. The largest and most spectacular of these is **Saddar Cave**, 27km (17 miles) southwest of town along the road to Eindu village. Steps lead to an entrance chamber featuring a row of Buddhas and *nats*, followed by a series of gigantic caverns whose walls ooze with amazing rock and crystal formations (bring a good torch). After half an hour underground you emerge on the far side of the hill, where an opening reveals a hidden lake – a truly magical experience.

Another enigmatic sight hereabouts is the **Kyauk Kalat Pagoda**, a small monastery complex centred on a weird finger of rock that juts vertically out of an artificial lake. Reached via a long footbridge, the site is set against a mesmerising backdrop of karst hills and crags, best viewed from the summit of the outcrop, which you can climb to via a flight of fifty steps.

Another local cave worth hunting out is the **Kawgun Cave** (daily 7am–dusk; charge), 12km (7 miles) southwest of Hpa-an. In use since the 7th century, the cave is packed with hundreds of Buddha statues seated around the floor of the cave and thousands more tiny terracotta Buddha figures affixed in frieze-like patterns to the caves jagged walls, with traces of ancient stucco painting visible here and there.

By far the most popular excursion from Hpa-an, however, is the **ferry ride to Mawlamyine** via the Thanlwin River. Services run daily and, unlike the ferries plying the northern Ayeyarwady or Chindwin rivers in Upper Myanmar, most of the passengers seem to be foreign backpackers. Nevertheless, the trip is worth making for the rural scenery the ferry chugs through – though be warned that if the boat leaves before sunrise, as is often the case, you'll miss the best of it – many people make the trip starting from Mawlamyine rather than Hpa-an precisely for this reason. You can also book a private boat ride.

Boarding a boat in Mawlamyine for the popular day trip upriver to Hpa-An.

Soldiers from the Mon National Liberation Army (MNLA).

⊘ ETHNIC CONFLICT

In January 1948, when the British withdrew from Burma, the stage was set for ethnic confrontation. In simple terms, the Bamar Buddhist majority tended to see the Kayin (Karen), who had fought for the British against the Japanese in World War II, as lackeys of the outgoing Raj. For their part, the Kayin were nervous about coming under a Bamar-dominated Buddhist government, and demanded their own state.

As a consequence, the Kayin rebelled against Yangon rule, embarking on a vicious, protracted and largely forgotten civil war that would span six decades and force tens of thousands of refugees across the border into Thailand. Its final flurry occurred in the wake of the 2010 elections, when Kayin and Burmese forces clashed in the town of Myawaddy. A series of ceasefires signed with various groups in 2011–2012, however, have brought a (hopefully) definitive peace to the region.

The Mon were slower to rebel, although the minority's principal armed faction, the MNLA, held out against Yangon in a few scattered and isolated border regions up until 2015, when a ceasefire was finally brokered – although fighting subsequently erupted between Mon and Kayin forces, continuing sporadically until the signing of a further ceasefire in 2018.

Despite the still potentially turbulent political situation, both Mon and Kayin states are today almost entirely open to foreign travellers.

A beach on an uninhabited island in the Myeik Archipelago.

MYEIK REGION

The remote, historically fascinating port of Myeik, with its neighbouring archipelago of unspoilt islands, is now becoming increasingly accessible to visitors.

Main attractions
Myeik
Myeik Archipelago

The coast of **Tanintharyi Region** (formerly known as Tenasserim), in the far south of Myanmar, is as beautiful as anywhere in Southeast Asia. Yet despite its proximity to neighbouring Thailand, on the opposite, eastern, flank of the Malay Peninsula, it has long been off the beaten track – largely thanks to the decades-old insurgency fought by Karen guerrillas along the mountainous international border. This has long been a politically sensitive zone. The main pipeline from the off-shore Yadana petroleum field also crosses the area, as does the controversial Ye-Dawei railway, which opponents of Yangon's former military regime claim was constructed by forced labour.

For the time being, the region's immense tourist potential, with its gorgeous beaches and sand-fringed coastal islet, remains largely untapped – although it is doubtless only a matter of time before development commences in earnest. In the meantime, the entire region remains enticingly unspoilt, while the almost complete lifting of travel restrictions means that foreigners are now allowed to head overland to Myeik (from where it's also possible to visit the alluring Myeik Archipelago either on a day-trip or by staying at one of the archipelago's three

Street market in Myeik.

upscale hotels), and can continue further south to Kawthaung, on the Thai border.

MYEIK

Although today a provincial backwater, **Myeik ⑤** – or "Mergui" as it was formerly known – served between 1350 and 1750 as the Thai capital's main sea port for trade between the spice islands and India. Overlooking the mouth of the Tanintharyi River, it was later occupied by the British, and still retains faint vestiges of colonial charm

Map on page 294

Bouldered island in the Myeik Archipelago.

Group of Moken children playing on the beach.

Kuthein Nayon Kyaung is another temple built in Mon style with characteristic square shrines. Myeik's real USP, however, is its fine harbour and the views from the waterfront to the nearby twin-peaked barrier island of **Kadan**, whose bulk protects the port from the cyclones of the Andaman Sea and has long ensured the town's viability as a year-round anchorage. Myeik harbour is also the principal embarkation point for ferries and launches bound for the Myeik Archipelago to the west.

MYEIK ARCHIPELAGO

along with some impressive local cottage industries – cashew farming and the making of *ngapi* (fermented fish paste – one of the staple ingredients of Burmese cuisine) are both major local commercial concerns.

Foremost among Myeik's Buddhist monuments is the central **Theindawgyi Pagoda**, a classic Mon-style temple lined with well-executed interior mosaic and high-quality bronze Buddha images. On the edge of town,

An archipelago of around 800 coral-fringed islands scattered off the coast of Tanintharyi, the **Myeik Archipelago ⑥** is a tropical paradise of the kind that has all but disappeared in Southeast Asia. The long-standing ban on independent travel imposed by the government has ensured that the islands remain much as they have for centuries, inhabited by communities of Malay fishermen and semi-nomadic Moken "Sea Gypsies"

(see page 305) who, like their contemporaries further south along the Malay Peninsula, spend the dry season on small boats and return to ramshackle villages on land during the monsoons.

The Japanese are engaged in lucrative pearl fishing in the archipelago, while the region's swifts' nests – found in cathedral-like limestone caves accessible only at low tide – are harvested for exotic bird's-nest soup.

After years of travel restrictions, the islands of the archipelago are now accessible as never before. It's possible to visit either on a live-aboard boat and dive tour; by staying at one of the archipelago's three officially sanctioned upmarket hotels); or, most affordably, on a day-trip from Myeik (combining visits to local villages, snorkelling and some time on the beach for around $80 per person). Alternatively, a handful of Thai scuba crews working out of Phuket run live-aboard cruises to the world-class dive sites in the area.

KAWTHAUNG

Kawthaung ❼, at the southernmost tip of Myanmar, is an unremarkable frontier town dominated by Thai trade. Many locals are bilingual in Burmese and Thai, and the *baht* is welcome everywhere – certainly more so than *kyat*.

There's not much to see in Kawthaung, although a walk around the town centre and along the seafront is sufficient to kill a few hours between transport connections. To the south of the harbour lies **Cape Bayinnaung**, a promontory named after the Burmese king of the same name who invaded Thailand several times via this route during the 16th century. A statue of the legendary warrior clad in battle armour and flourishing a sword at the nearby Thai coast serves to remind visitors of Myanmar's past military glories. Unspectacular accommodation is available at two or three small hotels in Kawthaung, while the offshore Grand Andaman resort offers upmarket surroundings for high-rollers intent upon golf, duty-free shopping and gambling – casinos are illegal in neighbouring Thailand.

⊙ Tip

Wander around the back lanes of Myeik to discover some wonderful old colonial mansions, teak houses and traditional wooden shopfronts.

Myeik town centre.

⊘ THE MOKEN SEA GYPSIES

The translucent waters of the Myeik Archipelago, off the coast of Tenasserim in southeastern Burma, are the last stronghold of seaborne nomads who call themselves the 'Moken' or 'Morgan'. Known in Burmese as 'Salone' or 'Selung', and in neighbouring Thailand as Chao Nam ('water people'), the group number between 2,000 and 3,000 and are unique for spending most of their lives at sea. Long-tailed diesel houseboats provide shelter and transport for families who subsist on what they catch and rarely return to dry land except to trade fish or shells for money to buy fuel.

In recent decades, the discovery of petroleum reserves in the region has posed a threat to the survival of the Moken's nomadic lifestyle. Attempts were reportedly made by the former military Burmese government to forcibly relocate them in settled villages – a life to which they are ill-suited.

The Moken made headlines in the wake of the tsunami of 2004, which they miraculously survived because they were able to perceive warning signals in the sea and flee to high ground ahead of the tidal wave. Another unusual attribute of the Moken is their ability to see clearly underwater – a faculty they develop in early childhood while diving for shells.

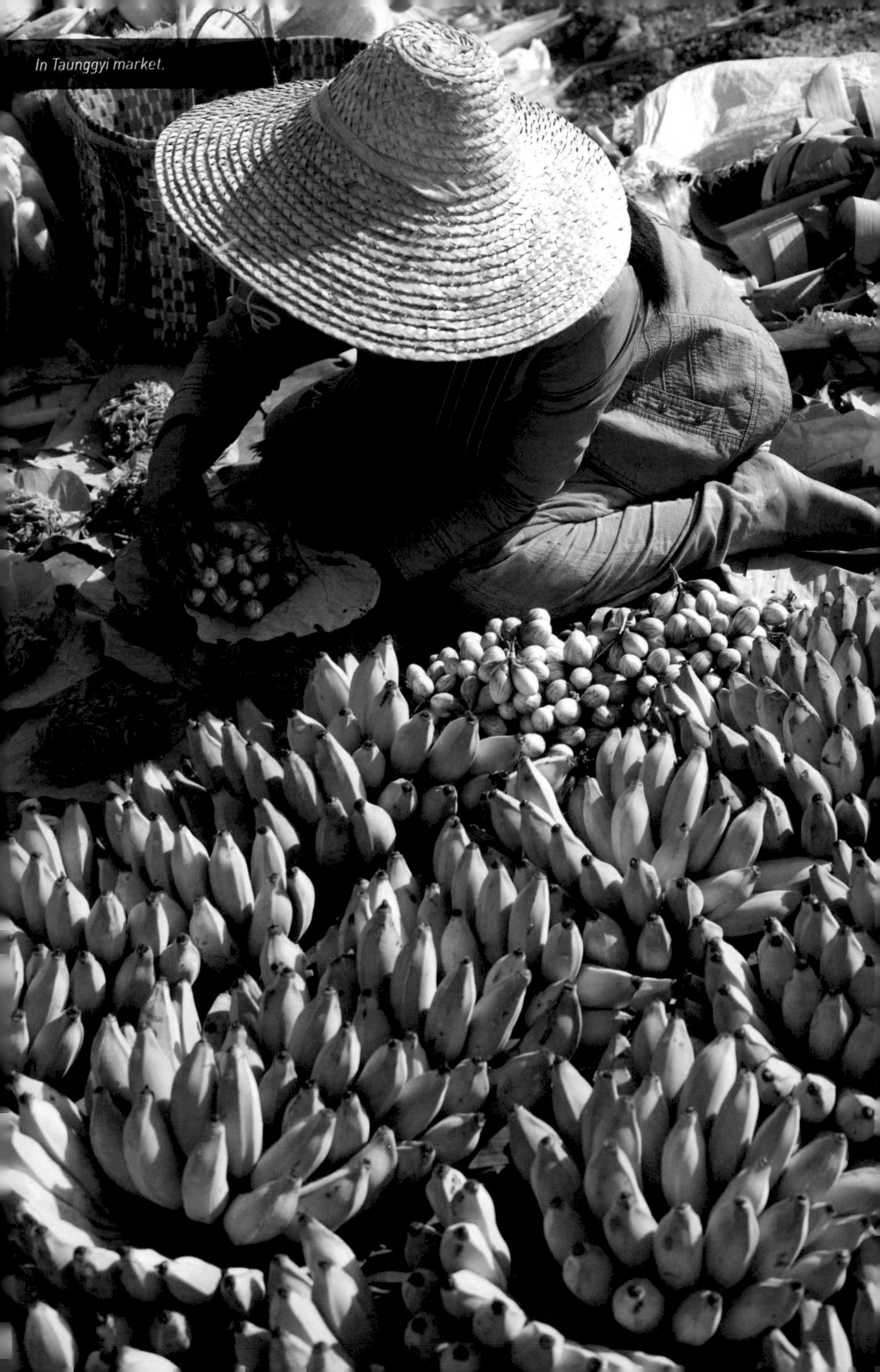
In Taunggyi market.

MYANMAR

TRAVEL TIPS

TRANSPORT

GETTING THERE

By air

Despite the rush of recent development, Myanmar is still poorly connected to international air networks. There are no direct flights from Europe or North America, meaning that you'll have to change either at Doha in Qatar or somewhere in Asia (Bangkok is most convenient, and there are also regular connections via Kuala Lumpur, Singapore, Hong Kong, Tokyo and Seoul). Most visitors fly into Yangon's Mingaladon Airport (www.yangonairportonline.com), although there are also increasing numbers of international flights to Mandalay and Naypyitaw.

Air Asia
Level 1, La Pyae Wun Plaza, Dagon, Yangon.
Tel: 09 254 049 991; www.airasia.com

Air China
Yangon International Hotel, cnr Pyay and Kaba Aye Pagoda roads, Yangon.
Tel: 01 655882; www.airchina.com

Bangkok Airways
Sakura Tower 339, Bogyoke Aung San Road, Yangon.
Tel: 01 255 122; www.bangkokair.com

Malaysia Airlines
335-357 Bogyoke Aung San Road (next to Central Hotel), Yangon.
Tel: 01 241 007; www.malaysiaairlines.com

Myanmar Airways International
Airport View Tower, 147 Pyay Rd, Mayangone, Yangon.
Tel: 01 967 0021; www.maiair.com

Qatar Airways
2nd floor, Centrepoint Towers, cnr Sule Pagoda Rd and Merchant St, Yangon.
Tel: 01 379 845; www.qatarairways.com

Singapore Airlines

Junction City Tower, cnr of Bogyoke Aung San Rd and 27th St, Pabedan, Yangon.
Tel: 01 925 3788; www.singaporeair.com

Thai Airways
11th Floor, Tower 1, HAGL Myanmar Centre Tower, 192 Kaba Aye Pagoda Rd, Bahan, Yangon.
Tel: 01 934 5210; www.thaiairways.com

Vietnam Airlines
Level 8, Tower 1, Myanmar Plaza, 192 Kaba Aye Pagoda Rd, Bahan, Yangon.
Tel: 01 934 5380; www.vietnamairlines.com

Overland

Myanmar shares borders with Thailand, China, India, Laos and Bangladesh, although the only straightforward land crossings are from Thailand. The solitary border crossings currently linking Myanmar with India and China require complicated permits, while the borders with Bangladesh and

Selling wares to train passengers.

Laos are entirely closed (although rumours of a new crossing with Laos continue to circulate). It is, however, relatively easy to navigate any of the four main border crossings between Myanmar and Thailand, although some are still subject to restrictions. In the far south, there are border crossings between the port town of Kawthaung and Ranong in southern Thailand, and (although it's difficult to reach) between Htee Kee in Myanmar and Phu Nam Ron in Thailand. Further north, visitors can cross between Mae Sot and Myawaddy in Kayin State, and between Mae Sai and Tachileik in southern Shan State (you'll need permission from the local tourist office to travel on to Kengtung from Tachileik, although this is easily arranged). A fifth crossing, at Three Pagodas Pass between Sangkhlaburi and Payathonzu, isn't currently open to foreigners.

Note that information about border crossings is highly susceptible to change and should be

always be checked in advance of travel with a reputable agent in Myanmar.

GETTING AROUND

Much of Myanmar is now completely open to foreign tourists, although some areas (mainly in the east and far north) remain off limits or require a permit. Exploring Myanmar on a pre-organised tour is a convenient option, saving you the hassle of dealing with the country's rudimentary and antiquated transport infrastructure – although equally it takes much of the adventure out a visit, as well as the chance to rub shoulders with ordinary Burmese during your journeys. Trains and buses will get you to most parts of the country, eventually, although given the parlous state of Myanmar's roads and railways, most travellers take at least a couple of internal flights using the country's well-developed domestic air network.

From the airport

In Yangon, both international and domestic flights arrive at **Yangon-Mingaladon Airport**, 19km (12 miles) north of the downtown area. Taxis can be arranged through one of the taxi booking counters; fares are around 8,000 kyat for the trip to the centre; some hotels and guesthouses offer free airport transfers as part of the room rate.

By air

Domestic air services have flourished in Myanmar, thanks to the country's size and rudimentary road and rail infrastructure. Around forty regional airports can be found across the country, with a growing number of operators and several flights daily to more popular destinations. Flights offer an easy way of getting between Yangon and Mandalay, Nyaung U (for Bagan) and Heho (for Inle Lake), while some other destinations which are either difficult or impossible to reach by road can also be easily accessed by air. Thandwe (for Ngapali Beach), for example, is just forty minutes by air from Yangon, compared to a gruelling sixteen hours-plus on the bus, while Sittwe (for Mrauk U), which is often cut off by land entirely due to

Ferry across the Ayeyarwady.

unrest in Rakhine State, is also easily accessible via Thandwe.

It generally works out cheaper to book your tickets through an agent in Myanmar rather than direct with the airline.

Domestic airlines

Air Bagan
56 Shwe Taung Gyar Street, Bahan, Yangon.
Tel: 01 514 861; www.airbagan.com
Air KBZ
5th Floor, Airport View Tower, 147 Pyay Rd, Mayangone, Yangon.
Tel: 01 967 0007; www.airkbz.com
Air Mandalay
1 Pyay Rd, 51/2 Miles, Hlaing, Yangon
Tel: 01 525 488; www.airmandalay.com
Asian Wings
56 Shwe Taung Gyar Street, Bahan, Yangon.
Tel: 01 515 259; www.asianwingsair.com
Golden Myanmar Airlines
Ground Floor, Sayar San Plaza, New University Ave, Bahan, Yangon.
Tel: 01 860 4035; www.gmairlines.com
Myanmar Airways
Airport View Tower, 147 Pyay Rd, Mayangone, Yangon.
Tel: 01 967 0021; www.maiair.com
Yangon Airways
No.166, Level 8, MMB Tower, Upper Pansodan Road, Mingalar Taung Nyunt, Yangon.
Tel: 01 383100; www.yangonair.com

By river and sea

With over 8,000km (5,000 miles) of navigable rivers and canals, boats have traditionally served as the most important means of transporting people and goods around the country. Gradual improvements in other

forms of transport are slowly eroding the importance of water-borne traffic, although luxury Ayeyarwady and Chindwin River cruises remain popular amongst well-heeled visitors, while there are also inexpensive local ferries on the same routes for hardier travellers.

Rivers

Myanmar has more than 5,000km (3,000 miles) of navigable river. Even at the height of summer, when water levels are lowest, it's possible to travel all the way from Yangon to Bhamo in the north of the country by ferry along the Ayeyarwady, and in the monsoons you can even reach Myitkyina. Other rivers serving as major transport arteries include the Chindwin, which joins the Ayeyarwady southwest of Mandalay, and the Thandlin, in the far southeast.

In colonial times, the redoubtable Irrawaddy Flotilla Company, or IFC, plied the country's waterways with its elegant, double-decker river steamers. A handful of these wonderful old tubs survive (some have been converted into luxury cruisers; see below), but nowadays most of Myanmar's ferry network comes under the jurisdiction of the government-owned Inland Water Transport (www.iwt.gov.mm), and its fleet of around 285 boats.

Taking to the water on a package tour, you're more likely to be travelling on a **luxury cruiser**. These vessels tend to be beautifully restored antique steamers, or else newly built replicas, complete with timber-walled cabins furnished in high colonial style, with sun decks, bars and restaurants. Trips typically last from five to around 13 nights, and include plenty of sightseeing excursions to towns and other places of interest along the way.

Popular river routes

The most travelled river route for tourists is the stretch of the Ayeyarwady between Mandalay and Bagan. Three private operators run boats along this stretch: Malikha River Cruises (www.malikha-rivercruises.com), Myanmar Golden River Group (www.mgrg-express.com) and Shwe Keinnery (http://www.rvshwekeinnerycruise.com). All three charge the same fares (currently $32 from Bagan to Mandalay, or $42 travelling in the other direction), with boats leaving daily at around 6am and taking around 10–12 hours to get from Mandalay to Bagan (or vice versa).

For a classic (albeit pricey) Burmese journey, book yourself on to one of the **luxury cruises** along the Ayeyarwady and/or the connecting Chindwin rivers, sailing in lavishly appointed vessels boasting a/c cabins, pools and top-notch restaurants. Itineraries last from between three to 16 days. Some longer cruises travel north from Mandalay via the Ayeyarwady's third and second defiles to Bhamo through a constantly changing riverscape, while there are also a growing number of extended cruises heading all the way south to (or north from) Yangon along

the Ayeyarwady. The ultimate river adventure trip, however, is the 20-night cruise up the untamed Chindwin, one of Myanmar's most scenic rivers, to the remote northern outpost of Homalin. Major operators including Belmond (www.belmond.com), Pandaw (www.pandaw.com) and Paukan (www.paukan.com), while other luxury vessels include the Strand Cruise (www.thestrandcruise.com) and the Sanctuary Ananda (www.sanctuaryretreats.com). Basic government ferries also cover the routes north along the Ayewarwady to Bhamo and up the Chindwin to Homalin.

Further south, basic government ferries travel (very slowly) south of Bagan to Pyay, taking two or three days to complete the journey; and also from Yangon to Myaungmya, near Pathein in the Delta (for details, see www.iwt.gov.mm). Government and private ferries also make the enjoyable trip (4–7hr) along the Kaladan River between Sittwe and Mrauk U, and down the coast from Sittwe to Taunggok (from where you can continue to Ngapali Beach). Further south, private boats make the beautiful trip down the Thanlwin from Mawlamyine to Hpa-An, as well as the journey down the coast of Tanintharyi. Memorable short boat trips include the one-hour cruise up the Ayeyardwady from Mandalay to Mingun, and the ten-minute hop across the Yangon River to Dalah, whisking you miraculously from

the hustle and bustle of downtown Yangon to the rural Delta in virtually the blink of an eye.

By train

Myanmar Railways comprises 5,402km (3,357 miles) of track, with Yangon's Central Railway Station at its hub. While the main Yangon–Mandalay line is reasonably quick, clean and efficient, the same can't be said of the rest of the network. Rolling stock ranges from shabby to decrepit and long delays are frequent. That said, if you're not in a rush, travelling by rail in Myanmar has its pleasures and offers an unrivalled chance to rub shoulders with local Burmese. If time is short, it's better to take the bus, or fly.

There are three classes: Upper (reclining seats); First (wooden slatted seats with padded leatherette bottoms); and Ordinary (bare slatted seats). Some services between Yangon, Mandalay, Bagan and Myitkina also have sleeper carriages – "standard" and "special" – with individual two- and four-bed compartments; "special" sleeper compartments come with their own private toilet and sitting area. Whichever class you're in, expect a noisy ride, and bring a fleece as it can get cold at night in winter.

Foreigners can purchase tickets through Myanmar Travels & Tours and a few other Yangon operators, or direct at the railway station they're leaving from, advisably 24 hours ahead of departure.

If you want to ride the rails but don't fancy a long journey by train, Yangon's Circle Line (see page 121) offers an enjoyable taste of Myanmar's railways in miniature.

Yangon to Mandalay

This is the country's premier line, boasting reasonably clean and comfortable rolling stock, though even here journeys can be hot and sticky, schedules erratic and delays frequent. There are three services daily in each direction, calling at Bago, Taungoo, Naypyidaw and Thazi and taking around fifteen hours to complete the journey. For the latest timetable info, photos comparing classes and trip reports, check www.seat61.com.

From Mandalay, there are train connections to the hill station of Pyin U-Lwin (Maymyo), 61km (38

Yangon city bus.

miles) east, from where you can continue across the famous Gokteik viaduct to Kyaukme and Lashio. Other useful rail connections include the following:

Yangon to Bagan

Bagan can be reached by train, departing Yangon daily at 4pm. The journey takes about 18 hours, compared to just an hour by plane.

Yangon to Kyaiktiyo and Mawlamyine

The main railway line south of Yangon heads down into Mon State via Bago to Kyaiktiyo (jumping-off point for visits to the famous Golden Rock Pagoda) and on to the historic town of Mawlamyine. There are three departures daily in each direction, taking roughly four to five hours to Kyaiktiyo, and around ten to Maylamyine. One service daily continues on to Dawei, in the far south, taking around 24 hours.

Mandalay to Myitkyina

The trip between Mandalay and Myitkyina is a bumpy one through rambling countryside that's been heavily logged but remains beautiful. Four trains cover the route daily, leaving at 10.20am, midday, 4pm and 6pm, and taking 18 to 21 hours to complete the journey. En route the train stops at Naba (for Katha, an Ayeryarwady embarkation point for river trips to Bhamo or Mandalay) and Hopin (for Indawgyi Lake).

By bus

Travelling by bus is generally faster and more reliable than taking the train, although still far from speedy, mainly due to the state of the country's main roads, most of which are narrow and congested, with trucks, cars, cyclists, pedestrians and livestock all fighting for space. Myriad private companies operate buses on different routes, along with government-run services. Vehicles themselves range from antiquated rustbuckets, stuffed with as many passengers as they can possibly squeeze in, through to the deluxe a/c express services which ply the main inter-city routes. All long-distance buses stop every two or three hours for food and drink breaks at roadside cafés.

Bus stations in larger cities are often located some way out of the centre of town. In Yangon, the two

Pick-up trucks are a common form of transport.

main terminals are Hlaing Thar Yar terminal (northwest of the city; services to the Delta); and Aung Mingalar terminal (north of the city; all other services), both of which are around 20km (12 miles) from the centre. Likewise in Mandalay, where departures are split between Kwe Se Kan (Main) Station (10km south of the centre; serving all destinations south) and Pyi Gyi Mat Station (3km east of the centre; for all destinations to the north-east). It's generally easiest to buy tickets through your hotel, guesthouse or a local travel agents – you may pay a dollar or two in commission but will save the bother of traipsing out to the bus station and buying tickets in person from the relevant bus company office.

Pick-up trucks

Pick-up trucks (*kaa*) – similar to the Thai *songthaew* – are often found on less-travelled routes where there's no bus service (or where bus services are infrequent). Cheap, cheerful and usually horrible uncomfortable, they don't follow a set schedule, simply leaving once the maximum number of passengers and cargo possible has been crammed into every last bit of available space.

Private transport

Trishaws and taxis

"Motorbike taxis" (where the passenger rides pillion behind the driver) are usually the fastest – if not the most relaxing – way of getting around the country's towns and cities. Slower but slightly more comfortable are motorised three-wheelers (*thoun bein*; effectively a motorbike with a kind of trailer attached, sometimes described as a "rickshaw", although it's completely unlike rickshaws found in India and Thailand). Slowest but most atmospheric are bicycle trishaws (*sai-kaa*). All three are usually widely available and cheap (except in Yangon and Mandalay, where taxis have taken over), generally charging around $1 for shorter journeys around town.

Taxis are ubiquitous and inexpensive in all the major cities, where they stand in ranks outside the main hotels and transport hubs. Meters rarely work, but few trips across town cost more than K3,000–5,000 ($3–5). For longer day trips out of town, expect to pay $50–60, depending on the age and condition of the vehicle.

Car and driver

Travelling independently, the easiest way to get around is to hire your own car and driver (paperwork and local road conditions mean that virtually no tourists drive themselves). Tourist cars tend to be no more than two or three years old and are usually air-conditioned. Expect to pay around $100 per day, including petrol, the driver's fee and expenses.

A

Accommodation

Despite the decades-long tourism boycott of the country, Myanmar offers a wide choice of accommodation in all its principal tourist centres, although. during the peak season from mid-November through January, vacancies in the most popular hotels can be hard to come by.

Accommodation ranges dramatically in cost, but is generally expensive by Southeast Asian standards. A basic en-suite room in a backpacker guesthouse generally goes for around $25 (although cheaper, and grubbier, rooms with shared bathroom are available in some places). A double in a decent mid-range hotel will cost anything from $50 to $100, while at five-star places you're usually looking at $200/night, and sometimes considerably more.

Budget guesthouses

The cheapest accommodation in Myanmar tends to be guesthouses tacked on to family homes. Standards vary wildly. Some places are homely, spotless and sociable; others are grubby, dark and depressing. Most rooms in lowland areas now come with a/c, a small TV (albeit it might not work, or receive only a few local channels) and often WiFi (although again this is often erratic). It's worth bringing a mosquito net and length of string to fasten it with as you're sure to encounter plenty of nocturnal insect life and also a torch for use during the country's occasional power cuts. A universal sink plug can also be handy, as can a roll of toilet paper.

Lower mid-range hotels

Basic hotels, costing $30–50 per night, tend to be in the Chinese mould: multi-floored concrete blocks with plain en-suite rooms off galleried walkways. Space tends to be at a premium; the more you pay, the larger the room, and more comfortable the facilities. There's generally some outside space. If you spend upwards of $50, however, you can expect a spacious en-suite room with air-con, a proper balcony or verandah, comfy mattress and tiled bathroom – and maybe the odd piece of Burmese handicraft or local textile to enliven the décor.

Upper mid-range

Things perk up considerably at around the $75 mark. Rooms at this price tend to be larger and more stylishly equipped, and you may also get a pool. There'll be private sitting space on a spacious verandah or balcony, furnished with wicker chairs. Some places may also have laundry and room service, a decent restaurant and a travel desk.

Expensive

Set in landscaped gardens, large and luxurious four- or five-star hotels account for the bulk of high-end accommodation in Myanmar, and they tend to try to accommodate both business visitors and foreign tourists; many are designed in traditional Burmese style, with plenty of carved wood décor and local handicrafts on display, while accommodation is often in individual villas or chalets rather than in large hotel blocks. Standards (and prices) are generally on a par with other countries in Asia, with spacious, well-furnished, air-conditioned rooms, and large pools with sunloungers and shaded sitting areas. There'll be a fitness room or gym with modern equipment; and probably a spa offering massage and herbal therapies. Dressed in semi-traditional Burmese uniforms, the staff will be courteous, professional and speak good English.

There should also be at least one good restaurant, plus bars. Most places also lay on nightly culture shows featuring local classical musicians, dancers and puppet troupes.

Most such places have rooms in various categories, differing in style and comfort according to their price. Views tend to cost extra (and can sometimes add dramatically to the price).

An alternative to the luxury, purpose-built five-star resort or city business hotel is offered by the country's growing number of more individual boutique hotels. These places tend to be smaller and less impersonal. The emphasis is on the look and heritage atmosphere created by the choice of fittings and furniture, drawing on local architectural styles. Think teak floors, carved railings, hand-made silk throws and brass Buddhas rather than imposing, marble-lined lobbies and bell boys in suits.

Über luxury

The very finest hotels in Yangon, Mandalay and the major resorts such as Inle Lake and Ngapali command room rates that sometimes approach $500 per night, and they're every bit as ritzy as you'd expect. Some, such as the Strand and Governor's Residence in Yangon, appeal to customers with their time-warped colonial feel, others pile on the regal Burmese style, with multi-tiered pagoda roofs and superb arts and crafts re-creating the feel of a Konbaung palace. Either way, you'll be offered a choice of at least half a dozen kinds of room and suites, plus the use of international-grade leisure facilities and gourmet restaurants.

Also in this category are a small number of exclusive boutique establishments such as Malikha Lodge in the far north of Myanmar, and a few of the designer resorts at Ngapali

Beach, where guests pay through the nose to stay at a very special location in the greatest of luxury.

Taxes and service charges

Wherever you stay, you'll pay a mandatory 10 percent government charge, while you may also pay an additional 10 percent service charge at more upmarket places.

Payment

Growing numbers of upmarket hotels now accept credit cards – although they may levy a 4 or 5 percent administration charge. If you pay cash, most places will accept either dollars or kyat. Some places prefer dollars but will probably accept kyat if you don't have dollars to hands – if you only have kyat it's a good idea to check when you arrive to see if this is likely to cause a problem. As always, dollar bills must be crisp and unblemished.

Booking

With the pressure on hotel and guesthouse beds as intense as it is these days, it's always a good idea to book ahead, ideally a week or more in advance. The vast majority of places are now available to book online – most commonly through www.booking.com, although many places also appear on other sites. You may have to pay a small surcharge for booking online, although most travellers consider this money well spent given the convenience and security of the process. It's also possible to book online directly with most larger hotels, an increasing number of whom now offer a "best price guarantee" for the rates quoted on their websites.

Addresses

Downtown Yangon and central Mandalay are both laid out on an easy-to-follow, numbered grid system, with corner addresses appearing as, for example, "2nd and 24th Street". Outside these main cities, formal addresses are only haphazardly used, with directions usually being given relative to major local landmarks rather than particular street names, few of which are signed, in any case.

Admission charges

For foreign tourists, entry to major archaeological and cultural sites, including those at Bagan, Bago, Mrauk-U, Pyay and monuments in and around Mandalay, is by government ticket, ranging from 5,000 kyat (around $4) in Mrauk-U up to $25 at Bagan. Some tickets (at, for example, Bagan, Mandalay, Bago and Mrauk-U) cover multiple sights and are valid for five days or a week. You can pay in foreign currency or the equivalent in kyat.

Other sights that tend to charge foreigners for entry include various museums ($2–5) and larger religious complexes (the Shwedagon Pagoda, for example, costs 8,000 kyat/around $6 to enter, while a few other pagodas levy entrance fees ranging between $1 and $3).

Budgeting for your trip

If you're travelling on a pre-arranged tour, where all the transport and accommodation costs are covered by the price of your holiday, your main expenses are likely to be dining and shopping. If you're not fussy about your surroundings, it's easy to find a filling meal for just US$5–10. Allow around $10–15 per head for a two-course meal in a regular, mid-scale restaurant, or $20–40 in a five-star hotel. The most upmarket establishments may cost a little more than this. Breakfasts are almost always included in hotel room rates. How much your souvenirs set you back will depend on your ability to haggle and can range from just a few dollars for a colourful Burmese parasol up to $100-plus for a high-quality piece of lacquerware.

Independent travellers will also need to factor in accommodation costs. It's difficult nowadays to find double rooms anywhere (including guesthouses) for less than $25, while you may end up spending at least double this for a clean modern room in a simple hotel, and over $100 if you want anywhere with a few frills. Transport costs are generally quite low, particularly buses, although naturally internal flights can rapidly blow your budget.

Children

Visiting Myanmar is not an easy option for families. The relentlessly hot and humid climate, uncomfortable public transport, unfamiliar food and absence of dedicated facilities for children mean you'll have to be resourceful. You'll also have to bring a supply of nappies to see you through your trip – difficult to find outside Yangon and Mandalay – though dealing with disposables causes inevitable problems in out-of-the-way locations, where refuse collection is non-existent.

Having said that, the Burmese love children and will do everything to make them comfortable, to the extent of taking them off parents' hands at every opportunity.

If you're travelling independently with children under 7, consider renting a car and driver for the duration as journeys by bus, in particular, can be long and gruelling, with no toilet facilities and few stops en route.

Child-friendly activities are rather thin on the ground, although most kids will enjoy the marionette shows in Mandalay (www.myanmarmarionettes.com), boat trips on Inle Lake, rides around the temples of Bagan or Inwa in a horse-drawn carriage, visits to the Green Hill Valley elephant camp near Kalaw, Naypyidaw's fine modern zoo and of course the country's various beaches.

Climate

Like all countries in South and Southeast Asia's monsoonal region, Myanmar's year is divided into three seasons: there are regional variations, but essentially it is hot and wet from May to October, cooler and dry from November to February, and hot and dry in March and April.

The Southwest Monsoon brings rains beginning in May, which are most intense between June and August. This is a time of high humidity – especially in the coastal and delta regions – and of daily afternoon/evening showers, as winds carry the moisture in from the Indian Ocean. The central inland region is drier than other parts of the country, but is also subject to much rain during this time. Travel during the rainy season can quite often be interrupted due to flooded roads and railway lines; it is made even more difficult as this information is not always made available through the media.

In October, the rains let up. From November through to May the Northeast Monsoon brings mainly dry weather, particularly away from the south. The cool season

(November–February) is the most pleasant time to visit. The average temperature along the Ayeyarwady plain, from Yangon to Mandalay, is between 21°C and 28°C (70°F and 82°F), although in the mountains in the north and east, the temperature can drop below freezing and snow can fall.

The hottest weather occurs during March and April, before the rains, with temperatures in the central plain, particularly around Bagan (Pagan), climbing as high as 45°C (113°F).

The annual rainfall along the coasts of Rakhaing and Tanintharyi ranges from 300 to 500cm (120 to 200in). The Ayeyarwady Delta gets about 150 to 200cm (60 to 100in), while the central Myanmar region, between Mandalay and Bagan, and the surrounding areas, averages 50 to 100cm (20 to 40in) of rain each year. In the far north, the melting snows of the Himalayan foothills keep rivers fed with water.

When to go

The best time to visit is during the relatively cool, dry winter months between November and February. This is peak tourist season, when the skies are blue for days on end and night time temperatures are pleasant. Up on the Shan Plateau around Inle Lake, you may even need a fleece in the evenings. Travel anywhere between May and early October is problematic: roads are routinely washed away, rail lines flooded and cyclones wreak havoc on the coastal plains and delta area.

Myanmar's festival calendar is jam-packed and you're sure to come across some kind of celebration during your trip, whenever you chose

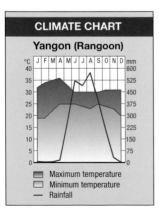

to come. The biggest events are the Thadingyut Festival of Lights in October and the raucous Thingyan in April, a nationwide knees-up when lots of drinking, singing, dancing and throwing of water marks the start of the Burmese New Year.

What to wear

Dress in Myanmar is casual but neat. Unless you are conducting business, you won't be expected to wear a tie anywhere. Long trousers for men and a dress or long skirt for women, lightweight and appropriate to the prevailing climatic conditions, is the generally accepted mode of dress for visitors. Quick-drying clothes are a good idea for visits during the rainy season or the Thingyan water festival. There's no law against shorts or short skirts, although skimpy clothing may attract strange looks or unwanted attention outside the beaches and the clubs of Yangon.

A sweater or jacket should be carried if you plan a visit to the hill stations or Shan Plateau, especially in the cool season. Open footwear, such as sandals, is acceptable, but remember to remove footwear when entering religious institutions. An umbrella is useful during the rainy season. Bring a hat for sun protection.

Crime and safety

Myanmar is a generally safe and welcoming place to travel. Muggings and petty thefts may have increased since the decline in the country's economic fortunes over the past couple of decades, but they're still rare – and much less frequent than in more developed Asian countries. Even so, take the same precautions as you would at home: don't wander about unfamiliar parts of Yangon or Mandalay on your own at night. Keep your passport and other valuables under lock and key at all times.

In addition, it's advisable to avoid all large gatherings and political rallies, and don't take photographs of soldiers, police, military installations or equipment.

Customs regulations

Formalities both on arrival and departure are now quite easy as long as you do not lose the various forms you have been given upon entry. Tourists are allowed duty-free import of limited quantities of tobacco – 400

cigarettes (or 50 cigars or 250g (8oz) of pipe tobacco) as well as two litres of alcohol and 150ml of perfume or eau de cologne and articles for personal use. Any foreign currency in excess of US$2,000 should be declared on arrival on a Foreign Exchange Declaration Form (FED), but you won't be required to obtain clearance for valuables such as a laptop or mobile phone. The import and export of Burmese kyat is technically forbidden (although you're very unlikely to be searched), and the export of foreign currency is limited to the amount declared upon entry.

Items you're not allowed to bring into Myanmar include counterfeit currency, pornography, narcotics, toy guns and remote-control toys, firearms and live animals/ birds. Leaving Myanmar, you are not allowed to export any antiques without a licence including old coins and documents, palm-leaf manuscript, or antique artworks and carvings.

D

Disabled travellers

Mobility-impaired travellers will find Myanmar a difficult proposition. The roads and walkways are mostly in an abysmal state, other wheelchair users a rare sight and access to public buildings such as railway stations, museums and archaeological sites frequently problematic – although river cruises are probably a viable option. As ever, the success of your trip will depend to a large extent on forward planning. The website www.disabledtravelersguide. com provides some useful pointers.

E

Embassies and consulates

Embassies in Yangon

Despite the fact that Naypyidaw is nowadays the official capital, virtually all foreign embassies and consulates remain in Yangon.
Australia, Vantage Tower, 623 Pyay Road
Tel: 01 230 7410; www.burma.embassy. gov.au
Singapore, 238 Dhamazedi Road, Bahan

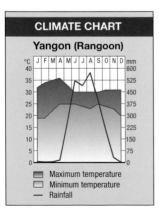

CLIMATE CHART

Yangon (Rangoon)

- ■ Maximum temperature
- □ Minimum temperature
- — Rainfall

Tel: 01 559 001; www.mfa.gov.sg/yangon
Thailand, 94 Pyay Road, Dagon
Tel: 01 222 784; www.thaiembassy.org/
yangon
United Kingdom, 80 Strand Road
Tel: 01 370 865; www.gov.uk/world/
organisations/british-embassy-rangoon
United States, 110 University Ave,
Kamayut
Tel: 01 536 509; https://mm.usembassy.
gov

Burmese embassies abroad

Australia
22 Arkana Street, Yarralumla ACT
2600, Canberra
Tel: 02 6273 3811; www.mecanberra.
com.au
Canada
336 Island Park Drive, Ottawa,
Ontario K1Y 0A7
Tel: 613 232 9990
South Africa
201 Leyds Street, Arcadia, Pretoria,
South Africa
Tel: 027-12341 2556; www.myanmar
embassysa.com
United Kingdom
19A Charles Street, London W1J 5DX
Tel: 020 7499 4340; www.londonmyanmar
embassy.com.
United States
2300 S Street, NW Washington DC
20008
Tel: 202 332 3344; www.mewashington
dc.org

Electricity

The standard electrical current is
230-volt/50 hertz and most sockets
take two round-pin plugs. Power cuts
are still fairly common in more remote
parts of the country, while rationing
means that in some towns the electrical supply is regularly turned off during parts of the day. Many hotels have
their own generators;

Etiquette

In common with most Asian countries, the Burmese are quite formal
(by Western standards) in the way
they engage strangers, especially
foreigners, and anyone of a different
gender. You'll find them painstakingly
polite, considerate and gentle – and
appreciative of those who respond
in a similar fashion, particularly in
homes and places of worship.

When introduced to people in
Myanmar, it is considered good man-
ners to call them by their full title
and full name, beginning with "U"

(the equivalent of "Mr") and "Daw"
("Mrs", "Ms" or "Madam").

It is particularly difficult for a
Burmese to address a Westerner
only by his Christian name, even
when they are close friends. Thus
Kau Reng will never call his friend
"Ronnie", but will address him as
"Ko Ronnie" or "Maung Ronnie".
Similarly, Nancy would be called
"Ma Nancy". Kau Reng expects that
he, too, will be similarly addressed
as "Ko Kau Reng".

Business etiquette

Handshakes are nowadays the con-
ventional greeting between businessmen. You shouldn't, however,
offer your hand to a woman, unless
she offers you hers first, in which
case it's fine to shake it; all other
physical contact should be avoided.

Business cards are used widely
and, as in most of Asia, should be
exchanged on first meeting. Use
both hands to present and receive
them (demonstrating respect), as
does taking a few seconds to read
the details. Do not put the card in
your pocket straight away as this
may also be deemed disrespectful.

Dress should be conserva-
tive. Lightweight suits for men are
acceptable, ideally worn with a tie.
Women should ensure that skirts are
of knee length or lower. Although the
majority of business people dress in
suits or formal shirts when meeting
foreigners, some – and nearly all
politicians – still wear the traditional
longyis or *htameins*.

Temple etiquette

A Buddhist place of worship is
unlike its equivalent in the West. You
might find a devout Buddhist in deep
meditation on any temple platform,
but you might also see whole families eating their lunches in front of
a Buddha image. You will see lines
of monks walking slowly around
the stupa, but you may also observe
hordes of children happily running
around. The temple ground is where
every Burmese village or city neighbourhood congregates in the evening. But don't let the "everydayness"
fool you. This is sacred space, and
there are certain rules you must
keep in order to show your respect.

Throughout the country, wherever
you enter religious grounds, you
must remove your shoes (or sandals) and socks. Appropriate clothing should also be worn, meaning

arms and legs should be covered,
while short skirts and skimpy shorts
should be particularly avoided.

It's traditional to walk around stupas in a clockwise direction – keeping the stupa on your right and thus
moving in the same direction as the
sun across the sky – although no
one will mind too much if you walk
around it in an anti-clockwise direction instead.

Festivals

January (Nadaw/Pyatho)
**Kachin Manao Festival (Kyitkyina,
Kachin)**
Traditional *manao* "totem poles"
form the focus of tribal dances by
Kachins dressed in traditional finery.
Ananda Pagoda Festival (Bagan)
Thousands of pilgrims descend on
Bagan's greatest temple for this
month-long religious celebration, with
accompanying funfair and market.
Naga New Year (Sagaing)
Most of the Naga tribespeople from
Sagaing and Chin states are Christian,
but their exuberant New Year's festi-
val, marked by spectacular group
dances and animal sacrifices, harks
back to their animist past.

February (Pyatho/Dabodwei)
**Mahamuni Pagoda Festival
(Mandalay)**
This intense Buddhist festival ven-
erates the country's most revered
statue, a massive gold seated Buddha
enshrined in a southern suburb of
Mandalay. Copious quantities of
incense are burned in large fires.
Salone Festival (Tanintharyi Region)
Traditional dances, feasts, rowing
and diving competitions mark this
government-sponsored homage to
the region's Moken "Sea Gypsies",
staged in Majungalet Village on
Bocho Island in Myeik.

March (Dabodwei/Tabaung)
**Shwedagon Pagoda Festival
(Yangon)**
Yangon's magnificent stupa becomes
the centre of a week-long period of
intense veneration, attracting huge
crowds from across Myanmar.
Kakku Pagoda Festival, Shan State
Marriages are fixed, deals struck
and *pwe* performed in the lively fair
that precedes the Pa-O people's

annual New Year celebrations at the extraordinary stupa near Inle Lake.

April (Tabaung/Tagu)

Thingyan Water Festival (Country wide)
Held annually from April 13 to 16, this massive celebration of Burmese New Year is easily the biggest of all Myanmar's festivals, with the entire country grinding to a halt and vast crowds taking to the streets, drenching all and sundry with endless buckets of water. Meanwhile, Buddha images are bathed in *thanaka* water as older Burmese retreat to monasteries and temples to pray.

Thanaka Grinding Festival (Rakhine)
While the women of Sittwe grind the roots of *thanaka* wood, the men play instruments, sing and dance in this festival dedicated to the fragrant paste worn by most Burmese women.

Shwemawdaw Pagoda Festival (Bago)
Singing and dancing competitions are the key part of this annual temple festival in the stupa-studded former capital.

May (Tagu/Kason)

Wesak (Buddha's Birthday)
Celebrated by the watering of Bodhi trees at temples and monasteries around Myanmar, Wesak marks the day of the Buddha's Enlightenment. Crowds of locals, carrying pitchers on their heads, walk in procession to their local temples, accompanied by troupes of musicians.

Chinlone Festival, Mahamuni Pagoda, Mandalay
The national *chinlone* (a local version of "keepy-uppy") competition, attracting the country's finest exponents.

August (Waso/Wakhaung)

Taungbyon Festival, nr Mandalay
For eight days running up to the full moon, this small town upriver from Mandalay hosts Myanmar's most frenzied *nat pwè* (*nat* spirit festival), with much drinking and dancing and appearances by the country's spectacularly dressed *nat kadaw* spirit mediums.

October (Tawthalin/Thadingyut)

Thadingyut
This three-day Festival of Lights is Myanmar's second-biggest nationwide event (after Thingyan), celebrating the end of Buddhist Lent. Festivities are held at pagodas nationwide, while houses are brightly illuminated with lanterns and candles.

Kyaiktiyo Pagoda Festival (Mon State)
Streams of pilgrims climb this sacred mountain in Mon State to venerate the famous Golden Rock Pagoda at this auspicious time.

Phaung Daw U Festival (Inle Lake)
This flamboyant festival on Inle Lake lasts for two weeks and features a re-created royal barge with a gigantic *karaweik* bird mounted on its prow.

November (Thadingyut/Tazaungmone)

Tazaungdaing (aka Tazaungmone)
Myanmar's second Festival of Lights, celebrating the end of the rainy season with events across the country on the full-moon night of the month of Tazaungmone. Special robe-weaving competitions (Matho Thingan) are held, and illuminated hot-air balloons released into the sky.

Taunggyi Fire-Balloon Festival (Inle Lake)
A local celebration of the Tazaungdaing Festival, held on the shores of Inle Lake and featuring hundreds of giant paper balloons and a deafening array of fireworks.

December (Tazaungmone/Nadaw)

Kayin New Year Festival
Colourful traditional dress is donned by Kayin (Karen) people to mark their New Year.

H

Health and medical care

Standards of healthcare in Myanmar are woeful – it's crucial that you have good travel insurance (see below) given that in the event of an emergency you may have to be airlifted to Thailand for treatment. It's best to talk to a doctor about the latest recommended immunisations for Myanmar (tetanus, hepatitis, typhoid may all be recommended), as well as to discuss appropriate anti-malarials. For longer stays, and if your travels should take you to outlying areas, consider bringing your own medical kit.

Entering Myanmar, you'll need to provide a certificate showing that you've been immunised against yellow fever if you're arriving within nine days of leaving or transiting an affected area. In addition, all visitors to Myanmar should take appropriate anti-malarial precautions before and after entering the country. The risk is highest at altitudes below 1,000 metres (3,000ft) between May and December. Many hotels have mosquito nets, but any hole makes them worthless. Bring your own mosquito net and carry mosquito coils to burn while you sleep. Note that Myanmar's eastern borders from Kachin State to Tanintharyi harbour a strain of malaria resistant to chloroquine and proguanil (Malarone), meaning that you may be recommended to take mefloquine or doxycycline instead.

Perhaps the two most common hazards to visitors are sunburn and intestinal problems. The best way to prevent sunburn is to stay under cover during the hottest parts of the day, and to wear a hat or carry an umbrella if you do go out. You'll see many Burmese, especially women and children, with yellowish *thanaka* powder applied to their faces to help screen out the sun. If you find yourself sweating a lot and feeling weak or dizzy, sit down (in the shade) and take some salt, either in tablet form or by mixing salt in a soft drink or tea.

Diarrhoea is an inevitable hazard of travelling in Myanmar, although many travellers have no problems. Taking care with what you eat and drink is obviously a major factor: never drink water which hasn't been purified and/or boiled, and avoid raw vegetables, fruit which you can't peel and any food which looks like it's been sitting around for a while. If you are struck down, various medicines such as Lomotil, Immodium (Loperamide) or charcoal tablets offer some relief. If symptoms persist for more than a few days you'll need to see a doctor to check for dysentery, which will require treatment with antibiotics.

Travel insurance

It's imperative that you take out travel insurance before travelling in order to ensure that you will receive proper medical attention in the event of an emergency – particularly crucial in Myanmar, where a clinical crisis might require you to be airlifted out of the country. Insurance also gives you the peace of mind that you're properly covered in the event that your trip is interrupted or cancelled, or if your belongings are lost, stolen or damaged in transit.

Medical treatment

Several hospitals in Yangon admit foreign nationals in emergencies. However, because of the generally lamentable state of the country's health-care facilities, travellers requiring serious care are generally flown to Bangkok; ensure your insurance covers such an eventuality.

Asia Royal Hospital

14 Baho Street, Sanchaung, Yangon

One of the few hospitals in the country offering international-standard medical services.

Tel: 01 538 055; www.asiaroyalhospital.com

International SOS Clinic

Inya Lake Resort

37 Kaba Aye Pagoda Road, Yangon

Tel: 01 657 922; www.internationalsos.com

Full outpatient and emergency services, delivered by a professional team of expatriate and national doctors.

Pharmacies

Yangon has several pharmacies, all with 24-hour counters:

May Pharmacy, 542 Merchant Street.

AA Pharmacy, 146 Sule Pagoda Road.

Global Network, 155 Sule Pagoda Road.

Internet access

WiFi is now available at virtually every hotel and guesthouse in the country, as well as a growing number of restaurants, although internet cafés are now increasingly rare, even in major cities and tourist centres. Connection speeds can be painfully slow, however, and WiFi networks can often go offline for no apparent reason, while frequent power cuts and surges are another problem.

The formerly oppressive levels of internet censorship have also been dramatically reduced in recent years, with most formerly banned websites (ranging from Skype through to sources of independent news and dissident bloggers) now unblocked.

Left luggage

There are no left luggage facilities in train or bus stations, or any other public places in Myanmar, though hotels may agree to store baggage.

LGBTQ travel

Homosexuality is technically illegal under the Burmese penal code, and punishable by anything up to life imprisonment in theory, although the law is rarely enforced.

Attitudes to same-sex relationships, whether gay or lesbian, remain conservative and shrouded in stigma and superstition. Many Burmese believe that being gay is a form of cosmic punishment for having had a bad relationship with a woman in a past life. Young men attracted to other men may be dispatched to a monastery to have their sexual orientation "corrected"; rape is also commonly used against lesbians for the same purpose. And ambiguously worded laws are routinely deployed by the authorities to harass anyone suspected of "dubious acts".

For fear of being ostracised by friends, work colleagues and family, lesbian, gay, bisexual and transgender (LGBTQ) Burmese rarely openly admit their sexuality. Apart from the odd "queeny boy" working the clubs in Yangon, the only obviously transgender people you're likely to come across are the oracles who perform at *nat pwe* festivals, such as the one at Taungbyon near Mandalay. And there are as yet no hundred-percent gay venues anywhere in the country; cruising areas, where they exist, tend to be well hidden.

Myanmar's conservative attitudes have had serious health implications. The Burmese government has found that HIV levels among gay men are almost 12 percent (and over 26 percent in Yangon) – far higher than infection rates in the rest of the population, while few of those who need anti-retroviral treatment are actually receiving it.

Even so, as Myanmar slowly modernises, public attitudes seem to be shifting – at least among the more monied, urban classes. 2016 saw the release of *The Gemini*, the first openly LBGTQ Burmese film, while

2018 witnessed the staging of the country's first public gay pride event.

&Proud

www.facebook.com/andPROUD

Leading local LGBTQ activist group, staging regular events including a popular LGBTQ film festival.

Utopia Asia

www.utopia-asia.com/tipsburm.htm

Detailed scene reports and gay info, mostly for Yangon.

Purple Dragon

www.purpledrag.com

LGBTQ-oriented tour operator.

Lost property

It's unlikely you'll gain any help from the Burmese police if you lose anything valuable while you're travelling in the country, although you'll probably need to report any theft and get a police statement before you can lodge a claim with your insurers.

If you lose your passport, your embassy in Yangon should be able to issue some form of emergency travel documentation, although the process will go much more quickly if you can provide a photocopy of the lost passport's information pages and your Burmese visa. You may be required to return to Yangon immediately to make an application.

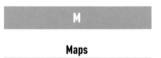

Maps

The best all-round maps of the country are the Reise Know-How *Myanmar (Burma)* 1:1,500,000, with exceptionally clear and up-to-date mapping printed on waterproof, non-tearable paper, and the similarly excellent Freytag & Berndt's *Myanmar* map, at a slightly larger 1:1,200,000. If you can't get hold of either of these, the *Myanmar map* (1:1,350,000) published by International Travel Maps (ITM) makes a passable substitute.

Free maps of major Burmese cities and tourist destinations are handed out by Myanmar Tours and Travels in Yangon. You can also download useful free maps of most large cities and towns from the Myanmar-based cartographers, Design Printing Services (www.dps-map.com).

Media

Newspapers and magazines

The lifting of draconian press censorship laws in 2012 is steadily, if slowly, transforming Myanmar's media – although censorship remains even under the new NLD government. The government's own mouthpiece, the turgid *New Light of Myanmar* (published daily in both Burmese and English, and readable online at www. moi.gov.mm/npe/nlm) features endless reports on visits by the generals to factories, schools and religious institutions. *More interesting is the Myanmar Times* (mmtimes.com), published five times weekly, although this too has suffered declining editorial standards in recent years. For the time being, the best source of independent, unbiased local journalism is *Frontier* magazine (published weekly and readable online at www.frontiermyanmar.net). Other good news websites include Burma News International (www.bnionline.net), the Democratic Voice of Burma (www.dvb.no) and The Irrawaddy (www.irrawaddy.org).

International newspapers are sometimes available at hotel newsstands, although it's generally easiest to read these online.

Radio and television

Myanmar broadcasts three free-to-air channels, all of them run by the government. TVs in more upmarket hotels usually feature a selection of satellite channels such as National Geographic, BBC World, CNN, ESPN and Fox Movies.

Visitors carrying shortwave radios will be able to pick up BBC Radio (www.bbc.co.uk) and Voice of America (VOA, www.voanews.com). The shortwave frequencies change according to the time of day; see their respective websites for further details.

Money

Myanmar's official currency is the *kyat* (pronounced "chet"), which comes in denominations of K1, K5, K10, K20, K50, K100, K200, K500, K1,000, K5,000 and K10,000, although the US dollar is widely used as a second, alternative currency, especially for larger transactions. Foreigners were formerly required to pay for certain services, such as air and rail tickets, in dollars, although these restrictions have now been dropped and visitors are free to pay for services in whichever currency

is most convenient (although some hotels, guesthouses and shops may prefer payment in dollars).

Accessing your cash is less problematic than it used to be. Until a few years back there wasn't a single ATM in the entire country; now, there's a growing network of machines, with at least one or two in any town of any consequence, and hundreds in Yangon and Mandalay. Having said that, they tend to go out of service with alarming frequency, dispense kyat only and also charge a (usually) $5 withdrawal fee on top of whatever fees your home bank levies. Credit cards are now accepted by a growing number of upmarket hotels, restaurants and shops, but don't expect to be able to use them in a local guesthouse or tea shop. In addition, you may also have to pay a small surcharge of a few percent if you want to pay by card.

It's therefore still a good idea to take at least some of the cash you'll need into the country with you in the form of dollars. Accredited money-changers are the best places to change dollars into kyat (some hotels also have exchange facilities); avoid dodgy money changers who approach you on the street, and who may well attempt to rip you off. Dollar notes should ideally be in **mint condition**; bills which are even slightly marked or worn are sometimes refused by money-changers, hotels and so on (or you may be forced to accept a poorer exchange rate). In addition, bills issued before 2008 are also often rejected. The higher denomination the bill, the better the exchange rate.

Taxes and tipping

Some pricier hotels and restaurants levy a 10 percent government tax and/or a 10 percent service charge on top of quoted prices. In fancier tourist restaurants where a service charge isn't levied it's polite to leave a 10 percent tip (assuming service has been acceptable). Tipping isn't really expected in local cafés and teahouses (or for that matter in taxis), although of course it's always appreciated.

Opening hours

Business hours for all government offices (including post offices) are 9.30am–4.30pm Mon–Fri,

9.30am–12.30pm Sat. Shops open between 8/9am and 6pm. Restaurants open at 8–9am, depending on whether they offer breakfast, and close at around 9/10pm, occasionally later in big cities and tourist centres.

Photography

Burmese are generally happy to pose for photographs, though as a courtesy it's always a good idea to ask permission first – easy enough through simple gesticulation and smiles (or try asking *"Da'-poun yai'-teh ya-deh naw?"*. People also love to see the photo you've taken afterwards. Avoid photographing any military personnel or police, and never point your camera at a barracks, army vehicle or anything that could possibly be deemed strategic.

Postal services

The Yangon General Post Office (tel: 01 285 499) is located on Strand Road at the corner of Bo Aung Gyaw Street and is open 7.30am–6pm Monday to Friday. All other post offices are open 9.30am–4.30pm Monday to Friday, and 9.30am–12.30pm Saturday. They are closed Sunday and public holidays.

For larger parcels, DHL is a faster and more reliable method of posting – though far from cheap. They have offices in Yangon (220 Insein Road, Hlaing, tel: 01 507 471).

Public holidays

In addition to the public holidays with fixed dates listed below there are also a number of holidays whose dates change annually according to the Buddhist calendar. These include the full-moon days of the Burmese months of Tabaung (March/April), Kason (May), Waso (July), Thadingyut (October) and Tazaungmone (November), as well as National Day (November).

All government offices are closed on the following days.

4 January Independence Day
Commemorates the date in 1948 that Burma became a sovereign independent nation.

12 February Union Day
Marks the date in 1947 that Aung San concluded an agreement with Burma's

ethnic minorities at Panglong in the Shan State. The Union of Myanmar (Burma) flag, which has been carried by runners to each of Myanmar's state capitals, is returned to Yangon amid the roar of hundreds of thousands of people from all over the nation.

2 March Peasants' Day
Honours the working population.

27 March Armed Forces (Tatmadaw) Day
Commemorates the World War II struggle against Japan. It is celebrated with parades and fireworks.

13–17 April Thingyan (water festival) and Burmese New Year

1 May Labour Day
The working people's holiday.

19 July Martyrs' Day
A memorial to the country's founding father, Aung San, and the eight members of his cabinet who were assassinated in 1947. Ceremonies take place at the Martyrs' Mausoleum, Yangon.

Non-Buddhist religious holidays: Minority groups celebrate holidays not on the Burmese calendar: the Hindu festival *Dewali* in October, the Islamic observance of *Bakri Idd* with changing dates, the Christian holidays of Christmas and Easter, and the Kayin (Karen) and Kachin New Year Festivals in late December or early January.

Shopping

Bustling, often borderline chaotic, markets *(zei)* provide the centrepiece and heartbeat of virtually every town in Myanmar. Larger markets or those in tourist areas usually sell traditional handicrafts and/or other souvenirs – great places to spend your money, as you can be sure most of it will reach local people who most need it. In addition, upscale hotels nearly all have souvenir boutiques, selling more upmarket merchandise, although often at inflated prices.

Another great place to hunt for souvenirs are the shops which line the stairways leading into many larger Buddhist pagodas. These specialise in quintessentially Burmese religious paraphernalia, from incense to mini Buddhas and prayer beads.

Among the well-heeled middle classes, modern air-con, multi-storey malls are the preferred places to shop, with an increasing number

in Yangon and Mandalay, although most of the merchandise on offer is pretty uninspiring.

Prices in mall and hotel shops are fixed. In markets bargaining is the order of the day: start at roughly 50 percent of what the vendor asks and work up from there, and don't be afraid to walk away (or even feign walking away) if you think you're being asked for too much. Smaller shops will generally have fixed prices, although there might be some scope for bargaining, especially if you're buying an expensive item, or making several purchases.

Smoking

Attitudes to smoke and smoking are relaxed by Western standards, although smoking is banned in all hospitals, clinics, stadiums, schools, colleges and universities, and some a/c hotels and restaurants may also be non-smoking (or have non-smoking areas). Elsewhere, non-smoking areas are largely nonexistent.

Telephones

The country code for Myanmar is 95.

When dialling from outside the country omit the 0 in the area codes given below. IDD (International Direct Dialling) is widely available in major Yangon and Mandalay hotels and at kiosks; costs are based on US$ rates plus a service fee. From the smaller towns it may be possible to call Yangon but not overseas. The cheapest way to call overseas is to use a VOIP service such as Skype.

Mobile phones

The cheapest way to make both local and international calls in Myanmar is to buy a local SIM card (something that was virtually impossible until a just a few years ago, but is now extremely straightforward). There are currently three local operators: Ooredoo (www. ooredoo.com), Telenor (www.telenor. com.mm) and MPT (www.mpt.com.mm) – Ooredoo and Telenor have more modern 3G networks, although MPT has more extensive coverage in out of the way places. Sim cards cost just a few dollars and are widely available from phone shops nationwide, who also sell top-up cards with which to

⊙ Area codes

Yangon: 01
Bago: 052
Lashio: 082
Mandalay: 02
Mawlamyine: 032
Monywa: 071
Myitkyina: 074
Pathein: 042
Pyay: 053
Pyin U-Lwin: 085
Sagaing: 072
Sittwe: 043
Taunggyi: 081
Taungoo: 054

refresh your balance. You'll need to show your passport when buying and, in a last bureaucratic hangover, register your card online (which only takes a few minutes).

Time zone

Myanmar Standard Time is 6 hours and 30 minutes ahead of Greenwich Mean Time, 11hr 30min ahead of US Eastern Standard Time, 14hr 30min ahead of US Western Standard Time, and 3hr 30min behind Australian Eastern Standard time. There are no daylight-saving time changes in Myanmar.

Toilets

Outside quality hotels, toilets tend to be of the basic squat variety. And don't expect them to be as clean as you may be used to back home. Paper is rarely provided (though it's available in most general stores) and will block the drain. A tap on the wall (or outside) is used to fill a small plastic hand bucket, with which you're then supposed to sloosh yourself.

Tourist information

The government tourist office at 122 Mahabandoola Rd, on the eastern side of Mahabandoola Gardens (tel: 01 252 859), is a useful source of the latest information. There are no Myanmar tourist offices abroad.

Travel to certain areas requires obtaining a government permit. Other areas are strictly off-limits. To arrange permits for restricted areas it's best to go through a reputable tour operator, who are also the best source of information about which areas are currently off limits to foreigners.

Tour operators

You can save a lot of money by arranging your holiday through a Burmese company rather than one based in your country (nearly all foreign tour operators use Burmese firms as ground agents in any case, adding a mark-up on top). Local travel agents are also essential if you wish to visit permit-only areas of Myanmar, such as the far north of Kachin State.

Recommended tour operators in Yangon
Asian Trails
635-J, Yoma Yeik Thar, Pyay Rd, Kamayut, Yangon
Tel: 09 453 411 155; www.asiantrails.info
Columbus Travels and Tours
1st Floor, 290 Pyay Rd (cnr of ZawTiKa St), San Chaung, Yangon
Tel: 09 257 352 754,; www.travel myanmar.com
Diethelm Travel
412 Merchant St (cnr of 45th Street),
Tel: 01 861 0458; www.diethelmtravel.com
Exotissimo
47 Shwegonedaing St, Bahan
Tel: 01 8604933; www.exotravel.com
Good News Travel
Building (D), Tha-Zin-Min Yeik Tha (nr YIS Private School), Thiri Mingalar Housing, Thingangyun, Yangon
Tel: 09 511 6256; www.myanmargood-newstravel.com
Myanmar Delight Travels & Tours
No.899, Kyaung Lane, Pyay Road, 10th Mile,
Sawbwagyigone, Insein, Yangon
Tel: 01 651 833; www.myanmardelight.com
Myanmar Shalom
No.70, 31 St, Pabedan
Tel: 01 252 814; www.myanmarshalom.com
Pegu Travels
15 Nawaday St, Yangon
Tel: 01 371 937; www.pegutravels.com
Santa Maria Travels & Tours
90 Kan-Road Condo, Kan Road, Quarter 10, Hlaing, Yangon
Tel: 01 537 191; www.myanmartravels.net

Recommended trekking agencies in Myanmar
A1 Trekking
Khone Thae St, Kalaw
Tel: 09 4958 5199; www.A1trekking.blogspot.com
Eagle Trekking
Aung Chan Tha St, Kalaw
Tel: 09 428 312 678
Mr Charles Guest House
105 Auba Street, Hsipaw
Tel: 082 80105

Harry's Trekking House
132 Mong Yang Road, Kengtung
Tel: 084 21620
Putao Trekking House
424/425 Htwe San Lane, Kaung Kahtaung, Putao
Tel: 09 840 0138; www.putaotrekking-house.com

Scuba diving agencies
A One Diving
www.a-one-diving.com
Asia Whale
www.travelmergui.com
Moby Dick Adventures
www.islandsafarimergui.com

Diving operators in Thailand
Dive Asia
Tel: (66) 091 894 8588; www.diveasia.com
Santana
Tel: (66) 096 298 6324; www.santana-phuket.com

Tours
A typical 18-day package tour will take in the main highlights, usually featuring the "Big Four" (Yangon; Mandalay, Inle Lake and Bagan) with perhaps a side trip to Ngapali Beach or a night or two on a luxury cruiser down the Ayeyarwady.

Travelling independently or on a tailor-made tour, obviously gives greater flexibility but will cost considerably more.

Either way, to cover much ground within the month allotted by a tourist visa, you'll have to take at least a couple of flights, and have a rented car and driver at your disposal for at least part of your trip – all of which is much more easily arranged through an agent than by yourself. Because agents also get hefty discounts from hotels, airlines and car companies, it may not even work out much more expensive.

Insight Guides (www.insightguides.com/holidays) offers holidays to numerous destinations around the glove, including Myanmar. You can book trips, transfers and a range of exciting experiences through our local experts, taking in all the major attractions and some off-the-beaten track highlights.

Tour operators in the UK
Audley Travel
Tel: 01993 838000; www.audleytravel.com
TransIndus
Tel: 020 8566 3739; www.transindus.co.uk

Tour operators in the US
Asia Transpacific Journeys

Tel: 800 642 2742; www.atj.com
TransIndus
Tel: 866 615 1815; www.transindus.co.uk
Indochina Oddysey Tours
Tel: 415 434 4015; www.indochinaodyssey tours.com

Visas and passports

All visitors to Myanmar require a visa and a passport valid for a minimum of six months after the proposed date of entry. Tourist visas (currently $50) can be obtained in advance at one of the country's overseas embassies or consulates, although it's much easier to get one online at http://evisa.moip.gov.mm; these are valid for entry at all airports and most land border crossings, apart from the Phu Nam Ron crossing with Thailand. Additional permits and conditions apply to entry at some of the country's other more obscure land borders – check with a reputable travel agent before arriving. Visas are usually processed within a couple of days, although anyone listing a media job on their application can expect a prolonged wait – consider declaring a suitably vague alternative, such as "consultant" or "teacher". A business visa on arrival is also available for those with appropriate documentation.

Tourist visas are valid for 28 days and cannot be extended, although the authorities are currently happy for you to overstay your visa for up to ninety days, for which you'll be charged a fine of $3/day.

Note that children above seven years of age, even when included on their parents' passport, must have their own visas.

Women travellers

Solo women travellers generally experience relatively little hassle in Myanmar compared to other countries in the region – although you'll probably find yourself the target of considerable curiosity. Brief shorts and skirts, or skimpy clothing in general is best avoided, and women will probably feel more comfortable wearing long trousers or an over-the-knee skirt. The traditional *longyi* is a good alternative.

LANGUAGE

SURVIVAL BURMESE

The Burmese language is tonal, like Chinese and Thai. The way in which a word is pronounced affects its meaning: a single syllable, given different stress, may carry several distinctly different meanings.

This may sound daunting, but in fact tones by themselves rarely obstruct survival communication. Other factors such as correct pronunciation of the vowels and consonants and having the proper rhythm are also important, however. The Burmese simplified pronunciation we are using is the John Okell method.

There are five tones in Burmese – three main tones plus two modifiers:

Creaky high tone. This is made with the voice tense, producing a high-pitched and relatively short creaky sound, as with words like "heart" and "squeak". It is indicated by an acute accent over the vowel, for example, ká, "dance".

Plain high tone. The pitch of the voice starts quite high, then falls for a fairly long time, as with words like "squeal", "car" and "way". It is indicated by a grave accent over the vowel, for example, kà which, conveniently, is the Burmese word for "car".

Low tone. The voice is relaxed, stays at a low pitch for a fairly long time, and does not rise or fall in pitch. It is indicated by no accent over the vowel, for example ka, "shield".

Stopped syllable. This is a very short syllable, on a high pitch, cut off at the end by a sharp catch in the voice (glottal stop). This is like the sound, "uh-oh", or the cockney pronunciation of the "t" in a word like "bottle". If you have trouble with this sound, try replacing it with a "t", but keep the syllable short. It is indicated here by a q after the vowel, for example kaq, "join". Note that the q is not pronounced.

Local ladies and goat, Bagan.

Reduced (or "weak") syllable. This is most commonly encountered as the first syllable of a two-syllable word, where the first – "reduced" – syllable is kept short and unstressed (as in the English "beneath", or for that matter, "reduced". It is indicated with a breve accent, ă.

CONVERSATION

Hello!/Hi! hălo, hèh-lo/hain
How are you? ne-kaùn-là?
Fine, thanks ne-kaùn-ba-deh-cè -zù-bèh
Excuse me! cănaw *m*/cămá *f* go- seiq-măshí-ba-néh
Do you speak English? k'ămyà *m/* shin *f* ìn-găleiq-zăgà-pyàw-dhălà?
What's your name? k'ămyà- *m*/shín *f* nan-meh-beh-lo-k'aw-dhălèh?
My name is... cănaw *m*/cămá *f* yèh-nan-meh-gá...ba
Nice to meet you. k'ămyà *m*/shín *f* go-twè-yá-da-wùn-tha-ba-deh
Where are you from? k'ămyà *m*/shin *f* beh-nain-ngan-gá-la-da-lèh?
What do you do for a living? Ătheq-mwè-wàn-caùn-bó-ătweq- k'ămyà *m*/shin *f* ba-ălouq-louq-lèh?
I work for... cănaw *m*/cămá *f*... ătweq-ălouq-louq-pa-deh.

ACCOMMODATION

Can you recommend a hotel? k'ămyà *m*/shin *f* ho-teh-tăk'u-hnyùn-pè-nain-mălà?
I made a reservation. cănaw *m*/cămá *f* co-tin-ăk'àn-yu-hmú-louq-k'éh-deh.
Do you have a room...? k'ămyà *m*/shin *f* hma...ăk'àn-tăk'àn-shí-dhălà?
for one/two lu-tăyauq/hnăyauq-ătweq
with a bathroom ye-ćo-gàn-tăk' ú-twèh-pa-déh
with air conditioning le-è- pè-zeq-pa-déh

DINING

A table for... please. cè-zù pyú-byí- lu... yauq-sa-zăbwèh- tă-lòun- pè-ba.
Can we sit...? cănaw *m*/cămá *f* dó- t'ain- ló- yá-nain-mălà?
here/there di-hma/Ho-hma
outside Ăpyin-hma
I'm waiting for someone. cănaw *m*/ cămá *f* tă-yauq-yauq-go-saún-ne-da.
Where are the toilets? ein-dha-beh-hma- shí- lèh?
The menu, please. cè-zù pyú-byì-ăsà-ăthauq-ămyi-săyin- bè-ba
What do you recommend? ba-sà-bó- k'ămyà *m*/shin *f* taiq-twu'n- mălèh?
I'd like... cănaw *m*/ cămá *f*... lo-jin-ba-deh.

Some more... please *cè-zù pyú- byì... nèh-nèh-t'aq-pè-ba.*

DIRECTIONS AND PLACES

How do I get to town? *myó-dèh-go cănaw **m**/cămá **f** beh-lo yauq-nain-mă-lèh?*
Where's...? *...gá beh-ne-ya-hma-lèh?*
the airport *le-zeiq*
the train station *yă-t'à bu-da-youn*
the bus station *baq-săkà-geiq*
the riverboat jetty *myiq-twìn-dhwà seq-hle (thìn-bàw) 'eiq-k'an-bàw-tă-dà*
Is it far from here? *èh-di-ne-ya-gá di-gá-ne wè-dhă-là?*

TIME

What time is it? *beh-ăćein-shí-bì-lèh*
It's midday. *ăk'u-né-leh*
At midnight. *nyá-dhăgaun-hma*
From one o'clock *tănayi -hmá-hnănayi*
Five past three. *thoùn-na-yi- t'ò -byì- ló-ngà-mí-niq*
A quarter to ten. *lè-na-yi- t'ò bó-śéh-ngà-mí-niq*
5:30 a.m./p.m. *măneq/nyăne-ngà-na-yi*

SHOPPING

Where's the market/ mall? *zè / zè-zain-dwe-shí-déh-ăs'ajq-ăù-gá-beh-ne-ya-hma-lèh ?*
I'm just looking. *cănaw **m**/cămà **f** mă-cí youn-cí-ne-da-ba*
How much? *beh-lauq-cá-lèh ?*
It's too expensive. *Èhdagá -ăyan-zè-cì-deh*
I have to think about it. *cănaw **m**/ cămà **f** èhdi-ăcaùn-sìn zà-meh*
I'll take it. *cănaw **m**/cămà **f** èhda go-yu-meh*

HEALTH

I'm sick. *cănaw **m**/cămá **f** ne-mă-kaùn-bù*
I need an English-speaking doctor. *cănaw **m**/cămá **f** in-găleiq-zăgà-pyàw-déh-śăya-wun-tăyauq-lo-aq-teh.*
It hurts here. *di-ne-ya-gá-na-deh*
Where's the pharmacy? *Śè-zain-beh-ne-ya-shí-lèh?*
What time does it open/close? *Èh-di-sain-gá-be-ăćein-p'wín/ peiq-thălèh?*

☉ Ana-deh

Every language contains expressions which don't lend themselves to translation. Burmese is no exception. The essence of Burmese courtesy stresses encouraging the other person to agree with you. Not imposing on others is the basic principle of *"ana-deh"*. The venerable Judson dictionary explains the term well as, "to be deterred by feelings of respect, delicacy, constraint, or by fear of offending." While all these feelings exist in Western countries, the concept as a single idea does not. *"Ana-deh"* must be learned and felt inwardly. It is true art to meet another person at a halfway point where neither side will lose face in the confrontation.

In the Westerner's dealings with Burmese authorities, he or she will often encounter this *"ana-deh"* approach to problems, coupled with a marked aversion to making a decision that will cause someone difficulty (such as turning down a visa extension application). In some cases, it can lead to considerable delays. Westerners must be patient and try to understand what other forces are influencing the individuals concerned.

What would you recommend for...? *ba-louq-p'ó-ătweq-thin-taiq-tùn-mălèh?*
How much do I take? *cănaw **m**/cămá **f** beh-louq-thauq-yá-măleh?*
I'm allergic to... *cănaw **m**/cămá **f**... néh-daq-mătéh-bù?*

NUMBERS

zero *thoun-nyá*
one *tiq*
two *hniq*
three *thoùn*
four *lè*
five *ngà*
six *ćauq*
seven *k'un-hniq*
eight *shiq*
nine *kò*
ten *tăs'eh*
eleven *s'éh tiq*
twelve *s'éh-hniq*

thirteen *s'éh-thoùn*
fourteen *s'éh-lè*
fifteen *s'éh-ngà*
sixteen *s'éh-ćauq*
seventeen *s'éh-k'un-hniq*
eighteen *s'éh-shiq*
nineteen *s'éh-kò*
twenty *hnăs'eh*
twenty-one *hnăs'eh-tiq*
twenty-two *hnăs'eh-hniq*
thirty *thoùn-zeh*
thirty-one *thoùn-zéh-tiq*
forty *lè-zeh*
fifty *ngà-zeh*
sixty *ćauq-śeh*
seventy *k'un-nă śeh*
eighty *shiq-śeh*
ninety *kò-śeh*
one hundred and one *tăyá-tiq*
two hundred *hnăyá*
five hundred *ngăyá*
one thousand *tăt'aun*
ten thousand *tăthaùn*
a million *tăthàn*

Book binder in Yangon.

GENERAL INTEREST AND TRAVEL

Rudyard Kipling. *From Sea to Sea.* Colourful account of Kipling's 1889 visit to Moulmein and Rangoon.

Emma Larkin. *Everything is Broken*. Harrowing account of life in the aftermath of Cyclone Nargis.

Emma Larkin *Finding George Orwell in Burma*. Part travelogue in the footsteps of Orwell; part examination of the 1984-like state of modern Myanmar under the generals.

Norman Lewis. *Golden Earth*. Classic account of the author's 1951 journey across the country.

Rory MacLean. *Under the Dragon: A Journey Through Burma.* Poignant travelogue focusing on the lives of four Burmese women.

Andrew Marshall. *The Trouser People*. Hugely entertaining account of the authors travels in the footsteps of Sir James George Scott (see below).

W. Somerset Maugham. *The Gentleman in the Parlour*. Interesting travel journals recounting Maugham's forays through Burma and Vietnam.

GENERAL HISTORY

Thant Myint-U. *The River of Lost Footsteps: A Personal History of Burma.* A highly readable account of the country's chequered history, both ancient and modern.

Thant Myint-U. *Where China Meets India: Burma and the New Crossroads of Asia*. Fascinating mix of history, travelogue and analysis of Myanmar's possible future role in the new Asia.

Sir James George Scott. *The Burman: His Life and Notions.* A goldmine of cultural information from a 19th-century British colonial official.

LITERATURE

Amitav Ghosh. *The Glass Palace*. Rollicking historical epic set in Burma, India and Malaya between 1885 and the end of World War II.

Orwell, George. *Burmese Days.* Bittersweet novel about British colonial rule. Orwell's two short essays on Burma – "Shooting an Elephant"

FURTHER READING

and "A Hanging" are also classics of their type.

CONTEMPORARY MYANMAR

Aung San Suu Kyi. *Freedom from Fear & Other Writings*. A collection of essays by and about the Nobel Peace Prize winner.

James Mawdsley. *The Heart Must Break*. Inspirational account by British activist Mawdsley of his time campaigning for democracy in Myanmar and subsequent imprisonment.

⊘ Send us your thoughts

We do our best to ensure the information in our books is as accurate and up-to-date as possible. The books are updated on a regular basis using local contacts, who painstakingly add, amend and correct as required. However, some details (such as telephone numbers and opening times) are liable to change, and we are ultimately reliant on our readers to put us in the picture.

We welcome your feedback, especially your experience of using the book "on the road". Maybe you came across a great bar or new attraction we missed. We will acknowledge all contributions, and we'll offer an Insight Guide to the best letters received.

Please write to us at:
Insight Guides
PO Box 7910
London SE1 1WE

Or email us at:
hello@insightguides.com

Pascal Khoo Thwe. *From The Land of Green Ghosts: A Burmese Odyssey*. Eloquent memoir describing the author's remarkable journey from remote Padaung villager to Cambridge University graduate.

Peter Popham. *The Lady and the Peacock: The Life of Aung San Suu Kyi.* Biography of Myanmar's Nobel-Prize-winning political leader.

Zoya Phan. *Little Daughter: A Memoir of Survival In Burma and the West*. Phan, a native Karen, became the face of a nation enslaved after this gripping 2009 memoir was published.

Justin Wintle. *Perfect Hostage: Aung San Suu Kyi, Burma and the Generals*. Published in 2007, this is still the best biography of Aung San Suu Kyi, although not quite as up to date at Peter Popham's study (see above).

ARTS AND CULTURE

Falconer, John et al. *Myanmar Style: Art, Architecture and Design of Burma.* A photographic survey of major design components in both traditional and contemporary Burmese design.

OTHER INSIGHT GUIDES

Companion volumes to the present title cover the Southeast Asian region comprehensively and include *Bangkok*, *Laos & Cambodia*, *Indonesia*, *Malaysia*, *The Philippines*, *Singapore*, *Southeast Asia*, *Thailand* and *Vietnam*. The **Insight Explore** series of itinerary-based guides includes *Bangkok* and *Singapore*. Insight's acclaimed laminated **Fleximap** series includes *Vietnam/Laos/Cambodia*, *Ho Chi Minh City* and *Bangkok*.

CREDITS

INSIGHT GUIDE CREDITS

Distribution
UK, Ireland and Europe
Apa Publications (UK) Ltd;
sales@insightguides.com
United States and Canada
Ingram Publisher Services;
ips@ingramcontent.com
Australia and New Zealand
Woodslane; info@woodslane.com.au
Southeast Asia
Apa Publications (SN) Pte;
singaporeoffice@insightguides.com
Worldwide
Apa Publications (UK) Ltd;
sales@insightguides.com
Special Sales, Content Licensing and CoPublishing
Insight Guides can be purchased in bulk quantities at discounted prices. We can create special editions, personalised jackets and corporate imprints tailored to your needs.
sales@insightguides.com
www.insightguides.biz

Printed in China by CTPS

First Edition 1980
Eleventh Edition 2019

Every effort has been made to provide accurate information in this publication, but changes are inevitable. The publisher cannot be responsible for any resulting loss, inconvenience or injury. We would appreciate it if readers would call our attention to any errors or outdated information. We also welcome your suggestions; please contact us at:
hello@insightguides.com

www.insightguides.com

Editor: Helen Fanthorpe
Author: Gavin Thomas
Head of DTP and Pre-Press:
Rebeka Davies
Update Production: Apa Digital
Picture Editor: Tom Smyth
Cartography: original cartography
Cosmographics, updated by Carte

CONTRIBUTORS

This new edition of *Insight Guide: Myanmar (Burma)* has been comprehensively updated to reflect the ongoing changes in the country by Gavin Thomas. Gavin is a freelance UK travel writer specialising in Asia and the Middle East, who has written and contributed to dozens of books over the past decade including *Insight Guides* to Sri Lanka, India, Morocco, Marrakech, Dubai, and Oman & the UAE. He builds on the work of David Abram, an Asia specialist who has since worked on more than a hundred books worldwide. Previous writers who have contributed to earlier editions include Andrew Forbes, Wendy Hutton, David Henley, Tan Chung Lee, Oliver Hargreave, Bertil Lintner, Wilhelm Klein and Günter Pfannmüller.

This edition was edited by Helen Fanthorpe. Most of the photography was provided by Corrie Wingate and picture research was by Tom Smyth.

ABOUT INSIGHT GUIDES

Insight Guides have more than 45 years' experience of publishing high-quality, visual travel guides. We produce 400 full-colour titles, in both print and digital form, covering more than 200 destinations across the globe, in a variety of formats to meet your different needs.

Insight Guides are written by local authors, whose expertise is evident in the extensive historical and cultural background features. Each destination is carefully researched by regional experts to ensure our guides provide the very latest information. All the reviews in **Insight Guides** are independent; we strive to maintain an impartial view. Our reviews are carefully selected to guide you to the best places to eat, go out and shop, so you can be confident that when we say a place is special, we really mean it.

Legend

City maps

	Freeway/Highway/Motorway
	Divided Highway
	Main Roads
	Minor Roads
	Pedestrian Roads
	Steps
	Footpath
	Railway
	Funicular Railway
	Cable Car
	Tunnel
	City Wall
	Important Building
	Built Up Area
	Other Land
	Transport Hub
	Park
	Pedestrian Area
	Bus Station
	Tourist Information
	Main Post Office
	Cathedral/Church
	Mosque
	Synagogue
	Statue/Monument
	Beach
	Airport

Regional maps

	Freeway/Highway/Motorway (with junction)
	Freeway/Highway/Motorway (under construction)
	Divided Highway
	Main Road
	Secondary Road
	Minor Road
	Track
	Footpath
	International Boundary
	State/Province Boundary
	National Park/Reserve
	Marine Park
	Ferry Route
	Marshland/Swamp
	Glacier / Salt Lake
	Airport/Airfield
	Ancient Site
	Border Control
	Cable Car
	Castle/Castle Ruins
	Cave
	Chateau/Stately Home
	Church/Church Ruins
	Crater
	Lighthouse
	Mountain Peak
	Place of Interest
	Viewpoint

INDEX

MAIN REFERENCES ARE IN BOLD TYPE

INSIGHT ⦿ GUIDES

OFF THE SHELF

Since 1970, **INSIGHT GUIDES** has provided a unique perspective on the world's best travel destinations by using specially commissioned photography and illuminating text written by local authors.

Whether you're planning a city break, a walking tour or the journey of a lifetime, our superb range of guidebooks and phrasebooks will inspire you to discover more about your chosen destination.

INSIGHT GUIDES

offer a unique combination of stunning photos, absorbing narrative and detailed maps, providing all the inspiration and information you need.

PHRASEBOOKS & DICTIONARIES

help users to feel at home, when away. Pocket-sized with a free app to download, they go where you do.

CITY GUIDES

pack hundreds of great photos into a smaller format with detailed practical information, so you can navigate the world's top cities with confidence.

EXPLORE GUIDES

feature easy-to-follow walks and itineraries in the world's most exciting destinations, with our choice of the best places to eat and drink along the way.

POCKET GUIDES

combine concise information on where to go and what to do in a handy compact format, ideal on the ground. Includes a full-colour, fold-out map.

EXPERIENCE GUIDES

feature offbeat perspectives and secret gems for experienced travellers, with a collection of over 100 ideas for a memorable stay in a city.

www.insightguides.com

London Borough
of Barnet

30131 05702092 4

A & H

19-Dec-2019

915.910454

Myanmar Eleventh edition
6218300

Greater Yangon

0   500 m
0   500 yds

DAGON MYOTHT

SOUTH
OKKALAPA

Nga Moe Yeik

Hlan Si
Gone

Thin Gan Gyur

Tarnwe

Than Thu Mar

Waizayandar

TARMWE

Myittar Nyunt

Kyauk Htat Gyi
Pagoda ★

Ma Hlwa Gone

Kandawgyi

Mat La Mu
Pagoda ★

Thu Damar

Harami

Kambe

Bauk Htaw

BAHAN

Yangon
Central

Yagu

Kaba Aye

Pagoda

Shwedagon
Pagoda ★

Mahabandoola

Strand

Pa Ywet
Seik Kone

Okkalarpa

Kyauk
Tae Twin

Tadalay

Gems
Museum ★

Kaba Aye
Pagoda ★

U Wisara

Pyay

MYANMAR
GOLF CLUB

Inya
Lake

Pyay

Ahlone
Road

Shu
Road

Yangon

Lawka Chantha
Abhaya Labha Muni

Mindhamma
Rd

Koe Htat Gyi
Pagoda ★

Pan Hlaing

Ahlanl Road

Yangon International
Airport

INTHEIN

Ah Lain Nga Sint
Pagoda ★

Hsin Hpyu
Elephant
Park

Insein

Okkyin

Tamine

Drug
Elimination
Museum ★

Ayee Min
Daing

Strand

Glygone

Thit Myaing

Kamaryut

Hledan

Hanthawaddy

Yangon

Bayint
Naung

Hlaing

★ N

BAHAN

Min

Kyauk Htat Gyi
Pagoda

Sasana Yeikhta

Shwegondaing

Nga Htat Gyi
Pagoda

Ngar Htat Gyi Pagoda

Bogyoke
Aung San
Museum

Bogyoke Museum

Wingabar

Nat Mauk

Aung San

BOGYOKE
AUNG SAN
PARK

Kandawgyi

Kyauk Myaung

Banyardala

Ni Yoe Gone

U Tin Myat

Kyaikkasan

Ma U Gar

Kandawgyi
Diplomatic
Hospital

Set

Pho Sein

Bahan

Kaba Aye Pagoda

KANDAWGYI

Kanmayut

Shwe Taung Gyar

Inya Myaing

Moe Hnying
Monastery

Mingon Dhama Wihara

GOLDEN
VALLEY

Ko Min Ko Chin

Old Yaetarshay

Gyar Taw Ya

Yaetarshay

Thwaysay

Thwaysay
Lake

Arzani

Shwedagon
Pagoda

Haung Bo

Inya

Thanlwin

Thanlwin

Shwegondaing

Martyrs'
Mausoleum

U Wisara

Dutpaung Su
Pagoda

Chin Twin

Dhammazedi

RESISTANCE
PARK

PEOPLE'S
PARK

Inya Gallery
of Art

Inya

Zawgyi

Panwar

Zawdika

Pyay

PEOPLE'S
PARK

People's
Square

Pyay

Barayar

Shinsawpu

Shinsawpu
Pagoda

Shwesandaw

Yangon
Brewery

→ Koe Htat Gyi Pagoda